Palgrave Studies in Educational Media

Eric Bruillard
ENS de Cachan
Cachan, France

Nigel Harwood
School of English
University of Sheffield
Sheffield, UK

Heather Mendick
Independent Scholar
London, UK

Eugenia Roldán Vera
Departamento de Investigaciones Educativas
CINVESTAV
Mexico City, Mexico

Neil Selwyn
Faculty of Education
Monash University
Clayton, VIC, Australia

Yasemin Soysal
University of Essex
Colchester, UK

There is no education without some form of media. Much contemporary writing on media and education examines best practices or individual learning processes, is fired by techno-optimism or techno-pessimism about young people's use of technology, or focuses exclusively on digital media. Relatively few studies attend – empirically or conceptually – to the embeddedness of educational media in contemporary cultural, social and political processes. The **Palgrave Studies in Educational Media** series aims to explore textbooks and other educational media as sites of cultural contestation and socio-political forces. Drawing on local and global perspectives, and attending to the digital, non-digital and post-digital, the series explores how these media are entangled with broader continuities and changes in today's society, with how media and media practices play a role in shaping identifications, subjectivations, inclusions and exclusions, economies and global political projects. Including single authored and edited volumes, it offers a dedicated space which brings together research from across the academic disciplines. The series provides a valuable and accessible resource for researchers, students, teachers, teacher trainers, textbook authors and educational media designers interested in critical and contextualising approaches to the media used in education.

Katja Gorbahn • Erla Hallsteinsdóttir
Jan Engberg
Editors

Exploring Interconnectedness

Constructions of European and National Identities in Educational Media

palgrave
macmillan

Editors
Katja Gorbahn
School of Communication and Culture
Aarhus University
Aarhus, Denmark

Erla Hallsteinsdóttir
School of Communication and Culture
Aarhus University
Aarhus, Denmark

Jan Engberg
School of Communication and Culture
Aarhus University
Aarhus, Denmark

ISSN 2662-7361 ISSN 2662-737X (electronic)
Palgrave Studies in Educational Media
ISBN 978-3-031-13959-8 ISBN 978-3-031-13960-4 (eBook)
https://doi.org/10.1007/978-3-031-13960-4

This Palgrave Macmillan imprint is published by the registered company Springer Nature Switzerland AG.
The registered company address is: Gewerbestrasse 11, 6330 Cham, Switzerland

Foreword

There is no education without some form of media. The field of educational media is a growing area of interest in education, as education policy papers on the 'digital agenda', the rapid expansion of media sections in national and international educational research associations, and the range of academic books on media in education show. Educational media are crucial to producing knowledge and shaping educational practices. Conflicts over the contents of textbooks and curricula, widely discussed in the daily news, illustrate how many different stakeholders are invested in sharing their particular understandings of our (shared) past, the current society, and potential imagined futures with the younger generation. Policymakers, politicians, and activists regard educational media as important tools which not only foster young people's media skills and world knowledge but also shape which ways of living are considered desirable or even legible. Textbooks and other educational media are deeply embedded in the socio-political contexts in which they are developed and used. Given this context, alongside the emerging interest in digital technology in education, the *Palgrave Studies in Educational Media* series takes stock of current research on educational media by focusing on three issues:

First, today's vibrant and dynamic research and scholarship on technology stems from a broad range of disciplines, including sociology, history, cultural studies, memory studies, media studies and education, and also information, computer and cognitive science. Traditionally, this research has drawn on textbooks and other educational media in order to engage with specific disciplinary questions, such as device-specific reading speed or social inclusion/exclusion. Studies on educational media are only beginning to be consolidated into the kind of inter- or transdisciplinary field which can build and develop on insights generated and exchanged across disciplinary boundaries.

Second, the majority of work in this field is focused on best practices, individual learning processes, or concerns over the risks involved when young people use technology. There are still relatively few studies which attend—empirically or conceptually—to the embeddedness of educational media in contemporary cultural, social, and political processes and to the historicity of the media used in education. If we see educational media as a highly contested and thus crucially important cultural site, then we need more studies which consider media in their contexts and which take a carefully critical or generative approach to societal concerns.

Third, current work emerging in this field has turned its attention to computers and other digital technologies. Yet, looking at today's educational practices, it is clear that (i) they are by no means predominantly digital, and simultaneously (ii) 'post-digital' practices abound in which the digital is no longer seen as new or innovative but is integrated with other materials in daily teaching and learning. The potentials and risks of digital education emit a fascination for politicians, journalists, and others concerned with the future of education and are undoubtedly important to consider. Empirical observations of education around the globe, however, demonstrate the reach and visibility of a broad range of media (textbooks, blackboards, LEGO™, etc.), as well as the post-digital blending of digital and non-digital media in contemporary educational settings.

Palgrave Studies in Educational Media aims to address these three issues in an integrated manner. The series offers a dedicated space which brings together research from across academic disciplines, encouraging dialogue within the emerging space of educational media studies. It showcases both empirical and theoretical work on educational media which understands these media as a site of cultural contestation and socio-political force. The focus lies primarily on schools, across the school subjects. The series is interested in both local and global perspectives in order to explore how educational media are entangled with broader debates about continuity and change in today's society, about classroom practices, inclusions and exclusions, identifications, subjectivations, economies, and global political projects.

This volume, edited by Katja Gorbahn, Erla Hallsteinsdóttir, and Jan Engberg, has come together via interdisciplinary and international collaboration between scholars inquiring into the complex relationships between national and European identities as expressed in educational media. The studies in this book, as diverse as they are in approaches, are informed by a strong shared interest in analysing the cultural and ideological backdrops to recent developments that have seen a renationalisation of European politics, serious challenges to concepts of European identity and unity, and—most recently—violent conflict in Europe. They do so by examining the embeddedness of educational media in such developments, recognising that these media are both catalysts of and informed by their specific geopolitical and socio-cultural contexts. Discourse analyses of educational texts unveil underlying assumptions, linguistic patterns, and narratives regarding the complex relationships between European integration and increasingly potent national agendas in our globalised world, showing how European and national identities are, paradoxically, both conflictual and intertwined—and in many cases constructed via language. Other studies apply technologies from the digital humanities to educational media, including eye-tracking, concept maps, and quantitative analytical software, to examine representations of identities in textbooks and students' knowledge and reception. Educational media as both the informants and products of a time intensely shaped by upheaval with regard to identities in and around Europe fulfil in this book, as so often, their unique function that continues to inform the work of the Leibniz Institute for Educational Media | Georg Eckert Institute.

Brunswick
Germany

Eckhardt Fuchs,
Felicitas Macgilchrist
June 2022

Acknowledgements

This book was rendered possible through the activities of the research network *Exploring Interconnectedness: Constructions of European and National Identities in Educational Media* (EurEd), which facilitated intense and productive interdisciplinary and international collaboration between the authors. The editors gratefully acknowledge a grant from the Independent Research Fund Denmark (https://dff.dk/en), which generously funded the activities of the network. We thank all its participants for sharing their expertise and knowledge. Furthermore, we express our gratitude to the managing editor of the book series, Wendy Anne Kopisch. Her support and expertise throughout the publication process was of invaluable help. Much appreciation also goes to Michaela Scioscia, who with enduring patience and a careful eye edited the draft manuscript.

Aarhus, Denmark
June 2022

Katja Gorbahn
Erla Hallsteinsdóttir
Jan Engberg

INDEPENDENT
RESEARCH FUND
DENMARK

Contents

Notes on Contributors

Anja Ballis is Professor and Chair of German Language Education at the University of Munich. In her university teaching she is responsible for teacher education in Germany. The focus of her research has been on Holocaust Education, teaching with digital media and textbook research. For her empirical studies, she uses a variety of qualitative and quantitative tools to gain insight into the field of Holocaust Education. Since 2018 she has been responsible for the project *Learning with Digital Testimonies*, exploring how interactive presentations of Holocaust survivors have learning effects on students. She is also known for her research on tour guides at Holocaust museums and memorial sites as an editor of *Holocaust Education – Historical Learning – Human Rights Education* (since 2019, Springer Science). Her recent publications include Ballis, A. & Schwendemann, L. (2022). '"In any case, you believe him one hundred percent, everything he says." Trustworthiness in Holocaust survivor talks with high school students in Germany'. *Holocaust Studies*, 28(2), 191–220 and Ballis, A. (2020). 'Die Migrationsgesellschaft als Herausforderung für Holocaust Education im Jugend-und Erwachsenenalter'. *Bildung und Erziehung*, 73(3), 226–241.

Katja Bethke-Prange was a research associate at the Institute for Scandinavian Studies, University of Kiel, Germany, from 2011 until 2021. She holds a PhD in Scandinavian linguistics and her research interests revolve around Danish as a neighbouring language, stereotypes in textbooks for Danish as a foreign language, translation from Scandinavian languages into German, higher education didactics in the field of Scandinavian linguistics, and language policy in Scandinavian countries. Her book, *Zeit des Verfalls – Verfall der Zeit: Zeit und Zeitwahrnehmung im skandinavischen Großstadtroman Ende des 19. Jahrhunderts* (Frankfurt: Peter Lang, 2012), examines time as a structuring element using selected examples of Scandinavian modernism.

Eckhard Bick is head of the Visual Interactive Syntax Learning project at the Institute for Language and Communication at the University of Southern Denmark, where he is engaged in the design and programming of grammatical tools. He holds a PhD in lexicography, and his research interests focus on natural language parsing and corpus linguistics. He specialises in Portuguese and Danish but has also developed constraint grammars for English, Spanish, French, and Esperanto. He is also an Esperantist and previously studied medicine at the University of Bonn.

Corinna Dettbarn is a research assistant at the University of Kiel. Her doctoral project focuses on the empirical identification of lexically and semantically bound knowledge about Europe as well as the language-didactic potential of concept maps. Her further research focuses on vocabulary didactics and cognitive linguistics.

Kimmo Elo is an adjunct professor and senior researcher at the Centre for Parliamentary Studies at the University of Turku (UTU). His research interests include German politics and history since 1945, theories and politics of European integration, Cold War and post-Cold War intelligence, theories and methods of network analysis, and computational social sciences, as well as knowledge visualization techniques. Elo's work revolves around all kinds of computational and digital research, including network analysis, computational discourse analysis, text/data mining, integration theories, EU theories, and geo-economics, as well as structuralist approaches to politics with a particular interest in Johan Galtung and agent-structure theory.

Jan Engberg is Professor of Knowledge Communication at the School of Communication and Culture, University of Aarhus. His main research interests are the study of cognitive aspects of specialised discourse and the relationship between specialised knowledge and text formulation. Much of his work is focused on communication, translation, and meaning in the field of law. In the context of conveying knowledge, concepts relevant for describing knowledge-communicative acts are central and have been used for studying legal institutions and the dissemination of basic legal concepts as well as by scientists popularising their own field in radio shows. Engberg has co-edited a number of books and special issues of international journals and is co-editor of the international journal *Fachsprache – Journal of Professional and Scientific Communication.*

Markus Furrer has been Professor of Contemporary History at the University of Teacher Education Lucerne (PH Luzern) since 2003. After receiving his doctorate from the University of Fribourg, he worked as a history teacher (1992–2003) and as vice-rector (1996–2001) at a teacher training college in Lucerne. He joined the University of Fribourg in 1998 as a part-time lecturer and held a position there as a covering professor from 2003 to 2006. His principal fields of research are European and Swiss contemporary history, with a focus on politics, culture, and social history and on the communication of history to the public. His publications include 'Neuzeit und Zeitgeschichte – die Zeit des heissen Erinnerns'. In *Geschichtskultur – Public History – Angewandte Geschichte. Geschichte in der Gesellschaft: Medien, Praxen, Funktionen*, edited by Felix Hinz and Andreas Körber, Göttingen: V&R, 2020, 543–556; and (edited with K. Messmer) *Handbuch Zeitgeschichte im Geschichtsunterricht* (Schwalbach am Taunus: Wochenschau, 2013). He received his Habilitation from the University of Fribourg, Switzerland, with *Die Nation im Schulbuch - zwischen Überhöhung und Verdrängung: Leitbilder der Schweizer Nationalgeschichte in Schweizer Geschichtslehrmitteln der Nachkriegszeit und Gegenwart.* Hanover: Hahn, 2004.

Katja Gorbahn is Associate Professor of German History and Social Studies at the School of Communication and Culture of Aarhus University, Denmark, and head of the research network *Exploring Interconnectedness. Constructions of European and National Identities in Educational Media (EurEd)*, funded by the Independent Research Fund Denmark. She is a trained teacher for history and German, received her PhD in history didactics from Augsburg University, and worked at the universities of Erlangen-Nuremberg and Siegen. Her research interests include textbook research, history and language education, digital analysis, and memory studies, with a strong focus on identity constructions. Her publications include studies on Europeanness in Aarhus 2017's programme of events, on regional history in Danish educational media, on national identity constructions in Danish movies and history magazines, and on the history of Ancient Greece as an 'identification offer' in German textbooks.

Stefan Hackl is a senior lecturer at the Chair of German Literature and Language Education and German as a Second Language at the Institute of German Philology at the University of Munich (LMU). His research focuses on learning with digital media in the teaching of German as a first and second language as well as stereotype research in the context of teaching and learning. He is a member of the interdisciplinary and international research network 'Interdisciplinary Research on Stereotypes (IDROS)'. His most recent publications include 'How to Deutsch. Zur Problematik von YouTube-Erklärvideos für das Unterrichtsfach Deutsch' in *Deutschunterricht im Zeichen der Digitalisierung* (Innsbruck: StudienVerlag, 2021, 116–129).

Erla Hallsteinsdóttir is Associate Professor of German Business Communication at Aarhus University, Denmark, with a PhD in German linguistics from Leipzig University. She has been a project leader in EU projects on stereotypes and the promotion of intercultural understanding in the Danish-German border regions and the author of several publications and research-based guidelines on Danish-German communication and cooperation. Her main research interests relate to language education, especially of German and Danish as neighbouring languages, intercultural communication and stereotypes, business communication, corpus linguistics, and cross-linguistic aspects of communication and vocabulary (multiword units). She is a board member of the European Society of Phraseology.

Tobias Heinz is a research associate in the project *LeaP@CAU - Lehramt mit Perspektive* (prospects for teachers in training) and at the Centre for Teacher Education of the University of Kiel, Germany. His previous positions include Acting Professor of language didactics and linguistics at the European University of Flensburg and lecturer at the Technical University of Braunschweig, with research interests in German teaching and history of science, semantics and lexical learning, and networking of knowledge in teacher education. His publications include Martina Ide / Tobias Heinz (eds) 2022. *Bild und Sprache im interdisziplinären Dialog universitärer Lehre. Forschendes Lernen vernetzt.* München: kopaed; and Tobias Heinz, Birgit Brouër, Margot Janzen, Jörg Kilian (eds) 2020. *Formen der Repräsentation fachlichen Wissens. Ansätze und Methoden für die Lehrerinnen- und Lehrerbildung in den Fachdidaktiken und den Bildungswissenschaften.* Münster, New York: Waxmann.

Nina Kalwa is a research associate at the Institute of Language and Literature at the Technical University of Darmstadt, Germany. She holds a PhD from the University of Kassel, where she wrote a linguistic study of discourse around conceptions of Islam. Her research interests centre around methods of text and discourse linguistics, culture-oriented linguistics, and meaning analysis. Her recent publications include 'Die kulturelle Bedingtheit (diskurs-)linguistischer Erkenntnis' in *Diskurs – ethisch*, edited by Heidrun Deborah Kämper and Ingo H. Warnke (Bremen: Hempen, 2020), 73–88; and 'Die Konstitution von Konzepten in Diskursen: Zoom als Methode der diskurslinguistischen Bedeutungsanalyse', in *Sprach(kritik)-kompetenz als Mittel demokratischer Willensbildung*, edited by Sandro Moraldo, Thomas Niehr and Jürgen Schiewe (Bremen: Hempen, 2019), 11–26.

Jörg Kilian is Professor of German Linguistics and Language Didactics at the University of Kiel, where he is involved in the Centre for Teacher Education and a member of the board of directors of the BMBF-funded teacher education project LeaP@CAU. His main research interests concern vocabulary teaching and learning, accuracy of teachers' judgements of German students' texts, discourse analysis in educational research, didactics of language criticism, pedagogical content knowledge for teacher education, and linguistic stereotypes. He is also co-editor of the scientific journal *Der Deutschunterricht*, of the online dictionary *Sprachdidaktik. Erstsprache, Zweitsprache, Fremdsprache*, of the handbook *Basiswissen Lehrerbildung: Deutsch unterrichten*, and author of the recently published monograph on vocabulary teaching and learning methodology *Wortschatz lernen und reflektieren* (Kallmeyer, 2021).

Hartmut E. H. Lenk is Professor Emeritus of German Language at the University of Helsinki, Finland. He has published work on text and contrastive media linguistics, contrastive onomapragmatics, and phraseology and maintains the web portal on contrastive media linguistics (www.kontrastive-medienlinguistik.net). From 2011 to 2018, he led the project 'Styles of Persuasion in Europe', in which around 20 colleagues from 9 European countries studied patterns and rhetorical means used in editorials and commentaries in daily newspapers from 13 countries, resulting in 5 edited volumes, further articles, and Master's theses. He is working on TV news cultures in the German-speaking countries and Finland. Two books he has recently co-edited are Lenk, H. E. H. & Giessen, H. (eds) 2020, *Persuasionsstile in Europa: Strategien und Mittel des Überzeugens in Zeitungskommentaren aus kulturkontrastiver Sicht*. Berlin: Frank & Timme (Sprachwissenschaft; no. 47), and Tienken, S., Hauser, S., Lenk, H. E. H. & Luginbühl, M. (eds) 2021, *Methoden kontrastiver Medienlinguistik*. Bern: Peter Lang (Sprache in Kommunikation und Medien; vol. 15).

Marcus Otto is a senior researcher at the Leibniz Institute for Educational Media | Georg Eckert Institute in Brunswick, Germany, and deputy head of the department 'Knowledge in Transition'. His research centres around decolonisation and memory politics in conflict contexts in education and the semantics of crisis in European textbooks. His PhD, from the University of Bielefeld, Germany, is an interdisciplinary study on the genealogy of political inclusion in France. He has worked on numerous research projects focusing on political inclusion, discourse theory, power and cultural assertiveness in interreligious communication, and peace and conflict in educational media. Otto's publications include the books

Der Wille zum Subjekt. Zur Genealogie politischer Inklusion in Frankreich (16. - 20. Jahrhundert), Bielefeld: transcript-Verlag 2014 and 'France' in *The Palgrave Handbook of Conflict and History Education in the Post-Cold War Era*, edited by Luigi Cajani, Simone Lässig and Maria Repoussi, London: Palgrave Macmillan 2019, pp. 233–244.

Mira Schienagel is assistant to the Chair of German Language Education at the University of Munich as well as a part-time Art and German teacher at a secondary school. Her research interests are learning and teaching processes with social media, hardware and software solutions, and textbook research.

Magdalena Telus is the academic director of the Polish Competence and Coordination Centre (*Kompetenz- und Koordinationszentrum Polnisch, KoKoPol*) in Ostritz, Germany. She studied Polish, Slavic, and German studies at the Universities of Wrocław and Bochum, with a PhD thesis on group-specific stereotypes (*Gruppenspezifisches Stereotyp: Ein Modell der Einbettung in die Textproduktion an russischem, polnischem und deutschem Material.* Frankfurt a. M.: Peter Lang, 2002). From 1997 to 2000 she coordinated a project at the Georg Eckert Institute for International Textbook Research, developing new history and social studies textbooks in the non-Russian CIS region with a focus on Ukraine. In 2016, she worked on the project 'European Identity as an authentic experience? Linguistic manifestations of a non-categorical semantics for Europe in material from German and Polish textbooks for history and geography' with the *Research Network Historical Authenticity* of the Leibniz Association. Her primary research interests are the linguistic construction of social reality, and identity and language policy in the German-Polish context, as reflected in her article: 'Semantyka przynależności vs. semantyka udziału: rozważania na temat koncepcji tożsamości europejskiej', *Etnolingwistyka. Problemy Języka i Kultury* 23 (2011): 145–166.

List of Figures

List of Tables

1

Introduction: European and National Identity Constructions in Educational Media

Katja Gorbahn, Erla Hallsteinsdóttir, and Jan Engberg

The 2008 financial crisis and its consequences revealed deep rifts within the European Union, and the refugee crisis fuelled the renationalisation of European politics. During the COVID-19 pandemic, Europe experienced strict national border controls, and the war in Ukraine presented new challenges to EU foreign and security policies. In a situation where meanings related to national and supranational identities are precarious, challenged and may have real consequences, as was evident in the United Kingdom's Brexit referendum, for example, it is essential to analyse the cultural and ideological background of such developments. Analyses of educational media are particularly relevant to this discussion, given their potential impact on individuals in their formative years, and textbook research has investigated the presentation of Europe and the European

K. Gorbahn • E. Hallsteinsdóttir (✉) • J. Engberg
School of Communication and Culture, Aarhus University,
Aarhus, Denmark
e-mail: katja.gorbahn@cc.au.dk; ehall@cc.au.dk; je@cc.au.dk

K. Gorbahn et al. (eds.), *Exploring Interconnectedness*, Palgrave Studies in Educational Media, https://doi.org/10.1007/978-3-031-13960-4_1

Union for some time (see Chap. 5, this volume). However, the specific question of European identity construction has received less attention, although a few studies exist (e.g. Soysal 2002; Augschöll et al. 2019).

This book investigates the interconnectedness of European and national identity construction in educational media. It presents the results of the activities of the international research network *Exploring Interconnectedness: Constructions of European and National Identities in Educational Media (EurEd)*, which was established in 2018 and funded by the Independent Research Fund Denmark (https://projects.au.dk/interconnectedness/). The volume explores the socio-cultural and media background of a critical and ongoing political challenge: the complex entanglements between European integration and strong national agendas in the context of globalisation. Denmark and Germany play important roles in this volume, serving as examples of how historical relationships and mutual perceptions are connected to and mirrored in the construction of Europe and associated narratives. The chapters in this volume thus address questions such as: How are European and national identities constructed through language? Which stereotypical attributes, which linguistic patterns and which narratives can be identified? How do different constructions of the European and various national identities relate to, compete and interact with each other? How might factors such as the perception of the size and power of a nation, or historical relations between nations, influence the discursive construction of identities from various group perspectives? How can different linguistic and discourse-analytical methods contribute to examining representations of identities from a cross-cultural perspective? And how can learners' reception of such representations and concepts of Europe and/or the nation be explored?

European and National Identities

'Identity' and 'Europe' are the focal points of the studies presented in this volume. 'Identity' is a highly ambiguous term (Brubaker and Cooper 2000), as is 'Europe'. Consequently, debates about European identity tend to be rather opaque and highly normative. The question of how European and national identities relate to each other on the 'battlegrounds of European identity' (Kohli 2000) is also controversial. Public debates about European unification often imply a dichotomous view of national and European identity. However, scholars have argued for the possibility of multiple identities (Smith 1992) and suggested that national and European identities should be understood as 'multi-layered' (Hettlage 1999) or 'nested' (Herrmann and Brewer 2004). Others have shown how multiple identities blend into one another, and should be analysed as 'intertwined' (Risse 2010) or 'entangled' (Ichijo and Spohn 2005). Indeed, constructions of national identity may incorporate references to Europe and the European Union, thus becoming Europeanised. Similarly, national identity discourses may also substantially influence the constructions of European identity. To make things even more complicated, other types of identifications (e.g. local, regional or social) may interact with national and European identity constructions. At the same time, phenomena such as globalisation and transnational migration challenge categorical approaches to European and national identity (Zappettini 2019), as the case of Denmark in particular demonstrates.

Denmark's relationship with Europe and European integration has often been debated in terms of Euroscepticism (Sørensen 2008), with reference to a strong Danish sense of a homogeneous national identity and desire for self-determination (Jenkins 2000, 161). At the same time, it has been argued that Danish society is one of the most globalised, cosmopolitan and, in fact, Europeanised, societies in Europe (Favell and Reimer 2021). This paradox (Wivel 2019) cannot be addressed via a simplistic model that contrasts European and national identity. Instead, the complexity of self-understandings and identity constructs must be taken into account. In the case of Denmark, other types of identification, for example those based on local affiliations (Jenkins 2000), on the understanding of being a Nordic country (Hansen 2002) or on Danish interests in the Arctic (Rosamond 2015), may affect and interact with Danish perceptions of Europe and the nation. Furthermore, debates around Danish national, Nordic, Arctic and European identity frequently—and often controversially—refer to Denmark as being—or not being—a small state (Østergaard 2000). While there is no clear consensus about how a 'small state' is to be defined (Baldacchino and Wivel 2020), Keohane (1969) has proposed taking a state's self-perception regarding size as a crucial factor. Browning—going one step further and adopting a discursive approach to small-state identity—argues with respect to the case of Finland that smallness may also be narrated in a positive way and utilised as a resource (Browning 2006). Narratives that address being a small or large state therefore need to be understood as constructions embedded in and stabilised by media discourses. This volume draws particular attention to the perspective of small states, and addresses European-identity discourses in the educational media of several countries that are often perceived as 'small': Denmark (Chaps. 3, 6, 7 and 9), Switzerland (Chap. 2) and Finland (Chap. 4).

Historical processes and historical narratives are crucial for the construction of identities. In the case of Germany, research has analysed the Europeanisation of German national identity construction, in particular in elite discourses, and demonstrated how national identity discourses have informed German constructions of Europe (Boldt 2011; Wenzel et al. 2007; Galpin 2017; Risse 2010). The Nazi past functions as the 'other' in the German construction of both the nation and Europe, and the progressive narrative of the nation's recovery after 1945, culminating in German unity in 1990, is closely entangled with the narrative of European integration. However, the role of Germany in the European Union has been—and still is—controversial. Concerns about a 'German Europe' have been expressed, as has the hope that a 'European Germany' may assume an important role in Europe (Beck 2013, Nedergaard 2015). Concerns about the 'big neighbour Germany' also occur in Danish discourses: Germany has had an important function as the 'other' since the emergence of Danish nationalism and the nation-state (Adriansen 2003). After 1945, the Danish view of Germany became entangled with the question of European integration: on the one hand, the Europeanisation of Germany was seen as a safeguard against German aggression, while on the other, fear and resentment of Germany had a significant impact on Danish discourses around European integration (Lammers 2005; Jenkins 2000). Danish and German constructions of 'Europe' in relation to the nation thus represent very different, if transnationally connected, cases. This volume analyses German identity discourses (Chaps. 5, 8, 9 and 11), investigates the construction of 'Germany' and 'Europe' in Danish discourses

(Chaps. 6 and 7) and explores cross-cultural perspectives, addressing the concept of Europe in the context of foreign-language instruction with German as the source or target language (Chaps. 3, 4 and 9).

The Construction of Identities in Discourse

Stuart Hall has described identity as 'a discourse—a way of constructing meanings which influences and organises both our actions and our conception of ourselves' (Hall 1992, 292). Educational media, which result from negotiations in the 'discourse arena' (Höhne 2003), reflect identity discourses and transform them into 'offers of identification' (Gorbahn 2012) in a didactic setting. However, discourses on Europe reach far back in time (Schmale 2000; Schmale 2008). In consequence, various understandings of Europe and European identity have emerged and may still be drawn upon in current discourses, often overlapping, permeating or even contradicting each other (Quenzel 2015). Analyses of European identity discourses need to take this complexity into account; Chaps. 2, 4, 7 and 9 thus focus on identifying various conceptualisations of Europe in the data collected, drawing on various methodological approaches.

This volume investigates identity constructions as concepts (Kalwa 2013) or as part of macro-level knowledge, as Engberg (2015) has elucidated. In line with Hall, we believe that meaning is produced and exchanged through language in ongoing processes and practices (Hall 1997). Hall and his colleagues have identified five cultural processes which together comprise the 'circuit of culture', and which need to be considered in the analysis of texts or artefacts: representation, identity, production, consumption and regulation (Gay et al. 1997). Together, these elements 'provide a shared cultural space in which meaning is created, shaped, modified, and recreated' (Curtin and Gaither 2007, 38). Digital communication may have further intensified the connections among these processes (Tombleson and Wolf 2017), for example by closely linking the aspects of consumption and production through social media practices.

To explore concepts of Europe and the nation in the cultural space of education, the chapters of this book address a wide variety of media, taking multimodality and multicodality into account (Chaps. 5, 10 and 11), and including learning material designed for history (Chaps. 2 and 6), foreign-language learning (Chaps. 3 and 4), geography (Chap. 5) and several other subjects or subject combinations (Chaps. 8 and 11). Textbooks and curricula are the focus of the first part of this volume and are also addressed in Chaps. 6, 9 and 11. They are important objects of analysis owing to their regulating function and authoritative status (Dreesen 2015), and older textbooks may also provide valuable insight into the development of discursive elements over time. Today, however, students have a wide variety of digital information sources at their disposal and use them in various ways and for various purposes, as international research on the use of Wikipedia suggests (Blikstad-Balas 2016). Further, the boundaries of formal and informal learning are blurred when it comes to social media (Greenhow and Lewin 2016), which both affect and reflect learning processes. The analysis of social-media discourses provides insight into the socio-political context of education and into current concepts of European and national identity at the crossroads of consumption and the production of meaning. To do justice to these developments, this volume's chapters address constructions of 'Europe' and 'the nation' in Wikipedia (Chap. 6), on Facebook and Twitter (Chap. 7), and on the website of the German Federal Agency for Civic Education, a public government institution (Chap. 8). Other chapters focus on the element of consumption by investigating learners' concepts and their reception of educational media. To accomplish this, the authors apply innovative methods to educational media research, such as concept maps (Chap. 9) and eye-tracking (Chaps. 10 and 11).

Analysing Constructions of Identity in Educational Media

Methodologically, educational media research relies on interdisciplinary collaboration. This book explores the potential of linguistic and corpus-linguistic approaches, which have recently received increased attention in textbook research (Ott 2017; Kiesendahl and Ott 2015; Nieländer and De Luca 2018). Linguistic methods may yield valuable results for the analysis of identity constructions, for example through critical discourse analysis (Wodak et al. 2009), stereotype analysis (Hallsteinsdóttir and Kilian 2016), cultural analysis (Bubenhofer 2009) or cross-cultural analysis (Minkov and Hofstede 2013). In particular, digital analysis methods provide new opportunities for research on educational media and identity constructions, addressing, for instance, the challenge presented by the fact that references to Europe, the nation or other categories of identity are often distributed throughout educational media products and may occur in various thematic contexts. Digital analysis also makes it possible to access large text corpora and to identify linguistic patterns that may not become apparent through hermeneutic analysis. While digital analysis draws on quantitative techniques, it is a fundamental assumption of this book that qualitative analysis remains crucial.

Chapter 6, which is intended as a kind of toolkit, provides an introduction to the use of digital techniques for analysing concepts of Europe and the nation. Throughout this volume, many authors use digital techniques such as frequency analysis, concordance and collocation analysis, comparison clouds, geographic analysis, vector analysis and network analysis (Chaps. 2, 3, 4, 6, 7, 8 and 9). However, not all the methods presented in this volume lend themselves to all corpus sizes, as Bick, Gorbahn and Kalwa point out in Chap. 6. A variety of methods is necessary to explore the cultural space of education and to deepen our understanding of the intersection of socio-cultural, cognitive and linguistic aspects of identity construction. Such an understanding is crucial not only for researchers but also for practitioners and students.

As Fuchs has pointed out, the challenges to Europe's identity cannot be met by establishing a single compulsory narrative (Fuchs 2011). Rather, an understanding of the diversity of national and transnational approaches to 'Europe' is essential if transcultural competence is to be established and communication about Europe is to succeed.

Part One

This volume is divided into three sections. Part One addresses constructions of European and national identity in textbooks for history, foreign-language teaching and geography. In Chap. 2 ('Europe and the Nation in

Current Swiss Textbooks'), Markus Furrer investigates two recent Swiss history books developed for schools in connection with the creation of a common Swiss national history curriculum (*Lehrplan 21*). As background to this study, he presents an overview of how the concept of 'European History' has been treated in the field of history research. There is an interesting contrast between the concept of Europe as a geographic entity—which, as such, is not of particular historical significance—and the various national and supranational developments for which Europe has constituted the point of departure. The latter aspect has been studied from a more political, more structural and more cultural perspective. As a second background point, Switzerland's special view of Europe is presented as an example of a small country's perception. Based on these aspects, the author has used the *AntConc* corpus tool to carry out a study of the use of the letter string *europ** in two Swiss history textbooks, focusing on six different categories of topics. The primary conclusion of this study is that recent history textbooks position Switzerland within more general European developments despite its being a small country. At the same time, its position as a bystander rather than a participant in European events is evident, resulting in a somewhat conflictual Swiss perception of Europe as presented in the country's history textbooks.

Chapter 3, by Katja Bethke-Prange ('A Corpus-based Discourse Analysis of the Frequency and Co-occurrences of *Danmark* and *Europa* in Textbooks for Danish as a Foreign Language'), also employs a corpus tool to empirically investigate the conceptualisation of Europe in textbooks for a small country, this time with regard to Denmark. However, this study focuses on textbooks for Danish as a foreign language—actually a neighbouring language—in a German setting, the border region of Schleswig-Holstein, and the associated curriculum text. Bethke-Prange focuses particularly on the linguistic construction of the national (Denmark and Germany) and the European, and the extent to which size and political power play a role. By using the *AntConc* tool for discourse analysis, the author specifically identifies constructions of conceptual knowledge. The results unveil cultural concepts related to being Danish, concepts related to Denmark as a nation, concepts of relations between Denmark and Germany, and concepts of relations between Europe, the

European Union and Denmark. Given the object of study (curriculum texts and textbooks), the constructed knowledge may be seen as what comprises the expected language reservoir for people learning Danish, and thus learning to understand the Danish. The constructions of the cultural concepts in question may thus be seen as perpetuating stereotypes around Danes as the 'other' for German students.

In Chap. 4, Hartmut Lenk ('Concepts of Europe in the Finnish Scholastic Curriculum and in German Textbooks for Finnish Secondary Schools') essentially follows the same methodological approach as that used in the preceding chapters (corpus studies using *AntConc* and *Voyant*). However, he focuses on the Finnish-German and European contexts, with a clear focus on the conceptualisation of Europe. As in Chap. 3, textbooks (here, two series of textbooks for teaching German to Finnish upper-secondary school students) and curricula are the objects of his empirical study, which seeks to determine the intended input for the students' development of key concepts of European identity in a small state. The curriculum texts display a clear preference for a positive attitude to Europe 'as an environment for individual and communal action', and this is taken up by the textbooks, which focus on Europe as a geographic entity, a cultural area, and a political and economic unit.

In the last chapter in this section, titled 'Constructions of European Identity, Crisis Stereotypes and the Discursive Embedding of the Subject in Textbook Assignments', Magdalena Telus and Marcus Otto investigate how learners are addressed as European subjects in textbook assignments in current German textbooks. This study's central hypothesis is that a European identity is propagated through non-categorical semantics that differ from the us-and-them semantics used when constructing national identities. After presenting some of the previous studies that have established these ideas and relating them to the concept of Late Modernity, Telus and Otto elaborate on the idea that European identity is inherently weak or fragile, and relate this to the types of exercises found in recent textbooks. Interestingly, the exercises focus on relations between the individual and the concept of Europe, and thus emphasise the constructed character of the latter. At the same time, the exercises relate this concept to another central notion of Late Modernity: crisis.

Part Two

The chapters in the second section focus on methods used in the digital humanities and their application to the analysis of educational media. In Chap. 6 ('Methodological Approaches to the Digital Analysis of Educational Media: Exploring Concepts of Europe and the Nation'), Eckhard Bick, Katja Gorbahn and Nina Kalwa analyse examples from Danish and German history textbooks and a corpus of texts from Wikipedia and social media. They demonstrate how to explore constructions of 'Europe' and 'the nation', first describing the fundamental steps of compiling a corpus, presenting the use of tools such as *AntConc*, *Voyant* and *Sketch Engine*, and types of analysis (word frequencies, keyword analysis, concordances, collocations and networks), including example analyses. They conclude by discussing the potential and limits of this approach, emphasising the importance of including qualitative approaches in the analysis of identity construction. Many of the methods used in the chapters of Part One are thus explained in this chapter.

Chapter 7, by Eckhard Bick ('Concepts of Europe in Danish and German Social Media: A Corpus-Linguistic Study'), offers a more elaborate application and explanation of some of the methods described in Chap. 6. Here, one specific corpus (a large Danish and a German corpus consisting of Facebook posts [approx. 87 million words] and Twitter Tweets [approx. 1840 million words] collected in 2017 and 2018) is used to find and qualitatively and quantitatively compare trends in the conceptualisation of Europe in German and Danish contexts. He finds a total of nine different conceptualisations of Europe in the Danish corpus, and compares Danish and German European identity concepts using vector analysis among other approaches. Here, the results indicate that both the Danish and the German contexts reveal traces of a nascent element of European identity, albeit more pronounced in the latter.

Chapter 8 ('How to Strengthen Awareness of 'Europe': A Digital Analysis of Informational Material from the German Federal Agency for Civic Education'), by Kimmo Elo, exemplifies another set of methods used in the digital humanities, applied to a specific case that involves the construction 'Europe' for young people. The focus of this study is German-language digital learning material about Europe from the Federal

Agency for Civic Education (*Bundeszentrale für politische Bildung*, bpb). By applying different tagging methods and statistically processing the data results in a text network analysis of the occurrence of 'European Union', the results can then be used to analyse and categorise the topics contained in large amounts of digitally available data.

Part Three

Whereas the chapters of the first two sections focus on analysing instances of communication, the contributions to Part Three explore learners' knowledge and reception processes. In Chap. 9 ('"Europe" in our Minds: Identifying Knowledge Models Using Concept Maps'), Corinna Dettbarn, Jörg Kilian and Erla Hallsteinsdóttir investigate students' knowledge of Europe with concept maps. They discuss the latter as an innovative tool for collecting data on linguistically bound knowledge, and methods of systematically interpreting the data. Further, corpus-based analyses of educational policy texts demonstrate how the relationship between learners' knowledge and curricula may be explored. Here we see the same interest in the impact of curriculum documents on teaching. But whereas Chaps. 3 and 4 compare curriculum documents with textbooks, here the focus is on the relationships between the intent of curriculum documents and actual learning outcomes. Interestingly, the results of the analysis indicate that concepts of Europe are less stereotyped than is usual for their national counterparts, which supports the conclusion in Chap. 5 that concepts of Europe may be structurally different from concepts of the nation.

The last two chapters in Part Three (Chaps. 10 and 11) work in concert and discuss eye-tracking as a method of collecting data on the reception of educational media and on learners' understandings of Europeanness. Chapter 10 ('Eye-Tracking as a Scientific Method for Analysing Educational Media—State of the Art and Potential'), by Stefan Hackl, includes a general introduction to this method. He begins with an overview of the fundamental concepts behind the use of eye-tracking for studies of reading perception. This is followed by a discussion of focused studies in the field of educational media, which presents a range of applications from investigating the interplay of text and image in the understanding of general reading research to assessing strategies of second-language acquisition and multimedia learning. In Chap. 11 ('Images and Perceptions of Europe: Exploring a Multi-Perspective Design that Comprises Visual, Textual and Subjective Elements'), Anja Ballis, Tobias Heinz and Mira Schienagel present an exemplary, multi-perspective analysis that employs eye-tracking as its principal method for examining the relationship between perceptions of Europe and perceptions of migration. To explore the interplay of text and image in the reception process of students training to become teachers, quantitative and qualitative data were collected with the help of eye-tracking technology. Parallel to these studies, the authors also conducted structured interviews on the topics of Europe and migration. The set of data that this yielded was analysed with the help of grounded theory and situational analysis. The results indicate that students view migration in Europe in terms of *Sicherheit*—how safe they feel, personally, and how they view the global situation.

References

Adriansen, Inge. 2003. *Nationale symboler i det Danske Rige, 1830–2000: Fra fyrstestat til nationalstater*. Copenhagen: Museum Tusculanum Press.

Augschöll, Blasbichler, Eva Matthes Annemarie, and Sylvia Schütze, eds. 2019. *Europa und Bildungsmedien. Europe and Educational Media*. Heilbrunn: Julius Klinkhardt.

Baldacchino, Godfrey, and Anders Wivel. 2020. Small States: Concepts and Theories. In *Handbook on the Politics of Small States*, ed. Godfrey Baldacchino and Anders Wivel, 2–19. Cheltenham: Edward Elgar.

Beck, Ulrich. 2013. *German Europe*. Cambridge: Polity.

Blikstad-Balas, Marte. 2016. "You Get What You Need": A Study of Students' Attitudes towards Using Wikipedia When Doing School Assignments. *Scandinavian Journal of Educational Research* 60 (6): 594–608.

Boldt, Thea D. 2011. European Identities Made in Germany. In *Europe, Nations and Modernity*, ed. Atsuko Ichijo, 60–82. New York: Palgrave Macmillan.

Browning, Christopher S. 2006. Small, Smart and Salient? Rethinking Identity in the Small States Literature. *Cambridge Review of International Affairs* 19 (4): 669–684.

Brubaker, Rogers, and Frederick Cooper. 2000. Beyond "Identity". *Theory and Society* 29 (1): 1–47.
Bubenhofer, Noah. 2009. *Sprachgebrauchsmuster: Korpuslinguistik als Methode der Diskurs- und Kulturanalyse*. Vol. 4 of *Sprache und Wissen* (SuW). Berlin: De Gruyter. https://doi.org/10.1515/9783110215854.
Curtin, Patricia A., and T. Kenn Gaither. 2007. *International Public Relations: Negotiating Culture, Identity, and Power*. Thousand Oaks: SAGE.
Dreesen, Philipp. 2015. Sprache—Wissen—Kontingenz. Die Konstrastive Diskurslinguistik in der Schulbuchforschung am Beispiel deutscher und polnischer Geschichtsschulbücher. In *Linguistik und Schulbuchforschung. Gegenstände—Methoden—Perspektiven*, ed. Jana Kiesendahl and Christine Ott, 53–84. Göttingen: V&R unipress.
Engberg, Jan. 2015. LSP Studies As a Quest For Meso-Level Regularities. In *Languages for Special Purposes in a Multilingual, Transcultural World, Proceedings of the 19th European Symposium on Languages for Special Purposes, Keynote Addresses*, 8–10 July 2013, Vienna, Austria, ed. Gerhard Budin and Vesna Lušicky, 14–25. Vienna: University of Vienna.
Favell, Adrian, and David Reimer. 2021. European Outliers? Rethinking Europeanisation and Euroscepticism in Britain and Denmark. *European Societies* 23 (2): 232–254.
Fuchs, Eckhardt. 2011. Current Trends in History and Social Studies Textbook Research. *Journal of International Cooperation and Education* 14 (2): 17–34.
Galpin, Charlotte. 2017. *The Euro Crisis and European Identities: Political and Media Discourse in Germany, Ireland and Poland. New Perspectives in German Political Studies*. New York: Palgrave Macmillan.
Gay, Paul du, Stuart Hall, Linda Janes, Hugh Mackay, and Keith Negus. 1997. *Doing Cultural Studies: The Story of the Sony Walkman*. Thousand Oaks: SAGE.
Gorbahn, Katja. 2012. Soziale Identität als geschichtsdidaktisches Konzept—11 Thesen zum Verständnis gruppenbezogener Identifikationen. *Zeitschrift für Geschichtsdidaktik* 11 (1): 148–162.
Greenhow, Christine, and Cathy Lewin. 2016. Social Media and Education: Reconceptualizing the Boundaries of Formal and Informal Learning. *Learning Media and Technology* 41 (1): 6–30.
Hall, Stuart. 1992. The Question of Cultural Identity. In *Modernity and Its Futures*, ed. Stuart Hall, David Held, and Tony McGrew, 273–316. Oxford: Polity Press.
———. 1997. *Representation: Cultural Representations and Signifying Practices*. Thousand Oaks: SAGE.

Hallsteinsdóttir, Erla, and Jörg Kilian. 2016. {German} and {Danish} in Stereotypes. The Worlds of Stereotypes and Their Linguistic-Cultural Constitution Forms. *Linguistik Online* 79 (5): 399–419.

Hansen, Lene. 2002. Sustaining Sovereignty: The Danish Approach to Europe. In *European Integration and National Identity: The Challenge of the Nordic States*, ed. Lene Hansen and Ole Wæver, 50–87. London: Routledge.

Herrmann, Richard, and Marilynn Brewer. 2004. Identities and Institutions: Becoming European in the EU. In *Transnational Identities: Becoming European in the EU*, ed. Richard Herrmann, Thomas Risse, and Marilynn Brewer, 1–22. Lanham, MD: Rowman & Littlefield.

Hettlage, Robert. 1999. European Identity—Between Inclusion and Exclusion. In *Nation and National Identity: The European Experience in Perspective*, ed. Hanspeter Kriesi, 243–262. Chur: Rüegger.

Höhne, Thomas. 2003. *Schulbuchwissen: Umrisse einer Wissens-und Medientheorie des Schulbuches*. Frankfurt am Main: Johann Wolfgang Goethe Universität.

Ichijo, Atsuko, and Willfried Spohn, eds. 2005. *Entangled Identities: Nations and Europe*. Aldershot, Hampshire: Ashgate.

Jenkins, Richard. 2000. Not Simple at All: Danish Identity and the European Union. In *An Anthropology of the European Union: Building, Imagining and Experiencing the New Europe*, ed. Irene Bellier and Thomas M. Wilson, 159–178. Oxford: Berg.

Kalwa, Nina. 2013. *Das Konzept 'Islam': Eine diskurslinguistische Untersuchung. Das Konzept 'Islam'*. Berlin: De Gruyter.

Keohane, Robert O. 1969. Lilliputians' Dilemmas: Small States in International Politics. *International Organization* 23 (2): 291–310.

Kiesendahl, Jana, and Christine Ott, eds. 2015. *Linguistik und Schulbuchforschung: Gegenstände—Methoden—Perspektiven*. Göttingen: V&R unipress.

Kohli, Martin. 2000. The Battlegrounds of European Identity. *European Societies* 2 (2): 113–137.

Lammers, Karl Christian. 2005. *Hvad skal vi gøre ved tyskerne bagefter? Det dansk-tyske forhold efter 1945*. Copenhagen: Schønberg.

Minkov, Michael, and Geert Hofstede. 2013. *Cross-Cultural Analysis. The Science and Art of Comparing the World's Modern Societies and Their Cultures*. Thousand Oaks: SAGE.

Nedergaard, Peter. 2015. Tyskland eller kaos. *Ræson* 22 (2): 34–37.

Nieländer, Maret, and Ernesto William De Luca, eds. 2018. *Digital Humanities in der internationalen Schulbuchforschung: Forschungsinfrastrukturen und Projekte*. Göttingen: V&R unipress.

Østergaard, Uffe. 2000. Danish National Identity: Between Multinational Heritage and Small State Nationalism. In *Denmark's Policy towards Europe after 1945: History, Theory and Options*, ed. Hans Branner and Morten Kelstrup, 139–184. Odense: Odense University Press.
Ott, Christine. 2017. *Sprachlich vermittelte Geschlechterkonzepte: eine diskurslinguistische Untersuchung von Schulbüchern der Wilhelminischen Kaiserzeit bis zur Gegenwart*. Berlin: De Gruyter.
Quenzel, Gudrun. 2015. *Konstruktionen von Europa. Die europäische Identität und die Kulturpolitik der Europäischen Union*. 1st ed. Bielefeld: Transcript Verlag.
Risse, Thomas. 2010. *A Community of Europeans? Transnational Identities and Public Spheres*. Ithaca, NY: Cornell University Press.
Rosamond, Annika Bergman. 2015. The Kingdom of Denmark and the Arctic. In *Handbook of the Politics of the Arctic*, ed. Leif Christian Jensen and Geir Hønneland, 501–516. Cheltenham, UK: Edward Elgar.
Schmale, Wolfgang. 2000. *Geschichte Europas*. Vienna: Böhlau.
———. 2008. *Geschichte und Zukunft der Europäischen Identität*. Stuttgart: Kohlhammer.
Smith, Anthony D. 1992. National Identity and the Idea of European Unity. *International Affairs* 68 (1): 55–76. Accessed June 3, 2022. https://doi.org/10.2307/2620461
Sørensen, Catharina. 2008. Danish Euroscepticism: Unique or Part of Broader Patterns. In *Danish Foreign Policy Yearbook 2008*, ed. Nanna Hvidt and Hans Mouritzen, 85–113. Copenhagen: Danish Institute for International Studies (DIIS).
Soysal, Yasemin Nuhoğlu. 2002. Locating Europe. *European Societies* 4 (3): 265–284.
Tombleson, Bridget, and Katharina Wolf. 2017. Rethinking the Circuit of Culture: How Participatory Culture has Transformed Cross-Cultural Communication. *Public Relations Review* 43 (1): 14–25.
Wenzel, Michael, Amélie Mummendey, and Sven Waldzus. 2007. Superordinate Identities and Intergroup Conflict: The Ingroup Projection Model. *European Review of Social Psychology* 18 (1): 331–372.
Wivel, Anders. 2019. Denmark and the European Union. *Oxford Research Encyclopedia of Politics*. New York: Oxford University Press.
Wodak, Ruth, Rudolf de Cillia, Martin Reisigl, Karin Liebhart, Angelika Hirsch, and Richard Mitten. 2009. *The Discursive Construction of National Identity*. Edinburgh: Edinburgh University Press.
Zappettini, Franco. 2019. *European Identities in Discourse: A Transnational Citizens' Perspective*. London: Bloomsbury Publishing.

Part I

Constructions of European and National Identities in Textbooks

2

Europe and the Nation in Current Swiss Textbooks

Markus Furrer

Introduction

In this chapter, I examine how Europe is represented in textbooks. I focus on current textbooks for lower secondary schools and ask how Europe appears in the teaching material. I also examine how it is presented and interconnected with perspectives on Switzerland. My focus is on history instruction material at a time when the question of the further development of the European Union is intensely debated, as is that of Europe's place in the world. This study touches on various topics. When considering how historical processes and spatial allocations are presented in teaching material, the fundamental question is what the science of history has to say about it. There is also the specific question of how historical processes may be represented in history textbooks for schools. History books have characteristic features and are subject to general conditions; this

M. Furrer (✉)
University of Techer Education Lucerne, Luzern, Switzerland
e-mail: markus.furrer@phlu.ch

K. Gorbahn et al. (eds.), *Exploring Interconnectedness*, Palgrave Studies in Educational Media, https://doi.org/10.1007/978-3-031-13960-4_2

must be considered. They also have specific socio-political functions in the educational system.

If we examine the question of how the European dimension is intertwined with the national and global dimensions in textbooks, then it is worth clarifying various preliminary questions. One is that of Europe as a theoretical concept in the study of history. What is European history and how may it be constructed? Europe consists of various nation-states, which are also integrated into the region in different ways. In the case of Switzerland, this raises specific questions concerning its representation of Europe, as the view and historical experience of a small state play a significant role here.

The Historical Dimension of 'Europe'

If one questions the representation of European history in textbooks, other fundamental questions emerge, which will be addressed in this chapter. First, is there such a thing as European history? What is the place of this history within national narratives? And what is its global framework? What is the consequence of European integration on the construction of a European history? What directions is research taking, and how do these differ? Has a European narrative emerged, and how do historians assess it?

The search for a common European history intensified with the European integration following the Second World War, and the ideas and goals related to a closer political union. In particular, it was connected with the debate about European identity (Duchhardt 2000, 7). At this same time, the national master narratives disintegrated. In Europe, the question arose as to whether Europe could take the place of the nation. As early as the end of the 1920s, the French historian Marc Bloch noted that there was no history of France, only one of Europe (Girault 1995); however, this was meant to be more declamatory than factual. Particularly in times of crisis, when European societies are in a state of disintegration, the demand for a European history arises. Social tensions in the societies of European countries promote forces that rely on national identity politics and promise solutions that suggest better management within the national context. At the same time, the countries of the European Union often disagree and defer solutions. The call for a common history is connected to questions about European commonalities and the recurring question: *quo vadis Europe*? With regard to Europe's history, there are answers to this question with respect to both the present and future. However, for most historians, it is clear that there is no common European history. Can continents even have a history? The English historian Eric Hobsbawm regards the history of Europe as a process, which in concrete terms means that its object is neither a historical period nor a human collective. Hobsbawm thus states that there is no historical, homogeneous Europe (1998, 275–86). European history, which saw the rise of modern state formation, has been characterised by two divergent forces: on the one hand, the constant rivalry between peoples or their rulers, with the resulting disputes and wars, and on the other hand, the longing for stability, unity and peace.

A European consciousness that has been carried by the political elite within the geographic borders of today's Europe is in fact a phenomenon of the seventeenth century, when Europe became a key concept in political and international law (Duchhardt 2000, 2). This was still the case in the nineteenth century, and this remained the preserve of a small class. Mostly, they belonged to the upper middle classes, the intellectuals and other cosmopolitans. But not until the First World War did an awareness of Europe emerge among the general population (Krüger 2006). During the interwar period, Europe was the embodiment of crises, problems and dangers. After 1945, conditions once again changed fundamentally. In the western European countries, the western form of parliamentary democracy stabilised in an almost unexpected way. Moreover, the peace narrative of 'self-civilisation' found expression (Rödder 2015, 382). The integrated Europe became a space where borders were transcended, and democracy and human rights were guaranteed. And after 1989, an integrated Europe contributed significantly to the stability of the east-central and south-eastern European regions.

The fact that the history of a continent was established is related to the process of change that began in Europe. Eric Hobsbawm writes, 'The questions of how and why capitalism and modern society came to full bloom in Europe alone are the fundamental questions of European history' (1998, 285). Since the end of the fifteenth century, European expansion made world history Eurocentric, and it remained so until the twentieth century. Nation states and industrialisation led to European (with the inclusion of the USA, also western) dominance, based on a capitalist economy, a modern administration and weapons technology (Mishra 2012). The continent was also perceived from outside in terms of this undeniable European superiority. Thanks to recent studies, we are aware of how this global hierarchy came about and, above all, how the rest of the world reacted to it (Mishra 2012). Europeanisation, which first occurred on the continent (Bartlett 1993), was extended globally by European expansion, and historians such as Andreas Eckert (2012) view it as the 'globally effective, unique form of existence of Europe'. If Europe had not changed itself and the world, there would be no such thing as a single, unified history of Europe (Hobsbawm 1998, 284). Understood in this way, 'Europeanisation' is a construct that is based on the idea of an entire set of commonalities between societies. 'Europeanisation' appears as various spatial and temporal dimensions, which then play a role in the analysis in this paper: On the one hand, it refers to a dramatic change that began in the High Middle Ages, during which a common sociocultural foundation was formed in large parts of Europe. This took place as a complex and multi-layered process that began in the Frankish centre and moved towards the European periphery. As Bartlett describes it, this process was warlike, and accompanied by 'conquest, colonization, and Christianisation' (Bartlett 1993). This also connected the step outward with colonial expansion. European naval empires subjugated the world to a new global hierarchy. Here, Europeanisation goes hand in hand with colonisation and imperial expansion. However, Europe is not only a continent, but also an idea (Bartlett 1993) connected to the transmission of certain values, norms and scientific and technological approaches. Europe is also perceived as such from the outside, which is a crucial factor. The transformation of Europe—and since modern times, the transformation of the world by Europe—creates a coherent European history. Another aspect of Europeanisation refers to the economic, cultural and, above all, political integration that took place in the post-war period, a time of deepened integration and also the expansion of the European Union to include new member countries. Europeanisation also refers to a process of alignment and 'social integration'. Similarities and rapprochements in European society affect not only the countries of the politically integrated Europe, but have always affected the entirety of western Europe, and, since 1989, they have spread and continue to affect some areas of Central Eastern Europe and South-Eastern Europe. The social integration of Europe has a different history to that of its political integration (Kaelble 2007).

The history of Europe is widely used in historiography. Three approaches have been identified for representing European history (Schmale 2008), along a chronological sequence up to the present.

The first approach is based on a geopolitical definition that is oriented towards today's Europe. Here, European history is simply conveyed within the assumed current geographic space and framework. This pragmatic view assumes a Europe that is not to be further discussed. However, it often resembles a juxtaposition of national histories. This raises the question of whether it makes sense to speak of a European history for a period when Europe was neither a political unit nor an important category of identity, when people had no awareness of living together on a continent.

The second approach sheds light on shared structural elements, and thus refers to peculiarities and commonalities evident in European history. Historical identities that go relatively far back in time have been constructed in this way. Such a contemporary European historiography is not limited to a historical creation of European identity, but focuses on more specific thematic areas, such as social orders, labour or migration. But there are also shared historical experiences, such as poverty and social suffering, the 1848 revolutions and the World Wars.

The third, cultural–historical perspective addresses how people perceived Europe in their time. From this perspective, Wolfgang Schmale (2000, 15) interprets Europe as 'the result of discourses and performative acts'. Schmale argues that the concept of Europe has been subject to constant change and describes Europe in terms of cultural references. Such approaches are primarily directed towards cultural–historical forms of representation, which focus on European memory (den Boer 2012) or bring together various European authors' perspectives (François and Serrier 2019).

Many historians are well aware of the fact that in reconstructions of European history, myth and reality may be difficult to distinguish. Trausch argues that the word 'Europe' has become the source of new myths since the Schuman Plan and the beginning of European integration following the Second World War (1995, 128). From cultural studies and cultural history perspectives, research has investigated the way in which narratives of Europe are constructed, and the functions of these constructions, establishing various classifications (Dülffer 2004; Forchtner and Eder 2017). For example, the narrative of Europe as having 'risen from ruins' (Dülffer 2004, 52) was highly influential: It is the story of a Europe that brought itself to the brink of self-destruction through national division and national hubris, but rose again, overcoming enmities, joining forces and securing the freedom of its citizens (Wirsching 2012, 72). This 'progressive narrative' (Dülffer 2004) was fundamental to the construction of Europe as a 'promise' and had particular impact after the fall of the Berlin wall.

It is usually much easier to narrate the history of European integration. This is due to the fact that, as historian Eric Hobsbawm points out, the history of Europe has neither a territory nor a people as its object: its object is the process itself (Hobsbawm 1998, 283–84). Early in the post-war years, most historians began to search for forces that drove integration. Subsequently, they divided the integration process into several phases. As the so-called European Coal and Steel Community and the later Economic Community (Treaty of Rome) led to today's European Union, other integration projects such as the Council of Europe and the European Free Trade Association were only marginally affected (Loth 2014, 323–29). In recent work, historians demonstrate their awareness of the danger of lapsing into simple teleological constructions and of offering a kind of 'Advent narrative' of the waves of entry, with the formula: 6–9–12–15–25–27/28. The success story, in the sense of a dynamic (unstoppable) genealogical and teleological process, is rightly suspect from today's scientific point of view. The process of European unification has never been without complications. The British–American historian, Tony Judt, views the European Union as largely unintentional (1996). In this sense, it emerged as a kind of by-product of decades of negotiations by western European politicians seeking to assert their national interests

(Mak 2012, 37). Recent representations of the history of European integration try to avoid explicitly simple constructions. They take a critical approach when they emphasise that a history of the European Union cannot simply be projected back to the 1950s (Patel 2018, 347). Many descriptions also overlook the fact that throughout the entire Cold War period integration occurred only in 'small western Europe'. Eastern Europe was unified as a socialist economy under the leadership of the USSR.

Switzerland and Europe: Historical References

Before we explore the representation of Europe in textbooks for Switzerland, it is worth looking at the country's specific relationship to 'Europe'. Switzerland seems to be bound to a special role in an integrated Europe. The country, which is geographically, culturally and economically closely interwoven with its European environment, remains sceptical about joining the European Union and prefers selective bilateral agreements. The reasons for this are many and varied. In addition to the economic and political ideas and motives that usually emerge over the short term, subjective concepts of history and objectifiable state structures are likely to play dominant roles (Furrer 2009b, 248).

A characteristic of Switzerland is its relative smallness. Small statehood is more than just a political science or historical category; it is also a mark of identity. Small size is also a relative size which, historically, has always been created differently and justified over the course of history. Switzerland's size is a result of the tradition of the Swiss Confederation being a loose, federal network of city republics in pre-modern times. Small-scale statehood was a structural feature of the Swiss cantons and then of the later federal state. By the fin de siècle, many countries had a size that was comparable to Switzerland's. However, centrally located Switzerland was surrounded by four major powers, and the relative sizes and potential were very unequal. Switzerland was also a 'pronounced border country'. Geometry contributes to this, as in a small country the perimeter is relatively long in relation to the area. Small statehood was also repeatedly presented in an idealised way, which is associated with the tendency to cultivate the image of 'pre-modern forms of community, idealised small statehood, transfigured ideas of self-sufficiency, and a limited understanding of culture'.

The small Swiss state is part of a conflictual pattern in the European balance, in which it also locates the basis of its existence (Holenstein 2014). During the First World War, the classic system of this European balance disintegrated, which also led to an unstable transition period for Switzerland, and, especially in the wake of the 'intellectual national defence', to a strongly separatist attitude that was reserved and distanced from the post-war European integration process. Small statehood and neutrality became powerful counter-myths. Switzerland's self-image and, in turn, its image of Europe were thus formed over the course of the twentieth century, a formula which historian Herbert Lüthy has referred to as an 'antithesis' (Holenstein 2014, 15). In Swiss historian André Holenstein's study, *Mitten in Europa* [In the middle of Europe], he extensively references the concept of the small state, and emphasises that a look at the 'longue durée' draws attention to patterns and strategies of action that have determined the long-term 'conditions d'être' of the small state of Switzerland in broader power constellations and geopolitical contexts. Europe is also the subject of persistent political debates. The Swiss semi-direct democratic system contributes significantly to this. There is probably no other European country where European questions are so frequently and intensively discussed in public. These always involve questions concerning the further development of Switzerland's cooperation with the European Union. In many ways, Switzerland also resembles a Europe in miniature, even if the Swiss model cannot be simply transferred to the larger Europe (Altermatt 2011, 218). Switzerland is repeatedly portrayed—sometimes ironically or even exotically—as presenting an anti-principle to the European mainstream. Friends and critics of Switzerland, as well as opponents and supporters of the European Union at home and abroad, use projections of this small neutral state in their arguments (Tanner 2015, 568).

For historical reasons, the question of the relationship of Switzerland and its population to the surrounding Europe is a question of identity. This also raises questions about Switzerland's identity and purpose. In 1971 Karl Schmid stated, 'Without a greater awareness [*Bewusstheit*] of the nature and aims of the Swiss Confederation, we will not be able to answer the question of integration clearly' (quoted in Weibel 1996, 11). The Old Confederation's political alliance system is probably the most enduring in world history (Würgler 2014, 133). A prerequisite for this was that the Swiss city republics could assert themselves in a European setting dominated by the nobility. After the French Revolution, modern Switzerland also developed out of close interrelations with the surrounding major European powers, namely France and the Habsburg Empire.

As far as the European integration process was concerned, Switzerland took note of it early on and was sceptical about it. The country was one of the founding members of EFTA (European Free Trade Association), which was intended as a direct 'alternative model' (Patel 2018, 28) to the European Economic Community. In 1972 Switzerland found a modus vivendi in a free trade agreement between the European Economic Community and Switzerland. Its neutral position made it impossible for Switzerland to be a member of the European Community during the Cold War. With the latter's end and the orientation of the European Community towards a political union, Switzerland came under unforeseen pressure. The 'fall of the wall' fundamentally changed the political situation in Europe. Neutral states such as Austria and Sweden joined the European Community. In a 1992 referendum, Switzerland decided against joining the European Economic Area by a narrow majority. It feared that this was a step towards full accession. It took another 10 years until Swiss participation in the European internal market was negotiated through bilateral agreements. Switzerland is also involved in the Schengen and Dublin systems. But scepticism about full EU membership remains high. There is no way to disregard this fact in history lessons, and take a critical look at the debates. Next, I consider textbooks, and explore the questions of how 'Europe' is used as a term and to identify a continent. and how specifically European integration is conveyed. To do this, I examine the curricula. I also consider the extent to which current history books are changing the way Europe is presented in the Swiss classroom, compared to the way this was done in earlier books.

Europe as a Subject in Earlier Swiss Textbooks

Before we turn to the question of the currently conveyed representations of Europe in Swiss textbooks, we consider the preceding representation. In older history textbooks of the entire twentieth century, Europe appears mostly in the descriptions of so-called general history. Some studies show that in Swiss textbooks, this history is usually given considerable space, (Furrer 2004). However, this primarily presents the histories of individual, mostly western European countries, and in terms of developmental steps and epochs: France is mentioned in connection with absolutism and the French Revolution; Great Britain stands for the Industrial Revolution; Germany is discussed with respect to the foundation of the German Empire, and Italy with the Risorgimento, whereas medium-sized and smaller countries, and, above all, the central and eastern European states are not mentioned (Furrer 2020). Also, this is not a European narrative in the true sense of the word. At best, Europe is viewed as a loose geographic vessel. The ideas of Europe and the Europe in which we live together appear underrepresented (Furrer 2009a, 70).

Discussions of European integration have little or no space in older Swiss teaching material. It should be noted that a historical narrative of European integration could only appear from the 1970s onwards, when historians began to address European integration, after the political scientists had. Nor was 'integration' a common term in contemporary usage until about 1950, when it appeared in everyday language in discussions of the consolidation of Europe. Until then, there was also no ongoing, politically determined and controlled integration of Europe. When the topic of integration is addressed in Swiss textbooks, it is always understood with reference to the temporal dimension. In Switzerland, references to western European integration penetrated the textbooks only slowly, and often only selectively. In most cases, 'integration' was not a concern. The textbooks barely addressed the importance of integration, which was viewed with significant concern well beyond the 1980s, and reduced to its economic aspect (Furrer 2009a, 73).

Until the 1980s, the presentation of European integration in Swiss school textbooks largely coincided with the officially disseminated views and pronouncements: the impossibility of accession due to its neutrality until 1991 and the insufficient economic attractiveness of the common market for Switzerland. The political dimension of Swiss involvement in Europe has largely been dropped. In a study from the 1990s, Anton Hauler demonstrated that the relationship between Switzerland and the integrated Europe was not adequately addressed in Swiss teaching material till the 1990s (Hauler 1994, 251). Typically, the relationship between Switzerland and the European Community was also considered from a purely economic perspective.

Integrating an Understanding of Europe into the Current Curricula

It is evident that in Switzerland, European integration was considered at a late date, and only marginally in Swiss curricula and teaching material. In Switzerland, the 1993 Conference of Cantonal Ministers of Education (EDK) decided on the question of Europe, and called for a bundle of measures to integrate the European dimension into teaching, and thus promote the concept of Europe. Therefore, the European dimension was to be included in the curricula. This took place through a lengthy process. Since 2014, there has only been a common curriculum for the entire country (subdivided according to language regions); there are no longer 26 cantonal curricula. The new Curriculum 21 for German-speaking Switzerland lists skills: 'Students can perceive and assess Switzerland's position in Europe and the world'. This skill-set is specified as follows: a) 'can describe selected goals and concerns, and the development of an international organisation of which Switzerland is a member (e.g. UN); b) can enumerate the phases of European unification and characterise Switzerland's position (e.g. neutral; Council of Europe; OSCE); c) can outline different positions on the relationship between Switzerland and Europe, and comment on them' (Lehrplan 21). European history is referenced only once more in the curriculum: in the context of world history, European expansion is mentioned.

As part of the implementation of Curriculum 21, which for the first time established language-region obligations for Switzerland, two new textbooks were presented in German-speaking Switzerland, which differed in their conception and in the way they were developed. Both adopt a skill-based orientation, and the specifications of the curriculum. Klett-Schulbuchverlag's *Zeitreise* (Time Travel) (2016–2018) is a textbook tailored specifically to Swiss schools (Swiss edition) and was integrated into the existing framework for a textbook used in Germany and South Tyrol. References to Switzerland, in existing textbooks and individual chapters, were respectively developed and incorporated into this textbook. In concrete terms, this means that many references to Europe reflect the perspective of a German textbook. Further references to Europe may also include the subsequent inclusion of Swiss-oriented chapters and adaptations. *Gesellschaften im Wandel* (Societies in Transition), a textbook published by Zurich's Lehrmittelverlag, takes a different starting position. It was developed from scratch. This textbook also raises the question of including the national level, and its link to and integration into the European and global dimensions, with regard to the curriculum. In other respects, the textbook is designed similarly to *Zeitreise*, and has additional work material, which is available online to registered users. This is not included in this analysis.

Textbooks and this Study's Methodology

This study focuses on current Swiss history textbooks. The two current textbooks, *Zeitreise* and *Gesellschaften im Wandel*, have been evaluated with the help of digital analytical tools. In this section, I refer to the specifics of textbooks, in order to classify their messages. There are three aspects that strike me as particularly important, and also influence the portrayal of Europe in these books.

Textbooks are a vehicle of knowledge transfer whereby socio-cultural knowledge is presented via a specific medium—as pedagogically coded, book-shaped, institutionalised, and historically and temporally condensed social knowledge (Höhne 2003, 73). History books for schools encounter challenges in their representation of Europe. This is due to their specific character. To begin with, a textbook needs to narrate events from the past in such a way that students can follow and understand the content, which inevitably results in a selection of topics and a kind of simplification, which also depends on the academic level in question. History textbooks have traditionally had a special status. They contain historical knowledge that is generally believed to be that which everyone should master. Through textbooks, historical information is selected and transmitted from one generation to another: 'History textbooks preserve and communicate cultural truths intergenerationally' (Grever and van der Vlies 2017, 288).

The development of history books for schools is a political question, because once published, history textbooks contribute to the common creation of meaning in a society (Gautschi 2006, 190). However, when comparing various textbooks, their different conditions of production must always be considered. This varies from country to country. As Grever and Vlies state, 'Because history textbooks are carriers of different social and political agendas, and function differently in various national and international contexts with various social and political demands, textbook research faces many more challenges than is generally assumed' (Grever and van der Vlies 2017, 289).

The communication of history is always narrative. From theories of history education, we know that the presentation of history cannot be achieved without a narrative and narrativity. Narrativity is, as it were, a historiological category. Therefore, an understanding of history is also a narrative understanding. But it is precisely here that teaching material encounters challenges. An excess of content is a major problem for authors of history-instruction material (Gautschi 2006, 183). As a result, textbooks do not always do justice to the narrative character of history, but often address events in isolation from each other and in a fragmented fashion.

The focus of this chapter is not the analysis of didactics or pedagogy, but the content of textbooks. First, we turn to the question of how Europe appears in the composition and structure of the books. The basis for this is a synopsis from which preliminary conclusions may be drawn. There is no compact narrative of a European history. Instead, references to Europe are distributed in thematically different chapters. These follow a kind of canon that takes up themes from antiquity to the present. The teaching material for the lower secondary level is usually divided into several volumes that together offer a compact overview. As a result, the European narrative conveyed in them is highly fragmented, and thematically linked to references to the Roman Empire, medieval feudal society, revolutionary Europe or the industrial revolution. This is to be expected, and is in the tradition of representations of Europe in history textbooks for schools.

What content is used to address European questions? And can a narrative, however fragmented, be discerned in it? To analyse the structures of a European narrative, I used digital analytical tools, such as AntConc, and systematically recorded and interpreted references to the term *europ**. The extended contexts of meaning surrounding *europ** were collected in lists and assigned to categories. This was done both deductively and inductively by combining historians' references and analytical perspectives on the history of Europe with the references made in the books, to form common categories. The following categories show how and in which contexts Europe is discussed, and with which theoretical references.

Space. Spatial references to Europe aim for geographic classification and allocation. At a deeper level, the following questions must be asked: Which spaces are mentioned (above all, large regions: east, west, north, south)? Is 'Europe' a toponym, with prepositions?

'Europe of Nations'. Where and how is Europe presented as a conglomerate of individual states, and what roles do the major nations (e.g. Germany) play in this?

'Cultural Europe'. 'Culture' refers to identification with Europe by identifying European cultural characteristics, and also by comparing them to non-European cultures. These characteristics range from religion (Christianity, but also secularisation) to cultural expression (Renaissance, Enlightenment, etc.). They may be used in an exclusive or inclusive way, with an essentialist underpinning, or even be purely descriptive.

The 'Europe of common processes' focuses on specific thematic areas, such as social orders, labour or migration, and also industrialisation and nation-state formation. Often, these are transnational developments in which the focus is less on a single European country, and more on developments that are recorded and interpreted at a pan-European level.

'Integrated Europe'. In everyday language, Europe is often equated with the European Union. In addition to an organised Europe, the aspect of an integrated Europe is thus also explicitly mentioned. Historically, too, this references a specific process that, in general terms, began with the ECSC (European Coal and Steel Community), and involved further forms of integration, up to the current European Union. It also includes the division of Europe during the Cold War and during the interwar period, through the rise of dictatorships. The integrated Europe also includes the naming and declaration of European organisations from the Council of Europe to the EFTA and the CSCE. Some, such as the EFTA, were competing organisations and others, such as the Council of Europe, are complementary organisations.

The Europe of 'Europeanisation'. The term 'Europeanisation' is understood broadly here, as I discussed at the beginning in the theoretical section, and is in keeping with the ideas of historians such as Hobsbawm. Essentially, it goes to the heart of what constitutes Europe's history and why it is possible to speak of something such as a 'European history'. This Europeanisation first created something like a common European frame of reference, and is also connected to colonial expansion up to the postcolonial present, and specific values, as Europe sees itself as a community of values. Thus, European history reveals itself as a process: if Europe had not changed itself and the world, there would be no such thing as a European history. This history is presented in textbooks that primarily address European expansion overseas in terms of colonialism and imperialism, up to the transmission of values (universalisation of the French Revolution, human rights), and also industrialisation and modernisation, for example, which initially emerged in Europe.

'Switzerland and/in Europe'. The connection of Switzerland with Europe refers to two areas: There is the matter of demonstrating in a comparative context that Switzerland is also affected by European developments, or that it differs from them. Thus, Europe is a frame of reference which the country is embedded geographically, politically and culturally. Furthermore, there are questions about the integration of

Switzerland in Europe with its involvement of various organisations, such as the EU, EFTA, the OSCE or special agreements, such as Dublin or Schengen.

Analyses of 'Europe' in Recent Textbooks

References to Europe occur frequently, as a digital analysis of word frequency indicates. A comparison of the most frequently mentioned terms shows how Europe may be classified. In the three volumes of *Zeitreise*, *europ** (Europe and European) appears with the following, also frequently mentioned terms: Switzerland (*schweiz*, 598 hits), people (*menschen*, 530 hits), war (*krieg*, 245 hits), history (*geschichte*, 214 hits), states (*staaten*, 217 hits), Europe and European (*europ* 196), and Germany (*deutschland*, 159 hits). Mentions of *europ** in *Gesellschaften im Wandel*, with its two volumes (Themenbuch 1 und 2), looks somewhat different. Here, the following words are the most important ones: people (*Menschen*, 469 hits), *europ* 259, Switzerland (*schweiz*, 259 hits), world (*Welt* 171 hits) and history (*Geschichte*, 119 hits). Without over-interpreting these relative results, this suggests that 'Europe' and 'European' are frequently mentioned terms. Moreover, and what the count alone does not yet show, the term is distributed across all the historical epochs represented. However, the analysis of all the findings revealed that the European dimension is most present in connection with the following historical topics (concordance plots): a) European expansion, discoveries b) the Napoleonic period and Congress of Vienna c) Racism, colonialism, imperialism, d) the world wars and their consequences (National Socialist extermination policy in Europe), e) the Cold War and f) European integration. The textbooks compared are similar in this respect, which is unsurprising. 'Europe' appears as a term in specific topics and is mentioned in various contexts. This raises the question of how the term 'Europe' is assigned. For this purpose, the hits for *europ** were assigned to the categories listed in Table 2.1. The term *europ** was mapped and analysed in connection with eight preceding and eight following words. The following table shows how these categorical classifications are distributed in the two history books examined here.

Table 2.1 Distribution of the categorised findings of *europ** in the textbooks (absolute and percentage of entries)

Categories	*Zeitreise* (Time Travel) (484 hits for *europ**)	*Gesellschaften im Wandel* (Societies in Transition) (541 hits for *europ**)
The spatial use of Europe	36 (7.5%)	22 (4%)
The 'Cultural Europe'	13 (2.7%)	40 (7.4%)
The Europe of common processes	88 (18.2%)	193 (35.7%)
The Integrated Europe	141 (29.1%)	76 (14.1%)
Europeanisation	101 (20.8%)	158 (29.2%)
Switzerland and/in Europe	105 (21.7%)	52 (9.6%)

This also includes repeated passages, as textbooks sometimes repeat statements with identical wording in exercises that appear in the authored text.

References to Space with Respect to Europe

With reference to Europe, the category of 'space' tends to be concerned with geography, allocation or classification. In terms of proportion, such references are only made sporadically. More interesting in terms of the evaluations are references made or not made to European regions (east, west, north, south). 'Eastern Europe' appears frequently (21 times in both textbooks together), whereas 'northern Europe' is non-existent, and 'southern Europe' (five times) and western Europe (seven times) are far less common than 'eastern Europe'. The more extensive use of 'eastern Europe' is a consequence of the selection of topics in the textbooks (wars of annihilation in the east during the Second World War, the Eastern Bloc during the Cold War and the eastward expansion of the EU). This may indicate that eastern Europe is perceived as a collective, whereas western Europe is represented in a more differentiated way through its nations, such as France or Great Britain. This fits well with research that indicates that eastern Europe serves as Europe's internal 'other' in discourses (Quenzel 2015).

'Cultural Europe': References to Identifiers

Europe was and is related to cultural characteristics in the fields of religion, art and music, and also education, politics and urban development, to list some of the topics in an unsystematic way. This cultural category also creates—intentionally or not—references to identifiers. For example, there are references to Christianity, architecture and styles, such as the Baroque, the Enlightenment epoch, and so on. This is found far more frequently in older textbooks. Cultural identifiers may have an exclusive or an inclusive effect, and they are sometimes essentialist. The cultural aspect of Europe appears in our books in various ways: a comparison between the two sets of teaching material shows that *Gesellschaften im Wandel* takes a broader approach, drawing attention to Europe's cultural heritage and to cultural similarities. This is also related to the different selections of topics in the textbooks. Antiquity and the Early Middle Ages are still treated as formative epochs from which the European heritage derives. Mainstays of such classifications are Greek and Roman antiquity, Christianity, socio-historical aspects of the Middle Ages, and epochal designations such as Humanism or Renaissance, Baroque and Absolutism. *Gesellschaften im Wandel* has a particular focus here, whereas *Zeitreise* addresses later epochs.

The Europe of Common Processes: A Structural View

There are many references to structural developments in the textbooks discussed here: for example, we learn that in many European countries, the awareness of belonging to a nation grew throughout the nineteenth century, and that in the 1970s and 1980s, parties developed from environmental movements in many European countries. The structural history approach is transnational and is not based on the additive naming of individual countries and states, but emphasises that developments are pan-European. On the one hand, the representation of actions, events and processes is oriented towards the European region, and further emphasises the implicit European character of such processes, such as the power struggles between great European powers, the (French) Revolution and Napoleon's expansion, or the formation of European nation states up to the formation of Europe-specific party movements. This area is predominantly represented in both textbooks. Today it represents a main approach to the representation of European history, and should also help to overcome national 'container' representations, in the sense of transnationally transmitted historical processes. Here, European references replace previous state histories (found in older textbooks).

The 'Integrated Europe': A Road to Unity?

As the results of my analysis demonstrate, both textbooks discussed here extensively discuss European integration, which they address in specific chapters on the topic. In connection with this, Switzerland's (current) role is frequently referenced ('What role should Switzerland play in Europe', *Gesellschaften im Wandel*, vol. 2, 122). As political education is primarily integrated into history lessons according to the Swiss-German curriculum, the history textbooks cover current topics, which sometimes have a strong contemporary historical character. In Switzerland's direct-democratic system, Europe—mostly with respect to questions concerning Switzerland's relationship with the European Union—is a practically permanent subject of political debate, which leads to referendums. Switzerland's semi-direct political system permanently links foreign, and by extension, European, policy with domestic questions, and presents these to the electorate for decision. Such debates are included in history textbooks. The topic of an integrated Europe is related not only to the European Union, but to the other European organisations previously mentioned, from the Council of Europe to the OECD and the OSCE. This is probably particularly typical of Swiss teaching material.

The textbook chapters on European integration ('Europe's road to unity?')—'Switzerland in Europe'—'Where is the EU headed?' (*Zeitreise*, vol. 3, 54–6) are problem-oriented and sober in their reporting. An opinion is avoided. *Gesellschaften im Wandel* (vol. 2, 122) addresses the fact that, thanks to the European Union, today Europe is predominantly a 'peaceful continent' and thus tends to take a stance on this, even if such statements seem historically reduced. But all such representations and explanations seem merely descriptive. While Europe's integration is no longer viewed through economic spectacles, unlike in older teaching texts, the further development of integration is left open, and many questions come to mind in a chapter on contemporary history.

Europeanisation: Global Europe

Here, 'Europeanisation' is used as a broad term that covers colonial expansion (including colonialism) and later imperial expansion, the so-called civilising mission, racist and Social Darwinist ideas, and the current role of the European Union in world affairs. The focus is on Europe in the world, as important European actors have played and continue to play an influential role. It may be assumed that this always includes Switzerland as a European country 'in the middle of Europe'. With the means of 'Europeanisation', the society of the colonial era is also included in colonial expansion. The focus is on interconnectedness instead of a simple representation that merely assigns discovery, conquest and colonialism to individual European states such as Spain or Great Britain. Colonial expansion assumes a European dimension in which European societies have been involved, including those of landlocked Switzerland. Thus, both history books—*Zeitreise* (vol 1, 40 and 42) and *Gesellschaften im Wandel* (vol 1, 74, 75 and 76)—repeatedly use the term 'European' in chapter titles and in the text when describing colonial expansion. This also includes Switzerland. Here, a change is apparent between the previously mentioned older history books and the new ones. This is an important change in Swiss history books. For a long time, people had the feeling that a country such as Switzerland, without colonies, had nothing to do with colonialism. Thus, one overlooked what today are called 'entanglements' (Purtschert et al. 2012; Furrer 2019). It was only the analytical approach to social and cultural history, and later in political history, that expanded the field, allowing events in Switzerland and social, economic, and cultural developments to be applied to the broader context and including transnational references (Furrer and Kaufmann 2020, 141). In concrete terms, Switzerland was now also considered part of Europe.

Switzerland and/in Europe

Conceptually, Switzerland is always related to Europe. The subject area, 'Switzerland and/in Europe', appears significantly more frequently in *Zeitreise* than in *Gesellschaften im Wandel*. This corresponds to the fact that, on the whole, the Swiss dimension is more evident in the former book, as was demonstrated above. In *Zeitreise*, *schweiz** [Swiss and Switzerland] is mentioned 598 times and in *Gesellschaften im Wandel* 259 times. This may be explained by the different conceptions conveyed by the textbooks. In the case of *Zeitreise*, the Swiss dimension was incorporated into an already existing version of *Zeitreise* in Germany. As a result, Swiss themes, presented in new, separate chapters and through specific references—'… also in Switzerland'—give the national dimension more weight in this history textbook than in the other, *Gesellschaften im Wandel*.

My analysis revealed that, essentially, there are three ways in which the relationship between Switzerland and Europe is mentioned. First, it is mentioned that historical events, such as revolutions or the Reformation, also took place in Switzerland, as a European country (*Zeitreise*, vol. 1, 48, 94 and 114). The effect is to demonstrate that the country is a participant in European history. Europe continues to be used as a general term for relationships and exchanges with various European states. In this way, transnational connections become apparent. Furthermore, Switzerland's function in Europe becomes a question, whether as a result of the influence of the major European powers on it, or as a result of Swiss politics. Switzerland is extensively referenced in the presentation of European integration, in order to present the country's positions and attitudes. As clearly as the books create European references to Switzerland, the integration project appears distanced and subdued. The current debate on Switzerland's future position in Europe is also interpreted soberly: 'Should Switzerland expand its integration with the European Union or instead cut its ties? The Swiss People's Party, the only party that is clearly opposed to such integration, has won more votes in the last twenty years. The other parties accept or even endorse the interdependence. In domestic politics, many questions are polarising' (*Zeitreise*, vol. 3, 94).

Conclusions

This analysis reveals that there is no coherent European narrative. This insight was obtained by creating a synopsis of the topics discussed here. A digital analysis also reveals that the hits for *europ** are distributed through all chapters analysed. However, the European dimension is distributed in various ways, as the preceding lists indicate. In *Gesellschaften im Wandel*, which briefly references early history and antiquity, this term is used primarily with respect to geography (spatial reference). In both textbooks, and thus also in *Zeitreise*, 'Europe' appears in the discussion of the early modern period, with its expansion to other continents (Europeanisation). Here, the spatial reference increasingly indicates a broad European development, and replaces the policy of expansion that focused solely on Spain or Portugal, and later purely British or French expansionism with imperialism. The expansive Europe ('The world is becoming European', in *Zeitreise*) replaces the mode of representation previously oriented towards national vessels. The pre-modern Swiss development is also presented as situated in Europe ('The Swiss Confederation and Europe', in *Gesellschaften im Wandel*) and the formation of the modern federal state of Switzerland is also mentioned in the context of the European revolutions ('Switzerland in Revolutionary Europe', in *Zeitreise*). Europe continues to emerge through industrialisation, nation-state formation, imperialism and in the age of catastrophes: 'Europe becomes a battlefield' (*Zeitreise*) and is caught in the field of tension between 'democracy and dictatorship' (*Zeitreise*). 'From Divided to United Europe' (*Zeitreise*) is another metaphor that covers the second half of the twentieth century. However, both textbooks repeatedly use Europe to contextualise Switzerland: 'Switzerland, a democracy in Europe' (*Gesellschaften im Wandel*).

What may be deduced from this analysis? Even if textbooks today no longer offer an actual narrative composed of a beginning, a main part, and a conclusion, an account of Europe's story may nevertheless be traced in a fragmented and pieced-together manner. With regard to this analysis, the presentation of Europe in the two current sets of teaching material may be summarised as follows.

In new history books, Europe has become a concept in which the nation-state and its society are closely involved. European developments are discussed thoroughly, and the history of Europe, defined as diffusely as is the continent, also shapes Swiss history. In contrast to older books, which established Europe's common ground on the basis of cultural references, new history books are oriented towards structural history approaches and the Europeanisation model. This has a significant effect: for example, Swiss society is included, with respect to its colonial entanglements. This is one of the biggest changes in the way Europe is presented, compared to its presentation in older history books, in which Europe still existed as loosely enumerated individual states. Because Switzerland and its society are situated in Europe, they are also involved in the history of Europe and the world. For a long time, this view remained underemphasised, and 'history' seemed to have taken place outside of 'happy' Switzerland.

As obviously as Switzerland is integrated into pan-European historical processes in the depictions in current teaching material, the presentation of the European integration process seems remote from it. The presentation of the history of European integration continues to be told in a sober, and above all, distanced manner, as in the older teaching material. Here, the history books appear open-ended with a critical view. Historians hold a similar position (Patel 2018). However, in contrast to the nation-states, the European project always raises the question of perspectives, which remain open and suggest a 'Swiss bystander' approach. Such representations do not promote European integration but instead establish an interpretative order, offering a variety of interpretations and points of view. Other forms of and possibilities for European cooperation aside from the European Union are also emphasised.

Although we may find interesting references in history books, these tend to be fragmentary and remain open to interpretation. History books for schools are also restricted by narrow frameworks. Nevertheless, and given these conditions, they are an interesting source that suggest how a historical topic and, in this case, a space such as Europe, emerges through discourse; they convey quasi-official knowledge. In this case, it is also evident that European representations and perspectives are closely related to the Swiss discourse on Europe. This in turn explains the somewhat paradoxical starting position: In the history books, Switzerland now appears well integrated into European historical processes. The country is part of it, and also reflects Swiss society's broad awareness of being European. On the other hand, widespread scepticism about European political integration is also expressed. This may be explained by the history of the small state, which shapes social perceptions and behaviour patterns. Its position in the middle of Europe also contributes to this. However, one should not speak too quickly of a 'special case': Europe is characterised by diversity and special cases.

What may we conclude? History textbooks depict social and political discourses, and they are interesting testimonies. They also present a discussion of current topics, interpretations and references, as currently underway in historical science and didactics. They should also be understood within precisely this framework and context.

Textbooks and Curricula

Gesellschaften im Wandel 1–2. 2017. Lehrmittelverlag des Kantons Zürich.
Lehrplan21.ch.
Zeitreise 1–3. 2004–19. Leipzig: Klett-Schulbuchverlag.

References

Altermatt, Urs. 2011. *Die Schweiz in Europa: Antithese, Modell oder Biotop?* Frauenfeld: Huber.

Bartlett, Robert. 1993. *The Making of Europe: Conquest, Colonization and Cultural Change, 950–1130*. London: Penguin Books.

Den Boer, Pim. 2012. Konzept Europa. In *Europäische Erinnerungsorte 1. Mythen und Grundbegriffe des europäischen Selbstverständnisses*, ed. Pim Den Boer, Heinz Duchhardt, Georg Kreis, and Wolfgang Schmale, 59–74. Munich: Oldenbourg.

Duchhardt, Heinz. 2000. Europa-Diskurs und Europa-Forschung. In *Jahrbuch für Europäische Geschichte/European History Yearbook 1*, ed. Institut für Europäische Geschichte, 1–14. Munich: Oldenbourg.

Dülffer, Jost. 2004. Europäische Zeitgeschichte—Narrative und historiographische Perspektiven. In *Zeithistorische Forschungen/Studies in Contemporary History*. Accessed May 17, 2022. http://www.zeithistorische-forschungen.de/site/40208144/default.aspx.

Eckert, Andreas. 2012. Globalisierung. Europa und die Welt. In *Europäische Erinnerungsorte 3. Europa und die Welt*, ed. Pim Den Boer, Heinz Duchhardt, Georg Kreis, and Wolfgang Schmale, 11–18. Munich: Oldenbourg.

Forchtner, Bernhard, and Klaus Eder. 2017. Europa erzählen: Strukturen Europäischer Identität. In *Europäische Identität in der Krise? Europäische Identitätsforschung und Rechtspopulismusforschung im Dialog*, ed. Gudrun Hentges, Kristina Nottbohm, and Hans-Wolfgang Platzer, 79–100. Wiesbaden: Springer.

François, Étienne, and Thomas Serrier, eds. 2019. *Europa. Die Gegenwart unserer Geschichte 1–3*. Darmstadt: Wissenschaftliche Buchgesellschaft.

Furrer, Markus. 2004. *Die Nation im Schulbuch—zwischen Überhöhung und Verdrängung. Leitbilder der Schweizer Nationalgeschichte in Schweizer Geschichtslehrmitteln der Nachkriegszeit und Gegenwart*. Hannover: Verlag Hahnsche Buchhandlung.

———. 2009a. Die Schweiz erzählen—Europa erzählen—die Welt erzählen … Wandel und Funktion von Narrativen in Schweizer Geschichtslehrmitteln. *Schweizerische Zeitschrift für Geschichte* 59 (1): 56–77.

———. 2009b. Konstanten im Europabild der Schweizerinnen und Schweizer. In *Europäische Geschichtskultur—Europäische Geschichtspolitik. Vom Erfinden, Entdecken, Erarbeiten der Bedeutung von Erinnerung für das Verständnis und Selbstverständnis Europas*, ed. Christoph Kühberger and Clemens Sedmak, 248–263. Innsbruck: Studien Verlag.

———. 2019. Colonial Complicity? The Impact of Post-Colonialism on History Teaching in Switzerland. In *History Education and (Post-)Colonialism. International Case Studies*, ed. Susanne Popp, Katja Gorbahn, and Susanne Grindel, 243–258. Berlin: Peter Lang.

———. 2020. The Polish–Lithuanian Commonwealth in Swiss History Textbooks: Concepts, Templates, and Omissions. *The Polish Review* 65 (1): 32–42.

Furrer, Markus, and Lyonel Kaufmann. 2020. Mittendrin' oder "aussen vor"? Fragen zur Gewichtung und Darstellung der Schweizer Geschichte in aktuellen Lehrmitteln aus der Romandie und der deutschsprachigen Schweiz. In *The Teaching of the History of One's Own Country*. In *International Experiences in a Comparative Perspective*, ed. Nadine Fink, Markus Furrer, and Peter Gautschi, 124–151. Frankfurt am Main: Wochenschau Verlag.

Gautschi, Peter. 2006. Geschichtslehrmittel: Wie sie entwickelt werden und was von ihnen erwartet wird. *Zeitschrift für Geschichtsdidaktik* 5: 178–197.

Girault, René. 1995. Das Europa der Historiker. In *Europa im Blick der Historiker*, ed. Rainer Hudemann, Hartmut Kaelble, and Klaus Schwabe, 55–90. Munich: Oldenbourg.

Grever, Maria, and Tina van der Vlies. 2017. Why National Narratives Are Perpetuated: A Literature Review on New Insights from History Textbook Research. *London Review of Education* 15 (2): 286–301.

Hauler, Anton. 1994. *Die Schweiz auf dem Weg nach Europa. Politikprobleme und Dilemmata politischer Bildung*. Bonn: Europa Union Verlag.

Hobsbawm, Eric J. 1998. *Wieviel Geschichte braucht die Zukunft*. Munich: Carl Hanser.

Höhne, Thomas. 2003. *Schulbuchwissen. Umrisse einer Wissens- und Medientheorie des Schulbuchs*. Frankfurt am Main: Universität Frankfurt, FB Erziehungswissenschaften.

Holenstein, André. 2014. *Mitten in Europa: Verflechtung und Abgrenzungen in der Schweizer Geschichte*. Baden: Hier und Jetzt.

Judt, Tony. 1996. *Große Illusion Europa. Herausforderungen und Gefahren einer Idee*. Translated by Susanne Hornfeck, Munich: Hanser.

Kaelble, Hartmut. 2007. *Sozialgeschichte Europas 1945 bis zur Gegenwart*. Munich: Verlag C.H. Beck.

Krüger, Peter. 2006. *Das unberechenbare Europa: Epochen des Integrationsprozesses vom späten 18. Jahrhundert bis zur Europäischen Union*. Stuttgart: Kohlhammer.

Loth, Wilfried. 2014. *Europas Einigung. Eine unvollendete Geschichte*. Frankfurt am Main: Campus.

Mak, Geert. 2012. *Was, wenn Europa scheitert*. Munich: Pantheon.

Mishra, Pankaj. 2012. *From the Ruins of Empire: The Revolt Against the West and the Remaking of Asia*. London: Penguin Books.

Patel, Kiran Klaus. 2018. *Projekt Europa. Eine kritische Geschichte*. Munich: C.H. Beck.

Purtschert, Patricia, Barbara Lüthi, and Francesca Falk, eds. 2012. *Postkoloniale Schweiz. Formen und Folgen eines Kolonialismus ohne Kolonien*. Bielefeld: transcript.

Quenzel, Gudrun. 2015. *Konstruktionen von Europa, Die europäische Identität und die Kulturpolitik der Europäischen Union*. Bielefeld: transcript.

Rödder, Andreas. 2015. *21.0. Eine kurze Geschichte der Gegenwart*. Munich: C.H. Beck.
Schmale, Wolfgang. 2000. *Geschichte Europas*. Wien: Böhlau.
———. 2008. *Geschichte und Zukunft der Europäischen Identität*. Stuttgart: Kohlhammer.
Tanner, Jakob. 2015. *Geschichte der Schweiz im 20. Jahrhundert*. Munich: C.H. Beck.
Trausch, Gilbert. 1995. Der Schuman-Plan zwischen Mythos und Realität. In *Europa im Blick der Historiker*, ed. Rainer Hudemann, Hartmut Kaelble, and Klaus Schwabe, 105–128. München: Oldenbourg.
Weibel, Ewald R. 1996. Einführung und Fragestellung. In *Schweizer Eigenart: eigenartige Schweiz. Der Kleinstaat im Kräftefeld der europäischen Integration*, ed. Wolf Linder, Prisca Lanfranchi, and Ewald R. Weibel, 11–16. Bern: Haupt.
Wirsching, Andreas. 2012. *Der Preis der Freiheit. Geschichte Europas in unserer Zeit*. Munich: C.H. Beck.
Würgler, Andreas. 2014. Tagsatzungen und Konferenzen. In *Die Geschichte der Schweiz*, ed. Georg Kreis, 132–135. Basel: Schwabe Verlag.

3

A Corpus-Based Discourse Analysis of the Frequency and Co-occurrences of *Danmark* and *Europa* in Textbooks for Danish as a Foreign Language

Katja Bethke-Prange

Introduction: Danish as a Foreign Language in Schleswig-Holstein

Danish has always been an important language in Schleswig-Holstein, owing to the geographic proximity of, and the historical and cultural relationships between, this federal state and Denmark. Still, the centuries of coexistence resulted in armed conflicts between Danes and Germans in Schleswig-Holstein during the nationalist movement of the 1860s, and language became an important aspect of the national identity of those on each side of the newly defined border. Following the reunion of Northern Schleswig and Denmark in 1920, the current border between Denmark and Germany was established. Thus, Danish became a minority language in Schleswig-Holstein, and German a minority language in Denmark. The new conditions once again raised questions about the national identity of the people in Schleswig-Holstein and Southern

K. Bethke-Prange (✉)
Institute for Scandinavian Studies, University of Kiel, Kiel, Germany

K. Gorbahn et al. (eds.), *Exploring Interconnectedness*, Palgrave Studies in Educational Media, https://doi.org/10.1007/978-3-031-13960-4_3

Denmark. Because of these specific circumstances, each language was recognised as a minority language in the other country, and was protected and promoted by the Bonn–Copenhagen Agreement of 1955. Since then, Danish has not only been taught at the schools of the Danish minority, but also as a foreign language in state schools in Schleswig-Holstein. In Denmark, German is taught as a minority language in the schools of the German minority, and as a foreign language in state schools. Both minorities do play an important role in the political relationship between Denmark and Germany, especially in Schleswig-Holstein. The successful cooperation between Denmark and Schleswig-Holstein is seen as a role model for other border areas in Europe. In the curriculum currently used in Schleswig-Holstein, Danish is no longer called a 'foreign language', but a 'neighbouring language'. Bearing in mind Schleswig-Holstein's eventful history, the struggle for, and the discourse concerning how national identity is constructed on each side of the Danish–German border has always been a part of the discourse about national identity in the mass media, and has found its way into the textbooks on Danish in Schleswig-Holstein, where it is part of the intercultural knowledge conveyed by teaching Danish.

In Schleswig-Holstein, Danish is part of L1 acquisition at the schools and kindergartens of the Danish minority. At state schools, Danish is the second or third foreign language, beginning in different years, as it is up to each school to decide whether or when Danish is offered as a school subject (see detailed overview, Jacob 2018, 18ff.).

At public schools in Schleswig-Holstein Danish is a minor subject, and only three textbooks are available: *Dansk for os* (Buchenau & Landesinstitut Schleswig-Holstein 1994 [*Do*] 1994), *Mere Dansk for os* (Buchenau et al., [*MDo*] 1998), and *Det er Dansk* (Brandt et al. [*DD*] 2004, 2011). These textbooks are designed for both beginners and advanced learners. They focus mainly on teaching grammar, rather than on intercultural aspects. The current curriculum for Danish represents the latest requirements of Schleswig-Holstein's foreign language policy. These requirements focus not only on Denmark, Denmark's national identity, and Denmark's relationship with Germany as a next-door neighbour, but also on Europe and the European Union as a common political, cultural, and economic background.

The focus on Europe as a cultural and economic area in a globalised and mediatised world renders foreign-language learning that aims for more multilingualism increasingly important, particularly in regions where neighbouring languages are in close contact with each other. (Ministerium für Schule und Berufsbildung des Landes Schleswig-Holstein. *Fachanforderungen Dänisch* [*FADan*] 2016, 13)

The analysis of textbooks in this chapter is to be viewed as a Scandinavian studies contribution to textbook research, with a focus on presenting concepts of the nation and content in textbooks on Danish. The aim is to identify and describe linguistically constructed concepts of 'the national' and 'the European' in the context of the Danish–German relationship in Europe. This chapter thus aims to answer the following questions: What concepts of 'the national' and 'the European' are found in textbooks and curricula for Danish as a school subject in Schleswig-Holstein, and how are these linguistically constructed and presented? And do size and political power feature in the concepts of 'the national' and 'the European'?

We begin with a short summary of linguistic approaches to textbook studies in general, and research on stereotypes, in particular. Then we present our study of how conceptualisations of 'the Danish' and 'the European' are constructed linguistically in three textbooks for Danish as a foreign language, and in the current curriculum for Danish as a school subject in Schleswig-Holstein. Part of the analysis presented in this article involves finding and describing linguistic constructions that may be interpreted as aspects of possible national and European identity constructs, and discussing their potential as stereotypes in the intercultural context of foreign language learning. Finally, we discuss our findings as components of the *expected* state of a learner's knowledge and thus as a potential part of national and European identity promoted in educational media.

Linguistic Approaches to Textbook Research

According to Ott (2015), there was a dearth of linguistics studies in textbook research for quite some time before it re-emerged as a field of interest in 2015, especially in linguistics and German studies, for example, in foreign-language teaching research, text linguistics, and discourse linguistics. Unfortunately, textbook research has never been a field of interest in Scandinavian Studies. The research presented here is therefore pioneering work and must rely on results from neighbouring disciplines, such as German studies and applied linguistics. The re-emergence of linguistics in textbook studies mentioned above was primarily influenced by English Studies and American Studies, where textbook research has always been a part of applied linguistics in the tradition of critical discourse analysis and educational media research. New methodological approaches have included corpus-based analysis (Ott 2015, 21). In 2015, Kiesendahl and Ott published an anthology of various methodological and text–linguistic approaches to textbook research, edited by the Georg Eckert Institute for International Textbook Research (GEI).[1] This anthology represents the state of the art of textbook research in Germany, with all its various focuses, perspectives and methods for examining the functions and influences of these specific types of texts on language teaching in general, and on teaching various topics, such as grammar, pragmatic elements, or cultural knowledge.

In our investigation, we implement some of these fundamental methodological approaches to analyse linguistic constructions of knowledge conceptualisations in educational media. Pfalzgraf (2015) discusses the possibility of a corpus-based approach to discourse linguistics, and Heinz and Pflaeging's (2015) adaptation of Lakoff and Johnson's (2003) Conceptual Metaphor Theory as a storehouse of specific knowledge transfer in textbooks. Here, metaphoric meaning is 'not just a matter of language, that is, of mere words' (Lakoff and Johnson 2003, 6). Metaphors carry information about linguistic structure, as well as the semantic content and pragmatic functions of words and phrases. Thus, the development of concepts in language use is an important part of mental processing, and therefore of language teaching and learning.

Textbooks are a specific text genre that manifests and mediates the conceptualisation of knowledge for its users. By 1980, Riemenschneider had already examined the constructions of the concept of 'nation' in foreign language textbooks. He argues that the content conveyed by language teaching is of utmost importance, as textbooks have always conveyed information about 'others' (Riemenschneider 1980, 29).

According to Lippmann ([1921] 2008), such information about others is encoded in stereotypes.

We are told about the world before we see it. We imagine most of the things before we experience them. And unless education has made us acutely aware, those preconceptions govern deeply the whole process of perception (Lippmann [1921] 2008, 79).

Textbooks for foreign language instruction often provide generalising stereotypes in the sense described by Lippmann. On the one hand, stereotypes are used to transmit cultural information. Often, textbooks are the only source of information for students learning about a country, its language, and its culture, until they have direct contact with the foreign culture. On the other hand, stereotypical perceptions of a foreign culture are critically discussed in the textbooks to convey a specific 'cultural awareness', as Byram and Grundy (2002) call it. According to Müller and Hallsteinsdóttir (2016), such critical discussion is necessary to raise awareness of the role of world views, notably the influence of stereotypes, in both native- and foreign-language teaching (ibid., 241).

Stereotypes, as complex mental constructs, became a matter of linguistic interest in foreign-language teaching and textbook studies in the first decade of the twenty-first century, and again at the beginning of the 2010s. Pieklarz (2008) provides an overview of the state of stereotype research in foreign-language teaching, especially of national stereotypes, and Broszinsky-Schwabe (2017) describes the influence of stereotypes on misunderstandings in intercultural communication in foreign-language teaching. In their study of stereotypes in foreign-language teaching in an intercultural, Danish–German context, Baunsgaard Koll and Heinz (2016) demonstrate how language and culturally sensitive approaches to teaching enable learners of a foreign language to develop an awareness of stereotypes in an intercultural teaching context, in particular, and an awareness and critical handling of the construction and function of stereotypes in intercultural contacts in general (Baunsgaard Koll and Heinz 2016, 383).

Hohenstein's 2017 article about Angelika Redder's important work on stereotypes summarises and discusses some of the important results of her and Redder's approaches to discourse- and communications-analysis-based research on stereotypes in textbooks. Hohenstein emphasises,

> …es sind mit anderen Worten die Wissensstrukturentypen per se noch nicht 'stereotypisierend' es ist die Art ihrer sprachlichen-mentalen Verarbeitung, durch die sie diskursiv in ein 'Stereotypisieren' umschlagen können
>
> (…in other words, the types of knowledge structure themselves do not stereotype; the cognitive processes related to language use turn them into stereotypes in discourse). (Hohenstein 2017, 524)

Such knowledge structures play a significant role in the understandings of 'the national' and 'the European'. Thus, the stereotype potential of mental models of national and European concepts, and their linguistic construction in the curriculum and the textbooks for Danish will be discussed in the interpretation of the findings of our analysis.

Analysis of Textbooks and the Curriculum for Teaching Danish

To answer the research questions concerning how concepts—as linguistically bound knowledge—of 'the Danish' and 'the European' are constructed through language use, and presented in textbooks on Danish as a foreign language and in the curriculum for Danish as a school subject in Schleswig-Holstein, we present a study of how concepts of 'the Danish' and 'the European' are linguistically constructed in textbooks for Danish as a foreign language, and the curriculum for Danish as a school subject in Schleswig-Holstein. The focus is on conceptualisations that include direct linguistic references to Europe, Germany, and Denmark. As does Lenk (Chap. 4, this volume), we maintain a specific focus on the concepts of nation size and political power (as Denmark is a small state), as a potential aspect of a national and a European identity, and, with the aim of identifying constructs that reflect the specific relationships between Denmark and Germany as Denmark's next-door neighbour and a large state, between Denmark and Europe respectively the European Union.

In our analysis, we first identify the constructions of linguistically bound knowledge that includes lexemes that refer to Europe and the European, Denmark and the Danish, and Germany and the German. Then we analyse the linguistic forms of the concepts and determine which aspects of conceptual knowledge may be identified through the linguistic structures. We consider conceptual knowledge as complex networks of knowledge units that form mental models of categories, classifications, stereotypes, and other constructs (see Chap. 9, this volume).

The three textbooks, *Dansk for os* (*Do* 1993 [Danish for us]), *Mere Dansk for os* (*MDo* 1998 [More Danish for us]) and *Det er Dansk* (*DD* 2011 [That is Danish]), and the *Fachanforderungen Dänisch* (Danish curriculum) for Danish as a foreign language at schools in Schleswig-Holstein (*FADan* 2016), represent all the available texts for Danish as a neighbouring language in Schleswig-Holstein. The books are published by the *IQSH* (Institution for Quality Development in Schools in Schleswig-Holstein) and available as .pdf files on the IQSH home page (https://fachportal.lernnetz.de/sh/faecher/daenisch.html).

For this study, the textbooks and the curriculum text were converted into txt files and searched with the open-source concordance tool, *AntConc* (Anthony 2005). The search included the lemmas (in a psycholinguistic sense, as a conceptual form of a word): *dansk*/dänisch** (Danish), *tysk*/deutsch** (German), *Danmark*/Dänemark* (Denmark) and *europ** (European) and the abbreviation, EU. The aim of the search was to identify linguistic constructs of Denmark, Germany, and Europe in the curriculum and the textbooks (Table 3.1).

Table 3.1 Search results for the textbooks and the curriculum

AntConc Findings					
lemmas	*dansk*/ dänisch**	*tysk*/ deutsch**	*Danmark*/ Dänemark**	*europ*/ Europa**	EU
Fachanforderungen für Dänisch (FADan) curriculum	7/86	1/35	10/25	17/6	2
Dansk for os	7/0	4/0	23/0	0	0
Mere Dansk for os	23/0	10/0	60/0	0	0
Det er dansk	152/0	71/0	58/0	1/0	14

Although the textual material for the curriculum tends to include suggested topics for teaching, tasks, and exercises, as well as subject-related didactic and political aspects of intercultural and transcultural foreign-language teaching, the textbooks' textual material includes the didactic implementation of these suggested topics. For this reason, the entirety of the textual material examined presents the process of foreign language didacticisation of educational policy requirements for foreign language teaching, and the actual implementation and linguistic design of the textbooks. So, although the findings in the curriculum indicate the required intercultural communication skills, the findings in the textbooks represent the actual state of didactic and linguistic implementation in the educational media. The search results yielded relevant linguistic data on all four texts, which were systematically collected and analysed. Their analysis and their interpretation are presented in the following sections.

The analysis indicates that the linguistic contexts of the above-mentioned lemmas refer to various constructions of concepts. In our analysis of the curriculum and the textbooks, we concentrate on the four main concept categories found in the data: cultural concepts related to being Danish, concepts of Denmark as a nation, concepts concerning the relationship between Denmark and Germany, and concepts concerning the relationships between Europe, the European Union, and Denmark.

These four categories are the result of a summarising abstraction of similar concept bundles found in the curriculum. The concepts relate to cultural, national, and intercultural aspects. The first one includes cultural concepts related to being Danish, the second the concepts of Denmark as a nation, and the third concerns the concepts concerning Denmark's relationship with Germany, which also includes the Danish and German minorities, and the fourth includes Denmark's relationship with Europe and the European Union. Even though the concepts of nation, culture and intercultural relations are analysed separately to maintain clarity, it is evident that they refer to each other, and this interconnectedness must be addressed in the discussion. The following analysis focuses on the contexts of the lemmas defined above, but some of the examples also include other linguistic constructions that occur close to the lemmas in the texts, and complement the verbalisation of the concept related to the lemmas in question.

Analysis of the *Fachanforderungen Dänisch*

In the first step of the analysis, the *Fachanforderungen Dänisch* (*FADan* 2016), was searched for the lemmas *dansk*/dänisch*, *tysk*/deutsch*, *Danmark*/Dänemark**, *europ*/Europa** and EU using *AntConc*. The curriculum is written partly in Danish and partly in German, therefore the search was conducted with search items in both languages. Table 3.2 summarises the findings, to provide a sense of the frequency of the search items.

As the results in Table 3.2 show, lemmas containing *dänisch**, *deutsch**, *europ**, and *Dänemark** appear frequently, which was expected because the curriculum content was for Danish as a school subject. Thus, the frequency of the results confirms the importance of the lemmas in the curriculum.

Table 3.2 Search results for the *Fachanforderungen Dänisch* (*FADan* 2016)

AntConc Findings: *Fachanforderungen für Dänisch (FADan)* curriculum					
lemmas	*dansk*/dänisch**	*tysk*/deutsch**	*Danmark*/ Dänemark**	*europ*/Europa**	EU
hits	7/**86**	1/**35**	10/**25**	**17**/6	2

Cultural Concepts Related to Being Danish

The search items *dansk** and *europ** occur in linguistic constructions of the concepts of Danish culture, in the sense that they verbalise cultural aspects of being Danish as instructional material. In 'The individual and society' subject area, the topic, 'Youth in Denmark', includes this sub-topic:

(1) *kulturelle, politiske og sociale aspekter af ungdom i dansk og europæisk/vestlig kultur* (cultural, political and social aspects of youth in Danish and European/Western cultures) (*FADan* 2016, 74)

In example 1, Danish culture is defined as a part of western European culture in general, and in example 2 as a part of Scandinavian culture and languages, in the sub-topic of 'Languages', in the 'Regional identities' subject area:

(2) *dansk og skandinavisk* (Danish and Scandinavian) (*FADan*, 75)

In example 3, Danish cultural heritage is highlighted as a possible topic in the curriculum's 'Culture and media' subject area:

(3) *Den danske kulturarv/kulturkanon* (Danish cultural heritage/cultural canon) (*FADan* 2016, 76)

Danish culture is related to two cultural regions: the western European and the Scandinavian. Concepts related to those cultural regions are not described in greater detail. The linguistic constructs refer to stereotypical ideas of western European culture as democratic, free, tolerant, and humanist (Schmale 2008, 15–19). Scandinavian cultures, connected through their closely related languages and common history, are also supposed to be egalitarian (Østergård 2002, 154ff.).

Cultural/national stereotypes are also thematised in example 4 in this sub-topic:

(4) *typisk dansk?—stereotyper og fordomme* (typically Danish?—stereotypes and prejudices) (*FADan* 2016, 76)

The concept of a uniform Danish culture is presented as a contrast to a multicultural society. That is quite interesting, because both Danish and German societies have been influenced by other cultures, in the past seventy years mostly by migration from southern and eastern Europe and the Middle East, and today Denmark and Germany may be considered multicultural societies. Nonetheless, the idea of a unique and pristine Danish culture as a national ideal is developed in the curriculum, as in example 5, which presents a possible topic for the 'Culture and media' subject area. Danish culture is contrasted with multiculturalism:

(5) *dansk enhedskultur vs. multikulturelt samfund* (homogeneous Danish culture vs. multicultural society) (*FADan* 2016, 76)

Danish culture is described as uniform and traditional, and contrasted with the concept of a multicultural society:

(6) *danskerne: et lykkeligt folk?* (the Danes: a happy people?) (*FADan* 2016, 75)

In example 6, as a sub-topic of 'Culture and media', the construction, 'Danes: a happy people', is written as a question, which expresses a critical view of the stereotype of the happy Danes. However, the influence of other cultures and countries on Danish culture is also mentioned in the curriculum, as another sub-topic of the topic presented in example 7 (*FADan* 2016, 76). And in 'The Individual and society' subject area, this sub-topic indicates a more differentiated concept of Danish culture in the curriculum:

(7) *integration i et multikulturelt samfund* (integration in a multicultural society) (*FADan* 2016, 74)

To summarise, the concepts of Danish culture—in the sense of being Danish—in this curriculum are constructed by comparing and contrasting it with concepts of other cultures, such as those of western Europe and Scandinavia, and, through the ideal of an outstanding and uniform Danish culture, sheltered from the influences of migration and historical–cultural contacts.

Concepts of Denmark as a Nation

Denmark—as a state, a nation, and a geographic, linguistic, or cultural area—is established as a predominant point of reference for the *Fachanforderungen Dänisch*. Thus, in many ways, Denmark defines the instructional material (*FADan* 2016, 38–39), and the topics and subtopics of the four main subject areas: 'The individual and society', 'History and politics', 'Regional identities' and 'Culture and media'. Aspects of concepts of Denmark as a nation may be found in topics such as 'Denmark' (*FADan* 2016, 39), 'Youth in Denmark' (*FADan* 2016, 74), 'The political system in Denmark' and 'Denmark's membership in the EU and role in northern Europe' (*FADan* 2016, 75).

Example 8 presents a cultural construct that includes national pride, which is thematised as a sub-topic of 'Culture and media':

(8) *den nationale stolthed* (national pride) (*FADan* 2016, 75)

Here, the construct of a proud Danish nation may be seen as an aspect of concepts of Denmark as a nation, even as something typically Danish. Although none of the search lemmas was part of the construction, national pride is probably related more strongly to *dansk** than to *tysk**. How this pride manifests is not mentioned, nor may it be deduced from the context. We interpret the thematisation of national pride as a stereotyped attribute, which is incorporated into German learners' intercultural competence as worth knowing. Hofmann and Hallsteinsdóttir were able to show in the results of the SMiK project (2015) that 'national pride' is a German stereotype of Danes (Hofmann and Hallsteinsdóttir 2016, 337). There is no critical classification of this concept. However, it is indicated that prevalent German perceptions of Danes may be based on stereotyped associations about what is typically Danish (see example 4). According to the curriculum, an essential part of students' intercultural competence is being aware of common views, prejudices, and stereotypes related to perceptions of their own and Danish cultures (*FADan* 2016, 33).

The curriculum does not directly mention either size or power in its construct of Denmark as a nation. So, to summarise, on the one hand, the concept of a nation is constructed very one-dimensionally as 'being Danish'; on the other hand, the concept of 'being Danish' should be critically discussed, because it is based on stereotyped assumptions.

Concepts Concerning the Relationship Between Denmark and Germany

The relationship between Denmark and Germany is a central aspect of the *Fachanforderungen Dänisch*. The linguistic construction of these concepts is manifested in twenty instances of *deutsch-dänisch** (German–Danish) and one of *dansk-tysk* (Danish–German), and two instances of

Dänemark und Deutschland (Denmark and Germany). The analysis of the contexts of the twenty-one instances of *deutsch-dänisch** and *dansk-tysk* yields:

the German–Danish border (*FADan* 2016, 13, 17, 50, 55)
the German–Danish border region (*FADan* 2016, 39)
the German–Danish neighbourhood (*FADan* 2016, 70)
German–Danish relationship (*FADan* 2016, 73, 88)
German–Danish cooperation (*FADan* 2016, 17, 55, 75)
German–Danish (student) encounters (*FADan* 2016, 13, 32, 54)
European and global aspects in the German–Danish context (*FADan* 2016, 75)
Knowledge of Denmark and German–Danish settings (*FADan* 2016, 70)
Aspects of Danish and German–Danish history (*FADan* 2016, 39)
German–Danish linguistic aspects in contrast (*FADan* 2016, 16, 54)

In the *Fachanforderungen Dänisch*, the relationship between Denmark and Germany is presented as a role model for intra-European cooperation, and closely related to the construction of a European identity, based on the topics presented below. This relationship is thematised as a topic in the curriculum's 'History and politics' subject area:

(9) *Danmarks Forhold til Tyskland* (Denmark's relationship with Germany) (*FADan* 2016, 75)

The foregoing topic is developed through sub-topics in many ways. For instance, the current relations between the countries are grounded in their common history, as evident in these sub-topics:

(10) *Aspekte dänischer und deutsch-dänischer Geschichte* (Aspects of Danish and Danish–German history) and *deutsch-dänische Grenzregionen* (German–Danish border regions) (*FADan* 2016, 39)

These belong to the topic of 'Denmark', in the 'country and culture' subject area. Other topics that refer to German–Danish subject matter include the history of southern Schleswig, the border regions of Southern

Jutland–Schleswig and the Fehmarn Belt region (*FADan* 2016, 14). In fact, the curriculum explicitly requires students to acquire knowledge of the border regions that connect Denmark and Schleswig-Holstein, and to learn about their special role (*FADan* 2016, 46).

The German–Danish relationship in the border regions is characterised as cross-border cooperation (*FADan* 2016, 75), which is especially influenced by minority politics, culture, language, and traditions. Thus, the minorities are presented as integral parts of the German–Danish relationship. And, as mentioned in the introduction, the languages are an important aspect of cross-border cooperation. Hence, the relationship between Germany and Denmark is effectively constructed through the relationship between two neighbouring regions, in which the neighbouring languages are closely related (*FADan* 2016, 50). According to the curriculum, neighbouring language competence is important for both the relationship between Schleswig-Holstein and Denmark, and for the relationship between Germany and the other Nordic countries (*FADan* 2016, 12, 46).

To summarise, the concept of the relationship between Germany and Denmark is determined by neighbourhood. Their two languages are central to this relationship. Therefore, they are seen as neighbouring languages, and not as foreign languages. The border is considered dividing but transparent, because of the common history and the current cooperation.

Concepts Concerning the Relationships Between Europe, the European Union, and Denmark

The regional aspect is an important part of the relationships between Denmark and the rest of Europe, and as example 11 shows, this is incorporated in the broader geopolitical context:

(11) *Themen mit regionaler, nationaler, europäischer und globaler Bedeutung* (Topics of regional, national, European and global significance) (*FADan* 2016, 73)

The geographic aspects expand hierarchically from the small, regional to the global scale, framing the national and the European levels. Therefore, we interpret size and power as parts of this construct. Denmark's national political influences are related to the European and global power structures. Here, the concept of nation is connected to international relations. On the one hand, Denmark's position in the European political relationships is defined thus:

(12) *Danmarks medlemskab af EU og rolle i Nordeuropa* (Denmark's membership in the EU, and its role in northern Europe) (*FADan* 2016, 75)

On the other hand, Denmark is also seen as an organic part of Europe:

(13) *Europa als Kultur- und Wirtschaftsraum* (Europe as a cultural and economic area) (*FADan* 2016, 50)

However, Denmark's membership in the European Union as a political entity is characterised by critical distance. Denmark is also part of the Nordic council, and therefore, at least geographically, it stands between the European Union and its Nordic allies. Although Europe is presented as a spatial concept based on geographic proximity and economic relationships, in contrast, the European Union is seen as an abstract construct based on common political interests. The two concepts are not congruent.

To summarise, there is a major difference between the concepts of the relationship between Denmark and Europe, and between Denmark and the European Union. The concept of Europe is based on shared geography and history, whereas the concept of the European Union is based on political power.

In the next section, the textbooks discussed here are searched for the same lemmas as above, and the constructs related to the concepts analysed above.

Analysis of the Textbooks *Dansk for os* (1993) and *Mere Dansk for os* (1998)

Dansk for os and *Mere Dansk for os* are interdependent and, as mentioned, were published prior to 2016, and therefore are not based on the requirements of the current curriculum. In many ways, their approach to teaching foreign languages, and intercultural topics in particular, seems outdated. The content is based mainly on teaching grammar and other linguistic structures.

In the *AntConc* search results, the lemmas, *dansk** and *Danmark** occur most frequently, whereas *europ** and EU are not found in these textbooks. Because of the small number of lemmas, the results are summarised and analysed together for both books (Tables 3.3 and 3.4).

Table 3.3 Search results for *Dansk for os*

AntConc Findings: *Dansk for os*					
lemmas	*dansk**	*tysk**	*Danmark**	*europ**	EU
hits	7	4	**23**	**0**	**0**

Table 3.4 Search results for *Mere Dansk for os*

AntConc Findings: *Mere Dansk for os*					
lemmas	*dansk**	*tysk**	*Danmark**	*europ**	EU
Hits	**23**	10	**60**	**0**	**0**

Cultural Concepts Related to Being Danish

We found no constructions that explicitly referred to a cultural concept. Our interpretation of the contexts of the lemmas results in constructions of cultural patterns, which are mentioned in these textbooks as stereotypical of Danish culture. For the most part, these patterns are related to Christmas traditions, and rites and habits, as mentioned in example 14:

(14) *Efter middagen danser de alle om juletræet og synger de gamle danske julesange.* (After dinner they all dance around the Christmas tree and sing the old Danish Christmas carols.) (*Do* 1993, 39)

The next example (15) shows how otherness is included in a cultural concept based on the contrast between everyday habits in Denmark and Germany:

(15) *Mahlzeiten Tyskland vs. Danmark, i Danmark siger man tak for mad/ tak for kaffe, tak efter alle måltider.* (Meals Germany vs. Denmark: in Denmark, one says thank you for the meal/thank you for the coffee; thank you after every meal.) (*Do* 1993, 27)

These knowledge structures are stereotypical patterns. There is no critical reflection on them: they are given as facts. Some of the habits are presented almost as cultural peculiarities, for example, the famous 'Danish evening coffee', as presented in example 16:

(16) *Man drikker aftenkaffe i Danmark* (In Denmark one drinks evening coffee) (*Do* 1993, 111)

The incorporation of otherness in concepts of culture is characteristic of an unreflective approach to teaching foreign languages. The result is the manifestation of stereotypes, rather than the fostering of intercultural competence. According to Byram and Grundy (2002), this is problematic because: 'The main aim of teaching the intercultural dimension is not the transmission of information about a foreign country' (Byram and Grundy 2002, 12). The same criticism applies to the construction of national identity, as analysed in the following section.

Concepts of Denmark as a Nation

One of the important symbols of a national identity is the national flag. In the second textbook, *Mere dansk for os*, the legend of the appearance of the Danish flag is described in a separate chapter, '*Sagn om Dannebrogen*' (The Legend of Dannebrog) (*MDo* 1998, 54). Because the legend is not integrated into a historical framework, its mention seems disconnected, and, like the habits analysed above, it is presented as historical fact, rather than legend. This construction contributes to a stereotyped understanding of national identity, with no critical reflection on, or explanation of it in the textbook. The flag is even personified (example 17).

(17) *Det danske flag hedder 'Dannebrog'* (The Danish flag is called 'Dannebrog') (*MDo* 1998, 54).

It is also connected to the concept of national power and worship (example 18).

(18) *Danskerne sejrede, og Dannebrog blev Danmarks flag.* (The Danes were victorious, and Dannebrog became Denmark's flag.) (*MDo* 1998, 54)

The Danish nation is described as one-of-a-kind and blessed by God, with a flag that confirms that. This concept is common among national narratives in general, and should be critically discussed and classified as such in a textbook for a foreign language.

Another aspect of the construction of a national concept of Denmark is that it is a kingdom (example 19):

(19) *Danmark er et kongerige.* (Denmark is a kingdom.) (*MDo* 1998, 7).

Although it is a fact that Denmark is a constitutional monarchy, its current form of government is a parliamentary democracy. In mentioning the legend of the appearance of the Danish flag and the fact that Denmark still has a queen, the textbook references the concept of a God-given nation that was promulgated as part of the emerging nationalism of the mid-nineteenth century. The fact that Danes elect their political leaders as the Germans do is omitted. Presenting such a concept of Denmark as a nation in a textbook seems alien to today's intercultural approaches to foreign-language learning. The function of this concept seems to be to accentuate the construction of the otherness of the Danish nation, from the textbook's German-centred perspective.

Concepts Concerning the Relationship Between Denmark and Germany

In the textbooks, as in the curriculum, the relationship between Denmark and Germany is reduced to the relations at the border region between Southern Jutland and Schleswig-Holstein (example 20):

(20) *Danmarks eneste landegrænse er grænsen mod Schleswig-Holstein* (Denmark's only land border is the border with Schleswig-Holstein) (*MDo* 1998, 7)

This is defined as Denmark's only land border, as its borders with other Scandinavian countries are on the sea. The Fehmarn Belt border region, with its sea border, and an important area for nautical traffic for Denmark and Schleswig-Holstein, is not mentioned at all. So, in the textbook, the relationship between Denmark and Germany is limited to and influenced by a conflicted past, whereas the relationship between Denmark and its Nordic neighbours is open and unrestricted. According to Østergård (2002), the contrast between the two concepts of border is historically grounded. 'Norden' (literally, 'the north') is a concept that evokes unequivocally positive associations for almost everyone in the Nordic countries, connoting ideas of a community of values that transcends boundaries of language and culture', whereas 'the two border areas, Sleswig and Karelia … share a similar historical experience in the sense that both provinces have been carved out of their original allegiance' (Østergård 2002, 156–57). These concepts contrast with the positive perception of the Danish–German border in the curriculum described above.

Concepts Concerning the Relationships Between Europe, the European Union, and Denmark

The concept of size is used to describe Denmark's relationship with Europe, and to explain Denmark's situation in Europe, as seen in example 21:

(21) *Danmark er et af de mindste lande i Europa.* (Denmark is one of the smallest countries in Europe.) (*MDo* 1998, 7)

Denmark's role in or relationship with the European Union is not mentioned in the textbooks.

To summarise, some constructions of Denmark as a nation that appear in the *Fachanforderungen Dänisch* appear in these two early textbooks, but the concepts to which they refer are different from those used in the textbooks. Denmark is defined as a nation in terms of a stereotyped national narrative, and its culture is defined by otherness and reduced to everyday habits that only Danes exhibit. The idea of a multicultural Denmark related to European culture and relations, as is required in the curriculum, cannot be found in these constructs.

Analysis of the Textbook, *Det er Dansk* (2011)

Det er Dansk (*DD*) is the newest textbook in our study. The *AntConc* findings indicate that the European Union is included as a relevant topic. The abbreviation, EU, does not occur as frequently as the other lemmas, but it is mentioned fourteen times, whereas *europ** occurs just once. As in the older textbooks, the lemma, *dansk** is most frequent, with 152 instances, and *tysk** occurs seventy-one times. There are but a few constructions that include all three lemmas; presumably, some of the concepts are strongly interconnected (Table 3.5).

Table 3.5 Search results for the textbook *Det er Dansk*

AntConc Findings: *Det er dansk*					
lemmas	*dansk**	*tysk**	*Danmark**	*europ**	EU
hits	**152**	**71**	58	**1**	**14**

Cultural Concepts Related to Being Danish, and Concepts of Denmark as a Nation

In *Det er Dansk*, several constructions refer to the same concepts of Danish culture and the Danish nation that occur in the older textbooks and the curriculum. In particular, the texts in chapter 12 (example 22) about the Danish minority in Schleswig-Holstein and about the German minority in Southern Jutland (example 22) contribute to the constructions of cultural and national concepts:

(22) *De danske skoler har en dobbelt opgave: De skal formidle kendskab til dansk sprog og kultur blandt eleverne og samtidig forberede dem til en tilværelse som borgere i Tyskland* (The Danish schools have a dual task: they must disseminate knowledge of the Danish language and culture among the students, while preparing them for a life as German citizens) (*DD* 2011, 133)

(23) *Det er en kæmpe fordel at gå i en tysk skole i Danmark, fordi man lærer både dansk og tysk kultur at kende* (There is a tremendous advantage to attending a German school in Denmark, because you learn about both Danish and German culture) (*DD* 2011, 137)

The members of both minority groups are described as ambassadors for their homeland's culture and language in the cultural environment of the majority. The voluntary membership of the minorities is based on a cultural concept, which is strongly related to their languages. Language as a national marker is part of the concept of 'nation'. It is mentioned that it is always:

(24) *godt at tale dansk i Danmark* (good to speak Danish in Denmark) (*DD* 2011, 138)

That indicates the importance of the national language to the Danish people, and their cultural concept of 'being Danish'.

Concepts Concerning the Relationship Between Denmark and Germany

Det er Dansk thematises the influence of the border on the relationship between Denmark and Germany in a chapter with the title 'Fra konfrontation til samarbejde' (From confrontation to cooperation) (*DD* 2011, 138). In this chapter, the lemmas *dansk**, *Danmark**, and *tysk** occur in the same context. The relationship described refers to the concept of political power as represented by a national border, and its establishment as the culmination of historical confrontations and current political cooperation between Denmark and Germany. As in the *Fachanforderungen*

Dänisch, the relationship between Denmark and Germany is described as an age-old coexistence (example 25), and explained by the history of the current border region of Southern Jutland and Schleswig-Holstein:

(25) *I det gamle hertugdømme Slesvig har danskerne og tyskerne altid boet sammen.* (Danes and Germans always lived together in the former Danish duchy of Schleswig) (*DD* 2011; 138)

Although national affiliation was not important to the people in this region in the post-national period, because of a general lack of national awareness, between the early sixteenth century and the nineteenth century (Østergård 2002, 153ff.), peaceful coexistence was an important part of the construction of the concept of the ongoing relationship between Denmark and Germany. The idea of coexistence functions as a guiding theme in *Det er Dansk*, and does not refer to just the relationship between Denmark and Germany, but to the relationship between Denmark and the European Union, too, as described in the next section. The concept of coexistence is closely related to the concept of political power and its balance between the two countries.

The changing history of the border between Denmark and Schleswig-Holstein (*DD* 2004, 138) is part of the construction of the relationship between Denmark and Germany. The historic Danish–German border is presented as a symbol of delimitation and estrangement during the national movement in Europe in the middle of the nineteenth century. The previously peaceful coexistence was then supplanted by national claims in both countries, as mentioned in example 26:

(26) *Danskerne ønskede den dansk-tyske grænse ved Ejderen, tyskerne derimod oppe ved Kongeåen.* (The Danes wanted the Danish–German border at Ejderen, the Germans at Kongeåen) (*DD* 2011, 138)

Each side tried to expand its territory. Thus, the concepts of size and power are also evident in the border narrative. The current border is described as having a significant impact on the stable political and economic relationship between Denmark and Germany (example 27):

(27) *Selvom modsætningerne ikke er forsvundet, betragtes den dansk-tyske grænse gerne som en model for, hvordan nationale konflikter kan løses fredeligt* (Although the contradictions have not disappeared, the Danish–German border area is considered exemplary for resolving national conflicts peacefully) (*DD* 2011, 139)

So, in *Det er Dansk*, the border undergoes a transformation, from being a symbol of separation and national enmity to symbolising the guarantee of peace and cooperation between the two nations. To summarise, the concepts of the relationship between Denmark and Germany are described and constructed in various ways, for instance, as a fight for national identity, territorial expansion, or increased political power on both sides.

Concepts Concerning the Relationships Between Europe, the European Union, and Denmark

In this section, we analyse the instances of the lemmas, *dansk**, *tysk**, and *europ** in a given context. Example 28 indicates that the relationship between Denmark and Europe is influenced by adverse experiences in the past, in a way that is similar to Denmark's relationship with Germany. But Europe is also the political framework that stabilises the relationship with Germany:

(28) *Mange tyskere og danskere, der begyndte at satse på et fælles Europa for at løse konflikterne uden våben. I denne sammenhæng er der i de sidste år blevet udviklet et godt samarbejde mellem danskere og tyskere* (Many Germans and Danes began to strive for a common Europe, to resolve conflicts without weapons. In this context, in recent years, Danes and Germans have collaborated amicably) (*DD* 2011, 139)

Hence, 'Europe' is presented as a positive construct of peaceful fellowship among nations. Europe guarantees the peaceful coexistence of Denmark and Germany. In example 29, the relationship between Denmark and the European Union is presented as more complex. The textbook refers to Denmark's much-discussed accession to the newly established European Union in 1993:

(29) *I 1993 talte man særlig meget om EU i Danmark* (In 1993, one talked a lot about the EU in Denmark)

The public discourse about Denmark's accession to, and Denmark's membership in the European Union, is described as very conflicted (example 30):

(30) *man kan tale både for og imod EU* (One may speak for and against the EU) (*DD* 2011, 154–55)

Although the relationship between Denmark and Germany is described as significantly influenced by Denmark's positive relationship with Europe, Denmark's relationship with the European Union is presented as quite the opposite. The concept of Europe as a peace-keeping alliance does not match the concept of the European Union as a political and economic organisation with great power and influence. Denmark prefers to be a part of Europe, but is sceptical of its role in the European Union.

Conclusions

The analysis of the search items yielded interesting results related to the questions of the linguistic construction of the concepts of DENMARK and EUROPE in the three textbooks, *Dansk for os*, *Mere Dansk for os*, and *Det er Dansk*, and in the *Fachanforderungen Dänisch*. All three textbooks were published before the current *Fachanforderungen Dänisch* (*FADan* 2016). Yet, these three textbooks are still used, and they represent all the available texts for Danish. We do not regard the large gap between the dates of the textbooks' publication and of the curriculum´s implementation as problematic, but as offering an opportunity to examine the development of the textbooks' content and requirements for Danish as a school subject over a period of approximately thirty years. The textbooks are based on an older curriculum, and the curriculum analysed here presents the current didactic requirements for Danish lessons in Schleswig-Holstein. Therefore, including the curriculum provides valuable insights into the latest developments in teaching topics, in contrast to the textbooks, regarding both the presentation of the concepts of 'the national' and 'the European', and the stereotyped traits and approaches to developing the learners' intercultural competence. However, the frequency of the lemmas *dansk**, *Danmark**, and *tysk**, and the related linguistic constructions demonstrate that Denmark and Germany are highly significant topics in the first two textbooks.

The lemma *europ** and the abbreviation, 'EU' are found in the curriculum for Danish and in the newer textbook, *Det er Dansk*. The much lower frequency of *europ** and EU in the early textbooks is explained by the textbooks' focus on language and cultural transmission. Europe is not discussed in the earlier curricula. In contrast, Europe and the European Union are important topics in *Det er Dansk* and the current curriculum. These describe Europe as guaranteeing a peaceful coexistence between Danes and Germans, although Denmark's accession to the European Union is presented as controversial in Denmark's public discourse.

In the textbooks, most of the concepts of 'the national' and 'the European' are connected to the relationship between Denmark and Germany, and between Denmark and Europe or the European Union. In turn, those concepts are linked to the concepts of national size and political power. Therefore, we conclude that national size and political power are relevant aspects of the constructions of the concepts that comprise a Danish national identity in all textbooks and in the curriculum. In the textbooks, this Danish identity may be seen as a frame of reference for the German pupils at schools in Schleswig-Holstein. This allows them to identify 'the Danes' as 'the others', as having a different identity with respect to a German perspective. This identity may be at least partly defined by stereotypes, and it does not necessarily reflect Danish identity in terms of how Danes see themselves.

The analysis of the contexts of the lemmas in the *Fachanforderungen Dänisch* indicates that they are part of, or connected to, several linguistic constructs related to a Danish national identity, the identity of the Danish minority in Schleswig-Holstein, a European identity, the relationship between Denmark and Germany, the relationship between Denmark and

Europe, and the relationship Denmark and the European Union. According to the instructions in the curriculum, these concepts are taught as part of the intercultural competence requirement for German students (*FADan* 2016, 50).

Constructs of 'the European' were found only in the newest textbook and the curriculum. Here we see differences in the concepts in terms of the constructions of the relationship between Denmark and the European Union, on the one hand, and between Denmark and Europe, on the other hand. Those differences in the concepts may even be interpreted as evidence of the existence of various European identities. In the data, the concept of 'the Danish' is closely related to concepts of the relationship between Denmark and Germany, and the relationship between Demark and Europe and the European Union. The concepts of size and power are apparent in the concepts. Denmark is presented as a small nation that depends on the peace-keeping power of the European Union within the European borders, and concurrently struggles with the size of its European neighbours, and the size and political influence of a powerful European Union.

In conclusion, the educational media we examined present and transmit various linguistically constructed concepts of 'the national' and 'the European'. Those concepts may be seen as elements of knowledge that correspond to the expected state of the learner's knowledge, as defined in the curriculum and apparent in the textbooks (see Chap. 9, this volume). Thus, these concepts include aspects of what the learners might interpret as parts of a Danish national identity and a European identity. The information about the 'others', in the sense that Riemenschneider (1980, 29) uses it, connects to the learners existing knowledge and stereotypes (in the sense used by Lippmann [1921] 2008), and therefore, an exploration of the learners' identities should be included in further research.

Note

1. Since 2021, the Leibniz Institute for Educational Media | Georg Eckert Institute (GEI).

References

Curricula

Ministerium für Schule und Berufsbildung des Landes Schleswig-Holstein. 2016. Fachanforderungen Dänisch [FADan]. Accessed March 10, 2021. https://fachportal.lernnetz.de/sh/fachanforderungen/daenisch-sek-i-ii.html

Textbooks

Brandt, Dieter, Jürgen Hansen, Renate Jacob, and Karin Vierecke. 2004. *Det er dansk. Lehrwerk für den Dänischunterricht* [*DD*]. 3rd edition, Kronshagen: Institut für Qualitätsentwicklung an Schulen, Schleswig-Holstein.

Brandt, Dieter, Jürgen Hansen, Renate Jacob and Karin Vierecke. 2011. *Det er dansk. Lehrwerk für den Dänischunterricht* [*DD*]. 9th edition, Kronshagen: Institut für Qualitätsentwicklung an Schulen, Schleswig-Holstein.

Buchenau, Rose-Marie, and Landesinstitut Schleswig-Holstein für Praxis und Theorie der Schule Arbeitskreis Dänisch. 1994. *Dansk for os—Lehrbuch* [*Do*]. Kronshagen: Institut für Praxis und Theorie in der Schule (IPTS)—Schleswig-Holstein.

Buchenau, Rose-Marie, Kerstin Ehmen, Eike Ketelsen, Claudia Paulsen, Kerstin Richert and Karin Nissen. 1998. *Mere Dansk for os—Lehrbuch* [*MDo*]. Kronshagen: Institut für Praxis und Theorie in der Schule (IPTS)—Schleswig-Holstein.

Tools

Anthony, Laurence. *AntConc* Homepage. 2005. Accessed March 16, 2020. http://www.laurenceanthony.net/software/antconc/

Further References

Baunsgaard Koll, Phillip, and Tobias Heinz. 2016. Didaktisch-methodische Perspektiven auf nationale Stereotype: Facetten einer unterrichtspraktischen

Konkretisierung. *Linguistik online* 79 (5): 381–398. Accessed May 5, 2022. https://doi.org/10.13092/lo.79.3350

Broszinsky-Schwabe, Edith. 2017. *Interkulturelle Kommunikation. Missverständnisse und Verständigung*. Wiesbaden: Springer.

Byram, Michael, and Peter Grundy. 2002. *Context and culture in language teaching and learning*. Clevedon: Multilingual Matters.

Heinz, Tobias, and Jana Pflaeging. 2015. Metaphern in Sprache und Bild—Zum Vermittlungspotenzial von Arbeitsmaterialien in Deutschlehrwerken. In *Linguistik und Schulbuchforschung: Gegenstände—Methoden—Perspektiven*, ed. Jana Kiesendahl and Christine Ott, 235–253. Göttingen: V&R unipress.

Hofmann, Annika, and Erla Hallsteinsdóttir. 2016. Deutsch-dänische Stereotypenwelten im SMiK-Projekt. *Linguistik online* 79 (5): 323–346. Accessed May 5, 2022. https://doi.org/10.13092/lo.79.3348

Hohenstein, Christiane. 2017. 'Stereotyp' – revisited. In *Form und Funktion: Festschrift für Angelika Redder zum 65. Geburtstag*, ed. Krause, Arne et. al., 511–532. Tübingen: Stauffenburg.

Jacob, Renate. 2018. Die Nachbarsprache lernen: Zur Situation des Dänischunterrichts an öffentlichen Schulen in Schleswig-Holstein. In *Nachbarsprachen in der Region Sønderjylland-Schleswig*, eds. Angela Jensen, Annika Carstensen, and Anne-Mette Olsen, 18–24. Padborg: Region Sønderjylland–Schleswig Regionskontor & Infocenter.

Kiesendahl, Jana, and Christine Ott, eds. 2015. *Linguistik und Schulbuchforschung: Gegenstände—Methoden—Perspektiven*. Göttingen: V&R unipress.

Lakoff, George, and Mark Johnson. 2003. *Metaphors We Live By*. Chicago: University of Chicago Press.

Lippmann, Walter. (1921) 2008. *Public Opinion*. New York: Harcourt, Brace and Company.

Müller, Katarina L., and Erla Hallsteinsdóttir. 2016. Stereotype im Fremdsprachenunterricht. In: Hallsteinsdóttir, Erla, Klaus Geier, Katja Gorbahn, and Jörg Killian, eds., *Perspektiven der Stereotypenforschung*, 233–256. Frankfurt am Main: Peter Lang.

Østergård, Uffe. 2002. Nordic Identity between "Norden and Europe". In *European Peripheries in Interaction. The Nordic Countries and the Iberian Peninsula*, ed. Luis Beltrán, Javier Maestro and Liisa Salo-Lee, 151–202. Alcalá de Henares: Universidad de Alcalá, Servicio de Publicaciones.

Ott, Christine. 2015. Bildungsmedien als Gegenstand linguistischer Forschung. Thesen, Methoden, Perspektiven. In *Linguistik und Schulbuchforschung:*

Gegenstände—Methoden—Perspektiven, ed. Jana Kiesendahl and Christine Ott, 19–37. Göttingen: V&R unipress.

Pfalzgraf, Falco. 2015. Zur Korpusdefinition in der Schulbuchforschung. In *Linguistik und Schulbuchforschung: Gegenstände—Methoden—Perspektiven*, ed. Jana Kiesendahl and Christine Ott, 39–51. Göttingen: V&R unipress.

Pieklarz, Magdalena. 2008. 'Zur Erforschung von Stereotypen in der Fremdsprachendidaktik—ein geschichtlicher Überblick über Forschun gsansätze und Darstellung eines Forschungsprojektes'. In *Auf neuen Wegen. Deutsch als Fremdsprache in Forschung und Praxis, Tagungsband der 35. Jahrestagung des Fachverbandes Deutsch als Fremdsprache 2007 an der Freien Universität Berlin*, ed. Christoph Chlosta, Gabriela Leder, Barbara Krischer, 35–52. Göttingen: Universitätsverlag Göttingen.

Riemenschneider, Rainer. 1980. Vorurteile Stereotypen und Klischees in Fremdsprachenlehrbüchern. Überlegungen zur Methode der Schulbu chanalyse. In *Internationale Schulbuchforschung, Zeitschrift des Georg-Eckert Instituts für internationale Schulbuchforschung*, ed. Karl-Ernst Jeismann, 29–40. Braunschweig: Westermann.

Schmale, Wolfgang. 2008. Geschichte der europäischen Identität. In *Aus Politik und Zeitgeschichte* 1–2, ed. Zentrale für politische Bildung, 14–19. Berlin: Societäts-Verlag.

4

Concepts of Europe in the Finnish Scholastic Curriculum and in German Textbooks for Finnish Secondary Schools

Hartmut E. H. Lenk

Introduction

Both Finland and Denmark are parts of northern Europe, and have comparatively small populations: Finland currently has about 5.5 million inhabitants (Finland in Figures 2019, 2). However, there are considerable historical differences. For a long time, Finland was part of neighbouring empires: the Swedish Kingdom until 1809 and the Russian Tsarist Empire from 1809 to 1917. Thus, Finland has been a sovereign state for only 105 years. Unlike Denmark, which was occupied by Nazi Germany during the Second World War, Finland was never occupied by German troops. Instead, the Finnish army and the German Wehrmacht saw themselves as 'brothers in arms' from 1941 to 1944. This alliance was ended by the Finnish Separate Peace with the Soviet Union on September 19, 1944, and the subsequent Lapland War, in which Finland had to drive

H. E. H. Lenk (✉)
Department of Language/German Philology, Faculty of Arts ,
University of Helsinki, Helsinki, Finland
e-mail: Hartmut.Lenk@helsinki.fi

K. Gorbahn et al. (eds.), *Exploring Interconnectedness*, Palgrave Studies in Educational Media, https://doi.org/10.1007/978-3-031-13960-4_4

from the country the formerly allied German Mountain Troops Division that was stationed there, which left behind scorched earth in revenge.

Finland's relations with Germany have been close since the late Middle Ages (Saarinen 2011). The founder of the Finnish written language, Bishop Mikael Agricola, studied in Wittenberg from 1536 to 1539 under Martin Luther and others. In the nineteenth century, the Russian Tsar sent German builders (especially Carl Ludwig Engel from Berlin) to Helsinki, to build the new Finnish capital. The Finnish national anthem was composed by the Hamburg-born music lecturer, Friedrich (Fredrik) Pacius. There was an active and economically successful German community in Finland, which in 1881 founded the German Library[1] and the German School Helsinki,[2] among other things. The German Church in Finland, as part of the country's Evangelical Lutheran State Church, still has civil powers today. Until the 1950s, German was the first foreign language learned by almost all secondary school pupils. In the 1960s English gradually took over this position, and in the twenty-first century, the number of students learning German at Finnish schools has unfortunately continued to fall dramatically. Nevertheless, Germany has been Finland's most important foreign trade partner for years, both in terms of exports and imports. Germany is the destination for a large number of Finnish exchange students, particularly through the Erasmus programme. There is a lively cultural exchange between the two countries, and Finland and Germany are also close partners in politics, agreeing on many fundamental questions.

Finland has been a member of the European Union since 1995 and was one of the first countries to introduce the euro as the common currency. Today, European Union membership is not seriously questioned by any of the parties represented in its Parliament, perhaps excepting the True Finns (*Perussuomalaiset*), who are regarded as right-wing populists.

Finland ranked first in the early PISA studies, and subsequently became the destination for numerous study trips by teachers and school politicians from Germany and other European countries, and delegations from other continents.

This chapter examines the conceptualisations of Europe in the current Finnish curricula for primary and secondary schools, and for upper secondary schools (partly corresponding to the 'sixth form' in England), and in the upper-secondary German-language textbooks that are currently on the market.

Research Questions, Corpus and Methods of This Study

Textbook analysis has a rich tradition in Finland (e.g. Julkunen 1988, or Väisänen 2005). It includes philology and German studies. Examples are the works of Maijala (2014), Tikkanen (2017), Järvinen (2018), Föhr (2018) and Bobkova (2019).

Research Questions

This study aims to find answers to the following questions:

1. How often, and with reference to what, do the lexemes with the stem *europ** (German) or *euroop** (Finnish) appear in the Finnish national framework curricula and in the current Finnish German-language textbooks for upper secondary schools?
2. In what way is 'Europe' conceptualised in the curricula and in the textbook presentations?

Corpus of Texts Analysed in This Study

Subcorpus 1: The Finnish Framework Curricula

Public schools in Finland are run by its municipalities. They establish guidelines, for example, those regarding the minimum group size for certain subjects (such as optional foreign languages), and may also determine which foreign languages are offered by the municipality's schools as the first, so-called A1, foreign language that will be taught from the first year on, beginning in 2020 (i.e. starting in the second half of the first school year, at the latest). There are also some private schools that are run by associations or denominational communities.

All schools, including private schools, are subject to the framework curricula issued by the Finnish Central Board of Education (*Opetushallitus*), which defines the general pedagogical and content-related objectives of the various school subjects. They are revised at various intervals, usually about every ten years, and usually take into account international developments in pedagogy and educational methodology. This is the basis on which special curricula for individual subjects are developed at the municipal or school level.

The first part of the study examines the texts of the Finnish framework curricula for general comprehensive schools (years 1–9) and for the upper secondary school (years 10–12), which were valid when the textbooks now used were developed.[3] The general comprehensive school is called *peruskoulu* in Finnish (literally, 'basic school'), the upper secondary school, *lukio*. Therefore, the documents in question are called *Perusopetuksen opetussuunnitelman perusteet* (Principles of the primary school curriculum), abbreviated as POPS, and *Lukion opetussuunnitelman perusteet* (Principles of the upper secondary school curriculum), abbreviated as LOPS. Both texts are available on the internet as .pdf and MS Word files. POPS (2014) comprises 169,868 words (tokens) and many tables. LOPS (2015) comprises 65,376 words.

Subcorpus 2: Two 'German as a Foreign Language' (DaF)[4] Textbook Series for Upper Secondary Schools in Finland

In Finland, each revision of a framework curriculum results in new textbooks. Although the number of students who take German as a foreign language continues to decline, there are still two publishers who market such textbooks in Finland. These are Sanoma Pro, the textbook division of the former publisher, Werner Söderström (WSOY), which now belongs to the Helsinki-based media group, Sanoma. The *Plan D* series is published here. The second DaF textbook series is published by the Otava media group. It bears the title, *Magazin.de*. Essentially, both textbooks follow the course structure at Finnish grammar schools, and consist of eight parts each; *Plan D* twice combines two parts in one volume. The authors are German teachers working in Finland, and the team usually includes a native German speaker. The bibliographic details of the volumes discussed here may be found in the index of the corpus.

(a) ***Magazin.de***

The *Magazin.de* subcorpus comprises eight documents (one per textbook) and 246,106 words (tokens) in 26,422 different word forms. The most common words are *bitte* and the digits *1–4* (due to the large number of tasks and exercises).

Figures 4.1 and 4.2 show the covers of two volumes of the *Magazin.de* textbook series. The individual volumes are structured as follows. The inside front cover shows a map of the German-speaking countries, followed by two blank pages. Pages one and two present the main title and

Fig. 4.1 Cover of the textbook, *Magazin.de 1*

Fig. 4.2 Cover of the textbook, *Magazin.de 6*

the imprint. On page three, under the title 'Mach die Tür auf!' (Open the door), there is a kind of letter from the book's authors to the students. The table of contents follows on pages four and five. On page six, under the heading 'Los geht's!' (Let's go!), there are seven self-assessment questions in Finnish and tips on how to improve one's German-language skills with the help of the internet. This is followed by a quiz entitled, 'Überblick' (Overview), with questions in German on knowledge of the country. Pages 8–16 are entitled 'Start' and include games, exercises on lexis, grammar, listening and reading comprehension, speaking, writing and internet research. Lessons 1–5 begin on page 17.

The lessons are structured as follows. After the introduction, under the heading, 'INTRO', the vocabulary for the lesson's topic is introduced under the heading, 'THEMA' (THEME), with corresponding exercises. This is followed by a 'TEXT' with corresponding exercises, then the 'RATGEBER' (ADVISOR) which explains grammatical structures. This is followed by a self-assessment section under the heading, 'ALLES KLAR?' (IS EVERYTHING CLEAR?), and at the end of each lesson, there is a 'KULTURCOUPON' (CULTURAL COUPON), which conveys cultural knowledge. The lessons are followed by a pronunciation guide and a grammar section (divided into word classes). The 'ALLES KLAR?' section then lists the solutions to the exercises, and the last page lists the illustrations and their copyright information. The last two pages and the inside back cover are blank.

(b) ***Plan D***

The *Plan D* subcorpus comprises six documents, one for each textbook: the series is published as four single textbooks and two double volumes. The number of words comes to 190,034 (tokens) with 27,105 different word forms. The most common terms are the digits *1* to *4* and the Finnish auxiliary verb, *on* (is).

On the inside front covers of the textbooks there are lists of everyday phrases. Pages one to three present the main title, a large photograph and the imprint. The table of contents follows on pages four and five. Page six includes photographs and short texts with partly amusing information about the German-speaking countries. Lessons 1–5 (or 1–10 or 12 for the two double volumes) begin on page seven.

The lessons include tasks and exercises for vocabulary, grammar, reading and listening comprehension, writing and speaking. There are monologues and dialogues, and various text types are used; generally they seem inauthentic and written specifically for the textbook. There are also (mostly bilingual) vocabulary lists in the lessons. After the last lesson there is a grammar section with rules, word lists (e.g. irregular verbs, separable verbs, country names), pronunciation hints and so on; the inside back cover, like the front cover (Figs. 4.3 and 4.4), has a list of phrases for everyday use.

Fig. 4.3 Cover of the textbook, *Plan D* 1–2

Methods

The two texts of subcorpus 1 (framework curricula) may be downloaded as Word files from the internet. Using MS Word's search function, all instances of *euroop** (Finnish for *europ**) were listed and then assigned to specific concept groups.

The above-mentioned textbooks are available as printed works. They were scanned as .pdf files, which were converted to the txt format with ABBYY FineReader.[5] The text-recognition software encountered

Fig. 4.4 Cover of the textbook, *Plan D* 5

significant problems. First, both textbooks are bilingual. This applies not only to the vocabulary lists, but also to most of the tasks (e.g. Fig. 4.5). Some texts, especially those that address background information about Germany, Austria or Switzerland, are written entirely in Finnish, but may include German lexemes. The main texts of the lessons are presented in German. Another complicating factor for electronic text recognition is that some texts are highlighted in colour, positioned diagonally in boxes or have graphic elements (lines, icons, pictures of objects and people).

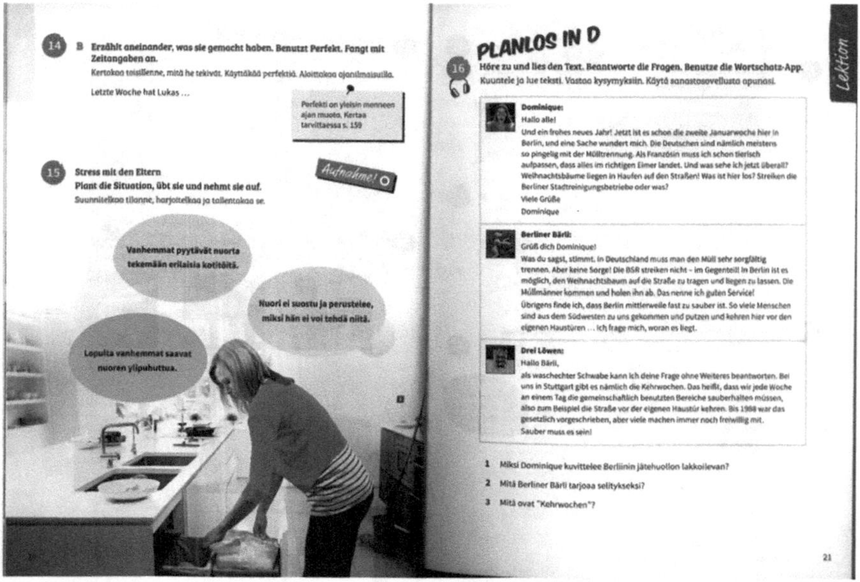
14 B Erzählt aneinander, was sie gemacht haben. Benutzt Perfekt. Fangt mit Zeitangaben an.
Kertokaa toisillenne, mitä he tekivät. Käyttäkää perfektiä. Aloittakaa ajanilmaisuilla.
Letzte Woche hat Lukas ...
Perfekti on yleisin menneen ajan muoto. Kertaa tarvittaessa s. 159
15 Stress mit den Eltern
Plant die Situation, übt sie und nehmt sie auf.
Suunnitelkaa tilanne, harjoitelkaa ja tallentakaa se.
Aufnahme!
Vanhemmat pyytävät nuorta tekemään erilaisia kotitöitä.
Nuori ei suostu ja perustelee, miksi hän ei voi tehdä niitä.
Lopulta vanhemmat saavat nuoren ylipuhuttua.

PLANLOS IN D
16 Höre zu und lies den Text. Beantworte die Fragen. Benutze die Wortschatz-App.
Kuuntele ja lue teksti. Vastaa kysymyksiin. Käytä sanastosovellusta apunasi.

Dominique:
Hallo alle!
Und ein frohes neues Jahr! Jetzt ist es schon die zweite Januarwoche hier in Berlin, und eine Sache wundert mich. Die Deutschen sind nämlich meistens so pingelig mit der Mülltrennung. Als Französin muss ich schon tierisch aufpassen, dass alles im richtigen Eimer landet. Und was sehe ich jetzt überall? Weihnachtsbäume liegen in Haufen auf den Straßen! Was ist hier los? Streiken die Berliner Stadtreinigungsbetriebe oder was?
Viele Grüße
Dominique

Berliner Bärli:
Grüß dich Dominique!
Was du sagst, stimmt. In Deutschland muss man den Müll sehr sorgfältig trennen. Aber keine Sorge! Die BSR streiken nicht – im Gegenteil! In Berlin ist es möglich, den Weihnachtsbaum auf die Straße zu tragen und liegen zu lassen. Die Müllmänner kommen und holen ihn ab. Das nenne ich guten Service!
Übrigens finde ich, dass Berlin mittlerweile fast zu sauber ist. So viele Menschen sind aus dem Südwesten zu uns gekommen und putzen und kehren hier vor den eigenen Haustüren ... Ich frage mich, woran es liegt.

Drei Löwen:
Hallo Bärli,
als waschechter Schwabe kann ich deine Frage ohne Weiteres beantworten. Bei uns in Stuttgart gibt es nämlich die Kehrwochen. Das heißt, dass wir jede Woche an einem Tag die gemeinschaftlich benutzten Bereiche sauberhalten müssen, also zum Beispiel die Straße vor der eigenen Haustür kehren. Bis 1988 war das gesetzlich vorgeschrieben, aber viele machen immer noch freiwillig mit.
Sauber muss es sein!

1 Miksi Dominique kuvittelee Berliinin jätehuollon lakkoilevan?
2 Mitä Berliner Bärli tarjoaa selitykseksi?
3 Mitä ovat "Kehrwochen"?

Lektion
21

Fig. 4.5 Example of a bilingual page in *Plan D* 5, lesson 1, pages 20–21

One text file was created for each textbook (eight for *Magazin.de* and six for *Plan D* with its two double volumes). Data were analysed and visualised with the help of the Voyant and AntConc[6] software. As both series of textbooks include German and Finnish texts, the search for lexemes that refer to Europe had to be carried out twice: for the Finnish search term, *euroop**, and the German search term, *europ**. Based on the KWIC lists provided by AntConc, the instances of the lexemes containing these roots were assigned to certain concept groups. Where necessary, the full context, as it appears in the text files, was checked.

Instances of *Europe* in the Curricula

As the text of POPS and LOPS is in Finnish, the search was conducted for words that included the *euroop** character string. Thus, all forms of the adjective *eurooppalainen* (European) and all forms of the noun *Eurooppa* (Europe) were found. Table 4.1 shows the number of instances in the two texts.

Table 4.1 Instances of *euroop** in POPS (2014) and LOPS (2015)

	Instances of *euroop**	Per 10,000 words
POPS	132	7.8
LOPS	55	8.4

In the two documents (POPS and LOPS), the Finnish expressions for Europe/European were mentioned in the following contexts:

1. Languages:

$$POPS:81(=88\%)\quad LOPS:15(=43\%)$$

Eurooppalainen kielisalkku (European languages).

Eurooppalaiseen viitekehykseen (Common European Framework of Reference for languages).

2. Religious education:

$$POPS:10(\sim 11\%)\quad LOPS:4(\sim 11\%)$$

juutalaisen tradition vaikutukseen eurooppalaiseen kulttuuriin ja tieteisiin (on the influence of Jewish tradition on European culture and sciences)

3. History and geography:

$$POPS:1(\sim 1\%)\quad LOPS:10(\sim 29\%)$$

historia syventää yksilöllistä, kansallista, eurooppalaista ja globaalia identiteettiä ([the subject of] history deepens individual, national, European and global identity)

4. Social studies and music:

$$POPS:—\quad LOPS:6(\sim 17\%)$$

opiskelija [...] osaa suhteuttaa ne [= *yhteiskuntajärjestelmän, oikeusjärjestelmän ja talouselämän perusteet ja toimintatavat*] *eurooppalaisiin ja kansainvälisiin yhteyksiin* (the student can relate them [= the social system, legal system and economic basics and practices—HL] to European and international connections).

Essentially, the conceptualisations of Europe that appear in the Finnish curriculum framework may be assigned to the following four concepts:

1. **Languages** belonging to the Indo-European language family or spoken **in Europe**
2. Europe as a diverse **community of cultures, values and faiths**
3. Europe as part of individual and collective **identities**
4. Europe as a historically rooted, globally anchored, changing **environment** for human activity

Conceptualisation of *Europe* in the Two Series of Textbooks

Instances of Lexemes that Reference Europe in *Magazin.de*

AntConc determined the following frequencies of the occurrence of German lexemes with the stem *europ** and Finnish lexemes with the stem *euroop** in the eight *Magazin.de* textbooks (see Figs. 4.6 and 4.7).

With the exception of the last (eighth), and to some extent the fourth, volume of the *Magazin.de* series of textbooks, lexemes that reference Europe occur in Finnish passages quite rarely. The contexts in which they are used are mostly explanations of special national or regional features, pronunciation, vocabulary and grammar, tasks and vocabulary lists. In volume 2, lexemes with this root are completely absent. Their uses in volume 8 (i.e. plot 7 in Fig. 4.6) are significantly connected to descriptions of European geography and history, including the European Union, which are a focus of this volume.

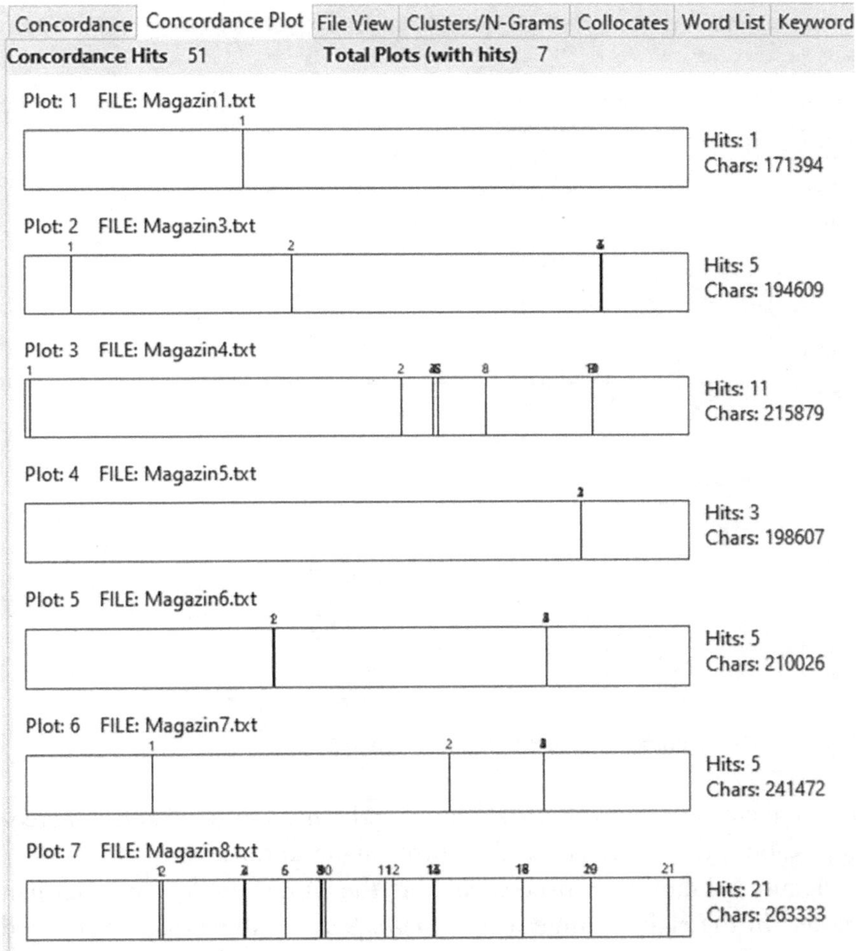

Fig. 4.6 Occurrence of *euroop** in *Magazin.de* 1–8

Figure 4.7 shows the number of instances of lexemes with the root *europ** in the German texts of *Magazin.de*. The total number of hits is even lower than in the Finnish passages. With 13 hits per volume, there is a relative increase in volumes 4 and 8, and in volume 8 they concern the geography and history of Europe (as in the Finnish passages). In volume 4 the 13, instances appear mainly in connection with references to

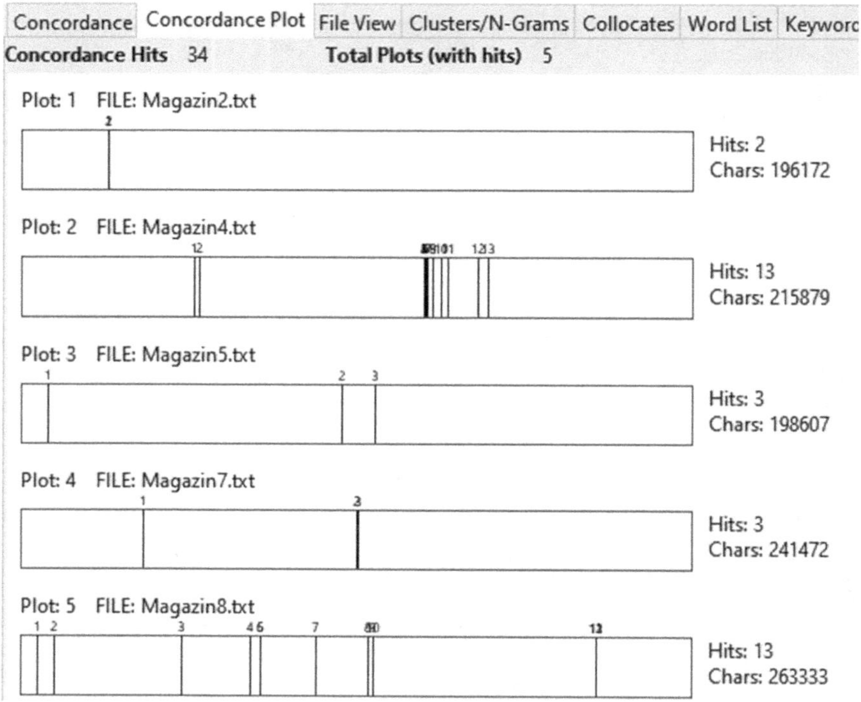

Fig. 4.7 Occurrence of *europ** in *Magazin.de* 1–8

cultural customs in northern, southern and central Europe, and to stereotypes about the behaviour of the people living in those regions.

Figure 4.8 shows the instances of both the Finnish *euroop** and German *europ** in the eight volumes of *Magazin.de* as a bubble diagram created with the help of Voyant.

A look at the KWIC lists provided by AntConc enables one to order the various contexts of use and the meanings of the lexemes that reference Europe. As a result, one may distinguish five categories of conceptualisations of Europe in the *Magazin.de* series of textbooks, which are mentioned below and are illustrated with (italicised) examples (owing to limited space, the examples are given as English translations only; those from Finnish passages are underlined). The order in which the categories are presented corresponds to their relative frequency.

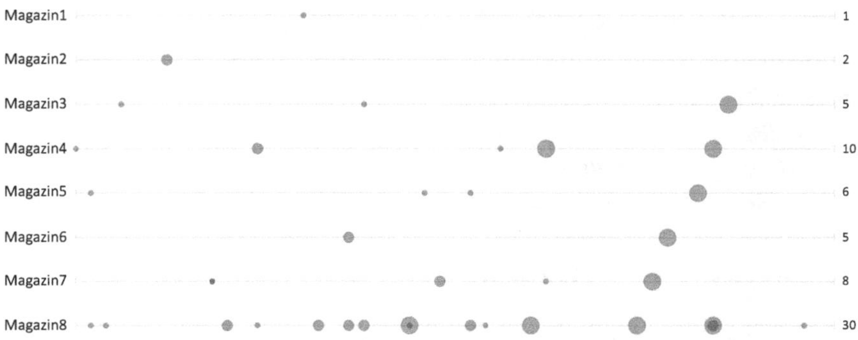

Fig. 4.8 Occurrence of *europ** and *euroop** in *Magazin.de* 1–8

1. Europe as a geographic entity

- *Europe's share of the world population…*
- *… in Germany and in many European countries as well.*
- *… the neighbouring countries in eastern and southern Europe.*
- *In southern Europe, it is at night …*
- *The names of Europe's rivers are mostly feminine*
- *The names of rivers outside Europe are mostly masculine.*
- *Western Europe's largest and highest mountains, the Alps*
- *The summer heat waves are increasing in Europe.*

2. The European Union (as a political entity)

- *… asylum seekers have entered Germany and Europe …*
- *Finland joined the European Union in 1995.*
- *… is the seventh largest city in the European Union …*
- *In terms of native speakers, German is the most spoken language in the European Union.*
- *Germany's role in Europe/the EU*

3. Ethnic European stereotypes (especially in *Magazin.de* 4)

- *northern, central and southern Europeans*
- *southern Europeans, for example, show joy and anger more openly.*

- *In Latin America, southern Europe and Russia, kissing on both cheeks is common.*
- *the typical southern-European joy*
- *northern Europeans are more reserved*
- *Feelings are more openly expressed in a) northern Europe, b) central Europe, c) southern Europe*

4. **Europe and/or the European Union as an economic entity**

- *establishing the European Economic Community*
- *Frankfurt a. M. is Europe's third largest airport*
- *... belongs to the Schengen area and the European Free Trade Association EFTA.*

5. **Europe as a (historical and current) cultural area**

- *One of Europe's biggest reggae festivals takes place in Cologne.*
- *Until early modern times, people in Germany and elsewhere in Europe had only one name.*

Occurrence of Lexemes that Reference Europe in *Plan D*

The following figures show the hits for lexemes that reference Europe in the Finnish (Fig. 4.9) and German passages (Fig. 4.10) in the six volumes (including two double volumes) of the *Plan D* series of textbooks.

In the Finnish passages in *Plan D*, lexemes that reference Europe occur rarely and in any case in smaller numbers than in *Magazin.de*. They are completely absent from volumes 3 and 4 of this series. On the other hand, the German-language passages in *Plan D* include significantly more lexemes that reference Europe, as shown in Fig. 4.10.

The number of instances of lexemes that reference Europe is particularly large in volume 5 (39 hits) and the double volume, 7–8 (36 hits). In volume 5, this number is due to a lesson about a visit to the *Europa-Park*

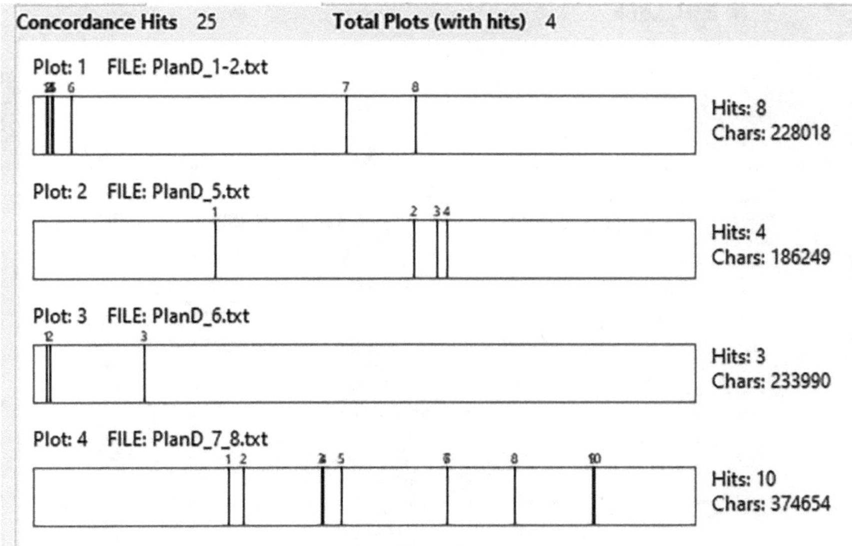

Fig. 4.9 Occurrence of *euroop** in *Plan D* 1–8

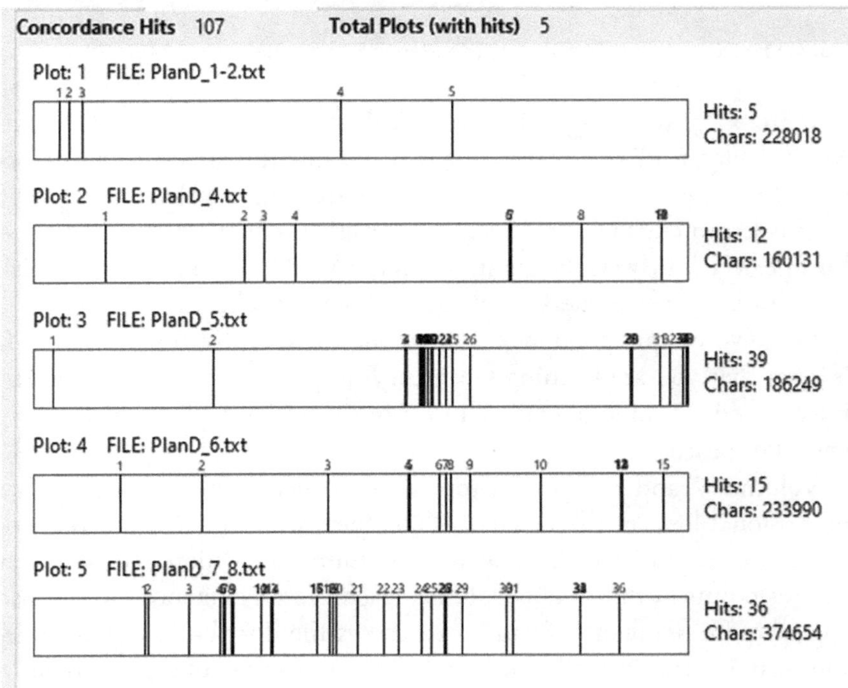

Fig. 4.10 Occurrence of *europ** in *Plan D* 1–8

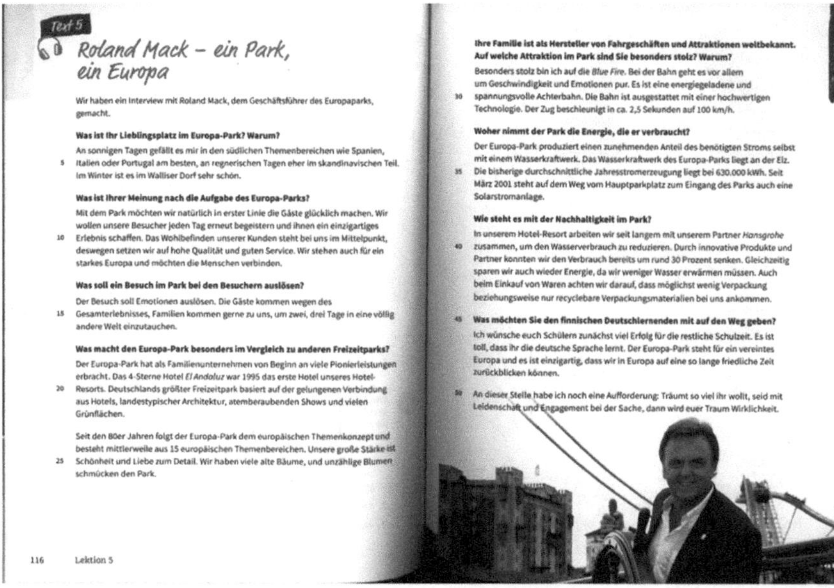

Text 5

Roland Mack – ein Park, ein Europa

Wir haben ein Interview mit Roland Mack, dem Geschäftsführer des Europaparks, gemacht.

Was ist Ihr Lieblingsplatz im Europa-Park? Warum?

An sonnigen Tagen gefällt es mir in den südlichen Themenbereichen wie Spanien, Italien oder Portugal am besten, an regnerischen Tagen eher im skandinavischen Teil. Im Winter ist es im Walliser Dorf sehr schön.

Was ist Ihrer Meinung nach die Aufgabe des Europa-Parks?

Mit dem Park möchten wir natürlich in erster Linie die Gäste glücklich machen. Wir wollen unsere Besucher jeden Tag erneut begeistern und ihnen ein einzigartiges Erlebnis schaffen. Das Wohlbefinden unserer Kunden steht bei uns im Mittelpunkt, deswegen setzen wir auf hohe Qualität und guten Service. Wir stehen auch für ein starkes Europa und möchten die Menschen verbinden.

Was soll ein Besuch im Park bei den Besuchern auslösen?

Der Besuch soll Emotionen auslösen. Die Gäste kommen wegen des Gesamterlebnisses, Familien kommen gerne zu uns, um zwei, drei Tage in eine völlig andere Welt einzutauchen.

Was macht den Europa-Park besonders im Vergleich zu anderen Freizeitparks?

Der Europa-Park hat als Familienunternehmen von Beginn an viele Pionierleistungen erbracht. Das 4-Sterne Hotel *El Andaluz* war 1995 das erste Hotel unseres Hotel-Resorts. Deutschlands größter Freizeitpark basiert auf der gelungenen Verbindung aus Hotels, landestypischer Architektur, atemberaubenden Shows und vielen Grünflächen.

Seit den 80er Jahren folgt der Europa-Park dem europäischen Themenkonzept und besteht mittlerweile aus 15 europäischen Themenbereichen. Unsere große Stärke ist Schönheit und Liebe zum Detail. Wir haben viele alte Bäume, und unzählige Blumen schmücken den Park.

116 Lektion 5

Ihre Familie ist als Hersteller von Fahrgeschäften und Attraktionen weltbekannt. Auf welche Attraktion im Park sind Sie besonders stolz? Warum?

Besonders stolz bin ich auf die *Blue Fire*. Bei der Bahn geht es vor allem um Geschwindigkeit und Emotionen pur. Es ist eine energiegeladene und spannungsvolle Achterbahn. Die Bahn ist ausgestattet mit einer hochwertigen Technologie. Der Zug beschleunigt in ca. 2,5 Sekunden auf 100 km/h.

Woher nimmt der Park die Energie, die er verbraucht?

Der Europa-Park produziert einen zunehmenden Anteil des benötigten Stroms selbst mit einem Wasserkraftwerk. Das Wasserkraftwerk des Europa-Parks liegt an der Elz. Die bisherige durchschnittliche Jahresstromerzeugung liegt bei 630.000 kWh. Seit März 2001 steht auf dem Weg vom Hauptparkplatz zum Eingang des Parks auch eine Solarstromanlage.

Wie steht es mit der Nachhaltigkeit im Park?

In unserem Hotel-Resort arbeiten wir seit langem mit unserem Partner *Hansgrohe* zusammen, um den Wasserverbrauch zu reduzieren. Durch innovative Produkte und Partner konnten wir den Verbrauch bereits um rund 30 Prozent senken. Gleichzeitig sparen wir auch wieder Energie, da wir weniger Wasser erwärmen müssen. Auch beim Einkauf von Waren achten wir darauf, dass möglichst wenig Verpackung beziehungsweise nur recyclebare Verpackungsmaterialien bei uns ankommen.

Was möchten Sie den finnischen Deutschlernenden mit auf den Weg geben?

Ich wünsche euch Schülern zunächst viel Erfolg für die restliche Schulzeit. Es ist toll, dass ihr die deutsche Sprache lernt. Der Europa-Park steht für ein vereintes Europa und es ist einzigartig, dass wir in Europa auf eine so lange friedliche Zeit zurückblicken können.

An dieser Stelle habe ich noch eine Aufforderung: Träumt so viel ihr wollt, seid mit Leidenschaft und Engagement bei der Sache, dann wird euer Traum Wirklichkeit.

Lektion

Fig. 4.11 Extract from lesson 4 of the *Plan D* 5 textbook, pages 116–17

near Freiburg, including an interview with the managing director, Roland Mack. When reading this text, one may feel that it is almost an advertisement for the largest theme park in Europe (see Fig. 4.11).

This lesson ends with a direct, very positive statement about a united Europe. Mack answers the question, 'What would you like to give Finnish German-language learners to take with them?' as follows:

I wish you pupils good luck throughout the rest of your school days. It is great that you are learning German. Europa-Park stands for a united Europe and it is unique that we in Europe can look back on such a long period of peace.

Volumes 7 and 8 focus on topics that concern the students' future professional life, on the language skills they need for this, and on economic development in Europe and the European Union. Therefore, at various points in this double volume, lexemes that reference Europe also appear quite frequently. Figure 4.12 shows the distribution of the relevant search terms in the Finnish and German passages of the six books in the *Plan D* series of textbooks as a bubble diagram created with Voyant.

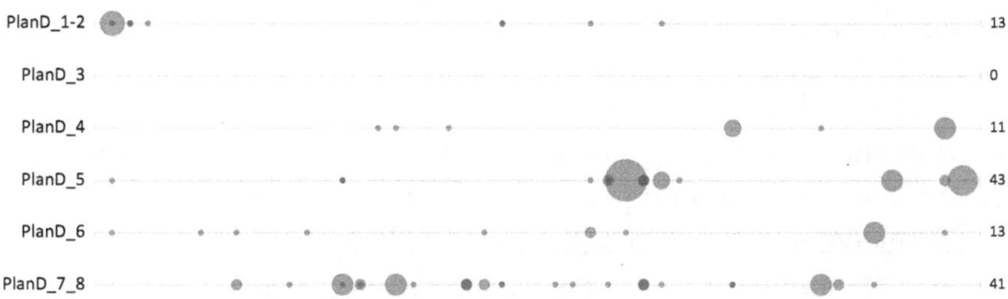

Fig. 4.12 Occurrence of *europ** and *euroop** in the six volumes of *Plan D*

With regard to *Plan D*, the KWIC list also made it possible to identify referential categories of the European lexemes. In this series of textbooks, there are eight different European concepts (see below), which again are provided with German and Finnish examples translated into English; the examples that were originally in Finnish are underlined. The order corresponds to their frequency.

1. **Europe as an [historical and current] economic entity**

- the long period of peace in Europe
- the Hanseatic League stretched over large parts of Europe
- deteriorating conditions for European businesses
- Germany as the largest economic power/as the economic centre of Europe
- Europe's oldest railway lines are in Switzerland[7]
- European integration
- Germany as a driving force for Europe's economy
- the single European market

2. **The European Union (as a political entity)**

- The whole of Europe is increasingly seen as a single market.
- European integration has also not been as successful as one would have wished.
- The united Europe
- Germany's role in Europe/the EU
- [Helmut] Kohl's view of European cooperation

3. Europe as a geographic entity

- The Netherlands is located in Europe.
- More than 100 million German-speaking people live in Europe.
- The largest dam in Europe, Grande-Dixence, is in Valais, Switzerland.
- The names of most of Europe's rivers are feminine.
- The names of most rivers outside Europe are masculine.
- European cities

4. Europe as a cultural region

- [Young Lena] became famous all over Europe in one evening.
- Finnish bands in Central Europe
- In most teams there is a 'European culture' and Italian cuisine …
- Her most famous hit, *Satellite*, has been played on the radio throughout Europe.
- Every year there are glamorous film festivals all over Europe.
- We expect a European school-leaving certificate.

5. Europe as a travel and holiday destination

- Fly somewhere in Europe
- Joe is in Europe for the first time.
- Interesting facts about health insurance in Central Europe may be …
- Europe's destinations

6. Europe as a centre of the sciences and research

- The Finnish___ students often travel to Europe to study at a German___ university.
- Europe's nuclear research centre, CERN

7. European championships

- Because of good results at the European Championships in Italy, I had the opportunity …

8. **The** ***Europa-Park*** (near Freiburg in Baden-Württemberg; high frequency in *Plan D* 5, see above)

Summary and Discussion

If the frequency of lexemes that reference Europe is related to the total number of words in the subcorpora, their relative frequency is shown in Fig. 4.13.

In the two framework curricula, lexemes that reference Europe occur comparatively frequently. The two series of textbooks differ considerably in this respect: *Plan D* contains almost twice as many lexemes with the roots *europ** or *euroop** as *Magazin.de*. This is partly owing to the lesson on Europa-Park near Freiburg in *Plan D* 5, in which a large number of these lexemes appear.

Table 4.2 gives an overview of the references and the contexts of the lexemes with the root *europ** or *euroop** in the framework curricula, and the current German textbooks for Finnish upper secondary schools.

With regard to the concept of Europe, it may be said that the framework curricula requirements are quite well-fulfilled by the two series of textbooks examined here. A positive attitude to Europe as an environment for individual and community action clearly predominates in the

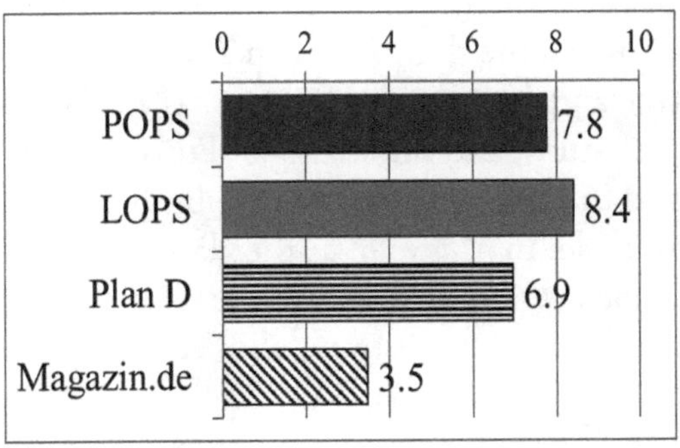

Fig. 4.13 Share of the lexemes *euroop** and *europ** per 10,000 words in the four subcorpora

Table 4.2 Overview of references and contexts of lexemes with the root *europ** or *euroop** in curricula and German textbooks for Finnish upper secondary schools

POPS & LOPS	*Plan D*	*Magazin.de*
Languages of the Indo-European language family or languages spoken in Europe	Europe as an [historical and current] economic entity	Europe as a geographic entity
Europe as a community of diverse cultures, values and faiths	The European Union (as a political entity)	The European Union (as a political entity)
Europe as part of individual and collective identities	Europe as a geographic unit	Ethnic–cultural stereotypes about Europe
Europe as a historically rooted, globally anchored, changing environment for individual human action	Europe as a cultural region	Europe and/or the European Union as an economic entity
	Europe as a travel and holiday destination	Europe as a historical and contemporary cultural area
	Europe as a Centre of science and research	
	European championships	
	The Europa-Park near Freiburg	

textbooks investigated here. Both series of textbooks have at least partly similar emphases, such as Europe as a geographic unit, as a cultural area, and as a political and economic unit. However, in addition to these similarities, there are also some differences. In *Plan D*, Europe is mentioned (only) as a travel and holiday destination, as a place for science and research, a place to study, and the setting of European championships for various sports and the Europa-Park near Freiburg in the German–Swiss–French border triangle. In *Magazin.de*, the glaring ethnic–cultural stereotypes about the behaviour of people from various regions of Europe (northern vs southern and western, and central vs eastern Europe) stand out.

The appearance of stereotypes about customs in various parts of Europe (and in some cases, of direct auto-stereotypes[8] related to Finland) may be surprising, but this is not unusual in modern Finnish textbooks, as Föhr (2018) has shown, for example. In the decades following the Second

World War, textbook authors tried to avoid national stereotypes as much as possible. With the spread of intercultural approaches to foreign language teaching since the end of the 1980s, stereotypes found their way back into textbooks, especially as objects of critical reflection. Negative prejudices and stereotypically attributed, neutrally assessed or positively viewed characteristics and behaviour patterns play a role here.

In general, it may be said that the conceptualisation of Europe that emerges from framework curricula and textbook series (apart from the geographic references to Europe as a continent, and the political references to the European Union as a political and economic entity) are very strongly influenced by the concept of culture.

Notes

1. See https://www.deutsche-bibliothek.org/index.php
2. See https://de.wikipedia.org/wiki/Deutsche_Schule_Helsinki and www.dsh.fi
3. A new curriculum framework for the upper secondary schools was developed in 2019, and came into force in 2021. It is not included here.
4. In German, *Deutsch als Fremdsprache.*
5. I would like to thank Heike Zinsmeister and Katja Gorbahn for their advice and support during this process.
6. Many thanks to Markus Furrer, who provided particularly useful information on the use of the software and on the methodology in general.
7. However, this information in the textbook is obviously wrong.
8. Regarding this concept, see Lehtonen (2005).

References

Corpus Texts

Opetushallitus, Helsinki. 2015. *'Lukion opetussuunnitelman perusteet' (LOPS).* https://www.oph.fi/sites/default/files/documents/172121_lukion_opetussuunnitelman_perusteet_2015-4-.docx. Accessed 5 May 2022.

Bär, Pia-Helena, Ines Paul, Ritva Tolvanen, and Heidi Äijälä. 2015. *Magazin.de 1*. Otava: Helsinki.
Bär, Pia-Helena, Ines Paul, Ritva Tolvanen, and Heidi Östring. 2016b. *Magazin.de 2*. Otava: Helsinki.
Bär, Pia-Helena, Ines Crockes, Ritva Tolvanen, and Heidi Östring. 2016a. *Magazin.de 3*. Otava: Helsinki.
Bär, Pia-Helena, Christian Busse, Ritva Tolvanen, and Heidi Östring. 2017b. *Magazin.de 4*. Otava: Helsinki.
———. 2017c. *Magazin.de 5*. Otava: Helsinki.
Bär, Pia-Helena, Christian Busse, and Ritva Tolvanen. 2017a. *Magazin.de 6*. Otava: Helsinki.
Bär, Pia-Helena, Christian Busse, Ritva Tolvanen, Heidi Östring, and Anu Hyypiä. 2018b. *Magazin.de 7*. Otava: Helsinki.
Bär, Pia-Helena, Christian Busse, Ritva Tolvanen, and Anu Hyypiä. 2018a. *Magazin.de 8*. Otava: Helsinki.
Haapala, Mika, Virpi Hatakka, Mikko Kervinen, Hanna Pyykönen, and Roman Schatz. 2016b. *Plan D 1–2*. Helsinki: Sanoma pro.
Haapala, Mika, Manuel Ackermann, Virpi Hatakka, Mikko Kervinen, Hanna Pyykönen, and Roman Schatz. 2016a. *Plan D 3*. Helsinki: Sanoma pro.
Haapala, Mika, Manuel Ackermann, Virpi Hatakka, Pia Hägglund-Viljanen, and Mikko Kervinen. 2017a. *Plan D 4*. Helsinki: Sanoma pro.
———. 2017b. *Plan D 5*. Helsinki: Sanoma pro.
———. 2018a. *Plan D 6*. Helsinki: Sanoma pro.
———. 2018b. *Plan D 7–8*. Helsinki: Sanoma pro.
Opetushallitus, Helsinki. 2014. *'Perusopetuksen opetussuunnitelman perusteet' (POPS)*. Helsinki. https://www.oph.fi/sites/default/files/documents/perusopetuksen_opetussuunnitelman_perusteet_2014.docx. Accessed 5 May 2022.

Further References

Bobkova, Jana. 2019. *Geschlechterrollen in finnischen Deutschlehrwerken der gymnasialen Oberstufe im 21. Jahrhundert*. Master's thesis, University of Helsinki. http://urn.fi/URN:NBN:fi:hulib-201905212011. Accessed 5 May 2022.
Finland in Figures. 2019. *Edited by Statistics Finland/Suomen tilastokeskus*. https://www.stat.fi/tup/julkaisut/tiedostot/julkaisuluettelo/yyti_fif_201900_2019_21461_net.pdf. Accessed 5 May 2022.

Föhr, Juha. 2018. *Nationale Stereotypen in finnischen Deutschlehrbüchern*. Master's thesis, University of Helsinki. https://ethesis.helsinki.fi/repository/handle/123456789/18722. Accessed 5 May 2022.

Järvinen, Martta. 2018. *Die Sprechfertigkeit im finnischen DaF-Unterricht an den gymnasialen Oberstufen—Eine Analyse der Sprechübungen in ausgewählten Lehrwerken vor und nach der Lehrplanerneuerung 2016*. Master's thesis, University of Helsinki. https://ethesis.helsinki.fi/repository/bitstream/handle/123456789/21144/Ja%cc%88rvinen_Martta_Pro_gradu_2018.pdf?sequence=1. Accessed 5 May 2022.

Julkunen, Marja-Liisa. 1988. *Oppikirja tekstianalyysin kohteena*. University of Joensuu: Kasvatustieteiden tiedekunta (Faculty of educational sciences).

Lehtonen, Jaakko. 2005. Stereotypes and collective identification. In *Cultural identity in an intercultural context*, ed. Diana Petkova and Jaakko Lehtonen, 61–85. Jyväskylä: Kampus Kirja.

Maijala, Minna. 2014. *Deutschland von außen gesehen. Geschichtliche Inhalte in Deutschlehrbüchern ausgewählter europäischer Länder*. Frankfurt am Main: Peter Lang.

Saarinen, Hannes. 2011. 'Von der Peripherie ins Zentrum Europas. Deutschland und Finnland im Laufe der Geschichte'. In *FINNLAND—Geschichte, Kultur und Gesellschaft*, edited by Hartmut E. H. Lenk, 19–31 (Beiträge zur Fremdsprachenvermittlung/Sonderheft 10). 2nd, extended and updated edition. Landau: Verlag Empirische Pädagogik.

Tikkanen, Emmi. 2017. *Interkulturelle Kompetenz im finnischen DaF-Unterricht der gymnasialen Oberstufe. Analyse der Lehrwerke Magazin.de 1 und Plan D 1 und Lehrerperspektive*. Master's thesis, University of Helsinki. http://hdl.handle.net/10138/229698. Accessed 5 May 2022.

Väisänen, Jaakko. 2005. *MURROS OPPIKIRJOJEN TEKSTEISSÄ VAI NIIDEN TAUSTALLA? 1960– ja 1990-luvun luvun historian oppikirjat kriittisen diskurssianalyysin silmin*. PhD diss., University of Joensuu. http://urn.fi/URN:ISBN:952-458-680-0.. Accessed 5 May 2022.

5

Constructions of European Identity, Crisis Stereotypes and the Discursive Embedding of the Subject in Textbook Assignments

Magdalena Telus and Marcus Otto

Introduction

Since the nineteenth century, education in general, and history and civics education, and the identity formation that takes place in this field in particular, have been discursively tied to the political form of the nation-state, both structurally and semantically. Yet, a range of political and epistemological discourses based on internal and external societal characterisations developed through history, geography and civics education throughout the twentieth century used the semantics of 'nation' and

M. Telus
Kompetenz- und Koordinationszentrum Polnisch (KoKoPol), Ostritz, Germany
e-mail: telus@kokopol.eu

M. Otto (✉)
Leibniz-Institut für Bildungsmedien | Georg-Eckert-Institut, Brunswick, Germany
e-mail: otto@gei.de

K. Gorbahn et al. (eds.), *Exploring Interconnectedness*, Palgrave Studies in Educational Media, https://doi.org/10.1007/978-3-031-13960-4_5

'Europe' in educational media to (in)form the learning subject. In the research on textbooks a plethora of studies is dedicated to discursive, narrative, visual and other constructions of Europe and European identity as well as the related processes of 'Europeanisation' (e.g. Patel and Conway 2010; Bluche et al. 2009). In view of the mutability, polyvalence and contingency of representations of Europe in textbooks and other educational media, set against the backdrop of various national, regional, transnational or globally oriented subject positions and constructions of Europe through narratives, images and spaces, this research project may draw on the work of the Georg Eckert Institute's 'Europe' department, with its multifaceted and comparative textbook analyses that address constructions of Europe (Bösch et al. 2012).

Analyses of how Europe is portrayed in textbooks are part of a controversial discussion as to whether education *for* Europe is acceptable, or even necessary, in addition to education *about* Europe (e.g. Borsche 2010, 269), or whether this would constitute indoctrination that resembles that practised in earlier nationalist (or communist) eras (Kühberger, 375; Slopinski and Selck 2014, 124–25; Eberstadt and Kuznetsov 2008, 125; Pingel 1995b, Pingel 2010; von Borries 2007; for the Polish discussion concerning the relationship between ideology and education, see Paszyński 2008; Chomczyńska-Rubacha and Pankowska 2011).[1] There is also disagreement about the role of the European Union in education-related matters. According to both the Maastricht Treaty of 1992 and the Lisbon Treaty of 2007, education and culture are not among the core focuses of the European Union, and an instrumental view of education as preparation for the European labour market has prevailed (Linsenmann 2002, 525). On the other hand, reference is made to the fact that the European Union 'shapes and endows' a European identity 'through political measures' (Marxhausen 2010, 84). The 'Resolution of the Council and the Ministers of Education meeting within the Council on the European dimension in education of 24 May 1988' is regarded as a key moment (Jobst 2004, 69; Leclercq 1995, 1) in which an awareness of a European identity was fostered via relevant measures carried out by the member states.

Since the 1950s the amount of space afforded to Europe in the textbooks of western European countries has steadily increased; however, it is not always possible to directly compare data from different studies, due to differences in how the various topic areas are defined. Challand (2009) identifies the space allocated to the theme of European integration in German, French and Italian history books as 0.52% in the 1950s and 5.35% after 2000 (Challand, 64). Even in the early 1990s, Wolfgang Mickel noted the marginal significance attributed to the topic of European integration in German curricula, despite recommendations by the Standing Conference of Ministers of Education and Cultural Affairs (*Kultusminister Konferenz*, KMK 2008) in 1978, and again in 1990, concerning 'Europe in the Classroom' (Mickel 1991, 14).[2] This changed slowly during the 1990s as, particularly after the Maastricht Treaty, a wave of publications and seminars were dedicated to a discussion of how the 'European dimension' might be taught, primarily in history lessons (van der Leeuw-Roord 2009, 157). The Council of Europe also became increasingly involved (Pingel 1995c, xvii). The international study, *Macht Europa Schule?* (Is Europe setting the school standard?), carried out by the Georg Eckert Institute for International Textbook Research in Brunswick (Germany) criticised the fact that European integration was portrayed as static, and that 'Europe' was equated with western Europe (Pingel 1995a). There was talk of an 'impeded identity' (*verhinderte Identität*) (Westheider 1995), accompanied by reports of Europe having a marginal presence in German geography books (Kirchberg 1995) and social studies books (Fritzsche 1995).

By the end of the 1990s the amount of space allocated to European topics in the broadest sense—that is, any topic with European relevance—had increased to between 30% and 40% in German (and in Italian and Spanish) history books (Pingel 2001, 214; the figure for south-eastern Europe and the Balkans was put at 10%). von Geyr and Moldenhauer (2007) noted a considerably lower count of 'European topics' in German textbooks for history, geography and social studies, namely between 1.5% and 13%, with the exception of single-topic booklets for A levels, dedicated entirely to the topic 'Europe' (Geyr et al., 278ff.).

A further project by the Georg Eckert Institute (Georg-Eckert-Institut n.d. [*Europabilder*]; also Nouvel 2011), on approaches to Europe in German, Italian and French textbooks (Challand 2009, 84),[3] has shown that European history is by no means constructed as a linear success story, that there are numerous narrative strands, that the constant presence of national narratives interferes with the European motives and, ultimately, that we may observe a gradual convergence in German and French textbooks. Visual material was particularly important in the analyses. In combination with findings from approaches to looking at places of memory (François 2013), it was revealed that the divergent meanings were attributed to the same images in different national narratives (Anklam and Grindel 2010 for German, French and Polish textbooks).

The above-mentioned analyses provide an initial point for orientation in this chapter. However, they also reveal that traditional approaches, generally anchored in an international perspective and primarily built around an analysis of the space allocated to European topics and their relevance (and thus remaining beholden to the national perspective) in fact tell us only little about *identity formation*, and specifically fostering a European identity. It is not possible to draw direct conclusions regarding identity construction from the manner and frequency with which Europe is portrayed in textbooks. It would be short-sighted to simply assume that the reception of a text or image—whether of national, international or European relevance—may be equated to forming an identity. Forming an identity, like developing knowledge and attitudes, does not work like the post office, modelled on the concept of sending a parcel from sender to recipient. Instead, identity formation is embedded in highly contingent, multi-layered and long-term semiotic processes, and subject to semantic shifts that typically occur in overlapping, polyphonic discourses. Identity formation is not a transition but a construction, and thus always involves an active subject.[4] It takes place at the iridescent, mutual cross-sections of the social and the individual, of the historico-cultural macro-perspective and the text-specific micro-level, and of deep structure and the surface of a text. To take into account all these facets and contingencies, it is necessary to consider not only the pictures of social reality proposed in textbooks but also the scripts for the behavioural responses offered to learners. In this respect, the newer approaches of discourse analysis and linguistic text analysis, as applied to textbooks, are of particular interest (Adamzik 2012; Kiesendahl 2013; Kiesendahl and Ott 2015), which are not yet widely used. Two such studies (Langner 2009; Marxhausen 2010) are specifically dedicated to the discursive construction of a European identity. Building on Wodak and Weiss 2004 (also Puntscher-Riekmann and Wodak 2003; Weiss 2003), both authors base their analyses on the assumption that construction of European identity in educational media takes place—if at all—with the same discursive means we encounter in processes of nation-building (Langner 2009, 96–97).[5] This paper assumes the opposite: European unity emerged in a different era to that of the European nations that have been mostly formed during Modernity at its peak, and at a different moment of Western cultural history. Jürgen Link called this the era of a 'flexible normalism', in contrast to a rigid 'proto-normalism' that began with the increasing naturalisation of social categories in the Modern era (Link [1996] 2006). Therefore, it seems unlikely that 'Europe' and 'nation' will be constructed with the same discursive semantics or generate the same subject positions.[6]

In recent and prominent broad historiographic representations (Judt 1996; Mazower 1999; Jarausch 2015; Patel 2017; Kershaw 2019), various aspects of Europe and its history in the twentieth century have been framed by master narratives of crisis, from various perspectives and to various degrees. Yet, the dictum that Europe is in crisis, as so many voices have claimed, with respect to the often-evoked European 'project', is in no way a new phenomenon; instead it represents a semantic topos that had already begun to crystallise by the beginning of the twentieth century, and since then has been articulated in a range of contexts over the course of the twentieth century. Therefore, the concept of 'crisis' became a topos in societies' portrayals of themselves throughout the twentieth century, as several recent studies have shown (e.g. Graf and Jarausch 2017). This applies to 'Europe' in particular, as a paradigmatic example of a discursive reference shaped by a variety of historically shifting semantics of crisis (Kaelble 2008, 2012). Kaelble lays out the ways in which various 'crises'—from the 'crisis of civilisation' to the 'integration crisis' to 'crisis management'—have established a corresponding topos in the representation of Europe throughout the twentieth century (Kaelble 2008, 2012). Furthermore, in connection with historical and sociological diagnoses of Modernity as a crisis of civilisation caught between the promise of progress and narratives of degeneration, Weiß (2016) studies discourses between Europeans and non-Europeans concerning Modernity and European decadence around 1900. The idea of a 'mission of civilisation' or a historically grounded European 'identity', along with its potential decline, became an expression of the 'crisis of Western civilisation' par excellence, especially in connection with the oft-evoked European crises that followed both World Wars, in the face of a perceived loss of significance. Finally, a study of French history textbooks (Otto 2013) positions itself at the nexus of European crisis semantics on the one hand, and on the other, the status of the self and the European subject position. Semantics of crisis have recently been identified as a seismographic topic in textbooks (Otto et al. 2020), and a crucial and topical challenge, especially for education on European politics and civics (Eis and Moulin-Doos 2018). This leads to the general question of the extent to which this significant semantics of crisis reflects a particular semantic modality of the discursive construction of a European identity, how this eventually affects the learning subject and how it is to be made apparent in textbook analysis.

Late Modernity and Its 'Weak Identities'

'Late Modernity'[7] produced 'weak identities'. These involve mentally embedding the subject in a societal space, whereas the relevance of belonging to a certain group is weakened in many ways with regard to this embedding. The latter occurs as a reaction to societal relations and requirements, which are different to those on which the collective identities of the heyday of Modernity were built. With reference to this development, Calhoun (2001) differentiates between *categorical* versus *relational identities*, and identifies the disparity between a national and a European identity as the prototype (47ff.; also see the terms *catness* vs. *netness* used by Brubaker and Cooper 2000, consistent with Charles Tilly's use). This pair of opposites plays an important role in debates concerning a possible European identity (see also Habermas 2006), despite persistent ambiguity regarding the nature of a post-national European society.[8] The nation remains the conscious or subconscious point of reference in identity research, and 'the most frequent yardstick with which the development of a European self-image is measured' (Kaelble 2001, 9; also Kaelble 2008, 437).[9] 'Critique that there has until now been no distinct

European identity, no real attachment of Europeans to Europe, no European symbols, no European people, always enlists the nation as its object of comparison' (Kaelble 2001, 9). Bearing in mind that the beginnings of a lifeworld European normality were established in the 1960s (Kaelble 2001, 242), that is, during a period of transition from the heyday of late-stage Modernity (Welsch 2008, 135ff.), it becomes clear that the semantic patterns of the national are incongruent with those of the European. If national identity is a point of reference for European identity, this may only be in a negative form: in other words, defining what it is not.

Studies from the 1980s and 1990s on the discursive construction of the nation (e.g. Wodak et al. 1998) examine the semantic principles according to which a categorical identity is structured. The social reality of the nation builds on the fundamental discursive–semantic figure (Dietrich Busse) of the *us–them* opposition (see also Telus et al. 1997). This opposition is static and is reinforced by myths, categorical homogenisation—via group stereotyping, for example—that assigns values in terms of positive auto-stereotypes and negative hetero-stereotypes, emotionalisation, heroisation, pathos and so on (Tajfel 1981; Telus 2002). The 'identity' of the individual is conceived of as membership in a group. In contrast, weak identities are intrinsically built on a dynamic nexus of relationships in which the subject (dynamically) positions itself in terms of its (communicative) acts, rather than on the principle of membership. Strong identities rely on statements and rules, on a narrative about who or what they are and on an explanation of what it means to be a member of that category.[10] On the other hand, weak identities tend to 'happen' imperceptibly; they simply materialise 'somehow': they unfold in everyday life and in concrete, discursive frames of reference.[11] They are practised as polyphonic fragments and idiosyncratic choices. Thus, Calhoun describes Europe as 'an institutional arena within which diversity and multiple connections among people and organisations can flourish partly because they never end up as a single, integrated whole' (Calhoun 2001, 38). He further argues that the differences in the discursive–semantic qualities of these two types of identity are so striking that one would be justified in asking whether weak identities may still be considered a continuation or rather a questioning of the identity project of Modernity (Calhoun, 37).

The social fabric of Late Modernity is different to that of the heyday of Modernity—on this, at least, contemporary social scientists such as Zygmunt (Bauman 1996), Ulrich Beck (1986, 2005), Anthony Giddens (1991), Herfried Münkler (2012), Wolfgang Welsch (2008) and Hartmut Rosa (Rosa 2002) largely agree. The social fabric of 'high' Modernity was built on homogeneous, static and discrete categories, like a uniform pattern stamped onto a cloth (Fig. 5.1). Single categories are conceived of as opposites, and subject positions adopted within these categories are equally static. On the other hand, in Late Modernity the patterns are irregular and woven into the social fabric, with knots and overlaps visible in the foreground (Fig. 5.2). The subject positions are more difficult to identify, as they materialise in and from the ongoing process of becoming that they, in turn, inform.

The Situation of the Subject

This section is based on the conception of a subject who is simultaneously self-aware of both their discursive subjugation and the discursive possibilities of their own essence as expressed through symbols and acts (Skarga 2015). A key moment in this concept of the subject is its contingency. It

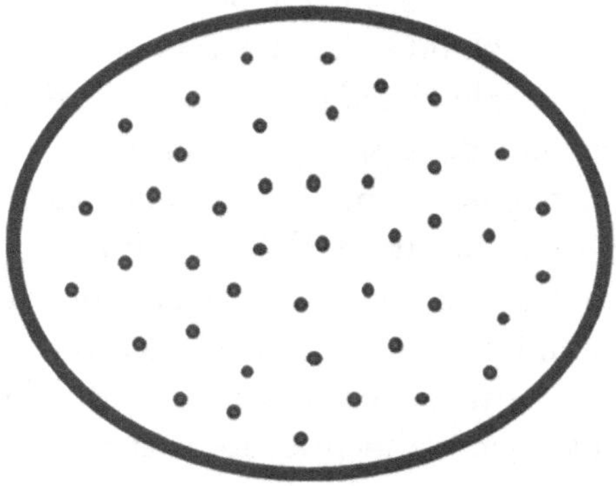

Fig. 5.1 The social fabric of 'high' Modernity (model design: Magdelena Telus)

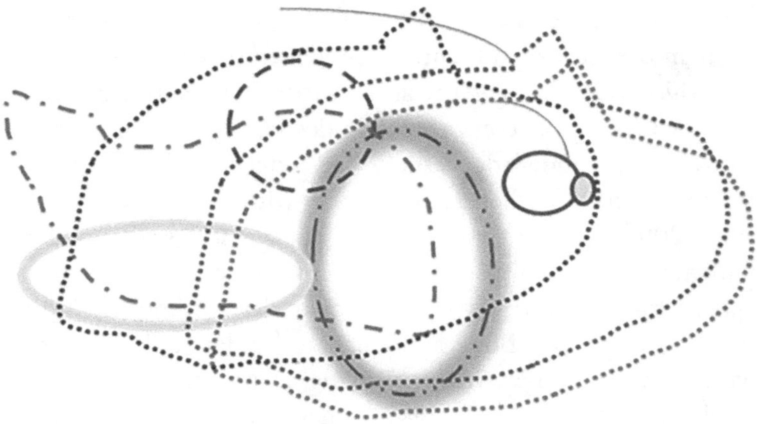

Fig. 5.2 The social fabric of Late Modernity (model design: Magdelena Telus)

is a 'subject of pluralisation' that has 'not only become contingent but also experiences itself as such' (Charim 2018, 101, below; also see the concept of the 'multi-vocal subject' in Hermans and Hermans-Konopka 2010). A core task of becoming a subject of Late Modernity is processing one's own plurality, the hallmark of which is termed 'authenticity'.

Social philosopher Charles Taylor has observed that in Late Modernity, people appear to increasingly measure the success of their lives in terms of themselves, and in this context, describe 'authenticity' as a social ideal. To be authentic means to orient according to one's inner compass, which, in Taylor's concept, is orientated around a communitisation, including a communitisation of life in Late Modernity, which is highly conditional and deeply rooted in cultural history. What counts as authentic, and in which direction the compass points, is determined by the subject, who, nevertheless, still requires social approval (Taylor [1991] 1995, 41ff.). Negotiation of the authentic is based on substantial arguments (Taylor identifies 'horizons of significance', in which such arguments must be rooted; Ferrara 2009, 27ff. discusses the complexity of justifying obligations entered into by an individual). In this conception of authenticity it is not a matter of 'genuineness' that indicates a person's 'true essence'; instead, it is a question of 'consistency', as the permanently materialising result of a successful exchange with one's social surroundings (both terms used here in the sense of authenticity presented by Parschalk 2012, 26).[12] It was in this sense that the term 'authenticity' entered the field of history didactics: achieving the competence to deconstruct myths, and to question conventional knowledge, established judgements and canons would allow pupils to have 'authentic experiences with themselves' (von Borries and Filser 2004). von Borries argues that engagement with plurality is the fundamental condition for such an 'authentic experience', which, in turn, is required for von Borries' postulate of understanding the 'other' and perceiving change (von Borries, 262ff.), and didactically flanked by the concepts of multiperspectivity (observing an object from various social standpoints), controversy (various judgements of circumstances) and plurality (various visions of the future) (von Borries, 292).

In her diagnosis of the times, Charim (2018) moves beyond the concept of authenticity.[13] She addresses three types of individualism, which she attributes to Modernity, Late Modernity and the present day (although at times they may occur simultaneously). The first type of individualism, that of 'high' Modernity with its large groups, is geared to disciplining the subject. On the other hand, since the 1960s, the second type of individualism has been based on the opposite: giving the subject the freedom to be, in accordance with its own wishes. It was during this period that the need for authenticity and its expression arose. The individualism of the present—the third type of individualism—is one in which identities exist in parallel, and on an equal footing, in pluralist societies. The daily experience that one's own identity is just one of many leads to a 'deduction of identity'—here Charim speaks of an 'identity-related precarity' (Charim, 48). This demands more effort from the subject than earlier, stable and unquestioned identities. 'The crucial question is not: *Who are you?* The crucial question is: *How true are you to what you are?*' (Charim, 214). This reframing is significant to our discussion, because it elucidates how identities that are weak (Calhoun) or diminished by plurality (Charim) require more intensive participation on the part of the (learning) subject.

Identity Constructions in Textbooks

For an observation of these social relations in textbooks it is insufficient to merely unveil the construction of social groups and the relationships between them; in other words, the outlines of social reality embedded within the authored texts.[14] We cannot infer from a portrayal of social reality in textbooks alone that the learning subject undergoes a particular construction of identity. Instead, the textbook analysis must encompass the options the textbook presents to the learning subject, by which one anchors oneself in, and negotiates these sketches of reality and constellations of knowledge. Therefore, it is not sufficient to ask, 'What is the student absorbing?'; instead, we must ask, 'How do the students engage with what they have absorbed; what are they doing with it?' Particularly relevant is the Late-Modern rejection of an essentialist concept of the knowledge and 'knowledge gain', mentioned above, in favour of the constructivist ideas that emerged in western European didactics at the end of the 1960s, and which influenced textbook design. Textbooks no longer consist of mere 'master narratives', but present multi-layered networks of various sorts of texts (*Textsortennetze*; Adamzik 2011): alongside texts written by the textbook authors themselves, the books also include source texts that present contrasting standpoints, requirements and suggestions for the pupils' project work, self-assessment tests, controversially arranged excerpts from academic literature, didactically presented illustrative material, links to selected and/or textbook-specific websites, methodological instructions and so on. The various types of text often include contradictory presentations of reality, which, however, refer to, question or complement one another, destabilising the horizons of what has previously been considered possible. Textbook authors are no longer mere producers of texts, but arrangers of a polyphonic, discursive learning landscape in which the learning subject has to orientate and position itself, with flexibility and self-reflection. Late-Modern textbooks stimulate the plurality of the learning subject, at the same time offering approaches for managing this plurality and thus qualifying for a claim to authenticity. Thus, the learning subject is addressed as exercising management in 'doing Europe'—and doing so within a discursive framework characterised by the semantics of crisis.

Doing Europe by Critique and Crisis Stereotypes: Interpellation of (European) Subjects in Textbook Assignments

The character of Europe as described above, in terms of non-categorical semantics, is often reflected in omnipresent, sceptical diagnoses of a deficient 'identity' or corresponding impotence of Europe as some kind of critical European metanarrative that is also a reflection of current political and societal discourses of European self-description in terms of crisis. Ultimately, this indicates the extent to which the discursive constitution of European 'identity', including an inherent diagnosis of its crisis, is advanced as a veritable formula for pathos and contingency in the Modern construction of historical and political meaning.

Within the dimensions of knowledge and power, the semantics of 'crisis' with regard to Europe in textbook tasks and exercises implies twofold, epistemologically and politically: with regard to knowledge and its dialogical construction it signifies the contingency of, and uncertainty about a (potential) identity and its current state of affairs. With regard to power and its performative exercise it exploratively challenges and eventually 'empowers' the subjects to make an individual, or even dialogical choice, rather than an imperatively categorical decision. Yet, in both these dimensions of knowledge and power, the discursive modality of the critique is involved as a complement to the political–epistemological (non-)category of crisis. Thus, the learning subject is addressed, interpellated and therefore eventually discursively embedded by textbook assignments (Otto and Spielhaus 2020; Otto 2018) to engage in a dialogical discussion of and introspective reflection on Europe as a non-categorical, 'experimental' object and subject of contingency.

According to the performative semantics of crisis, the inherent interconnection between knowledge and its negotiation, the modalities of exercising power and the discursive practices of the empowerment of the subject become manifest. Within this framework, the semantics of crisis serve as an expression of a programmatically precarious and uncertain, non-categorical identity that frames the exercising and embedding of 'Crisis Subjects' and corresponding critical subject positions through textbook assignments. Thus, Crisis and Critique serve as functions of governmentality in the Foucaultian sense (Otto 2014, 188–91), and contribute to the normalisation of representations of Europe in the interconnected dimensions of power and knowledge, and from the perspective of the self-fashioning of the learning subject. Although ideas of crisis serve as attention markers, and imply the focalisation of contingency, including an interpellation of decisions, the modality of critique configures power and knowledge, and the self-empowerment of subjects (positions). This educational governmentality through textbook assignments transforms the contingency by disaggregating categorical or even fundamental decision to individual choice and its limitations. Accordingly, dialogical and individualising practices, and iterative exercises in attention to, and criticism of, the crisis, invoke the self-fashioning of (European) subjects through education.

From a poststructuralist perspective, the corresponding subjects are discursively constituted as bearers of agency and experience within the discursive framework of power and knowledge. This also and especially applies to the formation of subjects within and through education, as it is institutionalised at schools. As we have already argued, although in terms of knowledge Europe is constructed in terms of non-categorical semantics, distinguished from the nation as categorical semantics, with regard to the dimension of power Europe is discursively constructed through the flexible normalisation of the subject whereas the nation traditionally serves the disciplinary normalisation of the subject. Maarten and Hodgson have analysed the interpellation and subjectivation of European subjects through education, within the theoretical framework of governmentality (Maarten and Hodgson 2012). This addresses the dimension of power in the context of governmentalised education focused on knowledge competence, and the corresponding subjectivation of students as 'European' (Maarten and Hodgson 2012). Therefore, in textbook assignments, Europe serves as an explorative, projected area for the (multi-)optional self-identification of the (individual) subject. This implies that Europe literally functions as a contingent and uncertain form that invokes the interpellation of the subject, to individually complete and eventually perform in, (re)iterate and supplement this form by constructing its flexible, liminal and (multi-)optional relationship to (constructions of) Europe. Within this discursive framework Europe is constructed as an experimental dispositive and exercises a 'laboratory' of stereotyped and idiosyncratic knowledge, and the learning subject's corresponding competence.

In the following example, there often dominates a perspective that addresses the question of the extent to which the subjects can identify with Europe, and what Europe literally and symbolically means to a given individual: 'What Europe means to me' (*Buchners Kompendium Politik*, 2016, 370).

In this example, the students refer to symbolically laden images, and are asked to state what the European Union means to them personally. This task and exercise imply self-reflection and self-positioning on the part of the students with regard to the European Union, which is identified here as the institutional figure of Europe (obviously, this presupposes a relationship between Europe and the learning subject).

Through various tasks and exercises, Europe is (critically) evaluated as a laboratory project and area of projection for the self-identification and self-evaluation, self-fashioning and self-positioning of the (Late-Modern?) subject. Thus, Europe eventually evolves into an individual and idiosyncratic life- and learning style. Furthermore, Europe serves as an experimental (epistemic) object in tasks and exercises, by explicitly challenging and eventually embedding the (individual) subject. In textbooks for history and civic education, Europe is a prominent topic and aspect of tasks and exercises. Indeed, Europe or the European Union and their construction are often evoked and manifested in tasks and exercises, as contemporary training instruments with regard to forming critical judgement and corresponding subject positions *par excellence*. The following examples from a current German textbook for civic education are representative and significant in this respect (Schaechterle and Willfahrt 2018, 292–93). In one example, under the suggestive heading, 'Should the EU regulate as much or as little as possible?', the assignment is to discuss the effects of the European Union on one's everyday life. Furthermore, the students are explicitly asked to judge eventually positive or negative aspects of EU regulations as such. This implies at least at an imaginary level that the institutional framework of the European Union is set as radically contingent from the perspective of the students' individual subject positions.

The subject is eventually discursively embedded in and through tasks and exercises concerning Europe as a project, real-life experiment and self-learning dispositive. This involves a performative interpellation of the self (Otto 2014, 140) of Europe and (the) European subject(s) through tasks and exercises, which eventually evokes self-referential introspection and a complementary dialogical self-exposition. This reflects the liminal status of Europe in terms of non-categorical semantics and its discursive implications, which repeatedly refer to scenarios of crisis and display the permanent liminal state of Europe and its corresponding European subject(s). Thus there emerges a twofold liminality that comprises *rites de passage* in the temporal dimension and an intermediate subject position between *alter* and *ego* in the social dimension. In the discursive framework of self- and other-stereotypes, this implies that the European subject has a liminal subject position that is framed as a neither 'we' nor 'the other'. The corresponding liminal stereotypes are then (re-)produced and eventually transformed through the prism of various co-existing and co-corresponding national perspectives that perform and re-enact 'Europe'. Thus, students' interpellation induces a doing of Europe and a corresponding positioning of the subject that also implies judging Europe.

The foregoing is somehow paradigmatically reflected in textbook assignments that induce and develop linguistic and semiotic stereotypical forms of and formulas for, Europe, as displayed in the 'Europe means to me' example. In such tasks and exercises the students are asked to 'do' Europe by creating, (re-)producing, invoking and acting out stereotypes. Thus, Europe becomes an object of 'idiosyncratic' stereotypes that are simultaneously collective. This is a remarkable paradox. Hence, discursively embedding the subject takes place through interdiscursive practices. Such inter-discourse manifests in the significant correspondence between idiosyncratic stereotypes on the one hand, and on the other hand, crisis stereotypes of Europe that are characterised by dramatising contingency and the consequential interpellation of subjective judgement, emphatic decisions and eventual action.

Conclusion: Critique of Identity, Crisis Stereotypes of Europe and the Discursive Embedding of the Subject

In the spaces of Late-Modern communication, Europe occurs as a 'hyphenated identity' (Giddens 2008, 56), a 'mélange identity' (Beck and Grande 2004, 193), a 'patchwork identity' (Parschalk 2012, 24), a 'nested identity' (Schmitt-Egner 2012, 42) or a 'marble cake identity' (Risse 2010, 25). Given this semantic backdrop, Europe cannot be conceived of as a reference group with a strong identity that overarches the nation while at the same time remaining semantically similar to it. Observations of changes in social relations demand revised methods of textbook research. These would include replacing the transmission approach to identity construction in educational contexts that has hitherto derived identity conceptions from portrayals of Europe with a constructivist or action-orientated approach. Thus, not only would knowledge about Europe be of interest, but so would the tasks demanded of the learning subject with reference to this knowledge. Developments in social studies subjects in western European didactics since the late 1960s may be considered isomorphic with respect to the 'softening' of categories that is characteristic of Late Modernity. The broader orientation of learning materials in the 1960s (material-orientated learning) was followed by a focus on selected problems (problem-orientated learning), and then in turn by the current emphasis on methods and competence (method-orientated learning, cf. von Borries and Filser 2004, 292; Popp 2010, 339). Empowering the learning subject via instruments for reflecting on identity (Kühberger 2010, 363) must be given greater prominence by textbook analyses that addresses Europe. European identity is weak, or perhaps more precisely, inherently fragile and liminal; it is not inspired by sentiment, as in the case of the nation, but by the subject's (self-)invocation of critical reflection and of an awareness of uncertainty that is particularly manifest in the use of 'crisis stereotypes' that invoke crucial situations of choice by the subject.

In general, there is a semantic and discursive coupling of Europe on the one hand and crisis on the other hand. This is particularly evident in textbook assignments and thus also affects the interpellation of the (learning) subject. Within this discursive framework the learning subject is challenged by the semantic emphasis on contingency and open future prospects of Europe as a genuine project whereas the concept of crisis serves as a programmatic formula for contingency and pathos. This presents Europe as an object of the learning subject's agency and experience. In this setting Europe means a current exercise and an object of deferral at the same time. Within the omnipresent and insistent discursive framework, the semantics of 'crisis' serves especially with regard to Europe as specifically insisting interpellation and embedding of the subject as a socialised bearer of potential agency (and demanded by the expectation of 'authenticity') by also recurring to collective and individualised experience. Thus, crisis furnishes the semantics of the normalisation of challenges, problems and threats through textbook tasks and exercises and of the learning and training subject within the educational framework of competence and method orientation. Therefore, textbook tasks and exercises experimentally transpose and stage contingency, both emphasised and normalised by the semantics of crisis. Moreover, crisis thus becomes an insisting marker of attention and interpellation of the subject and a semantic vehicle for the embedding of the subject as carrier of agency and experience. Textbook tasks and exercises related to the semantics of crisis transform undetermined contingency and uncertainty, especially with regard to Europe, into specified, determined contingency to be eventually resolved by the engaged and embedded individual. The corresponding educational practices of doing, experiencing and even experimenting Europe are significantly evoked by crisis stereotypes that serve as framing interpellations of subjects in textbook assignments. Thus, crisis becomes a dominant and significant semantic framework for making Europe in textbooks, and therefore, the learning subjects are performatively inscribed and embedded in the corresponding crisis discourse about Europe.

Appendix: Subject Construction in a European Context—An Exemplary Multimodal Analysis of a German Textbook

Based on the premises presented above, the following provide some insight into a geography textbook: *Terra Europa* (Klett publishing), supplementary material for years 11 to 13 (Boeti et al. 2016). It is reasonably up-to-date and discusses most of the recent European crises: the economic crisis, the refugee crisis, Euroscepticism, right-wing populism, the war in Ukraine and Russia's ambition to become a superpower, to name but a few. The book has seven chapters:

1. *Europa—zwischen Integration und Zerfall?* (Europe—Between Integration and Collapse/Disintegration?) (6–19)
2. *Europa—Migration und Bevölkerung* (Europe—Migration and Population) (20–35)
3. *Natürliche Grundlagen: Nutzung und Gefährung* (Natural Fundamentals: Usage and Threats) (36–59)
4. *Wirtschaftsraum Europa—Erfolgsgeschichte mit Schattenseiten* (Europe as an Economic Zone—A success Story with Drawbacks) (60–93)
5. *Zusammenarbeit in der Europäischen Union* (Collaboration in the European Union) (110–41)
6. *Globale Wirtschaftsverflechtungen der EU und Deutschland* (Global Economic Integration of the EU and Germany) (142–63)
7. *Arbeitsanhang* (Appendix: Tasks) (164–85)

These chapter headings reveal an interesting pattern. Headings 1 to 4 feature a binary structure (topos: *Two sides of one coin*; see below), which, despite the conjunction *und* (and) or the preposition *mit* (with), indicates a break. In headings 1, 3 and 4, the binary structure emerges via the juxtaposition of a positive and a negative term, whereby the former is relativised by the latter. In heading 2 the binary structure lies in the indirect opposition suggested by 'mobile' versus 'settled'. In contrast, headings 5 and 6 create a sense of cohesion: the term *Zusammenarbeit* (collaboration) in 5 directs the sense of the heading inwards (*in der Europäischen*

Union (in the European Union)); similarly, the term *Wirtschaftsverflechtung* (economic integration) in heading 6 gives the sense of an outward direction (*globale* [global]). The social reality of Europe presented here reveals ruptures and uncertainties, yet at the same time, reveals an internal cohesion and embedding in a global context. After working through these chapters, in Chap. 7 the learning subject is offered advice on, and support for exam preparation, and required to navigate this heterogeneous social world and find his/her place within it, via personal engagement with the world presented. Thus, the table of contents reveals a fundamental, discursive, semantic figure that may be summarised as: 'There are x and y (and z …), interwoven with respect to diverse points of reference—where are you in this nexus?' It is important to note that this figure's potential for generating a sense of identity is entirely different to that of the basic figure of *Self* versus *Other* or *them and us* (Busse 2000, 52). The difference lies not only in the fact that the first figure points to a multi-polar and interwoven structure of social reality, in contrast to the binary structure of the second figure, but also—and above all—in that the reader's sense of societal belonging in this second figure is predetermined by the text producer who decides who is 'them' and who is 'us' (furthermore, the second figure is based on the assumption that both text producer and reader belong to the same social group). We will see that the first figure—the one that indicates a blurring and dynamic plurality of the social world—is not only essential for the picture of the world suggested in the textbook, but also isomorphically forms the basic structure of the didactic concept on which the textbook is built.

Each chapter begins with a double-page introduction that consists of one or two images with captions and numbers, each with an authored text. This list of image captions corresponds to the images:

Chapter 1. Image 1: *Jubelfeiern in Kroatien beim Beitritt zur Europäischen Union 2013* (Celebrations in Croatia upon joining the European Union in 2013) (6)

Image 2 *Demonstration gegen Missstände in der EU* (Demonstration against shortcomings of the EU) (7)

Chapter 2. Image 1: *Europa: alternde Gesellschaften; Ziel von Arbeitsmigranten und Flüchtlingen* (Europe: Ageing societies; destination for migrant workers and refugees) (20–21)

Chapter 3. Image 1: *Krater des Vesuv vom Monte Somma nach Süden über den Golf von Neapel zur Halbinsel Sorrent* (Crater of Mount Vesuvius seen from Mount Somma to the south across the Gulf of Naples towards the Sorrento Peninsula) (36–37)

Chapter 4. Image 1: *Barcelona—pulsierende Wirtschaftsmetropole an der spanischen Mittelmeerküste* (Barcelona—vibrant economic metropolis on the Spanish Mediterranean coast) (62)

Image 2 *Industriebrache im niederländischen Maasmechelen* (Industrial wasteland in Dutch Maasmechelen) (63)

Chapter 5. Image 1: *Errungenschaften der EU: offene Grenzen als Markenzeichen 2011* (Achievements of the EU: Trademark open borders in 2011) (110)

Image 2 Flüchtlingskrise (Grenzkontrollen): eine Herausforderung für die Zusammenarbeit in der EU 2016 (Refugee crisis [border control]: a challenge for EU cooperation in 2016) (111)

Chapter 6. Image 1: *Paris—Flughafen Charles de Gaulle (im Bild: Terminal 1)* (Paris—Charles de Gaulle Airport [Illustration: Terminal 1]) (142)

Image 2 *Frankfurt am Main—bedeutende Schaltstelle der Weltwirtschaft (im Bild: EZB und Bankenviertel)* (Frankfurt am Main—significant global economic hub [Illustration: European Central Bank and the *Bankenviertel*]) (143)

Chapter 7. (Image without number or caption: four teenagers reading and writing at a table) (164–65)

Of the seven introductory pages, five are structured in a way that causes confusion or uncertainty. In Chaps. 1, 4 and 5 this occurs via contrasts: celebrating the European Union and Euroscepticism; a city landscape and an industrial wasteland; an open border and a border control. In Chaps. 2 and 3 the confusion arises indirectly through blurring. In Chap. 2, for instance, a double-page spread shows a group of people representing various generations, genders, skin colours and styles of clothing (Fig. 5.3). The middle of the photograph is in focus and in colour. To each side, the photograph is pale and grey. The point of transition from the sharp focus to the pale remainder of the picture forms a zigzag. Together with the chapter heading, *Europa—Migration und Bevölkerung* (Europe—Migration and Population), the picture creates confusion

Fig. 5.3 Detail from the introductory pages to Chapter 2, 20–21

regarding the status of the group that could be called the 'population of Europe'; it becomes clear that this is a case of a population permanently confronted with the topic of migration, remaining unclear as to which persons in the image are to be ascribed to the category of 'migrants' and which belong to the category of 'population'. Chapter 3 is introduced with a photograph of the crater of Mount Vesuvius before the backdrop of the Gulf of Naples. The image is unsettling as the volcano looms threateningly over the city.

The texts concerning the images on these introductory pages end with questions about the content of the chapters. Some of the questions are formulated so that the answers are unclear, or at least require discussion, for instance:

> *Wir müssen nicht nur fragen: 'Was wird aus dem Euro?', sondern auch: 'Was wird aus der EU?'*
>
> (We must ask not only: 'What will happen to the euro?' but also 'What will happen to the EU?' Chapters 1, 7)

> *Kann Zuwanderung tatsächlich dazu beitragen, die Probleme alternder Gesellschaften zu lösen?* (Can immigration really contribute to solving the problems of ageing societies?) (Chapter 2, 21).

Wo liegen die Grenzen des vereinten Europa?
(Where are the borders of a united Europe? Chapter 5, 111)

These questions are also interesting from the point of view of textual linguistics, because, with the exception of the introduction to Chap. 4, they are presented abruptly. In contrast, the examples below demonstrate an indirect transition from the authored text to the questions (intro. to Chap. 4, transition section in bold print); and a sudden transition without a preamble (intro. to Chap. 3, transition marked with [sic]):

Solche Schattenseiten entstehen jedoch nicht nur durch Krisen und Konflikte. Zu groß sind noch die Unterschiede zwischen einzelnen Ländern, aber auch zwischen einzelnen Teilregionen, als das die Erfolgsgeschichte des Wirtschaftsraums Europa schon fertig geschrieben wäre. ***Auf den folgenden Seiten werden hierzu Antworten auf unterschiedliche Fragen gegeben:***
Wie stellen sich Europas wirtschaftliche Vielfalt und Disparitäten räumlich dar?
Wie präsentieren sich einzelne Regionen zwischen wirtschaftlicher Krise und ökonomischem Wachstum? [...].
(Such drawbacks are not only the result of crises and conflicts. Differences between the individual countries, and also between regions are still too great for Europe as an economic zone to have completed its success story. **The following pages provide answers to various questions about this**:
How are Europe's economic diversity and disparities spatially distributed?
How do individual regions present themselves between economic crisis and economic growth? ...) (63).
Doch ist eine wirtschaftliche Nutzung oft mit Risiken verbunden, wie das Schrägluftbild der Bucht von Neapel eindrucksvoll zeigt. [...] Spektakuläre Ausbrüche in der Vergangenheit hatten oft schwere Zerstörungen zur Folge und forderten immer wieder auch eine hohe Zahl an Todesopfern. [sic].

Questions follow:

Welche Bedeutung haben die naturräumlichen Gegebenheiten in den verschiedenen Ländern und Regionen Europas für eine wirtschaftliche Nutzung?
Welche Gefährdungen sind mit der Nutzung verbunden? [...].

(Yet economic exploitation often involves risks, as the aerial photograph of the Gulf of Naples strikingly shows ... Spectacular eruptions in the past often resulted in severe destruction and, repeatedly, a high number of victims. [sic].

What is the significance of the natural circumstances in the various countries and regions of Europe with regard to economic exploitation?

What dangers does this involve? ...). (37)

Such abrupt shifts from the authored texts to sets of questions, as in the above quotation, refute the promise expressed in the previous example that the answers are to be found in the chapter's material. Furthermore, both the last two examples and the entire booklet exhibit a striking number of contrast (topos: *two sides of one coin*) and pluralisation (topos: *unity in diversity*): where there is 'utility' there are also 'dangers' or 'risks'; where there is 'crisis', 'growth' is never far away. The focus is on 'differences', 'diversity', 'disparities' and 'different countries and regions of Europe'. The penultimate example also features the topos of an open-ended project:

Zu groß sind noch die Unterschiede zwischen einzelnen Ländern, aber auch zwischen einzelnen Teilregionen, als das die Erfolgsgeschichte des Wirtschaftsraums Europa schon fertig geschrieben wäre.

(Differences between the individual countries and also between regions are still too great for Europe as an economic zone to have completed its success story) (63, quotation above).

From a discourse-analytical perspective, here we see the figure[15] of a rupture, an uncertainty, also visible in the headings of sub-chapters and paragraphs, for instance: *3.2 Geologisches Puzzle mit Risiken* (Geological Puzzle with Risks), *4.2 Tourismusräume zwischen Boom und Gefährdung* (Tourist areas between boom and threat), *6.3 Wirtschaftssanktionen—sinnvoll oder zerstörerisch?* (Economic Sanctions—Useful or Destructive?). The figure of the rupture is closely interwoven with the figure of vagueness and inconclusiveness, as in these examples, *2.2 Europa ohne Grenzen?* (Europe without Borders?), *6.2 Regionalisierung* vs. *Globalisierung* (Regionalisation vs. Globalisation), and the figure of plurality and diversity, as in *3.3 Klimavielfalt* (Climate Diversity), *4.1 Vielfalt der europäischen Raumstruktur* (Diversity of the European spatial structure), *5.4 Messung regionaler Disparitäten in der EU* (Measuring Regional Disparities in the EU). Equally characteristic is the figure of change and process, for example in *2.4 Demografischer Wandel* (Demographic Change), *3.3 Klimaänderungen* (Climate Change), *4.2 Altindustrielle Räume im Wandel* (Old Industrial Spaces Undergoing Changes).

As the textbook in question is designed for the final level of secondary school (*Gymnasium*), the tasks for the learners are divided into the three required areas (*Anforderungsbereiche: AFB*) of the *Abitur* examination: AFB I—reproduction; AFB II—reorganisation and transfer; AFB III—reflection and problem-solving. At the end of the textbook, the AFBs are described, and the specific 'operators' (verbs referring to the relevant actions required for the tasks in the given requirement area) are listed for each.[16]

AFB I: *nennen, beschreiben, darstellen, lokalisieren, herausarbeiten, charakterisieren* (name, describe, represent, localise, deduce, characterise)

AFB II: *ein-, zuordnen, kennzeichnen, analysieren, erläutern, erklären, vergleichen, anwenden, erstellen, begründen.*

(allocate and categorise, label, analyse, explain, elucidate, compare, apply, produce, justify)

AFB III: *erörtern/diskutieren, (kritisch) Stellung nehmen, überprüfen, beurteilen/bewerten.*

(debate/discuss, take up a [critical] position, validate, judge/assess) (reverse of inside cover, 184–85)

Each 'operator' is also given an explanation regarding the activity to which it refers, for example:

AFB I ***nennen:*** *Informationen/Sachverhalte ohne Kommentierung wiedergeben [...]* (**name:** reproduce information/content without comment ...)

AFB II ***ein-, zuordnen:*** *einem Raum/Sachverhalt auf der Basis festgestellter Merkmale eine bestimmte Position in einem Ordnungsraster zuweisen [...]*

(**allocate and categorise:** give a space/content matter a certain position on a grid based on specific features ...)

AFB III ***erörtern/diskutieren:*** *einen Sachverhalt unter Abwägen verschiedener Pro- und Contra-Argumente klären und abschließend eine schlüssige Meinung entwickeln [...].*

(**debate/discuss:** clarify content, taking into consideration the various arguments for and against it, and then develop your own logical conclusion) (... ibid.)

The 'operators' appear at the beginning of each chapter in the coloured strip marked *Kompetenzen erwerben* (Gaining Competencies). Furthermore, each task contains an 'operator' that clarifies the action to be undertaken and allocates it to one of the AFBs in such a way as to be clearly recognisable to the learning subject. The 'operators' signal to the learner which cognitive activity is expected for the task and at the same time allows for self-reflection regarding whether it is a matter of reproduction, reorganisation and transfer or of reflection and problem-solving.

Most of the required cognitive activities are dialogical in character, for instance:

> *3.2 Geologische Strukturen—eine Grundlage der Wirtschaft.*
> *Kompetenzen erwerben.*
> *—Die erdgeschichtliche Entwicklung Europas in Grundzügen beschreiben;*
> *—die Bedeutung geologischer Strukturen als wichtige Grundlage für die wirtschaftliche Nutzung erläutern;*
> *[...]*
> *—Chancen und Risiken der Nutzung alternativer geologischer Energiequellen in Europa diskutieren.*
> (3.2 Geological Structures—The Bedrock of the Economy.
> Gaining Competence.
> —Describe the geological development of Europe in an outline;
> —Explain the significance of geological structures as an important basis for economic exploitation;
> (...)
> —Discuss the opportunities for, and risks of using alternative geological sources of energy in Europe.) (40).

Describe, explain, discuss—the dialogic and self-reflective character of the knowledge thus developed becomes obvious when compared to the instructions in older textbooks, where it was customary to list questions after a long text (*'What is the significance of geological structures as an important basis for economic exploitation?').[17] Between the construction without an 'operator' and the one with it we see the evolution of the idea of knowledge that characterises the transition from 'high' Modernity to its late phase. The construction with the 'operator' presents a certain potential to train self-reflexivity. From the description of the operator 'explain', the learner knows that, by following these instructions, they will be 'clarifying factual connections with the aid of additional information' (*Sachzusammenhänge mit Hilfe ergänzender Informationen verdeutlichen*, 185). The knowledge is no longer a 'package' that is 'handed over' to the learner by the textbook author; nor is it a matter of 'possessing' knowledge. Rather, it is a question of carrying out certain cognitive activities in a dialogue and, at the same time, observing one's own actions from a meta-level. Knowledge thus becomes the outcome of communication. Moreover, the process of knowledge development is rendered observable by the learning subject, and it is precisely this observation that constitutes a crucial part of the didactic process. Another part of it is training the tolerance for ambiguity by subjecting the learner to contradictions and discontinuities in the diverse textbook material. The Late-Modern subject is positioned within more than one system of coordinates and acts as an intermediary between these systems by producing a permanently ongoing first-person narrative that goes on for a lifetime—and thus is not confined to the time spent at school. It is in this first-person narrative that the 'subject of pluralisation' constantly achieves communicative feats that derive from striving for authenticity.

Notes

1. The authors of the *Schulbücher als Vermittler der Europäischen Integration? Eine Studie zum politischen Fachunterricht* project, carried out in 2015 and 2016 by the Georg Eckert Institute and the University of Goettingen, refer to §23 (1) of the constitution, according to which the Federal Republic of Germany shall 'participate in the development of the European Union' (closing conference held 9 September 2016 in Goettingen).
2. For the revised version, see *Europabildung* 2008.

3. *Europabilder/Images de l'Europe.* The Georg Eckert Institute observed these developments by consistently monitoring portrayals of Europe in history and geography textbooks of various countries; the results have been available on the *EurViews* internet platform since 2014.
4. Terminology from Oberle et al. 2014.
5. Marxhausen's analysis of a special issue (no. 52, 2006) of the journal *Deutschland und Europa*, edited by the Baden-Wuerttemberg Federal State Office for Political Education (*Landeszentrale für politische Bildung Baden-Württemberg*), only partly confirms this hypothesis: the material analysed reveals the ambivalence that European identity is 're-presented [sic] as simultaneously static and dynamic; as a process and at the same time an essentialised phenomenon' (Marxhausen 2010, 317).
6. Historian Wolfgang Schmale writes: 'We cannot expect or conceive of an identity in terms of the essentialist model on which the nation-state or indeed the concept of the individual were built, neither for the present nor for the future. It will always be a matter of identities with complex structures in an intertwined nexus that enables the production of meaning' (Schmale 2008, 178).
7. The term 'Late Modernity' refers to a phase that followed the heyday of Modernity in the nineteenth century, and followed the two World Wars in the first half of the twentieth century. Bauman (2011) speaks of 'solid vs. liquid Modernity', whereas Ulrich Beck terms these periods the 'first' and the 'second' Modernity. Giddens (1991) terms the phase in question here, 'Late Modernity', and Touraine (1997) even uses the term 'demodernisation'. Welsch (2008) differentiates among three phases of Modernity: Phase 1 (from the seventeenth century to Romanticism), Phase 2 (the scientific and artistic Modernity of the twentieth century) and Phase 3 (Postmodernism, from 1945—and in literature, from the 1960s—on).
8. See Delanty (2014, 214): 'The idea of society today can no longer be conceived as a functional system underpinned by a foundational national ethnos or demos'. Similarly, Eder (2014, 219) states: 'The systemic crises of the state and the market in Europe are speeding up an evolutionary process of people-making, the outcome of which could be either the regression to a people with foundational identities or to a people without foundational identities. The latter will be described as a post-national society, which would make an emerging European society the first really modern society'.

9. See Ulrich Beck's critique of methodological nationalism in the social sciences (e.g. Beck 2009, 20).
10. Calhoun (2001, 49): 'Categorical identities require representation; they are not simply outgrowths of interaction but depend upon cultural labels and the production of ways of speaking about them'. At first glance this appears contradictory: When speaking of categories we blur them; the more definitions, the less clarity (see Bauman 1996). This contradiction is resolved if we recall Benedict Anderson's third paradox of the nation, which juxtaposes the political power inherent in the concept of the nation with the 'philosophical poverty' of that very concept (Anderson 1983). Discussion of categorical identities is based on stereotypical attributes in a stereotypical present. In a similar context, Charim (2018) addresses anti-pluralist identities that are dependent on symbols being 'closed down', prevented from circulating, and instead 'fixed' and 'naturalised' (Charim 2018, 103).
11. European identity, conceived of as an identity project and expressed with reference to specific topics and/or when approaching tasks, was the subject of the research seminar on 'European Identity—a semantics beyond group belonging?', which took place during the 2011 summer semester at the University of Magdeburg, Germany, as part of the European Studies degree course. It was directed by Magdalena Telus, with tutorial assistance from Hannes Köhler. See also Telus 2011.
12. Assmann (2012, 36ff.) discusses two biographical examples. As a young man, the Englishman Archibald Stansfeld Belaney (1888–1938) emigrated to Canada, where he lived under the name of Grey Owl, and claimed to be half Native American. He became well-known as a conservationist, but when his true origins were exposed, he was accused of fraud by the whites. However, Native Americans continued to hold him in high esteem, and today his lifestyle and work are remembered with respect. A different case was that of Bruno Grosjean, who published a falsified autobiography in 1995, under the pseudonym of Binjamin Wilkomirski, in which he described his (fictive) experiences as a child in the death camps of Majdanek and Auschwitz. Three years after its publication, it became known that Grosjean had actually spent his childhood with an adoptive family in Switzerland, and he was exposed as an imposter. Assmann points out that the difference between these biographies is that Grey Owl actually did live his role as a Native American conservationist. These examples show how Taylor's concept of authenticity involves a certain phenomenological affinity that poses a challenge to

discourse-orientated, constructivist approaches. Adamzik (2011) addresses this difficulty by replacing 'discourse' with 'series'. Using the example of a seminar completion certificate, which can exist only as the result of specific actions, such as seminar attendance, relevant achievements, meeting with the instructor, and so on, Adamzik shows how texts are fundamentally connected to actions.

13. For a critical reflection of the concept of authenticity, see also Straub 2012.
14. This was a widespread approach to discourse analysis in the 1990s; see Telus (1996, 2000).
15. 'Discursive basic figure' according to Busse (2000).
16. Whereas the three task areas are standard in all subjects in German school didactics, the verbs listed as 'operators' for each of them may differ slightly from textbook to textbook, and also with regard to single lists of such 'operators', as suggested by various professional societies (see *Bildungsstandards* ... 2020). In our discussion, it is crucial that the 'operators' used in tasks be explicitly listed and explained in the same textbook, thereby supporting the student's methodological competence.
17. This development may be traced back even further: for example, in the 1960s, West German history textbooks contained no questions at all and thus no elements of explicit dialogicity (see Pandel 2006, 26).

References

Textbooks

Bauer, Max, Helmut Becker, Stephan Benzmann, Peter Brügel, Steffen Kailitz, Susanne Kailitz, Hartwig Riedel, Karsten Tessmar, Martina Tschirner, Andreas Hamm-Reinöhl, et al. 2016. *Buchners Kompendium Politik*. Bamberg: Buchner.

Boeti, Pasquale, Wilfried Korby, and Arno Kreus. 2016. *Terra Europa*. Stuttgart, Leipzig: Klett.

Schaechterle, Lothar, and Wolfram Willfahrt, eds. 2018. *Politik entdecken 8–10*. Berlin: Cornelsen.

Further References

Adamzik, Kirsten. 2011. Textsortennetze. In *Textsorten, Handlungsmuster, Oberflächen. Linguistische Typologien der Kommunikation*, ed. Stephan Habscheid, 367–385. Berlin: De Gruyter.

———. 2012. Kontrastive Textologie am Beispiel des Schulbuchs. *Tekst i dyskurs* 5: 53–91.

Anderson, Benedict. 1983. *Imagined communities: Reflections on the origin and spread of nationalism*. London, New York: Verso.

Anklam, Ewa, and Susanne Grindel. 2010. Europa im Bild—Bilder von Europa: Europarepräsentationen in deutschen, französischen und polnischen Geschichtsschulbüchern in historischer Perspektive. In *Das Bild im Schulbuch*, ed. Carsten Heinze and Eva Matthes, 93–108. Bad Heilbrunn: Klinkhardt.

Assmann, Aleida. 2012. Authentizität—Signatur des abendländischen Sonderweges? In *Renaissance der Authentizität? Über die neue Sehnsucht nach dem Ursprünglichen*, ed. Michael Rössner and Heidemarie Uhl, 27–42. Bielefeld: transcript Verlag.

Bauman, Zygmunt. 1996. *Moderne und Ambivalenz. Das Ende der Eindeutigkeit*. Trans. Martin Suhr. Frankfurt am Main: Fischer Taschenbuch Verlag.

———. 2011. *Kultura w płynnej nowoczesności*. Cambridge: Polity Press.

Beck, Ulrich. 1986. *Risikogesellschaft. Auf dem Weg in eine andere Moderne*. Frankfurt am Main: Suhrkamp.

———. 2005. Das kosmopolitische Empire. Ein Plädoyer für ein Europa jenseits des Nationalstaats. *Internationale Politik* 7 (60): 6–12.

———. 2009. Critical Theory of World Risk Society: A Cosmopolitan Vision. *Constellations* 16, (1): 3–22. http://www.ulrichbeck.net-build.net/uploads/constell. Accessed 20 April 2014.

Beck, Ulrich, and Edgar Grande. 2004. *Das kosmopolitische Europa. Gesellschaft und Politik in der Zweiten Moderne*. Frankfurt am Main: Suhrkamp.

Bluche, Lorraine, Veronika Lipphardt, and Kiran Klaus Patel, eds. 2009. *Der Europäer—Ein Konstrukt. Wissensbestände, Diskurse, Praktiken*. Göttingen: Wallstein Verlag.

von Borries, Bodo. 2007. Europa als geschichtsdidaktische Herausforderung. In *Europa in historisch-didaktischen Perspektiven*, ed. Bernd Schönemann and Hartmut Voit, 21–44. Idstein: Schulz-Kirchner Verlag.

von Borries, Bodo, and Karl Filser. 2004. Kerncurriculum Geschichte in der Gymnasialen Oberstufe. In *Kerncurriculum Oberstufe II. Biologie, Chemie, Physik, Geschichte, Politik*, ed. Heinz-Elmar Thenorth, 236–321. Weinheim: Beltz.

Borsche, Tilman. 2010. Europa als Zukunft—Zukunft Europas. Philosophische Reflexionen. In *Europa—Europäisierung—Europäistik*, ed. Michael Gehler and Silvio Vietta, 257–269. Vienna, Cologne, Weimar: Böhlau.

Bösch, Frank, Ariane Brill, Florian Greiner, eds. 2012. Europabilder im 20. Jahrhundert. Entstehung an der Peripherie, Göttingen 2012.

Brubaker, Rogers, and Frederick Cooper. 2000. Beyond "identity". *Theory and Society* 29 (1): 1–47.

Busse, Dietrich. 2000. Historische Diskurssemantik. Ein linguistischer Beitrag zur Analyse gesellschaftlichen Wissens. In *Linguistische Diskursgeschichte. Sprache und Literatur in Wissenschaft und Unterricht* 31 (86), ed. Anja Stukenbrock and Joachim Scharloth, 39–53. https://www.phil-fak.uni-duesseldorf.de/fileadmin/Redaktion/Institute/Germanistik/AbteilungI/Busse/Texte/Busse-2000-04.pdf. Accessed 26 May 2016.

Calhoun, Craig. 2001. The virtues of inconsistency: Identity and plurality in the conceptualization of Europe. In *Constructing Europe's identity. The external dimension*, ed. Lars-Eric Cederman, 35–56. London: Lynne Rienner.

Challand, Benoît. 2009. European identity and external others in history textbooks (1950–2005) *journal of educational media. Memory, and Society* 1 (2): 60–96.

Charim, Isolde. 2018. *Ich und die Anderen. Wie die neue Pluralisierung uns alle verändert*. Vienna: Paul Zsolnay Verlag.

Chomczyńska-Rubacha, Mariola, and Dorota Pankowska. 2011. Władza, ideologia, socjalizacja. Polityczność podręczników szkolnych. In *Podręczniki i poradniki*, ed. Mariola Chomczyńska-Rubacha, 17–30. Kraków: Impuls.

Delanty, Gerard. 2014. Introduction. Perspectives on crisis and critique in Europe today. *European Journal of Social Theory* 17 (3): 207–218.

Eberstadt, Meike, and Christin Kuznetsov. 2008. *Bildung und Identität*. Frankfurt am Main, Berlin, Bern, Brussels, New York, Oxford, Vienna: Peter Lang.

Eder, Klaus. 2014. The EU in search of its people: The birth of a society of the crisis of Europe. *European Journal of Social Theory* 17 (3): 219–237.

Eis, Andreas, and Claire Moulin-Doos, eds. 2018. *Kritische politische Europabildung. Die Vielfachkrise Europas als kollektive Lerngelegenheit?* Immenhausen: Prolog-Verlag.

Ferrara, Alessandro. 2009. Authenticity without a true self. In *Authenticity in culture, self, and society*, ed. Phillip Vannini and J. Patrick Williams, 21–35. Farnham, Burlington: Ashgate.

François, Étienne. 2013. Geschichtspolitik und Erinnerungskultur in Europa heute. In *Geschichtspolitik in Europa seit 1989*, ed. Étienne François, Kornelia Konczal, Robert Traba, and Stefan Troebst, 541–558. Göttingen: Wallstein.

Fritzsche, Peter K. 1995. Europa in deutschen Politiklehrbüchern. In *Macht Europa Schule? Die Darstellung Europas in Schulbüchern der Europäischen Gemeinschaft*, ed. Falk Pingel, 81–94. Frankfurt am Main: Diesterweg.

Georg-Eckert-Institut—Leibniz-Institut für internationale Schulbuchforschung. Europabilder. n.d. http//europabilder.gei.de/projekt.html. Accessed 18 Aug 2016.

von Geyr, Maja, and Lisa Moldenhauer. 2007. *Die europäische Dimension in den Lehrplänen der deutschen Bundesländer*. Berlin: Europäische Akademie Berlin.

Giddens, Anthony. 1991. *Modernity and self-identity: Self and Society in the Late Modern age*. Stanford: Stanford University Press.

———. 2008. Acht Thesen zur Zukunft Europas. In *Europas Gedächtnis. Das neue Europa zwischen nationalen Erinnerungen und gemeinsamer Identität*, ed. Helmut König, Julia Schmidt and Manfred Sicking, 39–69. Bielefeld: transcript Verlag.

Graf, Rüdiger, and Konrad H. Jarausch. 2017. '"Crisis" in Contemporary History and Historiography', Version: 1.0. In *Docupedia-Zeitgeschichte*. https://doi.org/10.14765/zzf.dok.2.789.v1. Accessed 5 May 2022.

Habermas, Jürgen. 2006. Is the development of a European identity necessary and is it possible? In *The divided west*, 67–82. Cambridge, MA: Polity Press.

Hermans, Hubert, and Agnieszka Hermans-Konopka. 2010. *Dialogical self theory. Positioning and counter-positioning in a globalizing society*. Cambridge: Cambridge University Press.

Jarausch, Konrad. 2015. *Out of ashes. A new history of Europe in the twentieth century*. Princeton: Princeton University Press.

Jobst, Solvejg. 2004. *Schule zwischen Region und Europa. Zum Stellenwert der europäischen Bewusstseinsbildung in tschechischen und sächsischen Lehrplänen - theoretische Diskussion und vergleichende Analyse*. Münster: Waxmann.

Judt, Tony. 1996. *Große Illusion Europa. Gefahren und Herausforderungen einer Idee*. Munich: Hanser.

Kaelble, Hartmut. 2001. *Europäer über Europa. Die Entstehung des europäischen Selbstverständnisses im 19. und 20. Jahrhundert*. Frankfurt am Main: Campus.

———. 2008. Europäisches Selbstverständnis und gesellschaftliche Entwicklungen im 20. Jahrhundert. In *Selbstverständnis und Gesellschaft der Europäer. Aspekte der sozialen und kulturellen Europäisierung im späten 19. und 20. Jahrhundert*, ed. Hartmut Kaelble and Martin Kirch, 421–447. Frankfurt am Main, Berlin, Bern, Brussels, New York, Oxford, Vienna: Peter Lang.

———. 2012. Europa in der Krise: Zivilisationskrise - Integrationskrise - Krisenmanagement. In *Krisen verstehen. Historische und kulturwissenschaftliche Annäherungen*, ed. Thomas Mergel, 131–144. Frankfurt am Main: Campus.

Kershaw, Ian. 2019. *Achterbahn. Europa 1950 bis heute*. München: Deutsche Verlags-Anstalt.

Kiesendahl, Jana. 2013. Zum Exotenstatus der Linguistik in der Schulbuchforschung. *Eckert. Das Bulletin* 13: 76.

Kiesendahl, Jana, and Christine Ott. 2015. Linguistik und Schulbuchforschung. In *Linguistik und Schulbuchforschung*, ed. Jana Kiesendahl and Christine Ott, 5–16. Göttingen: unipress.

Kirchberg, Günter. 1995. Europa in deutschen Geographielehrbüchern. In *Macht Europa Schule? Die Darstellung Europas in Schulbüchern der Europäischen Gemeinschaft*, ed. Falk Pingel, 63–79. Frankfurt am Main: Diesterweg.

Kühberger, Christoph. 2010. Europäische Geschichte nach dem *spatial turn*. Geschichtsdidaktische Erkundungen zu transkulturellen Momenten. In *Europa—Europäisierung—Europäistik: Neue wissenschaftliche Ansätze, Methoden und Inhalte*, ed. Michael Gehler and Silvio Vietta, 353–378. Vienna, Cologne, Weimar: Böhlau.

Kultusminister Konferenz. 2008. *Europabildung in der Schule. Empfehlung der Ständigen Konferenz der Kultusminister der Länder in der Bundesrepublik Deutschland*. https://www.kmk.org/themen/allgemeinbildende-schulen/weitere-unterrichtsinhalte-und-themen/europabildung.html. Accessed 30 Oct 2016.

Langner, Carsta. 2009. *Vereintes Europa. Zur diskursiven Konstruktion einer europäischen Identität und ihrer Reproduktion in Schulbüchern*. Stuttgart: ibidem.

Leclercq, Jean-Michel. 1995. Die europäische Dimension im Geschichtsun terricht und in der staatsbürgerlichen Erziehung. In *Macht Europa Schule? Die Darstellung Europas in Schulbüchern der Europäischen Gemeinschaft*, ed. Falk Pingel, 1–14. Frankfurt am Main: Diesterweg.

van der Leeuw-Roord, Joke. 2009. Beyond the doorstep: The nature of history teaching across Europe. In *Teaching history and social studies for multicultural Europe*, ed. Semih Aktekín, 155–176. Ankara: Harf Eğitim Yayıncılığı.

Link, Jürgen. (1996) 2006. *Versuch über den Normalismus. Wie Normalität produziert wird*. Göttingen: Vandenhoeck & Ruprecht.

Linsenmann, Ingo. 2002. Die Bildungspolitik der Europäischen Union. In *Europa-Handbuch*, ed. Werner Weidenfeld, 523–530. Bonn: Bundeszentrale für politische Bildung.

Maarten, Simons, and Naomi Hodgson. 2012. Learned voices of European citizens. From governmental to political subjectivation. *Teoria de la Educacion* 24 (1): 19–40.
Marxhausen, Christine. 2010. *Identität—Repräsentation—Diskurs. Eine handlungsorientierte linguistische Diskursanalyse zur Erfassung raumbezogener Identitätsangebote*. Stuttgart: Franz Steiner Verlag.
Mazower, Mark. 1999. *Dark continent. Europe's twentieth century*. New York: Penguin Books.
Mickel, Wolfgang. 1991. *Lernfeld Europa. Didaktische Grundlagen einer europäischen Erziehung*. Opladen: Leske and Budrich.
Münkler, Herfried. 2012. Heroische und postheroische Gesellschaften. In *Krieg und Zivilgesellschaft*, ed. Dierk Spreen and Trutz von Trotha, 175–187. Berlin: Duncker & Humblot.
Nouvel, Maguelone. 2011. L'Europe en images: les représentations de l'Union Européenne dans les manuels scolaires d'histoire d'aujourd'hui. In *Signes, couleurs et images de l'Europe*, ed. Guillaume Bourgeois and Hélène Yèche, 239–255. Rennes: Presses Universitaires de Rennes.
Oberle, Monika, Eva Weschenfelder, and Georg Weisseno. 2014. Beliefs als Element professioneller Kompetenz bei Politiklehrkräften in Deutschland. In *Vorstellungen, Konzepte und Kompetenzen von Lehrpersonen der Politischen Bildung*, ed. Béatrice Ziegler, 124–137. Zürich: Rüegger.
Otto, Marcus. 2013. Dezentrierung des Weltbildes? Die Krise der westlichen Zivilisation, das Ereignis der Dekolonisierung und die Frage des Subjekts im Diskurs der Geschichtsschulbücher in Frankreich in den 1960er Jahren. *Comparativ. Zeitschrift für Globalgeschichte und vergleichende Gesellschaftsforschung* 23 (3): 117–137.
———. 2014. *Der Wille zum Subjekt. Zur Genealogie politischer Inklusion in Frankreich (16.–20. Jahrhundert)*. Bielefeld: transcript Verlag.
———. 2018. Inklusion/Exklusion und die Anrufung von Subjekten in der Migrationsgesellschaft. Die Adressierung der Lernenden in aktuellen Geschichtsschulbüchern. In *Geschichtsunterricht im 21. Jahrhundert. Eine geschichtsdidaktische Standortbestimmung. Beihefte zur Zeitschrift für Geschichtsdidaktik, Bd. 17*, ed. Thomas Sandkühler, Charlotte Bühl-Gramer, Anke John, Astrid Schwabe, and Markus Bernhardt, 205–220. Göttingen: Vandenhoeck & Ruprecht.
Otto, Marcus, and Riem Spielhaus. 2020. Schulbuch—Macht—Migration. Die Anrufung von Subjekten der Migration in Aufgabenstellungen. In *Migration*

und Bildungsmedien, ed. Sylvia Schütze and Eva Matthes, 279–289. Bad Heilbrunn: Verlag Klinkhardt.

Otto, Marcus, Steffen Sammler, and Riem Spielhaus. 2020. "Krisen" als Seismografen gesellschaftlichen Wandels und Gegenstand schulischer Bildungsmedien. In *Handbuch Krisenforschung*, ed. Frank Bösch, Nicole Deitelhoff, and Stefan Kroll, 93–108. Wiesbaden: Springer Verlag.

Pandel, Hans-Jürgen. 2006. Was macht ein Schulbuch zu einem Geschichtsbuch? Ein Versuch über Kohärenz und Intertextualität. In *Geschichtsdidaktische Schulbuchforschung*, ed. Saskia Handro and Bernd Schönemann, 15–37. Berlin: LIT.

Parschalk, Norbert. 2012. *Geschichte und Identität. Konstruktiver Geschichtsunterricht in Zeiten globaler Veränderungen*. Brixen: A. Verger.

Paszyński, Włodzimierz. 2008. Wychowanie w kontekście zmieniającej się polityki oświatowej—czyli od ideologii do ideologii. In *Wychowanie tom 4. Pojęcia—procesy—konteksty. Ku demokracji poprzez edukację*, ed. Maria Czerepaniak-Walczak and Maria Dudzikowa. Gdańsk: Gdańskie Wydawnictwo Psychologiczne.

Patel, Kiran Klaus. 2017. *Projekt Europa*. München: Eine kritische Geschichte.

Patel, Kiran Klaus, and Martin Conway, eds. 2010. *Europeanization in the twentieth century. Historical approaches*. London.

Pingel, Falk. 1995a. Europa im Schulbuch. In *Macht Europa Schule? Die Darstellung Europas in Schulbüchern der Europäischen Gemeinschaft*, ed. Falk Pingel, VII–XXV. Frankfurt am Main: Diesterweg.

———. 1995b. Europa im Schulbuch—Analyse und Perspektiven. In *Die europäische Dimension in Lehr- und Lernmitteln*, ed. Berd Janssen, 35–47. Bonn: Europa Union Verlag.

———. 1995c. Introduction. In *Macht Europa Schule? Die Darstellung Europas in Schulbüchern der Europäischen Gemeinschaft*, ed. Falk Pingel, VII–XXV. Frankfurt am Main: Diesterweg.

———. 2001. How to approach Europe? The European dimension in history textbooks. In *History for today and tomorrow. What does Europe mean for school history*, ed. Joke van der Leeuw-Roord, 205–228. Hamburg: Körber-Stiftung.

———. 2010. Geschichtsdeutung als Macht? Schulbuchforschung zwischen wissenschaftlicher Erkenntnis und politischer Erkenntnislogik. *Contexts. The Journal of Educational Media, Memory, and Society* 2 (2): 93–112.

Popp, Susanne 2010. Visualisierte Geschichte in den Lehrwerken Europas. Zwischen polysemantischen Vermittlungsstrategien und kanonischer Engführung. Ed. Michael Gehler, 337–359. Wien: Böhlau.

Puntscher-Riekmann, Sonja, and Ruth Wodak. 2003. '"Europe for All"—diskursive Konstruktionen europäischer Identitäten'. In *Europas Identitäten.* Mythen, Konflikte, *Konstruktionen*, edited by Monika Mokre, Gilbert Weiss and Rainer Bauböck, 283–303. Frankfurt am Main and New York: Campus Verlag.

Risse, Thomas. 2010. *Community of Europeans? Transnational identities and public spheres*. Ithaca and London: Cornell University Press.

Rosa, Hartmut. 2002. Zwischen Selbstthematisierungszwang und Artikulationsnot. In *Transitorische Identität. Der Prozesscharakter des modernen Selbst*, ed. Jürgen Straub and Joachim Renn, 267–302. Frankfurt am Main and New York: Campus Verlag.

Schmale, Wolfgang. 2008. *Geschichte und Zukunft der Europäischen Identität.* Stuttgart: W. Kohlhammer.

Schmitt-Egner, Peter. 2012. *Europäische Identität. Ein konzeptioneller Leitfaden zu ihrer Erforschung und Nutzung*. Baden-Baden: Nomos.

Skarga, Barbara. 2015. Die Identität des Ichs. In *Deutsch-Polnische Erinnerungsorte. Band 5: Erinnerung auf Polnisch*, ed. Peter Oliver Loew and Robert Traba, 213–227. Paderborn: Ferdinand Schöningh.

Slopinski, Andreas, and Torsten J. Selck. 2014. Wie lassen sich Wertaussagen in Schulbüchern aufspüren? Ein politikwissenschaftlicher Vorschlag zur quantitativen Schulbuchanalyse am Beispiel des Themenkomplexes der europäischen Integration. *Contexts. The Journal of Educational Media, Memory, and Society* 6 (1): 124–138.

Straub, Julia. 2012. Introduction. The paradoxes of authenticity. In *Authenticity. Studies on a critical concept*, ed. Julia Straub, 9–29. Bielefeld: transcript Verlag.

Tajfel, Henri. 1981. *Human groups and social categories. Studies in social psychology*. Cambridge: Cambridge University Press.

Taylor, Charles. (1991) 1995. *Das Unbehagen an der Moderne*. Trans. Joachim Schulte. Frankfurt am Main: Suhrkamp.

Telus, Magdalena. 1996. Textuelle Verfahren zur Konstruktion der Kategorien *wir* und *nicht-wir* in polnischen Schulbüchern für Geschichte in Anlehnung an das Thema Deutsche—Polen—Juden. In *Zwischen Abgrenzung und Assimilation—Deutsche, Polen und Juden*, ed. Robert Maier and Georg Stöber, 271–316. Braunschweig: Hahn.

———. 2000. Konstrukcja narodowego 'my' czyli dlaczego kochamy ojczyznę. *Język a Kultura* 14: 253–287.

———. 2002. *Gruppenspezifisches Stereotyp. Ein Modell der Einbettung in die Textproduktion. An russischem, polnischem und deutschem Material.* Frankfurt am Main: Peter Lang.

———. 2011. Semantyka przynależności vs. semantyka udziału: Rozważania na temat koncepcji tożsamości europejskiej. *Etnolingwistyka* 23: 145–166.

Telus, Magdalena, Marianne Krüger-Potratz, Jerzy Bartmiński, Michael Fleischer, Martin Giese, Andreas Meiser, Ulrich Kattmann, and Ram Adhar Mall. 1997. The "we" vs "they" opposition. *Internationale Schulbuchforschung* 19 (2): 137–162.

Touraine, Alain. 1997. *Pourrons-nous vivre ensamble? Egaux et Différents.* Cambridge: Polity Press.

Weiss, Gilbert. 2003. Die vielen Seelen Europas. Eine Analyse 'neuer' Reden zu Europa. In *Europas Identitäten*, ed. Monika Mokre, Gilbert Weiss, and Rainer Bauböck, 183–206. Frankfurt am Main and New York: Campus.

Weiß, Andreas. 2016. *Asiaten in Europa. Begegnungen zwischen Asiaten und Europäern 1880–1914.* Paderborn: Ferdinand Schöningh.

Welsch, Wolfgang. 2008. *Unsere postmoderne Moderne.* Berlin: Akademie Verlag.

Westheider, Rolf. 1995. Europa ist nicht Europa—zur Geschichte einer verhinderten Identität. In *Macht Europa Schule? Die Darstellung Europas in Schulbüchern der Europäischen Gemeinschaft*, ed. Falk Pingel, 15–62. Frankfurt am Main: Diesterweg.

Wodak, Ruth, and Gilbert Weiss. 2004. Möglichkeiten und Grenzen der Diskursanalyse. Konstruktionen europäischer Identitäten. In *Text und Kontext*, ed. Oswald Panagl and Ruth Wodak, 67–85. Würzburg: Königshausen & Neumann.

Wodak, Ruth Maria, Rudolf Kargl, Martin de Cillia, Karin Liebhart Reisigl, and Klaus Hofstätter. 1998. *Zur diskursiven Konstruktion nationaler Identität.* Frankfurt am Main: Suhrkamp.

Part II

Exploring Identity Constructions Through Digital Analysis

6

Methodological Approaches to the Digital Analysis of Educational Media: Exploring Concepts of Europe and the Nation

Eckhard Bick, Katja Gorbahn, and Nina Kalwa

Introduction

For research into the construction of European and national identities, educational media are particularly interesting due to their highly normative character. For instance, Dreesen, a discourse-linguistics researcher,

---

E. Bick (✉)
Institute of Language and Communication, University of Southern Denmark, Odense, Denmark
e-mail: eckhard.bick@mail.dk

K. Gorbahn
School of Communication and Culture, Aarhus University, Aarhus, Denmark
e-mail: katja.gorbahn@cc.au.dk

N. Kalwa
Department für Wissenschaftskommunikation, Karlsruher Institut für Technologie, Universitätsbereich/Campus Süd, Institut für Technikzukünfte (ITZ), Karlsruhe, Germany
e-mail: nina.kalwa@kit.edu

K. Gorbahn et al. (eds.), *Exploring Interconnectedness*, Palgrave Studies in Educational Media, https://doi.org/10.1007/978-3-031-13960-4_6

states that history textbooks represent a special order of historical knowledge, and are regarded as reliable and largely neutral sources that provide authoritative knowledge (Dreesen 2015, 55). However, references to categories of identity, such as Europeanness, are often distributed throughout texts, and both compete and are interwoven with other categories, such as 'the nation' or 'the global'. This presents a challenge for researchers, as the amounts of text and the variety of thematic contexts are considerable, even in a single textbook series, and even more so in larger samples or corpora. In consequence, research on the European dimension in textbooks has often focused on specific topics, such as European integration. Although such research may certainly provide valuable insights, it fails to encompass the manifold contexts in which the ambiguous concept of 'Europe' plays a role. The methods that have been developed by the digital humanities in recent decades have great potential to address this problem (Nieländer and De Luca 2018). In this chapter, we explore the possibilities and limitations of various digital methods of analysing identity discourses in educational media.[1]

'Identity' as a concept is as ubiquitous as it is contested (Brubaker and Cooper 2000). We approach it from a social constructivist perspective, and assume that language constructs knowledge of groups with which individuals may identify, or that they may or reject, thereby shaping their social identity (Fage-Butler and Gorbahn 2020, 19). Therefore, we are not interested in 'identity' as such, but we explore methods of investigating the knowledge and concepts on which constructions of identity may draw, and that are communicated through media discourses. Although concepts are often understood as cognitive units (e.g. Gardt 2008, 214), we understand them as complex meanings or contexts of meaning that are mapped and constituted by various more or less complex linguistic units in discourse. Like Teubert (2006, 291), we assume that concepts are shared by a discourse community. We do not look for concepts in people's heads, but identify them in texts in which the members of a discourse community exchange information and make the following fundamental assumptions: (i) concepts are not (only) cognitive phenomena but may be understood as something shared by a discourse community (Teubert 2006, 291); (ii) concepts are reflected in language; (iii) concepts are formed through language; (iv) an investigation of the linguistic surface facilitates a description of (historical) concepts.

Consequently, concepts are constantly generated in texts, and this is also true of educational media. With the help of digital analysis methods, the linguistic means that establish various concepts of Europe and the nation may be investigated in medium-sized and large text corpora. However, we do not advance a purely quantitative approach, but advocate the use of digital tools to support qualitative analyses.

As this chapter has a methodological focus, we will not provide a detailed analysis of a particular corpus. Instead, we use various examples to illustrate how various methods can be applied, including data sets of different sizes, as corpus size is an important factor in digital analysis.[2]

The foregoing provides a basis for demonstrating and discussing (a) methods that are suitable for smaller- and medium-sized amounts of text, and for (b) big data techniques. Also, our selection of examples reflects our broad understanding of educational media. Although we include traditional textbooks and the particular type of knowledge they represent, we acknowledge the fact that textbooks do not exist in a vacuum, but are part of a complex network of discursive practices. For better or worse, online resources and social media play a growing part in the acquisition of educationally relevant knowledge.

Though we are fully aware of the multi-modal character of educational media, this chapter addresses only the linguistic side. We first explain how to create a digital corpus, and present useful analysis tools. We then demonstrate how to acquire first insights into the corpus through frequency and keyword analysis. In the next step, we present possible ways of more specifically investigating the construction of concepts of Europe and the nation, discuss the question of search terms and address concordances, collocates and networks as possible approaches. In particular, we demonstrate the potential of employing grammatical information. This provides the background for a further exploration of ways of analysing identity-relevant concepts, using toponyms, demonyms and adjectives as a starting point, because of their unifying function. We conclude by discussing the role of corpus size, and recommend an approach that combines quantitative and qualitative methods of analysis.

Compiling a Corpus

In a linguistic context, a corpus is a structured digital collection of written or spoken-language data. Optionally, for instance in a Facebook or textbook corpus, such data sets may include visual data (images, video, graphics) as embedded or referenced context. Most corpora use structuring IDs for texts, utterances or tokens, and include meta-information about sources, genre, speaker, time, place and so on, and many are enriched with linguistic annotation (see the 'Employing Grammatical Information' section). Both information types are kept apart from the data itself by separating characters (word tagging) or in the form of xml markup (all information types). In addition to size, added structure and information determine the value of a corpus. Not least grammatical annotation is recognised as either an expensive (manual) or a challenging (automated) task. However, corpus end-users are often unaware of the initial labour cost involved in the very first steps of corpus creation, compilation and conversion. Also, some steps may involve basic programming, or command-line batch scripting in order to work with large data sets. This is particularly true of teaching material, which, unlike news sources, for example, comes in a wide variety of formats.

Non-digital sources such as printed textbooks with pictures of historical documents or handwriting present an obvious challenge. These need to be scanned and submitted to OCR (optical character recognition), or—in the case of poor print or conservation quality, and most handwriting—transcribed by hand. Often, an additional formatting step is necessary, because text sections such as footnotes or headers get mixed into the body text by the OCR system. Also, OCR systems may need to be re-trained for different texts or post-processed with a spellchecker. Well-known and robust open-source options[3] include OCRopus/ocropus3 and Tesseract.

The pdf format is common in online teaching material. It is digital, but not as easy to process as ordinary, editable text files (.txt, .docx, .odt etc.). This format was intended to be read-only, and re-conversion to text may result in line mixing across columns, loss of line-break separators following headlines and so on. Various platform-independent pdf2text tools are available.[4]

Webpages play a growing role in teaching, as teaching references or in student essays. They can be downloaded automatically, using the command-line Unix tool wget,[5] for example, which will crawl and save all sub-links on a page. However, that will include non-textual data such as .pdf, image and sound files, which need to be removed or processed (cf. a, b, above). The rest will be in html format, which is not exactly text, but may be filtered by stripping all <…> tags. Some programming languages have functions that do this, but individually programmed solutions may be better, if one wants to preserve meta-information, or insert newlines and other spacing in appropriate places.

Text documents, such as those found in unpublished didactic material, are the most straightforward corpus source, but come in different formats. Newer versions of both Word (.docx) and Open/Libre Office (.odt) save their files in .xml format with all non-text information in <…> brackets, which can therefore be processed more or less like the html formatting of webpages (c), using xml2txt[6] (or xml2text) software. The easiest-to-use source format of all is plain text (often marked .txt), as produced by non-graphical editors such as Emacs or Notepad. Although it will lose formatting upon saving, it is also an output option in text processors. For non-txt, non-xml versions, it may be necessary to open documents in the original text processor and re-save them in either .xml or .txt format before further processing.

For spoken-language data, such as online lectures on YouTube, it is necessary to transcribe the audio or video files. A manual transcription in standard orthography will take several hours, longer depending on the number of speakers and the audio quality. For some languages (German included) commercial tools can generate reasonable automated transcripts, reducing the workload of post-editing. However, if the objective is a linguistic/phonetic transcription, the process cannot be automated, and may take as long as one hour for each transcribed minute. Also, for discourse-analysis transcriptions, standard tools (e.g. the EXMARaLDA editor)[7] come with a huge overhead of manual work.

Proprietary electronic textbooks are usually published in a proprietary, closed format that cannot be converted into corpus text. Books in OpenDocument (ODF), .html, .xml or .pdf formats, on the other hand, can be automatically processed into corpus data (b, c, d).

For all of the above it should be noted that downloadability and convertibility do not necessarily imply permission to do so, and copyright restrictions may apply. For online material, even if permission is granted by the terms of use (TOS), this may be for personal use only, with restrictions on distributing derived products, such as a corpus. Depending on the source type (e.g. interviews and social media), it may be necessary to anonymise corpus data to comply with personal data protection laws (e.g. GDPR). Finally, the same legal provisions may limit data-storage time, and who may access the corpus.

Tools Used in This Study

Once a text corpus is established in digitalised form, researchers may choose among a variety of digital analysis tools, both free and paid for. Though many of them allow similar types of basic analyses, such as frequency analyses, the various tools often have specific advantages or capabilities. Next, we briefly present the most important tools we used to generate the results presented below, and we refer to more specific tools later in the text.

AntConc (Antony 2022a) is a comparatively simple to use, free tool, the newest version of which works with .txt, Word and .pdf files. *AntConc* allows the compilation of word frequency and keyword lists as well as the generation of concordances, collocations and n-grams. It does not offer rich visualisation options, but includes a useful concordance plot tool and a wordcloud tool. A significant advantage of *AntConc* is the fact that it makes it easy to shift between analysis results and full texts, which makes it especially suited to combining a corpus-analysis approach with qualitative methods.

Visualisation is a particular strength of *Voyant Tools* (Sinclair and Rockwell 2022; Alhudithi 2021). *Voyant Tools* is an open-source, web-based application, but may also be downloaded and run locally. *Voyant Tools* works with a variety of input formats, including Word and .pdf, and is popular in digital research in the humanities, for example, in literature studies. It offers a variety of tools such as word clouds, word trees, topic explorer and bubblelines, which may provide valuable insights but are less convenient when it comes to switching between analysis results and the findings in context.

Voyant Tools offers very helpful exploration tools, but does not employ grammatical information. However, grammatically informed analyses, such as part-of-speech and base-form (lemma) analyses, have great potential, as we demonstrate below, where we also recommend available taggers for German and Danish. *AntConc* can process text enriched with grammatical information, created by the related *TagAnt* tool, for example (Anthony 2022b).

Sketch Engine (Kilgarriff et al. 2014) is a commercial tool that automatically integrates part-of-speech-tagging in many languages. It enables a wide range of digital analyses and visualisations and computes the user's own data as well as integrated ready-to-use text corpora.

A corpus search interface which uses rich grammatical information is the multi-lingual, CQP-based CorpusEye (http://corp.hum.sdu.dk), which includes corpora in various languages, among them English, German, Danish and other Scandinavian and Roman languages. Though CorpusEye's corpora do not include school textbooks, they include texts that are relevant to teaching and learning, such as Wikipedia in various languages, although it is not possible for users to upload their own texts.

Finally, it is important to bear in mind that modern qualitative data analysis software packages such as at *ATLAS.ti*, *MAXQDA* or *NVivo* have started to integrate more and more language technology such as sentiment analysis, basic digital analysis functions such as word frequency queries or visualisations such as word clouds. Though these functions still are comparatively limited, they are especially useful when combined with the results of qualitative coding. However, QDA software may be expensive, and the most advanced functionalities are available only for major languages.

Getting to Know Your Data

Word Frequencies

'One of the first things that a user will do when analysing a new corpus is to generate a list of all the words in the corpus. Word lists are useful as they suggest interesting areas for investigation and highlight problem areas in a corpus' (Anthony 2005, 732). With the help of various corpus-linguistic tools, it is possible to create word lists that are sorted by frequency of all the words and word forms in the corpus. According to Gries and Newman (2013, 280), frequency lists represent 'the most basic corpus linguistic tool'. It is necessary to distinguish between absolute and relative word frequency. Absolute frequency means the number of occurrences of a certain word in the corpus. Relative frequency is the absolute word frequency divided by the corpus size (see Perkuhn et al. 2012, 78ff.). Grammatical annotation such as lemmatisation and POS-tagging improves the quality of word lists, as they resolve homonymy, and can relate various inflexion forms to the same lexeme.

In a word frequency list, function words usually will occupy the top positions, as they represent the most frequent words in natural language data. Although this may be revealing in some research contexts, research into identity constructions in textbooks will usually address specific function words only, such as the personal pronoun 'we'. 'We' indicates sameness and is highly relevant to the discursive construction of group identities (Wodak et al. 2009, 45–48). Thus, if we compare the German textbook series *Zeitreise* with the Danish *Historie*, a frequency analysis of the various word forms of the German *wir* and the Danish *vi* reveals that 'we' is more frequent in the German book (382 hits, 0.17% of all tokens) than in the Danish one (591 hits, 0.12% of all tokens). However, the use of 'we' is highly complex, and a word frequency list does not give information about the findings' use and contexts. Also, textbooks are complex media packages, and 'we' may be part of the authors' narrative or of source material. Thus, even if we ignore the fact that OCR problems may have an impact on the accuracy of the relative frequency, the explanatory value of the quantitative result is limited, if not misleading: as the qualitative analysis shows, the use of 'we' to denote a timeless national identity is clearly more pronounced in the Danish book, for example, where the author's text refers to a Danish 'we' when describing trade relations during the Bronze Age. In contrast, the German textbook contains more sources and other types of material, which often include the word 'we'.

Word lists may be more useful when it comes to content words that may provide insights in a corpus's or a specific text's focus area. Many tools allow the use of stopword lists, which automatically remove function words or, often, other frequently occurring words. Stoplists are available in many languages and in many versions, but should be used with care, as they may exclude words that may be important for the analysis. For instance, without a proper semantic-role analysis, prepositions may be the only means of distinguishing agent from patient, for example, 'attacked by Russia' versus 'attacked Russia', 'attack by/from/on/against' + name. However, the use of stoplists may help to obtain a quick overview, and may make popular visualisations such as word clouds more meaningful.

The decision about which words to take into account and which to filter out depends on the research question. For example, in a study of identity constructions, it could be helpful to particularly focus on nouns and adjectives, as they contain information about the groups in question. To give an example, Table 6.1 presents the most frequent nouns in the Danish textbook, *Historie*, and the German textbook, *Zeitreise*.

On the one hand, the results presented in the table reveal strong commonalities: both books' content centres around 'the nation', and extensively addresses states and conflicts with neighbouring countries. On the other hand, the word lists reveal minor differences in focus: social history seems to be more important in the Danish textbook series, whereas the European dimension seems to be more pronounced in *Zeitreise*. These quantitative results may contribute to forming hypotheses and guiding further analyses. However, they should be interpreted with caution, as many factors may have an impact on, and bias them—for example, OCR quality or the repetition of chapter titles—and necessitate supplementation with other types of analysis.

Table 6.1 Word frequencies in *Historie* and *Zeitreise* (case-insensitive, using Sketch Engine, Danish/German word forms in brackets; numbers refer to the total number of occurrences and their relative frequency as percentages)

Historie		*Zeitreise*	
1. source (kilde)	1430, 0.42%	1. human being/people (Mensch)	593, 0.27%
2. country/land (land)	1047, 0.31%	2. germany (deutschland)	421, 0.19%
3. year (år)	1010, 0.30%	3. year (jahr)	392, 0.18%
4. denmark (danmark)	953, 0.28%	4. war (krieg)	363, 0.16%
5. child (barn)	856, 0.25%	5. state (staat)	351, 0.16%
6. day (dag)	652, 0.19%	6. town (stadt)	347, 0.16%
7. king (konge)	634, 0.19%	7. life (leben)	274, 0.12%
8. war (krig)	600, 0.18%	8. way (weg)	269, 0.12%
9. people/nation (folk)	541, 0.16%	9. country/land (land)	259, 0.12%
10. people/human being (menneske)	485, 0.14%	10. photo (foto)	246, 0.11%
11. peasant (bonde)	473, 0.14%	11. woman (frau)	244, 0.11%
12. man (mand)	442, 0.13%	12. king (könig)	241, 0.11%
13. work (arbejde)	431, 0.13%	13. time (zeit)	240, 0.11%
14. picture (billede)	413, 0.12%	14. europe (europa)	237, 0.11%
15. town (by)	402, 0.12%	15. empire (reich)	205, 0.09%
16. state (stat)	395, 0.12%	16. peasant (bauer)	190, 0.09%
17. time (tid)	391, 0.12%	17. revolution (revolution)	190, 0.09%
18. part (del)	383, 0.11%	18. jew (jude)	158, 0.07%
19. society (samfund)	361, 0.11%	19. man (mann)	155, 0.07%
20. place (sted)	358, 0.11%	20. people/nation (volk)	154, 0.07%
29. europe (europa)	296, 0.09%		
34. germany (tyskland)	244, 0.07%	34. france (frankreich)	125, 0.06%

One way to identify possible bias factors in word lists is to carry out an n-gram analysis. N-grams are multi-word units that consist of n components. For example, n-grams for a textbook such as *Zeitreise* include 2-grams such as 'in the' (*in der*, 599), 3-grams such as 'in the GDR' (*in der DDR*, 35) or 4-grams such as 'Second World War and Holocaust' (*Zweiter Weltkrieg und Holocaust*, 30). Checking the findings for 'Second World War and Holocaust' will make it clear that the reason for this high frequency is the repetition of a heading due to the digitalised version's poor quality. This must be taken into account when interpreting the frequency of the word 'holocaust', which has 38 hits, and ranks 506 on the frequency list. Arguably, frequency-based lists of n-grams often do not have great value, as Bubenhofer (2008, 417) points out: they are very long and show language usage patterns that, although they represent frequent word combinations, are not necessarily typical of the corpus. To calculate the typicality, the n-gram list must be compared with the n-gram list of a reference corpus (Bubenhofer 2008). In the next section, we discuss the idea of 'keyness'.

Keyword Analysis

The fact that a word appears very often in a corpus or a textbook does not necessarily mean very much. Instead, as scholars in the field of linguistic discourse analysis have pointed out, it is important to identify the lexemes that are not simply frequent, but typical of a discourse. This may be achieved by matching a text or corpus with another. In this way, keyword lists are generated.

Essentially, keywords are words that appear more frequently in one corpus than another, and keyword lists may be used to identify the most significant and characteristic words in a study text or corpus, compared to a reference corpus. However, to calculate the keyness of words in a study corpus, several choices have to be made. First, the choice of the reference corpus needs to be well-considered. In the best-case scenario, the reference corpus should differ from the study corpus in one variable only. But as corpora 'are usually mixtures, [...] any two corpora vary in a multitude of ways' (Kilgarriff 2012, 14). Secondly, there are various mathematical options for calculating keyness, which may yield different results. To name just one important choice that needs to be made, keyword lists may be established via statistical significance metrics, such as log-likelihood, or via effect-size metrics, such as ratio, odds ratio, log ratio or difference coefficient (for a detailed discussion, see Gabrielatos 2018). Therefore, 'keyness is not a straightforward attribute. However objectively effect size and statistical significance are calculated, the identification of an item as key depends on a multitude of subjective decisions [...]. Simply put, a quantitative analysis does not necessarily entail objectivity' (Gabrielatos 2018, 253). Bearing this in mind, keyword lists may be useful instruments.

There are various ways of making keyword analysis useful in textbook research. For example, it is possible to identify the characteristics of one textbook when it is compared to another, if the books are in the same language. In this chapter, we used keyword analysis to compare the two Danish textbooks, *Klar, parat, historie* and *Historie*, in *AntConc*, where it is possible to use various significance and effect-size metrics. We found that the results were clearly most meaningful when sorted by effect size, as function words were less emphasised. The keywords for *Historie* reflect the fact that it includes sources and tasks, as indicated by keywords such as 'source', 'which', 'find', 'give reasons' or 'your', whereas *Klar, parat, historie* mainly consists of narrative text. The keywords for *Klar, parat, historie* revealed a strong focus on historical (including mythical) figures (bismarck, gisle, reign, kingdoms, caesar, knight, regnar, nero, mazarin, newton, profile, ss, gandhi, hanse, odysseus, czar). These findings were consistent with the results of the qualitative analysis. Europe, Denmark and Germany were not represented in the keyword lists.

Another way of using a keyword analysis in textbook research is to compare a textbook corpus to a reference corpus that represents another genre, for example, a public media discourse or a textbook collection from another historical period. Free reference corpora are available for many languages,[8] and may be used with free corpus tools such as *AntConc*. Sketch Engine, which is a commercial tool, offers numerous ready-to-use corpora in many languages, which may be used as reference corpora. For our purposes, we used Sketch Engine to match the two Danish textbooks *Historie* and *Klar, parat, historie* with a large Danish web corpus from 2020 (daTenTen20), thereby comparing history education with public media discourse. By using simple, effect-size metrics (see Kilgarriff 2009), Sketch Engine allows the user to focus on rare or common words with the help of an adjustable smoothing parameter. This is very useful, but yields highly variable results: choosing a very small smoothing parameter ($N < 1$) will yield keywords that are very specific, strange spellings or simply OCR mistakes. Choosing $N = 1$ will yield specialised terminology and give insights into the textbooks' topics (such as 'pirate', 'empire', 'napoleon'). A focus on very common words ($N = 10{,}000$ or more) will yield increasing numbers of function words. For our research question, a smoothing parameter between 100 and 1000 was most useful, as it filtered out both very frequent function words and words related to specific historical topics. For example, with N = 1000, the keywords and their ranking revealed the crucial role of the nation-state as presented in the history curriculum (2. king; 3. country; 5. Denmark). They also revealed the importance of Germany and Europe (10. German; 13. Europe; 20. Germany) in the two history textbooks, always compared to the reference corpus.

Exploring the Construction of Concepts of Europe and the Nation

In the previous section, we focused on initial insights into a text or text corpus. Though this implies decisions that may be connected to a specific research question, at this point we had not yet searched for specific words or terms. Next, we will discuss ways of more specifically exploring the construction of concepts of Europe and the nation. In doing so, our epistemological focus is directed towards the serial, the recurring, the typical or the pattern-like.

Determining Search Terms

Determining the search terms that are relevant to the reconstruction of a given concept is a very important step. However, it is challenging to find a search pattern that helps to identify the concept in question and does not miss important cases, and, at the same time, does not yield too many false positives. In our case, *europ*—case-insensitive and with asterisks as placeholders for zero or more additional letters—is a very characteristic letter sequence that covers various search terms that include this string. Intuitively the same appears to be true of *deutsch*/*tysk* (*german*), *dänisch*/*dansk (*danish*) and *däne*/*dansker* (*dane*) or *dänemark/danmark*. However, after executing a first search, it becomes apparent that these strings need to be grammatically (and thereby semantically) constrained, because the nation adjective is identical to the name of the language, diluting the search results with false positives. As language names are nouns, in German the problem may be addressed by using a case-sensitive search that excludes the uppercase. In Danish, which does not use the upper case for nouns, this is not enough, and we need proper part-of-speech (POS) tagging. The iterative process of refining one's search terms and adding linked grammatical conditions constitutes a hermeneutic circle and is typical of corpus exploration. In a less premeditated scenario, even *europ* may have begun as just *euro* and prompted many compounds with the currency name as their first component. Another problem that may arise is that of homonyms: for example, a search for *Europa* in a German corpus may yield findings that relate to the record label of this name. In short, no search pattern survives contact with a real corpus.

To reconstruct the concept of Europe or of the nation, other letter sequences than those mentioned above may also be relevant. This includes not only abbreviations such as EC or BRD, but also synonyms. To investigate the concept of 'Europe' in German-language data, a thesaurus[9] may help to identify search terms such as *Abendland* or *Okzident*. Without a thesaurus, search term synonyms may be identified by translating and back-translating words with a dictionary tool such as *Linguee* (https://www.linguee.com), or even fully automatically, using vector similarities in word embedding.[10] It is also possible to inspect contexts (one by one, or in a sorted fashion) in a first round of concordances.

Concordances and Collocations

A concordance is a list that displays each hit for a search word (or pattern) with a fixed number of co-occurring words on either side in a KWIC view (Keywords in Context). The KWIC view provides insights into the qualitative use of the search term, and is especially valuable if the tool allows you to switch between the KWIC view and the original text. However, the number of results may be overwhelming: our search for the letter string, *euro*, in the digital textbook collection of the Georg Eckert Institute yielded 79,048 hits, and the search in our sample of 96 historical textbooks from Imperial Germany yielded 1987 findings. Even in smaller text corpora or single textbooks, a manual analysis of all findings may be too time-consuming. Therefore, it is important to sort the results in a meaningful way. For example, *AntConc* offers the option of ordering the results alphabetically by up to three words to the right or left of the search term, or—even more usefully—by frequency, thus revealing the most common patterns in the data.

Further steps of digital analysis may help to provide insights, define focus areas or identify particularly relevant findings. For example, it may be helpful to analyse the distribution of relevant search terms by calculating the relative frequency of the letter sequence *euro* in various files. Thus, in our sample of historical textbooks, it is possible to quickly identify the books with the strongest European dimension. However, relative frequencies may be misleading, as they do not take into account the underlying distribution patterns: a word may be distributed evenly throughout a text, or may be clustered in a specific context (Kilgarriff 1997, 138–39; Brezina 2018, 47). This is very important, as there is a significant difference in identity construction if the European dimension appears frequently throughout the text, or if it is frequent, but connected to one specific topic only. One way of investigating a word's distribution pattern is to calculate its dispersion throughout a text or corpus, which may be carried out with *AntConc*'s plot function, for example. However, calculating dispersion raises statistical questions regarding which measures to choose, and, as Brezina points out, the 'decision about which dispersion measure to use is thus closely connected with the research design of our study and the design of the corpus used' (Brezina 2018, 47, with a discussion of a number of dispersion measures). Therefore, it is important to not view dispersion values as unambiguous results.

When it comes to distribution, visualisation may be particularly helpful, and is especially useful when working with medium-sized amounts of text, such as our historical textbook sample. *AntConc* allows the user to generate a 'bar-code' dispersion plot, which visualises the position and frequency of a search term in each file of a corpus (Anthony 2018, 213). Similarly, *Voyant Tools*' 'bubblelines' function visualises the frequency of a term in the text's segments through the size of bubbles on a horizontal line. When investigating identity constructions, it is especially helpful to visualise the distribution of various search terms in various colours and in overlay mode. Thus, it is possible to obtain insights into the extent to which, and where in the text, the European dimension and the national dimension are separate or intertwined. For example, it is possible to very quickly identify passages where references to Europe and Germany appear in close proximity to each other. As *AntConc*'s particular strength lies in the easy connection between the findings and the original text, such passages may be a useful starting point for an initial analysis.

In the next step of digital analysis, it is possible to approach a search term's meaning by investigating the words with which it is associated. As J.R. Firth, who introduced the term 'collocation' to linguistics, famously remarked: 'You shall know a word by the company it keeps!' (Firth 1962, 11). Collocations may be broadly understood as 'combination of words that habitually co-occur in texts and corpora' (Brezina 2018, 67). For our purposes, it is important to bear in mind that we do not aim to identify fixed, structured lexical or syntactical units, as in some linguistics-oriented approaches. Instead, we are interested in the proximity of words on the text surface, in order to establish the concepts that underlie and cause this proximity (Evert 2009, 1218).

To begin with, it should be noted that it is possible to generate a simple frequency list of two-word combinations that include the letter sequence *euro*, by using *AntConc*'s cluster function. The results from our sample of historical textbooks from Imperial Germany reveal that there are at least two linguistic constructions of Europe: Europe as an entity[11] and Europe as consisting of its parts, especially the nation-states.[12]

To gain a deeper understanding of the use of a word, it is possible to investigate which words appear within a certain distance from it, that is, within a collocational span, which usually ranges from three to five words to the left and/or right of a search term. However, a frequency-based list of collocates within the chosen span will include many words that are merely very frequent in the text, without being especially connected to the search term. Various association measures may be used to address this bias, including measures of effect size, such as MI (mutual information), and measures of significance, such as z-score, t-score or log-likelihood (for a discussion of measures, see Evert 2009 and Brezina 2018). The question of which measure to use is not a trivial one, however, because various measures have different strengths and problems, and may yield quite different results. As a 'one and only association measure' does not exist, a recommendable strategy may be to apply various measures, in order to obtain various perspectives on the data, as Evert suggests (Evert 2009, 1229). This is especially meaningful when collocate lists serve as a heuristic tool, and are combined with a qualitative analysis of the findings.

In *AntConc*'s collocate tool, it is possible to choose the collocation span as well as various statistical measures, and results may be sorted by frequency, likelihood or other statistical measures. It is also possible to choose a minimum frequency of words and files that should be considered. This is an important functionality, as effect size measures, especially MI, emphasise low-frequency words (including misspelled words in a text with poor OCR quality). For example, we calculated the collocates of *euro* in our sample of 96 textbooks from Imperial Germany, using MI as an effect size measure, and taking into account co-occurrences with a frequency of 20 or more in a minimum of 10 books (Table 6.2). The results indicate that the concept of Europe as a space where power struggles occur is very evident in the data. However, it is important to bear in mind that this result represents only one particular—if certainly intuitively meaningful—perspective on the data. Still, the result may suggest a direction for further investigation.

To gain an insight into changes and shifts in the construction of concepts of Europe and the nation, it is interesting to investigate how collocations develop over time. This is possible with DiaCollo, an open-source software tool for diachronic collocational analysis (Jurish 2018). DiaCollo makes it possible to detect semantic changes over time, and has been applied in particular to German-language corpus archives, including the GEI-Digital-2020 corpus, which comprises the Georg Eckert Institute's digital collection of 5036 textbooks published between 1648 and 1921

Table 6.2 Collocates of *euro* in a sample of 96 historical German textbooks

Collocate	Rank	FreqLR	Likelihood	Effect
gleichgewicht (balance)	1	30	196.960	6.131
großmacht (great power)	2	38	237.250	5.899
großmächte (great powers)	3	55	335.564	5.796
mächte (powers)	4	86	451.069	5.171
mächten (powers)	5	28	135.662	4.877
mächtigste (most powerful)	6	24	105.590	4.546
vorherrschaft (supremacy)	7	30	129.175	4.475

(https://diacollo.gei.de/, Nieländer und Jurish 2021).[13] For example, various visualisation techniques allow a quick overview of the proximity of various national categories to the term 'Europe' over time. However, a qualitative analysis of the findings is essential to interpreting the results, as words such as 'Germany', 'Russia' or 'America', though associated with the word 'Europe', may relate to it in very different ways.

When calculating collocations using a certain span size, it is important to bear in mind that irrelevant words may be included and relevant words excluded, even more so in languages with comparatively free word order. Therefore, Sketch Engine takes a word's grammatical relations into account. For example, 'word sketches' make it possible to see which adjectives modify 'Europe', or which nouns use it as a genitive object. Though this approach may exclude words that provide interesting insights into important contexts, word sketches offer structured insights, and facilitate focused comparisons, for example, regarding the use of 'Europe' compared to the use of 'Germany'. Therefore, they are a good example of how the quality of results may be improved when grammatical information is employed, as we discuss next.

Employing Grammatical Information

Linguistic annotation may be useful or even indispensable for identifying more sophisticated, category-based patterns, or simply to execute more efficient corpus queries. At the most basic level, this will involve lemmatisation (especially for inflection-rich languages), part-of-speech (POS) and word and sentence boundaries. Annotation at the syntactic, semantic and discourse levels (e.g. rhetorical structure) is less common and more difficult, but functional and structural relations (e.g. modifiers, verb arguments and dependency links) are more informative than simple (word) adjacency, and semantic types (ontologies) or semantic function (semantic roles) may facilitate systematic inspection, for example, a search for nationality nouns, or ambiguities such as 'Europe' used as a place, a political entity or an agent.

For large corpora, manual annotation is impossible, and automated tools must be used. In most cases, with the exception of machine learning data, this is true even of smaller corpora, because the limited use in a single project does not justify the workload of manual annotation. Also, the performance of automated annotation tools has reached impressive levels for many tasks and languages (e.g. 97–99% correct POS and up to 90% labelled dependency attachment), and for corpus inspection and statistics, a certain error rate is a small price to pay for instant access to annotation. Only the pragmatic level, and aspects such asimplicature, metaphor, irony and sarcasm continue to remain out of reach of automatic annotation.

For the basic POS level, an example of a robust tagger with multi-language support is Treetagger (Schmid 1994), which uses an HMM method based on decision trees. For syntactic analysis and dependency trees, many state-of-the-art systems employ machine learning (ML) based on so-called treebanks, usually combined with an external tokeniser and lexicon extension. Well-known examples are the MALT parser (Nivre et al. 2006) and the Stanford parser (Chen and Manning 2014), both available for many languages. The MATE tools (https://code.google.com/archive/p/mate-tools/) combine ML-based dependency (Bohnet and Nivre 2012) parsing and semantic-role labelling (Björkelund et al. 2009).

There are a number of systems that were specifically developed and optimised for German, such as the TnT tagger (Brants 2000) and the UIMA tagger (Giesbrecht and Evert 2009) for the POS level, Sennrich et al.'s (2009) hybrid syntactic parser with a finite-state morphology module, or GerGram (Bick 2020), a Constraint Grammar-based system that covers all levels up to semantic annotation (ontologies, frames and semantic roles). A sister system for the latter exists for Danish (DanGram, http://visl.sdu.dk/da/).

Using tags assigned by the GerGram parser, Figure 6.1 illustrates, in graphical form, the grammatical analysis of the sentence, *Kaum spricht man das Wort Burka aus, sind alle Europäer Faschisten.* ['Just mention the word "burka", and all Europeans are fascists']. Words have numbered IDs and are linked by dependency arrows with syntactic function labels (e.g. @SUBJ = subject). For inflecting words, a lemma is provided in brackets. Each field contains an uppercase tag string for POS (e.g. N = noun, V = verb) and morphology (e.g. M = male, P = plural,

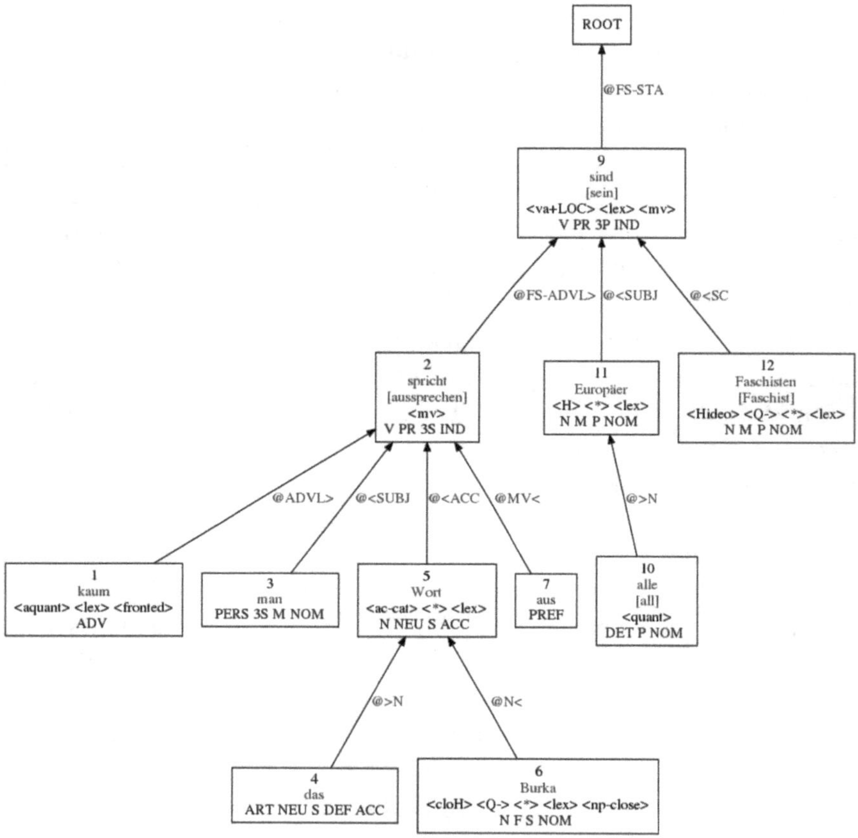

Fig. 6.1 Grammatical analysis—tree structure

NOM = nominative). Secondary information is given in angle brackets, for example, subcategories (<mv> = main verb), sentiment (<Q-> = negative polarity) or semantic class (<Hideo> = "ideological" human).

All the foregoing information may be made accessible through a corpus search interface, such as the multi-lingual, CQP-based[14] CorpusEye (http://corp.hum.sdu.dk). For example, it is possible to search for instances of 'Europe' as a subject, with a main verb to the right and no conjunctions between them (or simply with a main verb as dependency head). This will yield a concordance such as the following:

&pulseofeurope Imre Kertézs: **Europa wird untergehen!**
Alles was **Europa ablehnt nehmen** wir mit Kusshand
Sehr gut, das letzte was **Europa jetzt braucht** ist Veränderung
Erst muss **Europa rechristianisiert werden**.
Bitter—**Europa ist gefallen**.
gen wir unter dem Radar ¤ Wo **Europa daheim ist:** in der Gemeinschaft der Cafébesucher
Die #FPÖ will, dass **Europa europäisch bleibt** und tritt gegen #Islamisierung
Schuhe zu mir. ¤ Warum sich **Europa neu erfinden** muss … ¤ Kluger Artikel von twitter
Versprechen gebrochen, dass **Europa Wohlstand bedeutet** ¤ Wer Neoliberalismus wählt
für den Ausschuss Afrikas soll **Europa verantwortlich sein** ?😳 ¤ https:twitter.com
Die Chinesen werden warten bis **Europa sich abgeschafft** hat und dann wirds wohl ein

For a large corpus, inspection and evaluation are iterative processes, with search refinements prompted by the examples found (or not found), and alternate qualitative and quantitative steps. Thus, our example search could be constrained to cognitive and speech verbs, or to include prefiltering for sentiment emojis. If there are too many examples, a statistical–quantitative step may follow, to provide an overview. In the case of CorpusEye, each search or context field (or n-grams) may be sorted for absolute or relative frequency of word form, lemma or other tag types (e.g. semantics). For verb lemmas with 'Europe' as a (left) subject (5221 hits), this will yield the following list (Table 6.3). Note that the items have been reranked by comparing them to norm frequencies in a background corpus (first column) rather than sorting by absolute frequency in the local corpus (last column).

Networks

Network representations (of words in a text) are mathematically based representations that are useful for identifying and visualising the centrality (or peripherality) and connectivity of words occurring in the same text, as well as the statistical strength of their relations. For instance, one

Table 6.3 Relative frequencies of verbs with 'Europa' as their subject

Lemma	Freq²/norm	Freq/corp × 10^8	Freq/conc, %	Num
wählen	6199.80	4.8	2.4	130
zerstören	2971.50	3.32	1.7	90
islamisieren	616.67	1.52	0.7	41
verändern	424.08	1.26	0.6	34
umpflügen	424.08	1.26	0.6	34
überrennen	287.61	1.04	0.5	28
aufhören	161.78	0.78	0.4	21
schützen	146.74	0.74	0.3	20
aufwachen	133.71	2.0	1.0	54
schließen	82.54	0.56	0.2	15
überleben	71.90	0.52	0.2	14
gründen	71.90	0.52	0.2	14
heißen	71.90	0.52	0.2	14
untergehen	62.73	2.11	1.0	57
übernehmen	61.99	0.48	0.2	13
gehören	52.82	0.45	0.2	12
fluten	52.82	0.45	0.2	12
führen	44.38	0.41	0.2	11
zusammenrücken	36.68	0.37	0.1	10
abhängen	36.68	0.37	0.1	10
kämpfen	29.71	0.34	0.1	9

could create an overview of the characters in a play, film or novel, based on name co-occurrences and attributed family relationships. The network tool presented here, *Cytoscape* (Shannon et al. 2003), was originally designed for visualising molecular interaction networks in bioinformatics, but has since been adopted for linguistic uses, too. In our case, network nodes are not molecules, but words or lemmas, and relations may be either (a) simple adjacency, perhaps skipping so-called stopwords (non-content words), or (b) real (directed) syntactic dependencies. Both nodes and relations can have attributes, such as POS or semantic type for the former and syntactic function for the latter.

Once a network is generated, it can be searched, labelled, zoomed, edited and laid out in various ways, and both nodes and relations may be sorted for various statistical measures, such as frequency, connectedness, centrality, maximal distance and in- or out-going relations. The method words well for small (book-size) data sets, but for large corpora it may become noisy and computationally problematic, so a frequency threshold needs to be defined for node words that are part of the network itself or its visualisation.

The input for *Cytoscape* are so-called csv files with (comma-separated) node/word pairs and their relation, plus optional attributes for both nodes and relations. The csv files may be automatically generated from a corpus by using bigrams or dependent-head pairs, as well as relevant grammatical tagging. In the least informed version, naked wordforms are used, but particularly for inflecting languages, lemma or lemma_POS is useful for reducing ambiguity and limiting the number of nodes in a meaningful way. Further complexity reduction and salience may be achieved with minimum occurrence thresholds for nodes and relations, or by weighting node pairs.[15] For instance, using the product or sum of the relative frequencies of two related nodes will prioritise strongly related node pairs (with high mutual information) over more random pairs. If available, semantic classes may be useful as attributes, because they will allow searching and filtering the network on the fly, highlighting people, places or events, for example.

For large corpora, more tractable subcorpora may be generated by pre-filtering for sentences that contain the concept or word types to be studied, for example: 'Europa', 'europäisch', 'Europäer' (cave derivations/compounds: uneuropäisch); places (<[L[a-z]+>), or even just countries (<Lcountry>) or towns (<Ltowns>); people (e.g. character networks) or nationality nouns (<Hnat>); or verbs of motion (Framenet types) and direction prepositions

Table 6.4 shows a *Cytoscape* table after csv import, for texts from http://vimu.info/ prefiltered for sentences containing words indicating nationality, places or the pattern 'europ.*'. Relations are called edges, following graph theory conventions, or interactions, inspired by biochemical applications. In the example, relations (interactions) are verb lemmas or 'naked' attributive dependencies (attr). Nodes are verb arguments (subjects, objects etc.) or a modifier and head (attributive np relations). Node attributes are semantic class[16] for nouns or adjectives, and valency class[17] for verbs (edge attributes). The table is sorted for 'EdgeBetweenness' (Ebn), that is, highest number of shortest paths that pass through a given edge/relation. This means that the word triplet 'Europa'—ændre(s)—'revolution' is central to the network in the sense that if you search for a shortest path between two randomly selected nodes, this path is very likely to pass through it.

Figure 6.2 shows a graphical network representation for the same data, with a network entry threshold of minimum of two occurrences for

Table 6.4 *Cytoscape* data table after csv import (top 8 lines only)

Name node attribute	Interaction	Ebn	Source node attr.	Edge attr.	Target
Europa (ændre) revolution	ændre	314	<Ltop>	<vt>	<event>
revolution (sprede) Denmark	sprede	186	<event>	<vt>	<Lcountry>
Danmark (beskyttet) stormagt	beskyttet	97	<Lcountry>	<vt>	<HH>
Danmark (få) stormagt	få	97	<Lcountry>	<vt>	<HH>
1800-tal (få) idé	få	51	<temp>	<vt>	<sem-c>
stormagt (arbejde) kamp	arbejde	48.5	<HH>	<vi>	<fight>
Den industrielle revolution (knyttet) 1800-tal	knyttet	44	<occ>	<vt>	<temp>
Europa (ændre) bysamfund	ændre	39	<Ltop>	<vt>	<HH>

Fig. 6.2 *Cytoscape* network (unzoomed), highlighted for country nodes and their relationships

relations and three for nodes, and a row maximum of three hundred, sorted by the sum of the relative frequencies of paired nodes.

The network illustrates the tight mesh of relations between the nodes for Europe, Germany (*Tyskland*) and Denmark, but it also demonstrates the readability limits of a graphical overview of a complete network, even for a small, filtered corpus. The solution is a kind of search- or click-based zooming, where only a small portion of the network is shown. Figure 6.3 presents such an excerpt, focusing on the *Danmark* and *Europa* nodes only, including their labelled relations to neighbouring nodes.

Figure 6.4, another network excerpt, shows the shortest path between two peripheral nodes, Sydkorea [South Korea] and Slesvig-Holsten [Schleswig-Holstein].

The virtues of *Cytoscape* are not limited to visualisation. More powerful, and more efficient for large networks, are the tool's statistical measures of network and node properties. Table 6.5 illustrates some of these features with a history textbook, where both sentences and node pairs

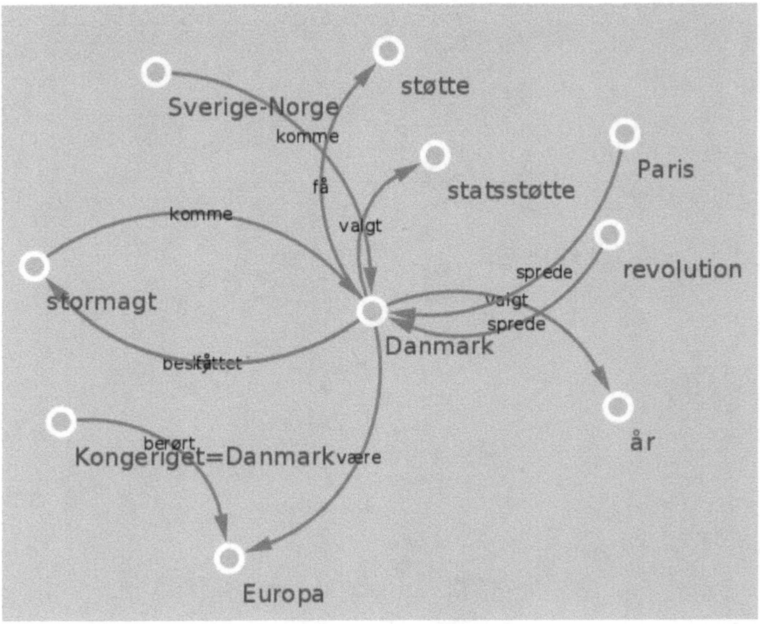

Fig. 6.3 Network excerpt: Denmark and Europe

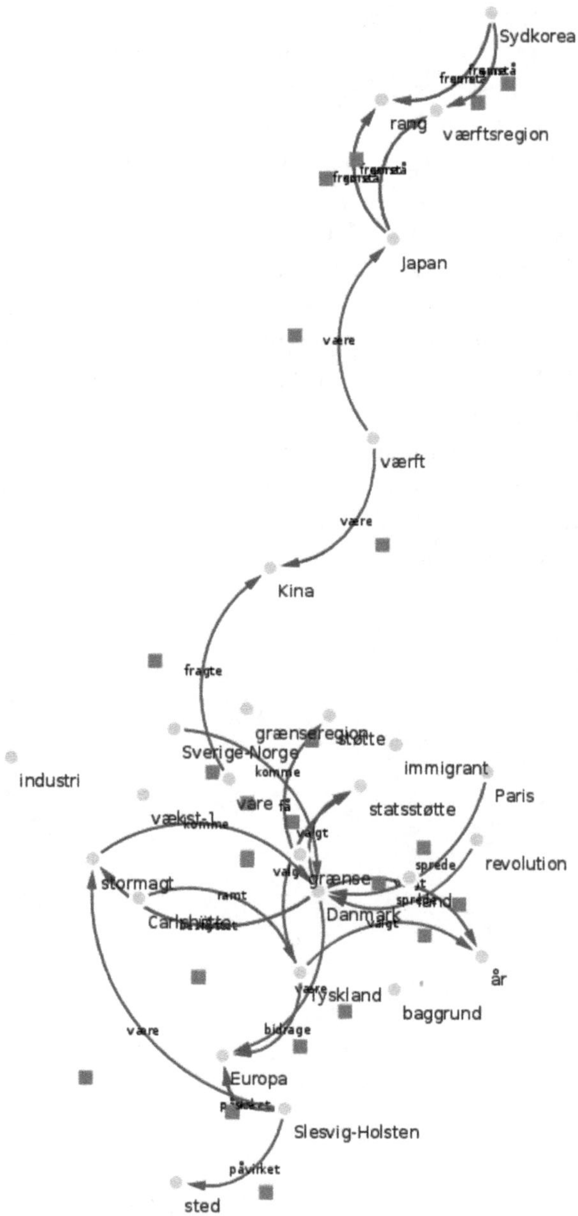

Fig. 6.4 Network excerpt: shortest path Sydkorea–Slesvig-Holstein

Table 6.5 Node table with network feature columns

Name	Average share	Partner of	Excentr.	Stress	EdgeCount	Indegree	Outdegree	Bn	Neighborh.
Danmark	1.72	57	3	12891	251	58	193	0.11	3.97
Tyskland	2.35	15	4	6732	59	22	37	0.05	11.1
Storbritannien	3.20	8	5	5905	34	22	12	0.05	13.2
Frankrig	3.59	12	6	5540	67	37	30	0.05	5.7
stat	2.56	4	4	4471	12	3	9	0.04	21.2
Europa	3.55	8	5	3924	26	25	1	0.03	11.7
krig	3.70	9	6	3438	51	43	8	0.02	20.6

were filtered for populated place nouns, institutions, events and nationality or geography adjectives. The table is a node table, where each column represents a different network feature. As presented, the table has been sorted for stress, defined as the number of shortest paths passing through a given node. With this feature, Denmark tops the list, and it also tops the edge count (number of relations)—a not unreasonable finding in a Danish textbook.

Two interesting and informative measures are outdegree and indegree, which are available for networks with directed relations. In the linguistic interpretation used here, the former covers cases where the node functions as a subject, whereas the latter covers object and adverbial use. One interpretation is that entities with a large outdegree/indegree ratio are active players in the text, whereas entities with an indegree overweight play a more passive role. In that sense the United States, Germany and, to a certain extent, the Soviet Union appear to take the initiative, whereas Great Britain, Israel, Africa and, to a lesser degree, France, are—at least syntactically—positioned at the receiving end, or simply mentioned as locations. Finally, a mention of the Neighbourhood connectivity feature is in order. This feature measures the average connectivity (number of direct relations) of a node's neighbouring nodes. Interestingly, the highest-ranking terms for neighbourhood connectivity are *stat* [state] and *krig* [war]. Though these are not the most central nodes, they are important because they indicate what connects the most central nodes in the text. In this case, war.

Identifying Identity?

The discursive construction of group identity draws on a vast number and variety of linguistic means that may be used to construct unification, sameness or difference, among other things, as Wodak et al. point out (Wodak et al. 2009, 35). To facilitate digital analysis, we decided to use various word forms that refer to important facets of group construction as our point of departure.

1. Toponyms such as 'Europe', 'Germany' and 'Denmark': spatial references play a crucial role in the construction of groups, even more so in the age of the territorially bounded nation-state. However, spatial concepts such as 'Europe' are culturally constructed, which is reflected in the fact that the definition of Europe's geographical borders has shifted over time. Besides, a toponym such as 'Europe' does not necessarily refer to a spatial entity, but may, directly or through metonymy, denote a group or a social actor, as in this example:

   Europa wiederum war über die wachsenden Exporterfolge Japans beunruhigt, dem es wirtschaftlichen Protektionismus vorwarf. (Europe, for its part, feared Japan's growing export successes, and accused the latter of protectionism). (Beckedorf 1992, 374)

   Here, 'Europe' has the grammatical role of experiencer and speaker subject, matching a verb-projected restriction of 'human', rather than 'location', which indicates a strong notion of European unity. Therefore, the investigation of group-related concepts benefits from the analysis of toponyms, if their function is taken into account.
2. Adjectives such as 'European', 'German' or 'Danish': the analysis of adjectives may provide important insights into what is considered typical of the group in question. Thus, it may serve as a first step when analysing the attributes that are discursively assigned to a given group.
3. Demonyms such as 'European(s)', 'German(s)' and 'Dane(s)': in the linguistic construction of identity, personal references play a prominent role. In particular, demonyms are very clear indicators that a group is constructed as a unit. Interestingly, in history textbooks, the European as a person appears only in specific contexts, in particular, in chapters on colonialism, gaining an (a European) identity only when confronted with the indigenous 'other'.

Next, we discuss how these concepts and distinctions may be studied in a large corpus of social media data (Twitter).

Beyond the Toponym

In its prototypical 'place' sense, we would expect the proper noun 'Europe' to appear in corpus data in location or direction adverbials and with verbs of motion, and linked to topics such as climate, nature and geography. To trace a possible 'country', 'nation' and 'group of people' sense, we need to excerpt and examine sentences in which the term is used as a subject or object, or in connection with attributes unrelated to place. Given sufficiently advanced corpus annotation, this may be achieved by searching for patterns such as the following:

1 word="Europa" & role="(Agent|Cognizer|Speaker|Donor)"
dass uns ganz Europa geholfen hat, unsere selbstverschuldete Kacke wieder aufzuräumen
Europa darf nicht den Eindruck erwecken, seine Währung sei ihm wichtiger als …
Masseneinwanderung—was kann Europa von Israel lernen?
Europa erntet grade die Früchte der Appeasement-Politik gegenüber
Was hat Europa Marokko getan, dass sie uns ihre Sexstraftäter exportieren?

2 word="Europa" & role="(Experiencer|Patient|Receiver|Beneficiary)"
Papst Franziskus rügt Europa für seine Flüchtlingspolitik
Ganz Europa leidet wieder unter d. #Zeitumstellung
Europa erlebt momentan den Krieg der Köpfe
Ganz Europa hasst Merkel?
Ja, mein Schnuckelchen, die Amis wollen Europa versklaven

We may also use adjective collocates as simple method for shedding light on which attributes are typically associated with the concept of Europe, as opposed to the German and Danish nation-states. In a POS-annotated corpus, for identifying prenominal adjective attributes, search pattern (a) will work, but in a dependency-annotated corpus, (b) could also be used. Attributes may also be harvested from subject complements, and here, because of German word order rules, and possible interfering verbs or adverbials, a POS search (c) is more complicated, whereas dependency annotation will allow a straightforward sister search (d). In the query language used here, '+' separates words, '&' combines features of the same word and '*' indicates optional constituents.

(a) pos = "ADJ" + lemma = "Europa"
(b) pos = "ADJ" & head lemma = "Europa"
(c) lemma = "Europa" & func = "@SUBJ" + morph = "VFIN"* + pos = "ADV"* + pos = "ADJ" & func = "@SC"
(d) pos = "ADJ" & func = "@SC" & sister lemma = "Europa" & func = "@SUBJ"

Search (b), with an additional condition for +HUM adjectives (semantic class tags such as <jpsych>, <jsoc>, <jbio>, <jemo> or <jsick>), will yield examples such as the following:

Nur ein Vereintes Europa sichert unsere Grenzen
leider gibt's in dem kleinkarierten Europa nicht so recht Platz dafür ☹
sie stand auf keiner Liste und soll nun das lahme Europa anführen 👍 😂
Rahmenbedinungen für ein klimafreundliches Europa
was heißt das dann für ein zukünftig kriegerisches Europa?

Adjectives

To shed light on which concepts are typically associated with the concept of 'Europeanness', we may also invert the previous chapter's ADJ + N search, using 'European' as a fixed attribute and searching for N as a variable (a, b). If we instead search for noun collocates of 'German' and 'Danish', we can compare traits of nation concepts with each other and with the ones associated with Europe.

(a) lemma = "europäisch" + pos = "N"
(b) lemma = "europäisch" & head = "N"

Since this kind of search, in a large corpus, will yield thousands of hits, frequency sorting may be used to facilitate inspection and interpretation of results. However, frequency alone does not imply conceptual information. Neutral words, such as 'weather' or 'town', which also frequently occur with other nation adjectives, are not interesting, whereas an association between 'German' and 'car', and between 'Danish' and 'furniture' is more informative because it reveals typical product associations. Therefore, it is often useful to sort by relative frequency, where in-corpus frequency is divided by a norm frequency value taken from a neutral background corpus (Tables 6.6 and 6.7).

A comparison of the Danish and German collocates for 'European' shows a marked difference. For instance, football is more important in the former, while politics appear mostly in general terms (*venstrefløj* [left wingers], *fagbevægelse* [unions], *socialdemokrater* [social democrats]). The exception, Centralbank, may be explained by the fact that 'European Central Bank' is a fixed term and, as such, sensitive to relative frequency ranking. The German collocate list, on the other hand, is more specific with respect to politics, with many collocates evoking the image of Europe as embodied by the European Union, and relating to EU

Table 6.6 Danish noun collocates for nation adjectives

Europæisk + N (11.4%)	Tysk + N (8.3%)	Dansk + N (80.3%)
gruppespil, værdier, fællesskab, venstrefløj, sammenhæng, sæson, løsninger, tømmermænd, ligaer, økonomi, Centralbank, fagbevægelse, melodigrandprix, kulturhovedstad, søjle, æggeskandale, gruppespil, forår, undersøgelse, socialdemokratier	grænse, jøder, FDP-leder, smågrise, økonomi, besættelsesmagt, vejskat, rockerklub, sejlbåd, forbundsdag, besættelse, vælgere, mænd, børn, ubåd, gæster, hær, politi, slagtesvin, krigsubåd, supermarkedsangreb, efterretningschef, grænsebutikker	værdier, økonomi, børn, hær, mænd, grænse, fængsler, jøder, landmænd, sundhedsvæsen, tøs, økonomi, folkebedrag, værdi, håndbold, forældre, velfærdssamfund, fødevarer, læger, familiefilm, fodboldkvinder, vækst

Table 6.7 German noun collocates for nation adjectives

europäisch + N (12.8%)	deutsch + N (86.3%)	dänisch + N (0.8%)
Lösung, Bürger, Bevölkerung, Kulturerbejahr, Solidarität, Flüchtlingspolitik, Außengrenze, Identität, Bürgerinitiative, Datenschutz-Grundverordnung, Einlagensicherung, Datenschutz-grundverordnung, Gerichtshof, Kurzhaar, Protesttag, Fußball, Währungsfonds, Datenschutztag, Küche, Großstadt, Währungsunion, Behörde, Gemeinschaftswährung, Wasserschutz, Verteidigungsunion	Pass, Küche, Bürger, Bevölkerung, Mädchen, Staatsbürger, Behörde, Fußball, Staatsbürgerschaft, Übersetzung, Umwelthilfe, Straße, Großstadt, Staatsangehörigkeit, Täter, Wähler, Leitkultur, Börse, Fernsehpreis, Trailer, Volk, Rapper, Außenminister, Kanzlerin, Gefängnis	Kamin, Bettenlager, Königin, Künstler, Königshaus, Verhältnis, Containerschiff, Hinauszögern, König, Nordseeküste, U-Boot-Bauer, Ministerpräsident, Glücksrezept, U-Boot-Erfinder, Staatsbürgerschaft, Prinzgemahl, Königsfamilie, Bitcoin-Baron, Schülerin, Pass, Integrationsministerin, Netflix-Serie, TÜV, Behörde, Vanillesoße

monetary and data protection initiatives. It is also much more suggestive of a European identity, with terms such as *Bürger* [citizen], *Identität* [identity], *Außengrenze* [outer border] and *Behörde* [institution]. The closest equivalent in the Danish data is the high rank of *værdier* [values].

In the German 'auto-collocates' (deutsch + N), citizenship also ranks high, but is accompanied by down-to-earth topics such as football, *Mädchen* [girls] and *Küche* [cuisine]. The citizenship focus is probably linked to immigration,[18] and combines with *Leitkultur* [host culture], for example. The corresponding Danish 'auto-collocate' list is very different, and focuses on values, family and agriculture. The two nations' hetero-collocates are also interestingly different. Thus, Danes associate *tysk* [German] with a border, the piglet trade, the economy and war. Germans talk—corpus-wise—about Danes far less than vice versa, but when they do, they associate the topic with furniture, royalty and happiness.

Demonyms

A quantitative method for investigating the existence of a European identity is to compare—in both Danish and German—demonym frequencies (a German, a Dane, a European), both with each other and with the corresponding toponyms and adjectives (German, Danish, European). Table 6.8 provides the frequencies of these terms in Danish and German Twitter data, per million words.

In the adjective group, the self-adjective dominates equally in both languages, but the cross distribution is asymmetrical: *tysk* [German] is much more frequent in the Danish corpus than *dänisch* [Danish] is in the German corpus. In both corpora, the adjective 'European' is more frequent than the non-self national adjective (i.e. than 'German' in Danish or 'Danish' in German), and the fact that the demonym 'European' is only three times less frequent in Danish than the noun *tysker* [German], and six times as frequent in German than *Däne* [Dane] may indicate a nascent European identity. Also, the ratio of adjective to noun is not much higher for 'European' than for 'German' and 'Danish', suggesting that the European demonym—at least on Twitter—has entered the general vocabulary on par with the nation demonyms:

> europäisch/Europäer (de) = 5:1, europæisk/europæer (da) = 8:1 deutsch/Deutscher (de) = 3.3:1, dansk/dansker (da) = 3.3:1 dänisch/Däne (de) = 3:1, tysk/tysker (da) = 4:1

Table 6.8 DK, DE, EU part-of-speech frequencies

dansk/deutsch	1061/713
tysk/dänisch	102/6
dansker/Deutscher	297/225
tysker/Däne	27/3
euopæisk/europäisch	71/93
europæer/Europäer	9/19

Discussion and Conclusion

In this chapter we have discussed the analysis of word frequency, of keywords, of concordances and of collocates, as well as network analysis as an approach to investigating concepts of Europe and the nation in educational media, which may be relevant to the construction of identity. We hope we have demonstrated that the various methods of digital analysis offer new and abundant possibilities for research in educational media: they contribute to making medium-sized and large amounts of text accessible. They may reveal patterns that may not be apparent in traditional approaches to analysis, thereby functioning as a heuristic instrument and encouraging further analysis. However, in concluding, we wish to emphasise two important factors: first we wish to note that the size of a corpus is an important factor of which researchers must be aware; secondly, we wish to emphasise that the integration of quantitative and qualitative procedures is essential to the approach we propose.

Size Matters!

Not all methods lend themselves to all corpus types, or at least, not on their own. Corpus size, in particular, is an important factor, as some quantitative methods may require a minimum corpus size to work reliably. Thus, the significance of a certain word or construction that occurs more often in a target corpus than in a background corpus (keyness) is dependent on frequency (i.e. corpus size).[19] This illustrates that size matters, but also that lemmatisation is important, because it may reduce the vocabulary and necessary corpus size. The richer a language's morphology, the larger this effect will be.

In principle, the same argument holds for n-grams, and since n-grams are less frequent than the words they comprise, even larger corpora are needed to achieve statistical significance. Again, linguistic analysis offers alternatives. In addition to lemmatisation, other word-level annotation may be useful. For instance, n-gram frequencies will rise if so-called complex n-grams (Bubenhofer 2015) are used. Here, one or more context words in an n-gram are replaced with their POS or a morphosyntactic feature combination. If provided by available parsers, semantic class tags could be a more lemma-near alternative.

A third example of size-dependence is word clustering using word embeddings (distributed representations, Mikolov et al. 2013). In this technique, a word's semantic elements are approximated by a vector in multi-dimensional space, where dimensions are co-occurring words. Words are regarded as similar if they have a small cosine vector distance. Without a sufficiently large corpus, no robust vectors can be computed, and the resulting language model risks overfitting, with rarer words having their meaning 'skewed' by the few existing examples. Usually, corpora with hundreds of millions of words are used, and 10 million may be considered a lower limit. For restricted medical domains, Gu et al. achieved vocabularies of 10,000 to 30,000 words with document collections containing 5 to 15 million tokens (Gu et al. 2018). Given the size-sensitivity of this method, it is more useful for background corpora such as Wikipedia, rather than traditional educational media.[20]

Some explorative methods require less, rather than more, data, to allow relevant patterns to emerge, and therefore are particularly appropriate for the smaller, more selective data sets found in teaching material. For instance, to avoid pattern dilution, it is possible to apply topic-filtering to history textbooks, by using only chapters that are relevant to the concept of 'Europe', including sentences that do not contain the term itself, but excluding other chapters. At the word level, downsizing vocabulary may be useful for some visualisations. In network analysis, for instance, a lower granularity, with only a few hundred items (rather than the full lexicon), enhances the readability of the representation. Reduction may be achieved by using frequency thresholds, or by replacing some word categories with a semantic class.

Qualitative Analysis Matters Too!

Though digital analysis often draws on quantitative techniques, qualitative analysis is crucial for the methodology we propose. As Eve points out, as a tool, the computer may serve as both a telescope and a microscope (Eve 2017), and facilitates not only distant, but also close reading.

Although quantitative analysis seems ideal for identifying certain patterns in the concept formation, it often fails to take into account that meaning formation may be very subtle. However, a purely qualitative evaluation of large corpora risks overlooking important information, or generalising from isolated examples.

Corpus-linguistic analysis may be used to 'evaluate the data material more systematically and carefully' (Ziem 2010, 159), and to provide insights into vast amounts of text. On the other hand, a detailed analysis of a smaller amount of text may capture subtle forms of meaning formation, which occur in complex and less obvious ways, as Kalwa points out (2019, 15). Detailed text analysis also makes it possible to establish how individual actors or groups of actors construct certain concepts linguistically, and at which levels of language the constitution of meaning occurs: lexically, syntactically and pragmatically. As educational media usually contain a large variety of text types, such as author accounts, source material and tasks, and as they are often the result of collaborative work, this is a very important aspect to consider. As a result, it may be stated that each approach—the corpus-linguistic analysis of large text corpora, the qualitative analysis of a smaller text corpus, or the very detailed analysis of specific texts or text passages—has considerable potential for describing concepts in discourses, and specific limitations.

We suggest that quantitative and qualitative methods should combine in an iterative fashion; once a corpus is compiled, bottom-up data exploration through the calculation of word frequencies, keywords and n-grams helps to understand the characteristics of the data, though the results should be interpreted cautiously, as they may vary, depending on certain preliminary decisions. Next, search terms must be chosen that contribute to the investigation of the concepts in question, a crucial and anything but trivial step in the research process. Then, distributions, concordances and collocations may be generated and interpreted qualitatively. Employing grammatical information significantly improves the quality of the results, and visualisations such as networks may be helpful heuristic tools. At the same time, the thorough qualitative analysis of concordances and collocations is indispensable for establishing their relevance with regard to the formation of a particular concept, and to check for bias due to characteristics of the data or statistical measures. Distributions, concordances and collocations also make it possible to identify significant passages in a text that may otherwise have been overlooked, but should be analysed in detail, as even small constituents of a text may constitute separate units or layers of meaning, or be key vehicles for the text's overall meaning. Such detailed analyses may form the basis for new hypotheses, which initiate a new cycle of analysis. To fully exploit the potential of this approach, it is helpful to use digital tools that allow the user to switch easily between corpus-analysis results and the original texts, as is the case with *AntConc*.

To analyse linguistically constituted concepts of the nation and Europe in medium-sized and large corpora, we suggest that quantitative and qualitative methods should mesh in an iterative fashion in the various steps of analysis. As Kalwa points out, this may be compared to the way a camera zoom works (Kalwa 2019, Kalwa 2013). Through the use of digital methods, quantitative and qualitative analysis may inform each other, which offers new potential for educational-media research.

Notes

1. The authors are grateful to Heike Zinsmeister, with whom we collaborated while working on this chapter and who contributed important input and very helpful comments on the text.
2. In particular, we refer to the following examples: (i) two Danish (*Historie*, *Klar, parat, historie*) and one German (*Zeitreise*) history textbook series, and examples from a website on the history of the Danish–German border region (Poulsen et al. 2009–2014; Hemmingsen and Hostrup 2007–2012; Christoffer et al. 2017–2019, http://vimu.info/); (ii) the Georg Eckert Institute's digital collection of historical textbooks (gei-digital.gei.de), in particular, a randomly selected sample of 96 history textbooks from Imperial Germany, that is, from the period between 1871 and 1918; and (iii) examples from Wikipedia or social media, in particular the Facebook and Twitter sections of the XPEROHS corpus, a two-billion-word Danish–German social media corpus compiled for hate speech research (Bick 2020).
3. For a thorough comparison of tools, with test examples, see https://source.opennews.org/articles/so-many-ocr-options/.

4. For example, https://sourceforge.net/projects/pdf2textpilot/ (open source).
5. https://www.gnu.org/software/wget/ (open source) or http://gnuwin32.sourceforge.net/packages/wget.htm (Windows).
6. http://xml2txt.sourceforge.net/ (open source).
7. https://exmaralda.org/de/partitur-editor-de/.
8. For example, https://www.clarin.eu/resource-families/reference-corpora
9. For example, with the help of https://wortschatz.uni-leipzig.de or www.openthesaurus.de.
10. For more details about this method, see the 'Size matters!' section.
11. *in europa* = 'in europe', frequency 422; *ganz europa* = 'the whole of europe', 181; *nach europa* = 'to europe', 163.
12. *europäischen staaten* = 'european states', frequency 84; *staaten europas* = 'states of europe', 64; *europäischen mächte* = 'european powers', 51; *fürsten europas* = 'princes of Europe', 27.
13. As corpus size matters, this is not the tool of choice for minor languages with very limited diachronic corpus data, such as Danish.
14. The 'Corpus Query Protocol', an open-source Corpus Workbench (Evert 2005).
15. These and other adaptations mentioned here need to be programmed separately, and depend on the type and quality of existing corpus annotation, or the availability of a tagger/parser for the language in question.
16. For semantic tag explanations, see https://visl.sdu.dk/semantic_prototypes_overview.pdf (nouns) and https://visl.sdu.dk/semantic_prototypes_adj.pdf (adjectives).
17. Here, <vt> means 'transitive', <vi> intransitive and <va> a bound adverbial argument.
18. This should be checked in context, and is a good example of the interplay of quantitative and qualitative analysis, where intuition about the former leads to focused inspection of the latter.
19. For instance, if a keyword candidate occurs 80 times in a target corpus of 1 million words, but only 50 times in a background corpus of the same size (i.e. a 60% over-occurrence), this yields a log-likelihood measure of 6.99, and is significant at the 1% percentile ($p < 0.01$). A 20-to-32 difference (also 60%) does not even reach the 5% significance percentile ($p < 0.05$). The problem is that, according to Zipf's law, frequency is inversely proportional to frequency rank. For German, a frequency of 50 ppm, roughly equal rank 1600, and 20 ppm rank 4000. In other

words, if a word is not among the top 4000 German words, a 60% deviation is not significant at the 5% level, and only a very basic vocabulary will make the 1% threshold in a million-word corpus. Typically, however, real keywords are specific noun terms that are much rarer. However, a large German print dictionary, such as *Duden*, contains 200,000 lemmas, probably equivalent to at least half a million inflected forms. According to Zipf's law, over half of these words (the ones under rank 160,000) would have a frequency 100 times lower than is needed for our significance threshold. In other words, we would need a 100-million-word corpus; more, if the observed difference is under 60%, less if it is over 60%.

20. For an example of how this method may be used to compare the concept of Europe to traditional concepts of nationality, see Bick's Chap. 7, this volume.

References

Alhudithi, Ella. 2021. Review of Voyant Tools: See through your Text. *Language Learning & Technology* 25 (3): 43–50.

Anthony, Laurence. 2005. AntConc: Design and Development of a Freeware Corpus Analysis Toolkit for the Technical Writing Classroom. In *Professional Communication Conference*, 729–37. IPCC.

———. 2018. Visualisation in Corpus-based Discourse Studies. In *Corpus Approaches to Discourse*, 197–224. Taylor and Francis.

———. 2022a. AntConc (Version 4.0.5) [Computer Software]. Tokyo, Japan. Waseda University. https://www.laurenceanthony.net/software.

———. 2022b. TagAnt (Version 2.4.0) [Computer Software]. Tokyo, Japan. Waseda University. https://www.laurenceanthony.net/software

Beckedorf, Jürgen, ed., and Dieter Tieman (deutsche Ausgabe). 1992. *Europäisches Geschichtsbuch*, 374. Ernst Klett Schulbuchverlag.

Bick, Eckhard. 2020. An Annotated Social Media Corpus for German. In *Proceedings of the 12th International Conference on Language Resources and Evaluation (Marseille, May 2020),* ed. Calzolari, Nicoletta et al., 6129–37. LREC2020. ACL/ELRA.

Björkelund, Anders, Love Hafdell, and Pierre Nugues. 2009. Multilingual Semantic Role Labeling. In *Proceedings of The Thirteenth Conference on Computational Natural Language Learning*, 43–48. CoNLL, Boulder, USA.

Bohnet, Bernd, and Joakim Nivre. 2012. *A Transition-Based System for Joint Part-of-Speech Tagging and Labeled Non-Projective Dependency Parsing*, 1455–1465. EMNLP–CoNLL.

Brants, T. 2000. TnT—A Statistical Part-of-Speech Tagger. In *Proceedings of the 6th Applied Natural Language Processing Conference*, 224–31. ANLP.

Brezina, Vaclav. 2018. *Statistics in Corpus Linguistics: A Practical Guide*. Cambridge: Cambridge University Press. https://doi.org/10.1017/9781316410899.

Brubaker, Rogers, and Frederick Cooper. 2000. Beyond "Identity". *Theory and Society* 29 (1): 1–47.

Bubenhofer, Noah. 2008. 'Diskurse berechnen? Wege zu einer korpuslinguistischen Diskursanalyse'. In *Methoden der Diskurslinguistik: Sprachwissenschaftliche Zugänge zur transtextuellen Ebene*, ed. Ingo H. Warnke and Jürgen Spitzmüller, 407–34. Berlin/New York: De Gruyter. https://doi.org/10.1515/9783110209372.6.407.

———. 2015. Muster aus korpuslinguistischer Sicht. In *Handbuch Satz, Äußerung, Schema*, ed. Christa Dürscheid and Jan Georg Schneider, vol. 21, 485–502. Berlin/New York: De Gruyter.

Chen, Danqi, and Christopher D. Manning 2014. A Fast and Accurate Dependency Parser Using Neural Networks. In *Proceedings of EMNLP 2014*, 740–50.

Christoffer, Sven, et al. 2017–2019. *Zeitreise*, vol. 3, 1–3. Stuttgart: Klett.

Dreesen, Philipp. 2015. Sprache—Wissen—Kontingenz: Die Kontrastive Diskurslinguistik in der Schulbuchforschung am Beispiel deutscher und polnischer Geschichtsschulbücher. In *Linguistik und Schulbuchforschung. Gegenstände—Methoden—Perspektiven* (= Studien des Georg-Eckert-Instituts zur internationalen Bildungsmedienforschung 137), ed. Jana Kiesendahl, and Christine Ott, S. 53–83. Göttingen: V&R unipress.

Eve, Martin Paul. 2017. 'Close Reading with Computers: Genre Signals, Parts of Speech, and David Mitchell's Cloud Atlas'. *SubStance* 46 (3). Johns Hopkins University Press: 76–104. https://muse.jhu.edu/article/676240.

Evert, Stefan. 2005. *The CQP Query Language Tutorial. Institute for Natural Language Processing*, University of Stuttgart. www.ims.unistutgart.de/projekte/CorpusWorkbench/CQPTutorial.

———. 2009. Corpora and Collocations. In *Corpus Linguistics: An International Handbook*, ed. Anke Lüdeling and Merja Kytö, vol. 2, 1212–1248. Berlin: De Gruyter Mouton.

Fage-Butler, Antoinette, and Katja Gorbahn. 2020. Europeanness in Aarhus 2017's Programme of Events: Identity Constructions and Narratives. *Culture, Practice & Europeanization* 5 (1): 16–33.

Firth, John Rupert. 1962. A Synopsis of Linguistic Theory 1930–55. In *Studies in Linguistic Analysis*, ed. John Rupert Firth, W. Haas, M.A.K. Halliday, W.S. Allen, R.H. Robins, R.K. Sprigg, F.R. Palmer, J. Carnochan, and T.F. Mitchell, 1–32. Oxford: Blackwell.

Gabrielatos, Costas. 2018. Keyness Analysis: Nature, Metrics and Techniques. In *Corpus Approaches to Discourse*, ed. Charlotte Taylor and Anna March, 225–258. Routledge.

Gardt, Andreas. 2008. Kunst und Sprache. Beobachtungen anlässlich der documenta 12. In *Literatur—Kunst—Medien: Festschrift für Peter Seibert zum 60. Geburtstag*, ed. Achim Barsch, Helmut Scheuer und Georg-Michael Schulz, 201–24. München: Peter Lang.

Giesbrecht, E., and S. Evert. September 2009. Is Part-of-speech Tagging a Solved Task? An Evaluation of POS Taggers for the German Web as Corpus. In *Proceedings of the Fifth94 Web as Corpus Workshop*, 27–35.

Gries, Stefan Th., and John Newman. 2013. Creating and Using Corpora. In *Research Methods in Linguistics*, ed. Robert J. Podesva and Devyani Sharma, 263–293. New York: Cambridge University Press.

Gu, Yang et al. 2018. Optimizing Corpus Creation for Training Word Embedding in Low Resource Domains: A Case Study in Autism Spectrum Disorder (ASD). In *Annual Symposium Proceedings of AMIA*, 508–17.

Hemmingsen, Søren E., and Hans Hostrup. 2007–2012. *Klar, parat, historie*, 3–9. Copenhagen: Aliena.

Jurish, Bryan. 2018. Diachronic Collocations, genre, and DiaCollo. In *Diachronic Corpora, Genre, and Language Change*, ed. R.J. Whitt, 41–64. Amsterdam: Benjamins.

Kalwa, Nina. 2013. *Das Konzept 'Islam'. Eine diskurslinguistische Untersuchung*. Berlin, Boston: De Gruyter.

———. 2019. Die Konstitution von Konzepten in Diskursen: Zoom als Methode der diskurslinguistischen Bedeutungsanalyse. In *Sprach(kritik)-kompetenz als Mittel demokratischer Willensbildung*, Greifswalder Beiträge zur Linguistik, ed. Sandro Moraldo, Thomas Niehr, and Jürgen Schiewe, vol. 12, 11–26. Bremen: Hempen Verlag.

Kilgarriff, Adam. 1997. Putting Frequencies in the Dictionary. *International Journal of Lexicography* 10 (2): 135–155. https://doi.org/10.1093/ijl/10.2.135.

———. July 2009. Simple Maths for Keywords. In *Proceedings of Corpus Linguistics Conference CL2009*, ed. M. Mahlberg, V. González-Díaz, and C. Smith. UK: University of Liverpool.

———. 2012. Getting to Know Your Corpus. In *Text, Speech and Dialogue*, Lecture Notes in Computer Science, ed. P. Sojka, A. Horák, I. Kopeček, and K. Pala, vol. 7499. Berlin, Heidelberg: Springer.

Kilgarriff, Adam, Vít Baisa, Jan Bušta, Miloš Jakubíček, Vojtěch Kovář, Jan Michelfeit, Pavel Rychlý, and Vít Suchomel. 2014. The Sketch Engine: Ten Years On. *Lexicography* 1 (1): 7–36. https://doi.org/10.1007/s40607-014-0009-9. http://www.sketchengine.eu.

Mikolov, Thomad, Ilya Sutskever, Kai Chen, Greg Corrado, and Jeffrey Dean. 2013. Distributed Representations of Words and Phrases and Their Compositionality. In *Neural Information Processing Systems (NIPS)*, 3111–19.

Nieländer, Maret, and Ernesto William De Luca. 2018. *Digital Humanities in der internationalen Schulbuchforschung*. Göttingen: V&R unipress. https://doi.org/10.14220/9783737009539.

Nieländer, Maret, und Bryan Jurish. 2021. D* für Anfänger:innen: Ein Tutorial Einfache und komplexe Suchanfragen, Frequenzanalysen und diachrone Kollokationsanalysen in der D*-Korpusmanagement-Umgebung, Juli. https://repository.gei.de/handle/11428/321

Nivre, J., J. Hall, and J. Nilsson. 2006. MaltParser: A Data-Driven Parser-Generator for Dependency Parsing. In *Proceedings of the fifth international conference on Language Resources and Evaluation (LREC2006), May 24–26, Genoa, Italy*, 2216–19

Perkuhn, Rainer/Keibel, Holger/Kupietz, Marc. 2012. *Korpuslinguistik*. Paderborn: Fink.

Poulsen, Jens Aage et al. 2009–2014. *Historie*, 3–9. Copenhagen: Gyldendal.

Schmid, Helmut. 1994. Probabilistic Part-of-Speech Tagging Using Decision Trees. In *Proceedings of International Conference on New Methods in Language Processing, Manchester, UK*, 44–49.

Sennrich, Rico, Gerold Schneider, Martin Volk, and Martin Warin. 2009. 'A New Hybrid Dependency Parser for German'. In *Von der Form zur Bedeutung: Texte automatisch verarbeiten / From Form to Meaning: Processing Texts Automatically. Proceedings of the Biennial GSCL Conference 2009*, edited by Christian Chiarcos, Richard Eckart de Castilho, and Manfred Stede, 115–24. Tübingen: Narr. https://doi.org/10.5167/uzh-25506.

Shannon, P., A. Markiel, O. Ozier, N.S. Baliga, J.T. Wang, D. Ramage, N. Amin, B. Schwikowski, and T. Ideker. November 2003. Cytoscape: A Software

Environment for Integrated Models of Biomolecular Interaction Networks. *Genome Research* 13 (11): 2498–2504.

Sinclair, Stéfan, and Geoffrey Rockwell. 2022. Voyant Tools. Web. http://voyant-tools.org/

Teubert, Wolfgang. 2006. Über den fragwürdigen Nutzen mentaler Konzepte. In *Von Intentionalität zur Bedeutung konventionalisierter Zeichen: Festschrift für Gisela Harras zum 65. Geburtstag*, ed. Kristel Proost, Edeltraud Winkler, Von Kristel Proost, and Edeltraud Winkler, 289–325. Tübingen: Narr.

Wodak, Ruth, Rudolf de Cillia, Martin Reisigl, Karin Liebhart, Angelika Hirsch, und Richard Mitten. 2009. *The Discursive Construction of National Identity*. Translated by Angelika Hirsch, Richard Mitten, and J. W. Unger. Edinburgh: Edinburgh University Press.

Ziem, Alexander. 2010. Kollokationen, Konkordanzen und Metaphern: Krisenszenarien im SPIEGEL. *Aptum. Zeitschrift für Sprachkritik und Sprachkultur* 6: 272–288.

7

Concepts of Europe in Danish and German Social Media: A Corpus-Linguistic Study

Eckhard Bick

Introduction

At first glance, Denmark and Germany, size aside, appear to be very similar countries in economic, social and cultural terms, and often rank similarly in international comparisons.[1] However, possibly because size does matter and because of small-state fears of larger neighbours, both attitudes and politics related to Europe and the European Economic Community (EEC)/European Union have been distinctly different in these two countries since the early days of the European integration project, with Denmark joining later (1973) and exhibiting a marked, albeit nuanced, Euroscepticism (Sørensen 2004), which manifested in close-call referendums (the last in 2015), footnotes, citizens' rights exceptions,[2] a 40-year-old Leave party with European Parliamentary (EP) representation (until 2019) and popular slogans such as 'Holger og konen siger nej

E. Bick (✉)
Institute of Language and Communication, University of Southern Denmark, Odense, Denmark
e-mail: eckhard.bick@mail.dk

K. Gorbahn et al. (eds.), *Exploring Interconnectedness*, Palgrave Studies in Educational Media, https://doi.org/10.1007/978-3-031-13960-4_7

til unionen',[3] whereas the larger German–French axis more consistently tended to view European integration as a peace project with shared values.

Though media coverage went from decidedly EEC-hostile in the 1980s and 1990s, with an almost exclusive focus on national interests and sovereignty, to more neutral coverage up to the EP election in 2004 (Ørsten 2004), European topics figured only in the (Danish) national consciousness and media as a pragmatic necessity to be largely ignored—with the exception of the recurring sovereignty referendums. However, against the background of Brexit, Trump and the refugee/immigrant crisis, times appear to be changing. Over a period of a few years, European questions have started to be a normal part of the daily media discourse in Denmark, and if the 2019 EP election is any indication, most Danes now seem to perceive political Europe more as part of the solution than part of the problem. Arguably, a nascent European identity is also being strengthened, albeit 'via *negationis*', by distancing 'ourselves' from American politics, totalitarian regimes or African economies. In the research presented here, we attempt to document these trends, as well as the traditional, negative Danish narrative in two mainstream social media, Facebook (FB) and Twitter (TW), identifying and exemplifying competing conceptualisations of Europe and the European Union. Because only 34% of Danes (47% of Germans) with populist views trust the news media (Pew Research Center 2018), we expect social media to be a better source of populist stereotypes than are mainstream media. Also, lexical frequencies suggest that social media texts are linguistically closer to spoken language than are print media (e.g. Scheffler 2014, for German Twitter), and in light of this, we expect such data to be more spontaneous, less premeditated and less self-censored and therefore to include more personal and more stereotype-laden expressions of opinion.

The Corpus

We applied various corpus-linguistic methods to a collection of public posts, Tweets and comments (on both FB and TW) that span a one-and-a-half-year period from late 2017 to early 2019, and compare the Danish data to corresponding German data, as we try to identify and—where possible—measure various concepts of Europe. Our working hypothesis is that the refugee/immigrant crisis, and possibly Brexit, has provoked a discourse on identity in both countries, not only in terms of nationality and ethnicity, but also with regard to what people perceive as 'European'. That said, there were significant and interesting differences between Danish and German Europe-related stereotypes. Thus, for some, the historical Danish, German-fearing narrative is being 'raised' and translated into a Europe-fearing narrative: Little Red Riding Hood going to be eaten by the big bad wolf world. For Germany, there is a conflict between two narratives—one of historical guilt and anti-nationalism with a strong pro-European sentiment, and one of knowing better how to run things and resenting having to share the wealth with 'lazy cousins'.

Our social media corpus was developed at the University of Southern Denmark (SDU) as part of an ongoing hate-speech project, XPEROHS (Experiencing and Perceiving Online Hate Speech),[4] and is focused primarily on discourse that targets immigrant minorities. Owing to data harvesting constraints, in both the Danish and German Facebook material, this focus is reflected in the choice of FB pages (those of media, political parties and a few public figures), whereas the Twitter data were harvested using high-frequency search words, and represent a more comprehensive and almost complete cross-section[5] of the period in question. All in all, the bilingual corpus contains almost two billion words (Table 7.1). Population sizes and harvesting differences explain why there are more German than Danish data, and more Twitter than Facebook material.

The corpora were grammatically annotated with the DanGram (Danish) and GerGram (German) parsers,[7] using the CG3 version of the Constraint Grammar formalism (Bick and Didriksen 2015), and may be searched for lemma, part-of-speech, inflection and syntactic function.[8] In addition, there is some annotation of 'nonverbal' items, in particular emoji/smileys, with a ten-class sentiment annotation, sentiment polarity markers for most adjectives and a range of high-frequency verbs and nouns. Content words are assigned to one or more lexical–semantic types, with ontologies organised in shallow hierarchies for nouns (~ 200

Table 7.1 Corpus sizes[6] (in millions of words)

	Danish	German
Facebook	21.6	65.3
Twitter	140	1700

categories), adjectives (~ 120 categories) and proper nouns (20 categories). The highest annotation level consists of 500 framing classes and about 50 semantic roles that are assigned not only to verbs and their complements, but also to many argument-taking nouns and adjectives, subclauses and adverbials. Figure 7.1 illustrates the structural and morphosyntactic annotation levels as a dependency tree graph with numbered tokens followed by CG tag fields, and function labels for the node edges, for the following sentence:

> *Kaum spricht man das Wort Burka aus, sind alle Europäer Faschisten.*
> (Just mention the word 'burka', and all Europeans are fascists.)

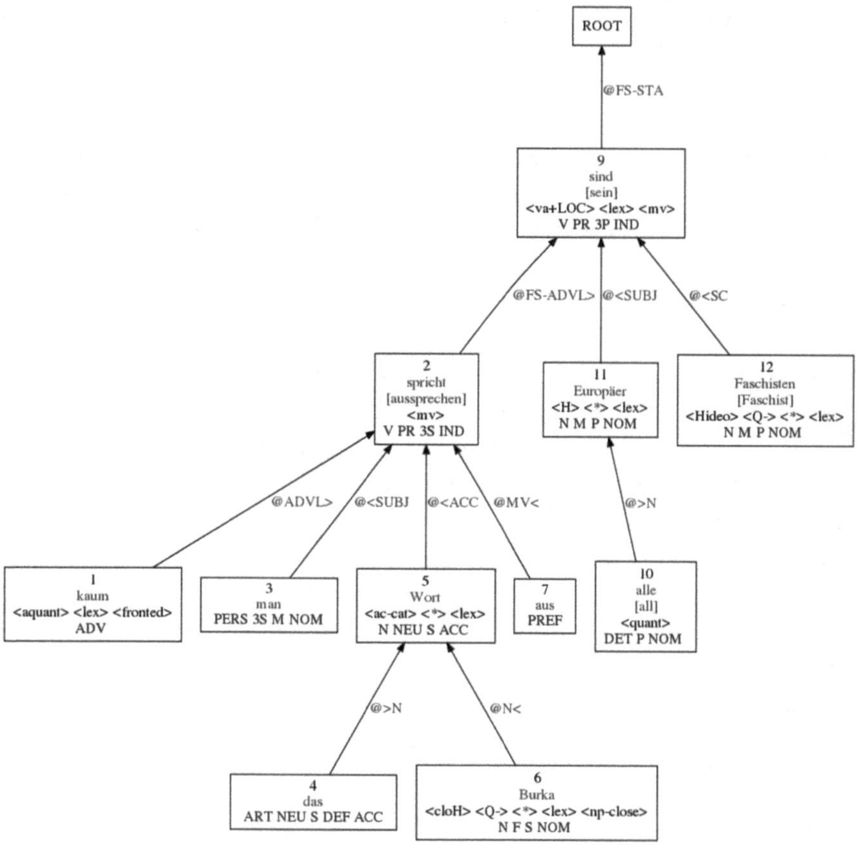

Fig. 7.1 Parse tree

Sample Annotation Fields

12 → 9 dependency link	2 → 9 dependency link
Faschisten wordform ('fascists')	*spricht* wordform ('talks')
[Faschist] lemma: 'fascist'	[aussprechen] lemma (with prefix 7!)
<Hideo> 'ideological human'	<mv> main verb
<Q-> negative polarity marking	<lex> lexicalised
<*> uppercase	V PR verb, present tense
N M P NOM noun, male, plural, nominative	3S IND 3rd Person indicative
@SC subject complement of 9	@FS-ADVL adverbial subclause of 9

Using measures such as relative frequency and mutual information,[9] it is possible to linguistically map potential concept features, for instance as adnominal or predicative collocates (to identify typical attributes) or subject/agent or object/patient relations to typical verbs (to identify typical roles). Similarly, the generalising—inclusive or exclusive—use of pronouns (all, we/you, our/your), and n-gram frequencies may help to identify stereotypes and identification/othering constructions, associating speaker-assigned attributes with either an in-group or an out-group. Although quantitative evaluation is inherent to some of these techniques, because they are based on statistical salience ('Collocation Studies' section) or mathematical models ('Word Embedding' and 'Using Vector Distances for Measuring Conceptual Differences: A Danish–German Comparison' sections), quantitative findings were not the only, or even the main, objective, and in many cases, corpus annotation was used simply to facilitate the inspection and qualitative exploration of a billion-word corpus. Thus, our first goal was to identify concepts, rather than to quantify them ('Qualitative Overview and Examples' section), using statistics only to support this process ('Linguistic Indicators of Conceptual Change: Place or Agent?', 'Europe on German Twitter' and 'Word Embedding' sections). In a separate, purely quantitative step, we tried to determine the scale of some conceptual dimensions ('Using Vector Distances for Measuring Conceptual Differences: A Danish–German Comparison' section), focusing in particular on place-hood, agency, statehood and shared identity, as well as cultural differences between the Danish and German data.

Danish Concepts of Europe

Qualitative Overview and Examples

For the qualitative analysis we used an iterative corpus inspection technique, where broad searches based on known keywords are expanded and refined in subsequent searches using salient words and patterns found through co-occurrence analysis and relative frequencies from the preceding searches. All in all, we found nine main conceptualisations of 'Europe' in the Danish social media data from the period studied. The examples below were chosen with an eye on the immigrant/refugee discourse.

The concepts may be ordered in a two-dimensional space with a ±identity axis (1–2–3) and a place/agent axis (a–b–c). Thus, in the upper-left corner of Table 7.2 we find a view of Europe simply as a non-Danish space, often perceived as a kind of Greater Germany (1a) or a European 'United States', an evil empire (1b), big and threatening.[10] In the lower-right corner is 'Fortress Europe' (3c), embattled and holding off the barbaric hordes at its southern borders. This Europe offers a shared identity based on shared fears and calls on agent metaphors (often involving fighting and conflict). This concept had particular significance in Denmark

Table 7.2 Danish concepts of Europe

- European identity +			
+ Place	1a) Greater Germany	2a) common market shared rules space	3a) identity via *negationis*: not the USA, not Africa
	1b) United States of Europe (U.S.E.), evil empire	2b) shared values shared institutions	3b) active othering home/we—there/they
+ Agent	1c) remote Brussels meddling bureaucrats	2c) cogniser, agent living being	3c) FortressEurope

during the 2017–2018 refugee crisis, because it suggested a solution to the immigration crisis, a problem that a record number of Danes ranked as one of the (two) main problems facing the European Union (71%) and Denmark (57%), more than in any other EU country at the time (European Commission 2016 [Eurobarometer 85]). Later, attention shifted to a shared-value concern (climate change), with EU/national percentages of 46%/26% (ranks 10 and 3) for the former and 43%/49% (ranks 3 and 2) for the latter (European Commission 2019 [Eurobarometer 92]). It is interesting that even in a low-threat situation, Danes still outrank other countries on the immigration question in the national setting (rank 3).

Another traditional Danish concept of Europe is that of a distant, but meddlesome, bureaucracy (1c). Here, agency is conceded, but common identity is not. Conversely, there is also recent evidence of a high-identity, low-agency concept of Europe (3a) 'via *negationis*', as a 'not Africa' or 'not the United States'. Agent-hood may be added by proxy, linguistically seen as othering (3b) (we—they/you, in here—out there), and often leading to a call for action and a Fortress Europe mentality (3c). As concepts go, the middle ground is represented by Europe as a (political) project with (market) rules (2a) and (human) values (2b). In the Danish discourse, the critical version of this concept, that of the meddlesome and distant bureaucracy (1c) epitomised by Brussels, is slowly giving way to a more positive and identifying view of European values, driven by comparisons with other, intrusive cultures. Sometimes, this process leads to linguistic personification, with Europe conceptualised as a biological entity (2c) that can die by drowning and that thinks, feels, suffers, wants and acts.

1a) *Værnemagerne har taget magten i Europa*

(The Wehrmachters have seized power in Europe)

egentlig burde Europa have fået nok af tyske førere(Europe ought to have seen enough of German Führers)

EU Europas Undergangs nye Diktator HR . Martin Schulz. Sig Heill(EU—the fall of Europe—new dictator MR Martin Schulz. Sieg Heil)

1b) *Glem aldrig den underliggende dagsorden; U.S.E United States of Europe. Europahæren er endnu et skridt på vejen. Spørg bare hyperføderalisten Jean Claude* [sic], *eller en anden ikke folkevalgt kleptokrat i Europakommissionen* (Don't forget the underlying agenda: U.S.E United States of Europe. A European army is yet another step on that path. Just ask Jean Claude [sic], or another unelected kleptocrat in the European Commission)

1c) *dansk lovgivning dikteret af EU* (Danish legislation dictated by the EU)

EU-liderlige politikere (EU-lusting politicians)

[Danmark] fanget i edderkoppens spind ([Denmark] caught in the spider's web)

2a) *Europa overlever ikke hvis ikke magt liderlige liberalister begynder at LYTTE til folket og vågne op* (Europe will not survive if the power-hungry liberalists won't LISTEN to the people and wake up)

2b) *Rædselsfuldt, at VI ikke stemte for forbuddet mod de midler, der ødelægger livet for bierne! GODT vi har EU!* (Terrible that WE didn't vote to forbid the substances that destroy bees' lives! So GOOD we have the EU!)

Hele idéen med EU er solidaritet(The real purpose of the EU is solidarity)

2c) *Europa graver sin egen grav* (Europe is digging its own grave.)

Europa dør …. Trist. Kvindeundertrykkelse er blevet til fashion.(Europe is dying … Sad. Oppressing women has become fashionable.)

3a) *retur til jeres Afrika* (back to your Africa)

derfor må Europa gå sammen med de øvrige demokratiske lande(This is why Europe needs to work together with the other democratic countries.)

3b)*de høre ikke til her i Europa* (They don't belong here in Europe)

de forpester vore lande (They contaminate our countries)

Bliv hvor I er—vi har ikke plads (Stay where you are—we don't have room [for you])

3c) *Hvis Europa ikke snart står sammen og bekæmper den erobring muslimer har gang i*(If Europe doesn't soon act as one and fight the conquest Muslims are plotting)

ud af EU og tilbage med de der nasser (Out of the EU, send back those parasites) *de prøver at koloniser os konstant* (They are constantly trying to colonise us)

Note that although these examples illustrate the various concepts, this chapter (in contrast to 'Using Vector Distances for Measuring Conceptual Differences: A Danish–German Comparison' section) does not make any claims regarding their prevalence. Also, concepts overlap and combine at the individual level. For instance, the meddlesome-bureaucracy concept is also found closer to home, in the context of the Danish state bureaucracy, and does not mean that Danes in general feel underrepresented in the European Union. In fact, according to Eurobarometer 85 and 92 (European Commission 2016, 2019), Danes score second highest (63% yes) on the question of whether they think that their voice counts in the European Union; this is true, given the numerical overrepresentation of small countries in both the European Parliament and the Commission.

Linguistic Indicators of Conceptual Change: Place or Agent?

Based on societal and political changes, and the growing newsworthiness of European/European Union topics in the Danish news media, our working hypothesis was that we would find the growing conceptualisation of both Europe and the European Union as acting units rather than places or (market) spaces. Linguistically, this should translate into a change from adverbial/location use to subject/agent use, involving verb frames that denote actions, cognition, emotions and physical processes, as exemplified by the following corpus examples:

Action Verbs

Europa kan kun gøre en ting, holde disse horder ude (Europe can do only one thing, keep those hordes out)

Cognitive Verbs

Europa bør … forholde sig/indføre … (Europe should … react/introduce') (Constructions with 'ought to', 'should', 'must', suggest conscious control of actions.)
Europa kan ikke løse … (Europe cannot solve …).
hele Europa begynder at fatte … (All Europe is beginning to understand …).
Europa begår selvmord … (Europe is committing suicide).

Emotion Verbs

Europa har fået nok (Europe has had enough)
Hvad med at Europa stiller krav (What with Europe making demands)

Biological Verbs (Animate Subjects)

Det stopper ikke før Europa vågner (It will not stop until Europe awakens)
hvis Europa skal overleve (If Europe is to survive)
Når hele Europa bliver voldtaget og misbrugt (When all Europe is being raped and abused)

Human Adjectives and Personification

Europa er alt for blødsøden (Europe is far too forgiving).
Europa er ved at vågne af sin tornerosesøvn (Europe is awakening from its Sleeping Beauty slumber).

As the Danish corpus was automatically annotated with frames and semantic roles, it was also possible to explore the conceptual location–agent shift in quantitative terms. In Table 7.3, sum frequencies for unambiguously 'human' roles (agent, speaker, cogniser, donor and experiencer) are compared with place roles (location, destination, origin and path). As expected, 'EU' is more associated with +HUM semantic roles than *Europa,* but based on a comparison with a news corpus that dates back

Table 7.3 Semantic role distribution

	Europa		EU	
	Twitter	K2010	Twitter	K2010
Word frequency (per million words)	197	214	427	280
+HUM roles: AG, SP, COG, DON, EXP	6.1%	4.3%	16.9%	20.1%
Place roles: LOC, DES, ORI, PATH	46.3%	57.2%	22.5%	27.1%
HUM/LOC ratio	0.13	0.08	0.75	0.74

ten years (DSL's Korpus 2010),[11] the location-to-agent change (HUM/LOC ratio in Table 7.3) is more pronounced for the latter, possibly because in many contexts, Europe is now seen as equivalent to the European Union. Together, the terms 'Europe'/'EU' are more prevalent in the recent Twitter corpus than in the older news corpus, with a large increase for 'EU', and a slight decrease for *Europa*, again suggesting that conceptually, the European Union is taking over the European space.

In light of the refugee crisis, it is interesting that although the concept-of-Europe change from place to agent is quite generalised, Danes are still split into two camps in their interpretation of this, where one calls on the European Union to act firmly and resolve the crisis, whereas the other insinuates that there is a hidden German/European agenda of actively encouraging immigration or even Islamising Europe. The latter is often linked to the concept of Europe as a 'wealth drain':

*Europa kan ik være verdens socialkontor (*Europe cannot be the world's welfare office)

Danmark ska selv bestemme hvem vi lukker ind i landet. EU ka rende os i R … !!!!!!!!!! (Denmark must decide for itself who we accept into the country. The EU can lick our A … !!!)

Europe on German Twitter

'We Europeans': In or Out?

As in the Danish discourse, Europe is a frequent topic in the German-language immigration discourse on Twitter. Thus, the root *Europ** occurs in 5% of the Tweets containing a word meaning *refugee*, *foreigner* and *immigrant*. 'Europa', with a frequency of 1000 per million words, is the most frequent term, followed by *Europäer* (350 per million words) and *europäisch* (250 per million words). The frequency of the demonym, in particular, is interesting, as it may be interpreted as a sign of a nascent European identity. It also marks a crucial difference between Denmark and Germany, as the corresponding Danish term (*europæer*) is very rare in the corpus. Similarly, the linguistic identity marker 'We Europeans' is almost non-existent in the Danish data, and more common in the German data (444 instances).

Inspection/statistics confirmed the suspicion that most German Twitter users had reservations about immigration: 80% of Tweets that mentioned refugees or immigrants expressed the desire to keep them out of Europe, 10% were neutral or unclear and 10% were instances of counter-speech.

However, in terms of discourse aggressiveness, and possible hate speech, there is a difference between 'keeping out' and 'throwing out'. We used directional prepositions to roughly quantify these two perspectives, comparing the frequency of 'to Europe' (*nach/til Europa*) and 'out of Europe' (*hinaus aus/ud af Europa*) in the two languages (Table 7.4).

Although in both languages the aggressive variant ('out of') is much less common, it is eight to nine times more frequent in Danish than in German, consistent with the impression received from the qualitative analysis, that the anti-immigrant discourse is more pronounced in Denmark. Similarly, place adverbs may be used to examine the extent of European identity: Does the speaker see himself as within, or outside, Europe? On Danish Twitter, the constructions 'here in Europe' (*her i Europa*) and 'out there in Europe' (*ude i Europa*) have roughly the same frequency:

Table 7.4 In/out perspective on Europe

Per million words	Danish	German	ratio da/de
Nach Europa *Til Europa*	23.4	15.8	1.5
Raus/hinaus aus Europa *Ud af Europa*	1.7	0.2	8.5

Socialismen som vi kender den ***her i Europa*** *kan muligvis samle stumperne af det Demokratiske Parti i USA* (Socialism as we know it here in Europe may yet save the day for the Democrats in the USA)

Men har Løkke så været ***ude i Europa*** *og søge opbakning til en regelændring eller er det bare tom snak?* (But has Løkke [Danish Prime Minister] been out there in Europe to seek support for a change in rules [on immigration], or is that just empty talk?)

But although the German data show a similar frequency for *hier in Europa* (here in Europe), there are virtually no examples of *draußen in Europa* (out there in Europe) and almost none for *dort in Europa* (there in Europe). For Germans, unlike Danes, it seems to be cognitively impossible to see oneself as 'not in Europe'. That said, many of the Danish 'out there [in Europe]' are used when speaking of sport, whereas the immigration topic may provoke an 'in here' perspective of Europe in both Danish and German.

Collocation Studies

Using collocations ranked by relative frequency, we searched for typical nouns and verbs associated with the concept of Europe in the German Twitter data. Table 7.5 shows the top-ranking terms for three different patterns: (a) nouns collocated with the adjective *European*, (b) verbs governing *Europe* as a syntactic object and (c) verbs that take *Europe* as their subject.

The nouns we found align broadly with the concepts of *Europe* suggested by Danish, with significant weight on political and cultural initiatives (concept space 2b and a less critical version of 1c). The space concepts of identity (3a and 3b) and the Fortress Europe concept (3c) become apparent in the verb+object relations, with a narrative dominated by metaphors of war, invasion and catastrophe (*zerstören* [destroy], *stürzen* [overthrow], *überrennen* [overwhelm], *überschwemmen* [inundate], *erobern* [conquer]). Europe as a subject has an affinity to cognitive (*beschließen* [decide], *erwägen* [ponder], *ankündigen* [announce]) and political verbs (*erhöhen* [increase], *verkürzen* [cut], *fördern* [subsidise], *verschärfen* [tighten]),

Table 7.5 Syntactic collocation analysis

Context	Search focus	Twitter hits ranked by relative frequency
europäisch (European) **@>N** (prenominal)	**N** Noun	Kulturerbejahr, Nachbarschaftspolitik, Datenschutztag, Zukunftsfonds, Identität, Flüchtlingspolitik, Kulturhauptstadt, Datenschutz …, Grundwert, Außengrenze, Mädchen, Schnapsidee, Währungsfonds, Filmpreis, Gerichtshof, Lösung, Bürger, Aufklärung, Solidarität, Kurzhaar, Zentralstaat, Bevölkerung, Pestizidverordnung, Leistungsschutzrecht, Geheimnisschutz, Referenznetz, Bürgerinitiative, Gläubiger, Leitkultur, Muslim, Plastiksteuer
Europa (Europe) **@ACC** (object)	**V** Verb	zerstören, verändern, islamisieren, stürzen, löschen, überrennen, fluten, kämpfen, rechristianisieren, schützen, überschwemmen, führen, erobern, übernehmen, spalten
Europa (Europe) **@SUBJ** (subject)	**V** Verb	erhöhen, kürzen, beschließen, erwägen, verhängen, unterstützen, erklären, prüfen, gehören, führen, verlängern, stärken, veröffentlichen, mögen, zerstören, verklagen, verschärfen, fördern, verkürzen, schützen, kämpfen, ankündigen

which is consistent with concepts 2a–b, 1c and 2c. However, although the human 'agenthood' of 2c, includes concrete action verbs such as *führen* [lead], *schützen* [protect] and *kämpfen* [fight], is not a prominent aspect of the biological/body metaphors found (*die*, *wake up*, *suffer*). Concepts 1a and 2b do not really seem to play a role in the German data; that is, Europe is not seen as an external power that threatens Germany, and certainly not as a former war enemy in disguise (France?), trying to dominate the country (a fear sometimes expressed in Denmark and Great Britain). It is also interesting that the European citizen and European culture are prominent in the Europe of values and institutions (concept 2b), with collocates such as *Bürger* (citizen), *Bürgerinitiative* (grassroots initiative), *Identität* (identity), *Filmpreis* (film prize), *Kulturerbe* (cultural heritage) and several terms ending in *-schutz* (protection). Finally, in both the Danish and German data, the Common Market concept of Europe (2c) is, somewhat surprisingly, not much of a concern, and even those commercial terms that do appear, such as *Pestizidverordnung (*pesticide directive) or *Plastiksteuer* (plastic tax), are more relevant to environmental or grassroots agendas than to the economy.

Word Embedding

As a supplement to traditional corpus inspection and collocation studies, we also drew on (neural) word embedding to delineate the contextual semantics of terms such as 'Europe' and 'EU', using the word2vec neural net technique (Mikolov et al. 2013) and the TensorFlow suite (Abadi et al. 2016). For each target word (or lemma), this method calculates a vector in a multi-dimensional space, where the dimensions are hundreds or thousands of other words that either occur (value=1) in the same text unit (typically a sentence) or do not (value=0). The method may be seen as a data-driven approximation of lexical semantics, where categories correspond to multi-dimensional vector bundles. In the bag-of-words approach, simple (sentence) co-occurrence is used as context, whereas the skip-gram method uses adjacent content words only. Vector distances may then be used to examine conceptual aspects such as term clustering (relatedness), and to compare Danish and German data. For instance, the terms 'Europe' and 'EU' may be interpreted as more synonymous in one language than the other, if their vector distance is smaller. In our approach, we used morphosyntactically analysed data, so content words were identified based on POS (N, ADJ, PROP and V), rather than by using a list of so-called stopwords (word exclusions). To further increase the quality of the training data, we chose a skip-gram model with lemmas rather than words, and dependency links rather than just adjacency. Both adaptations increase the number of instances per skip-gram, simulating a larger training corpus.

Once computed, a vector-space may be represented graphically. As Siirtola et al. (2011) point out, methods of information visualisation for large text corpora, although still little used in sociolinguistics, are an important means of making distributed/structural/quantitative information accessible to the human mind, and are more effective for browsing large data collections than inspection/reading or even frequency tables. In our study, it allowed us to identify groups of meaningfully related words that could be used to widen concordance searches, and it may also be used to identify candidates for stereotypes or concept clusters. Thus, in a flattened, two-dimensional map of the German vector space (Fig. 7.2), *Europe* and *EU* end up together with *Deutschland* (Germany), *Welt*

Fig. 7.2 Flattened vector space (1500 words), zoom detail (~ 50 words)

(world) and *Nation*, whereas *USA*, *Israel* and *Iran* occupy a separate space, an interpretation of which may be that place-hood (*Welt*) and nation-hood (*Nation*/*Germany*) concepts may blend together, and that *Europe*/*EU* covers aspects of both, whereas the cluster of *USA*, *Israel* and *Iran* evokes a narrative of conflict. An example of synonym clustering that is useful for widening concordance searches is the word group *Ausländer* (foreigner), *Migrant*, *Flüchtling* (refugee), *Asylbewerber/Asylant* (asylum seeker). That the bundle is located just below *kriminell*, *abschieben* (repatriate) and *Terrorist*, and below and to the left of Turkey and Syria, also tells an interesting story. Note that for illustrative purposes, Fig. 7.2 has fairly low granularity, and shows a 50-word close-up of a 1500-word space. With a lower frequency threshold and a consequently larger number of words, the synonym lists become longer, more terms may appear in the vicinity of Europe/EU and more traces of concept bundles may appear.

However, because of its dimension loss, the two-dimensional, flattened map is necessarily a simplification of the multi-dimensional vector-space, which sacrifices some relations in order to show others. Therefore, when examining and comparing Danish and German concepts of Europe, we will use true, pairwise vector distances (Figs. 7.3, 7.4, 7.5 and 7.6). For instance, the hypothesis that Danes view the European Union as a kind of extended Germany may be tested by comparing the vector distance between 'EU' and 'Germany' with that between 'EU' and other country names. As far as concepts may be reduced to prototypical terms, or at least to a set of potential synonyms, these terms may be used as proxies for vector distance measurements. Thus, this technique allows us to determine whether 'Europe' is conceptualised as a place/location or as a country/state, by looking at the vector distances between the term itself and individual or generic country words on the one hand, and prototypical place words on the other.

Using Vector Distances for Measuring Conceptual Differences: A Danish–German Comparison

'Europe': Statehood or Place?

One of the central questions in research on European identity is whether Europe is seen as (just) a geographic region, or whether the concept has acquired some degree of statehood, occupying a semantic space similar to that of country names. To determine this, we compared the 'Europe' vector to that of seven major countries and the terms *EU* and *Bruxelles*, and the common nouns, *state*, *country* and *continent*. In Fig. 7.3, the values given are 'vector similarities' between 0 (completely unrelated) and 100 (completely synonymous). The left-hand columns refer to German data, right-hand columns to Danish. For comparison, we provide 'calibration similarities', calculated with the same training parameters, for a set of noun pairs with a growing degree of semantic similarity:

'apple'—'house': 16.4 (*Apfel—Haus*)
'apple'—'food': 41.2 (*Apfel—Essen*)
'house'—'building': 56.1 (*Haus—Gebäude*)
'apple'—'fruit': 61.8 (*Apfel—Obst*)
'apple'—'pear': 69.7 (*Apfel—Birne*)

In the country comparisons, 'Germany' stands out in both languages, matching the (expected) vector similarity of 'EU—Europe' (or, for calibration, that of 'apple—pear'), and indicating that the mental–linguistic space occupied by the concept of 'Europe' resembles that of Germany

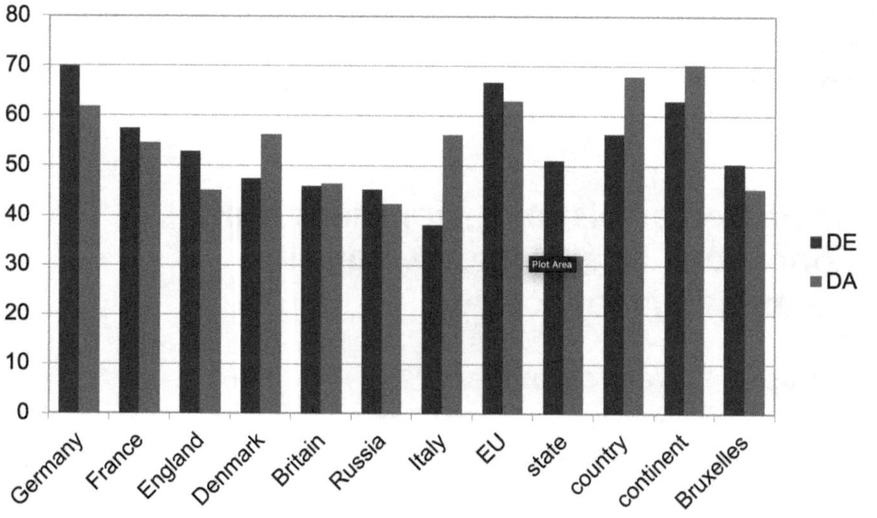

Fig. 7.3 Statehood or place?

more than that of other countries, or at least shares many of its functions and attributes. The pars-pro-toto relation between Brussels and the European Union is quite entrenched, with a similarity level that is higher than for some countries. Interestingly, the statehood test yields different results for Danish and German data. In the Danish data, the concept of 'state' scores lower, and the concept of place, 'continent', higher than any other item in Fig. 7.3. The difference is much less pronounced in the German data, with 'state' above the 50% similarity threshold. This finding supports the narrative about the Eurosceptic, footnote-toting, referendum-holding Danes and the nationally self-effacing, European-Union-paying Germans. However, although statehood represents a deeper commonality than place-hood, a third concept may be more important for conveying identity, and easier to develop than political structures. Thus, Chopin (2018) notes that it is difficult to build a European identity based on a concept of place, because neither Europe nor the European Union covers a distinct territory. Thus, the eastern limits of the European 'place' are not well-defined, and political Europe is a set of overlapping spaces (Internal Market 27 states, Schengen 22+4 states, Euro-zone 19 states, etc.) that cautiously uses the term *area* rather than 'territory'. He instead suggests that the 'Europe of values' concept is a more realistic vehicle for a joint (political) identity and claims that such a set of identity-building core values does now exist.

'European' (Noun): Citizen or Inhabitant?

In light of the foregoing, the demonym *European* is interesting, because, unlike 'Europe' and the adjective 'European', even linguistically it presupposes some kind of European concept of identity. In both German and Danish, the noun is morphologically distinct from the adjective and easy to identify. Figure 7.4 views the term through the similarity-filter of other demonyms, and also compares it to the statehood-implying 'citizen' and the concept-of-place-implying 'inhabitant'.

The first two column pairs suggest that for a German, the prototypical European is French, and for a Dane, he is German. Interestingly, Brexit or not, at least on Danish/German Twitter, the British share the same

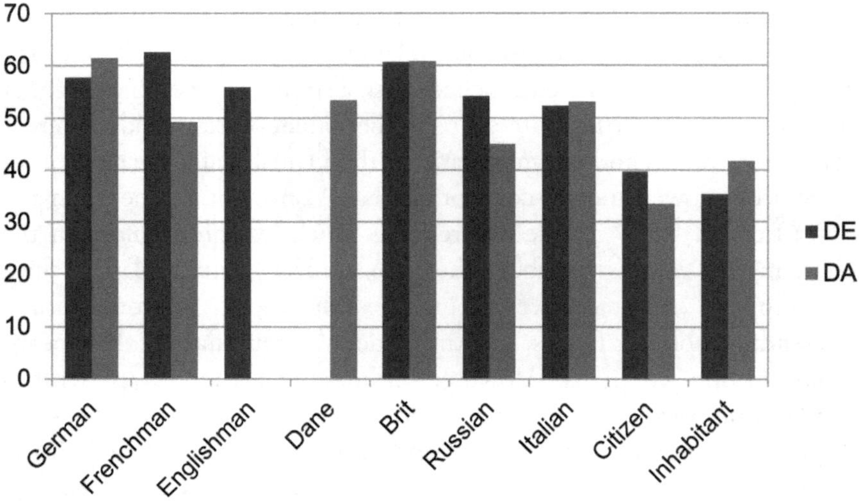

Fig. 7.4 Demonym similarity

semantic space as Europeans. The Danish word for 'Englishman' (*englænder*) (*briter* [Brits] is used instead), and the German one for 'Dane' [*Däne*] were too rare to pass the model's frequency threshold (50,000 most frequent words). The statehood test was positive for German (citizen > inhabitant) and negative for Danish (inhabitant > citizen). Note that this test measures the existence of the linguistic/mental concept of a European citizen *as such*, not whether one regards *oneself* as a citizen of the European Union when asked directly. Interestingly, in 2016 both Danes and Germans answered 'yes' to that latter question, with an almost identical 77% and 78% (European Commission 2016 [Eurobarometer 85]), but yielded lower and different values after the refugee crisis, with 72% for Denmark (rank 1) and 61% for Germany (rank 5).

'European' (Adjective): Specific or Not?

Demonym adjectives were included in our comparisons, because they may indirectly indicate the existence of a concept of European identity, measuring whether there are things that are perceived as 'typically

European' in the same sense as (typically) 'German cars', 'French wine' and 'Danish dairy products'. Thus, in Fig. 7.5, a greater vector similarity means 'less specific' (i.e. projecting less identity), because that would mean that there are few things significantly associated with only one of the adjectives. The fact that the German columns are shorter than the Danish ones suggests that the former have a better-defined, more distinct concept of Europe than the latter. This interpretation is supported by the comparison between the country (statehood) adjective, 'Japanese', and the regional (place) adjective, 'Asian'. Here, Danes score higher for the 'regional' interpretation of 'European', whereas Germans favour the 'statehood' interpretation (Fig. 7.5).

The very low German similarity scores for 'English' and 'Danish' may be explained by the fact that the former is also frequently used as a noun, to denote the English language (i.e. influencing the word vector by mixing language contexts with nationality contexts), whereas the latter is influenced by the fact that only very few Danish things are talked about in Germany (e.g. furniture and royalty).

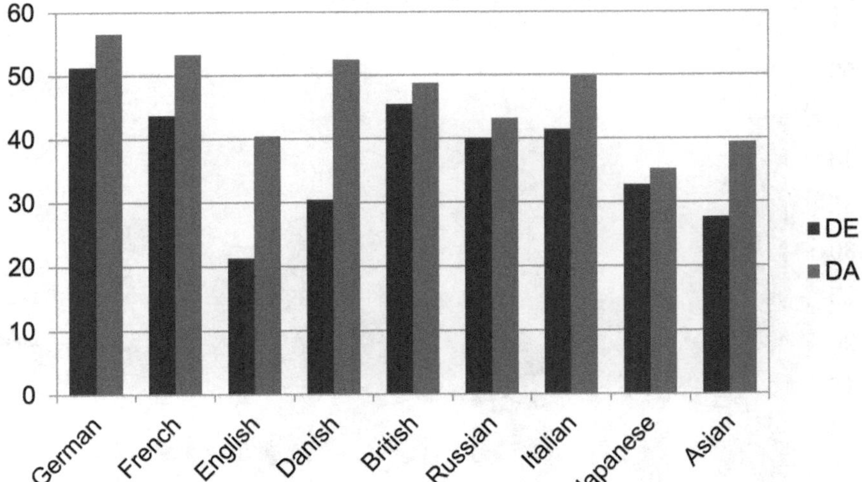

Fig. 7.5 Demonymic adjectives

A European Index of Corruption

So far, we have used word embedding to measure *whether* and to what extent there are concepts of Europe in Denmark and Germany that go beyond the concept of place, and involve some measure of statehood or national identity. However, a positive answer to this question does not tell us specifically *what kind* of state or nation Europe is associated with, other than indicating that Europe is perceived as more like Germany and France than Italy or Russia. Therefore, our last word-embedding analysis focuses on one more specific trait, *corruption*, prompted by the concept of a 'corrupt, aloof bureaucracy' found in our qualitative analysis.

Figure 7.6 makes it quite clear that in terms of corruption, the European Union is not Europe, with the former scoring much higher than the latter. In other words, Brussels is seen as approximately as corrupt as Italy, and although this is only a relative comparison, the vector space behind Fig. 7.6 corroborates the existence of the concept of a 'corrupt bureaucracy'. A secondary finding is that the German corruption judgement is much harsher than the Danish one, not just with respect to the European Union, but also for all other countries included in Fig. 7.6.

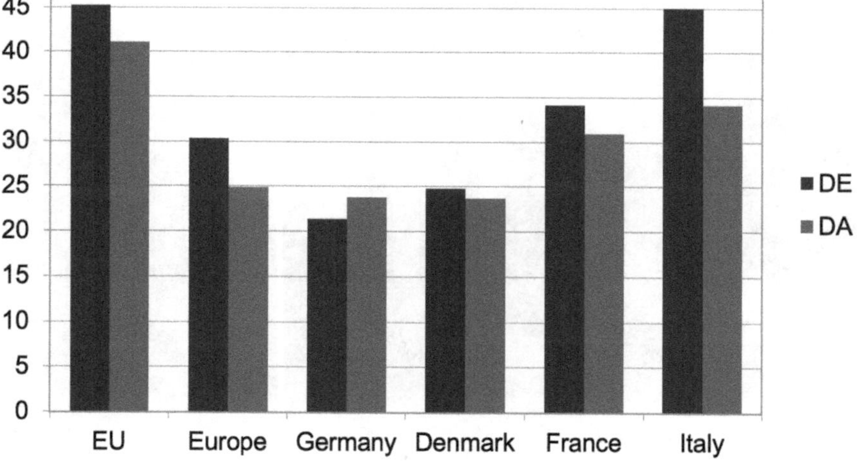

Fig. 7.6 Corruption index

There is only one exception to this—Germany itself. Thus, both Germany and Denmark are considered the least corrupt states, even—remarkably—in each other's opinions, but the human condition still prevails, and Germans tend to see themselves in a better light than Danes do, and Danes think they are less corrupt than Germans think they are. The shared Danish/German association of southern Europe (here: Italy) with an increased level of corruption is not unexpected and matches a stereotype also identified by Van Hecke (2017), who, in his study of European political cartoons, concludes that the Euro-crisis is perceived as a crisis of responsibility in northern Europe, whereas a crisis of solidarity is the dominant framework in southern Europe.

Conclusions and Outlook

We have identified and examined nine leading concepts of Europe that occur in Danish social media discourse, based on a qualitative analysis and examples from the period of the refugee crisis. A nascent element of European/European Union identity may be observed, as is a shift from constructions of space, to agent and experiencer constructions. Using quantitative methods—in particular, word embedding vectors—to perform a cross-language comparison, we found European statehood, citizenship and identity to be more pronounced in the German data than in the Danish data. Also, although the German perspective is positioned firmly in Europe ('here in Europe', 'we Europeans'), the Danish data also still clearly include a competing, more nationalistic perspective, wherein Europe is seen as a threatening and/or meddlesome *outside* entity.

It is not yet clear whether Brexit and the refugee crisis will have long-term effects on the balance among the various concepts of Europe, and whether recent events will accelerate the development of a European identity in the Danish and German populations. Nor is it clear, given Twitter's limited reach in Denmark and Germany, whether these findings are specific to social media users, or whether they are shared by mainstream media and the general population. Also, the advent of climate change as a greater threat than immigration could mean a shift in favour of the shared-values concept. Therefore, future research should aim to apply our methodology to further, diachronic data, and other genres and topics, and perhaps also include interview data, to reach those sections of the populace that still maintain social-media silence.

Notes

1. For a long list of comparisons, see https://www.nationmaster.com/, or, for a European-Union perspective, https://ec.europa.eu/eurostat/data/statistics-a-z/abc.
2. For instance, a rule that limits holiday home ownership in Denmark to Danes.
3. In English: 'Holger and his wife say no to the European Union', a long-lived campaign pun from the 1992 Maastricht referendum, playing on the first name of a Europhobic left-wing politician (Holger K. Nielsen) and the legendary warrior *Holger Danske* sleeping under his mountain ready to awaken and protect the Danish nation.
4. https://www.sdu.dk/en/om_sdu/institutter_centre/c_ccs/xperohs_side.
5. Search-word seeding is also an effective language filter. However, it should be noted that 'complete cross-section' applies only to the target language, not to a country's Twitter output as a whole. Thus, Tweets in Denmark are only 30% of Tweets from Denmark are in Danish, and 46% are in English (Laitinen et al. 2018). Although English is essentially a lingua franca in Scandinavia, it is still probable that in general, English Tweets represent better-educated people; arguably, the rest, mostly in immigrant languages, would present very different opinions and stereotypes.
6. These numbers refer to the 2019 version of the corpus that was used for this analysis. The XPEROHS corpus has since grown and incorporated data from a time period influenced more by the COVID-19 crisis than by the refugee crisis.
7. Parser demos are accessible at http://visl.sdu.dk, under the respective language sections.
8. The GUI used is a custom-made graphical adaptation of the CQP engine (http://cwb.sourceforge.net/links.php), offering an added layer of search options (e.g. dependency heads) and statistics (e.g. relative frequencies).
9. In probability theory, 'mutual information' is a measure for the mutual dependence between two variables. In corpus linguistics, this means

dividing the co-occurrence frequency of two words by the individual frequencies of the words.

10. Historically, this concept has its roots in a negative stereotype of Germany that is framed by Nazism and WWII, and in a broader timeframe, the Prusso–Danish war of 1864. However, as Hofmann and Hallsteinsdóttir (2016) point out in their questionnaire-based work on Danish–German stereotypes, this is no longer a dominant narrative. That we can find it in social media is relevant, but as linked to individuals and not representative in statistical terms.
11. This corpus was compiled by the Danish Society for Language and Literature and is accessible at https://korpus.dsl.dk/resources.html. The annotated version has 42.2 million words.

References

Abadi, Martin, Paul Barham, Jianmin Chen, Zhifeng Chen, Andy Davis, Jeffrey Dean, Matthieu Devin et al. 2016. 'TensorFlow: A system for large-scale machine learning'. In *Proceedings of the 12th USENIX Symposium on Operating Systems Design and Implementation (OSDI 16), Savannah, GA*, 265–83.

Bick, Eckhard, and Tino Didriksen. 2015. CG-3—Beyond classical constraint grammar. In *Proceedings of NODALIDA 2015, may 11–13, 2015, Vilnius, Lithuania*, ed. Beáta Megyesi, 31–39. Linköping: LiU Electronic Press.

Chopin, Thierry. 2018. *Europe and the Identity Challenge: Who are "We"?*. Fondation Robert Schuman policy paper: European Issues 466. https://www.robert-schuman.eu/en/european-issues/0466-europe-and-the-identity-challenge-who-are-we. Accessed 5 May 2022.

European Commission. 2016. Standard Eurobarometer 85. http://ec.europa.eu/COMMFrontOffice/publicopinion/index.cfm/Survey/getSurveyDetail/instruments/STANDARD/surveyKy/2130. Accessed 5 May 2022.

———. 2019. Standard Eurobarometer 92. https://europa.eu/eurobarometer/surveys/detail/2255. Accessed 5 May 2022.

Hofmann, Annika, and Erla Hallsteinsdóttir. 2016. Deutsch-dänische Stereotypenwelten im SMiK-Projekt. *Linguistik online* 79 (5): 323–346. https://doi.org/10.13092/lo.79.3348. Accessed 5 May 2022.

Laitinen, Mikko, Jonas Lundberg, Magnus Levin, and Rafael M. Martins. 2018. The Nordic Tweet Stream: A Dynamic Real-Time Monitor Corpus of Big and Rich Language Data. In *Proceedings of the Digital Humanities in the*

Nordic Countries 3rd Conference (DHN 2018 Helsinki), edited by Eetu Mäkelä, Mikko Tolonen and Jouni Tuominen, 349–362. Aachen: CEUR.

Mikolov, Tomas, Ilya Sutskever, Kai Chen, Greg Corrado and Jeffrey Dean. 2013. Distributed representations of words and phrases and their compositionality. In *Advances in neural information processing systems—Proceedings of NIPS 2013*. 3111–3119.

Ørsten, Mark. 2004. *Nyhedsmediernes dækning af valget til Europa-Parlamentet.* Danmark: Modinet, Center for medier og demokrati i netværkssamfundet.

Pew Research Center. 2018. In Western Europe, public attitudes toward news media more divided by populist views than left-right ideology. https://www.journalism.org/wp-content/uploads/sites/8/2018/05/PJ_2018.05.14_Western-Europe_FINAL.pdf. Accessed 1 June 2019.

Scheffler, Tatjana. 2014. A German Twitter snapshot. In *Proceedings of the 9th international conference on language resources and evaluation (LREC '14), Reykjavik, Iceland*, ed. Nicoletta Calzolari, Khalid Choukri, Thierry Declerck, Hrafn Loftsson, Bente Maegaard, Joseph Mariani, Asuncion Moreno, Jan Odijk, and Stelios Piperidis, 2284–2289. Paris: ELRA.

Siirtola, Harri, Terttu Nevalainen, Tanja Säily, and Kari-Jouko Räihä. 2011. Visualisation of text corpora: A case study of the PCEEC. In How to Deal with data: Problems and approaches to the investigation of the English language over time and space. Ed. Terttu Nevalainen and Susan M. Fitzmaurice. Vol. 7 of *studies in variation, contacts and change in English*. Helsinki: Varieng.

Sørensen, Catharina. 2004. *Danish and British Euroscepticism compared: A sceptical assessment of the concept*. Danish Institute for International Studies Working Paper 2004/25. DIIS: Copenhagen.

Van Hecke, Matti. 2017. Imag(in)ing the Eurocrisis: A comparative analysis of political cartoons. *National Identities* 19 (1): 129–147.

8

How to Strengthen Awareness of 'Europe': A Digital Analysis of Informational Material from the German Federal Agency for Civic Education

Kimmo Elo

Introduction

In the member states of the European Union (EU), the topic 'Europe' has a special status in primary and secondary education, but also as part of general civic education (Becker 2012; Keating 2014, 79–84). Understanding the essential facts and topics that concern the European continent's past and present is seen as an important cornerstone of general education and civic competence. This broader European context should also help us to understand the interplay between national and supranational political, economic and societal developments. Hence, in more general terms, educating Europe should contribute to the development of historical and political awareness among adolescents and young adults. From this perspective, learning about Europe may be seen as a part of (political) socialisation that seeks to educate people to become

K. Elo (✉)
Centre for Parliamentary Studies, University of Turku, Turku, Finland
e-mail: kimmo.elo@utu.fi

K. Gorbahn et al. (eds.), *Exploring Interconnectedness*, Palgrave Studies in Educational Media, https://doi.org/10.1007/978-3-031-13960-4_8

functioning members of a society, by providing them with some fundamental information about what is important and valued by a particular culture. Consequently, since the 1990s, the European Union has allocated substantial resources to political education, to strengthen civic competence and knowledge of (European) politics (Benei 2005; Becker 2012; Keating 2014; Hodgson 2016; Kennedy and Brunold 2016).

Europeanism is a central element of Europe's collective identity. This identity is rooted in a shared understanding of Europe's present and past, and creates an 'imagined community' (Benedict Anderson) of Europe. At the same time, there is a strong connection to a general knowledge of politics: without a proper understanding of European history, politics and contemporary questions, 'it is difficult for [the citizens] to understand political events or to integrate new information into an existing framework' (Galston 2001, 223; for a similar argument, also Downs 1957, 79, 234; Graber 1994, 334–35). In other words, sufficient and relevant knowledge of politics is necessary, when it comes to evaluating and understanding events, institutions and processes in the surrounding society and the world (Massing 2012).

During the 2010s and 2020s concepts such as 'disinformation', 'alternative facts' or 'hybrid influencing' have been used to describe modern threats and challenges to democracy. Ordinary people are increasingly subject to campaigns that seek to question political or economic leaders, or freedom of speech or the press. These developments are catalysed by algorithm-based social media networks, where users are fed customised information that supports their beliefs and opinions, and causes so-called internet bubbles to emerge. These 'bubbles' bring together similarly minded users, and strengthen their values, beliefs and opinions, but also increase distance and complicate interaction between people with different opinions (e.g. Garimella et al. 2018).

Many scholars see informed citizens as the foundation of a functioning democratic system, especially when it comes to political and civic participation (for a comprehensive introduction, see Massing and Breit 2003; also Converse 1975, 79). Although many studies have shown that citizens' factual knowledge of politics is remarkably varied (Delli Carpini and Keeter 1991; Elo and Rapeli 2008, 2010), trusted sources of information—for example friends, schoolmates, colleagues, parties, educational institutions—play an important role as 'shortcuts', that compensate for gaps in factual knowledge (Iyengar 1990; Lupia 1994).

This chapter focuses on the German Federal Agency for Civic Education (*Bundeszentrale für politische Bildung*, hereafter, bpb), as a public, government institution for strengthening civic competence. This chapter presents a computational analysis of Europe-related content offered by the bpb on its home page (https://www.bpb.de/). Hence, this chapter has two principal aims. First, it seeks to exemplify how digital data-mining methods may be used to explore a large collection of online material, to gain an understanding of the topics and themes that comprise the collection. In this respect, this chapter may be understood as a contribution to the digital humanities, a rapidly evolving field of research that seeks to connect the humanities to computational science. Second, based on the results of my digital analysis, this chapter discusses how the bpb presents 'Europe', and how the information available on its home page reflects the broader goals set by German and European civic education.

The structure of this chapter is as follows. The first section discusses the role of the bpb as a government institution for civic education. The second section presents the data and the methods used in the analysis. The third section presents and discusses the results of the analysis. This chapter is rounded off by a conclusion that summarises and contextualises the main results.

The German Federal Agency for Civic Education (*Bundeszentrale für politische Bildung, bpb*) as a Platform for Civic Competence

As a government institution for civic and citizenship education, the German bpb is somewhat unusual in Europe and the world. Founded in 1952 as *Die Bundeszentrale für Heimatdienst*—The Federal Agency for Homeland Services—the centre intended to strengthen the development of democracy and the self-organisation of the German people. Originally, the idea of establishing a centre for political education was presented by the US military administration in 1949, as a part of the denazification programme. Hence, the centre was deeply rooted in the legacy of the Second World War, but also in Germany's division and the early years of the Cold War. In the early 1950s, a political struggle revolved around the question of whether the Federal Agency for Homeland Services should be established as a successor to the earlier *Reichszentrale für Heimatdienst* (Reich Agency for Homeland Services) or as a new institution. The connection to the Weimar agency was rapidly dropped, with the argument that the Reich Agency for Homeland Services had failed in its task to educate the citizens about democracy. There was also a widespread, negative impression that the Reich Agency had, albeit unwillingly and unintentionally, supported the rise of National Socialism by strengthening nationalist, authoritarian political attitudes. Interestingly, the federal government's press and information services pushed for a concept whereby the Agency would spread 'state propaganda' as a part of government policy. Finally, the Federal Agency was established as a politically independent federal institution tasked with spreading and consolidating democratic and European attitudes among the German people. Carl-Heinz Lüders, head of bpb supervision in the early 1950s, noted that the bpb should concentrate on promoting the democratic and European idea (*die Werbung für den demokratischen und europäischen Gedanken*; Hentges 2012, 40). In 1963 the Agency was renamed the *Bundeszentrale für politische Bildung* (Federal Agency for Civic Education). The reasons for this were, first, that the concept of *Heimat* (homeland) was frequently misunderstood as indicating the 'politics of deported persons' (*Vertriebenenpolitik*), and second, the new name was to indicate and identify the state's responsibility for ensuring the effectiveness of democratic, political education (Hentges 2012, 35–38, 40, 43).

Since the 1960s the bpb has attained a strong, effective position as an important platform for civic education. At its core the bpb is—as the term *Bildung* (education) in its name indicates—an institution that is intended to strengthen citizens' political knowledge and competence. This objective of civic education is also included in the bpb's own guidelines, according to which the Federal Agency for Civic Education is a federal public authority providing citizenship education and information on political issues for all people in Germany. 'Citizenship education' in this connection broadly means educating and encouraging citizens to actively participate in society and in the democratic process. The bpb's work focuses on fostering an awareness of what democracy is and on furthering participation in politics and social life.[1]

Generally speaking, the above-mentioned self-understanding is consistent with the scientific definition of civic education, rooted in civic competence. Civic competence refers to a normative concept that identifies the people's ability to understand questions of, and participate in, public politics, and of the institutional, government arrangements for teaching civic competence.[2] The theoretical framework of this chapter draws on a four-dimensional model of civic competence (Detjen et al. 2012), which consists of a person's political knowledge, her political attitudes and interests, her ability to evaluate political questions and her ability to take political action. All four dimensions are interlinked and influence each other, for example, political knowledge is required to evaluate political questions or to take appropriate civic action, if one wants to participate in politics.

Conceptual knowledge of politics is the core element of one's political competence. There is an important, significant difference between this conceptual knowledge and fact-based knowledge, on the one hand, and on the other hand, professional knowledge. Conceptual knowledge is about understanding and categorising attributes and characteristics that are typical of political topics (Massing 2012, 24), about an 'understanding of processes and structural components associated with developing public events' (Genova and Greenberg 1979, 89) and about 'cognisance of the basic forces relevant to some given field of operations' (Downs 1957, 79). This conceptual, structural knowledge is—as Elo and Rapeli (2010, 141) conclude—'knowledge of those basic and rather unchangeable facts about politics (institutions, rules etc.)', which is mostly gained through civic education. First, a robust understanding of one's own conceptual knowledge makes it possible to integrate new concepts, or correct misunderstandings and misinterpretations, by abandoning or correcting incorrect or incomplete concepts. In contemporary politics, which are plagued by disinformation, false or 'alternative' facts, barefaced lies and widespread conspiracy theories, the importance of solid conceptual knowledge cannot be overemphasised.

Political attitudes and interests define a person's cognitive and affective orientation towards political issues, and may motivate one to act (Massing 2012, 27–28; also Barber 1984; Galston 2001; Davis 2005; Jensen and Espino 2006; Campbell 2008). An interest in politics has also proven to be one of the most important predictors of political knowledge (e.g. Holmberg and Oscarsson 2004; Grönlund 2007; Tranter 2007; Elo and Rapeli 2010). In turn, one's ability to evaluate political questions helps one to confirm or reject the truthfulness of political questions. This is often seen as a prerequisite for normative actions, such as reassessing one's political values and opinions, or actions prompted by normative assessments (Massing 2012, 25–26). Finally, the ability to take appropriate civic action consists of communicative and participatory activities. Among other things, communicative actions refer to participation in political discussions and debates, and following political communication in various media landscapes (internet, social media, newspapers, TV etc.). Communicative actions are used to acquire knowledge, to express political opinions and to learn civic argumentation and reasoning in various circumstances. Participation refers to voluntary activities, such as voting in general elections or being involved in civic protests or organisations (Massing 2012, 26–27).

When evaluated with respect the foregoing framework, the bpb may be classified as a government institution that seeks to foster its users' civic competence by providing up-to-date, fact-based material that covers a wide range of historical, political and cultural topics. This also accounts for the 'Europe' topic. Material published by the bpb is intended to help interested citizens to understand European current affairs. From this perspective, the bpb's material also reflects an institutional understanding of the most topical European questions and subjects of which its citizens should be aware and informed. However, although the bpb also clearly has the task of supporting civic involvement, its impact at the individual level is rather difficult to assess. Contemporary societies are complex, and individuals have multiple sources and channels for accessing political information. Hence, to generally assess the impact of a single institution is virtually impossible. One encouraging perspective is provided by Faas and Leininger's recent study (2020), which focuses on the impact of the wahl-o-mats[3] provided by several of the bpb's regional offices. According to this study, the wahl-o-mat provided by the bpb had a rather significant impact on young, first-time voters. This is consistent with the analytical framework, as the wahl-o-mat is used to obtain relevant information that supports the planned activity, that is, voting in general elections. We may carefully generalise this by stating that interested citizens may also use the bpb as one source of information about current European questions.

Material and Workflow

This chapter explores the bpb's German online material, published on the bpb's official website (https://www.bpb.de/). We explore online educational material available under *Lernen* (learning) and *Unterrichtsthema* (Topics for lessons) on the bpb website (https://www.bpb.de/lernen/themen-im-unterricht/). The educational material provided by the bpb covers a wide range of topics. We used the 'wget' web-scraping tools to gather educational material broadly understood as linked to 'Europe'. In this material, we focused on the topics *Europäische Union* (European Union), *Deutsch–deutsche Geschichte* (German history), *Nationalsozia lismus* (National Socialism, Nazi Germany) and *Wahlen* (election). We also decided to gather further material from other parts of the website, on *Europa* (Europe) from *Internationales* (international affairs), on *Zeitgeschichte* (contemporary history) and *Deutsche Einheit* (German unification) from *Geschichte* (history), and *Extremismus* (extremism) from *Politik* (politics), because those topics have a strong connection to Europe.

We collected our source material on 13 to 15 May 2020. The raw source material consists of hundreds of web pages written in HTML and stored locally as text files. Most of the collected web pages are lengthy text documents written by experts on the topics in question, but the material also includes shorter informative texts. The material does not just provide information about current topics, such as the refugee crisis or the conflict in Ukraine; it also delivers historical and political fundamentals and analyses, providing in-depth background knowledge, country-based facts or additional background information.

Once we had collected all the source material, it was processed to yield data. First, non-textual material, such as videos and images, was excluded from the material. This was a deliberate, method-based decision, as this chapter applies digital methods and tools designed and developed for text-based material. Second, all the remaining material was processed with dedicated Linux command line tools (sed,[4] awk,[5] pup[6]) to extract metadata and textual content from the collected HTML files, and to store the extracted metadata in a database, and the extracted content in separate text files. After this, all textual content was processed with the command-line tagger and lemmatisator, *TreeTagger*,[7] to annotate all textual content with part-of-speech and lemma information.

In the last step, all data sets were imported to the open-source statistical computing environment, R (https://www.r-project.org/), for further analysis. The corpus of the final material comprises 15,137 documents with approximately 32,000,000 words and approximately 104,000 unique lemmas. The documents were originally tagged with 7058 unique keywords, and covered a period from 2000 to 2020. For network analysis and visualisation, we used the open-source, platform-independent *Visone* software (http://visone.ethz.ch/).

As this chapter also contributes to the digital humanities—an area of research that fosters the application of computational science methods, tools and algorithms in the humanities and social sciences[8]—all analyses presented in the next section exploit specific digital methods, and are made with dedicated digital tools. The analysis begins with a geospatial analysis that analyses the geographic coverage of the material, followed by an in-depth content analysis that explores the corpus with selected text mining methods, accompanied by text network analysis that focuses on the thematic structures hidden in the corpus. Hence, the analysis section also seeks to exemplify and provide evidence of how computational methods may be used to explore a large textual corpus by distant reading methods, to gain various perspectives.

Results

Temporal Analysis

The publications of an institution such as the bpb, which is strongly involved in civic education, should fulfil two complementary tasks. First, it should provide its users with the elementary background knowledge needed to develop robust structural knowledge of current political affairs. Second, it should publish timely information about current questions, to help its users to evaluate and assess current affairs, to integrate new information or to correct misunderstandings and misinterpretations. Hence, if we inspect publication timelines, we may expect to find peaks every time something interesting happens.

Figure 8.1 supports this expectation, as evidenced by a relatively strong variation in publication intensity, with respect to various topics, and over time. However, this variation accurately reflects political and societal developments linked to a given topic. For example, the peak in 2009

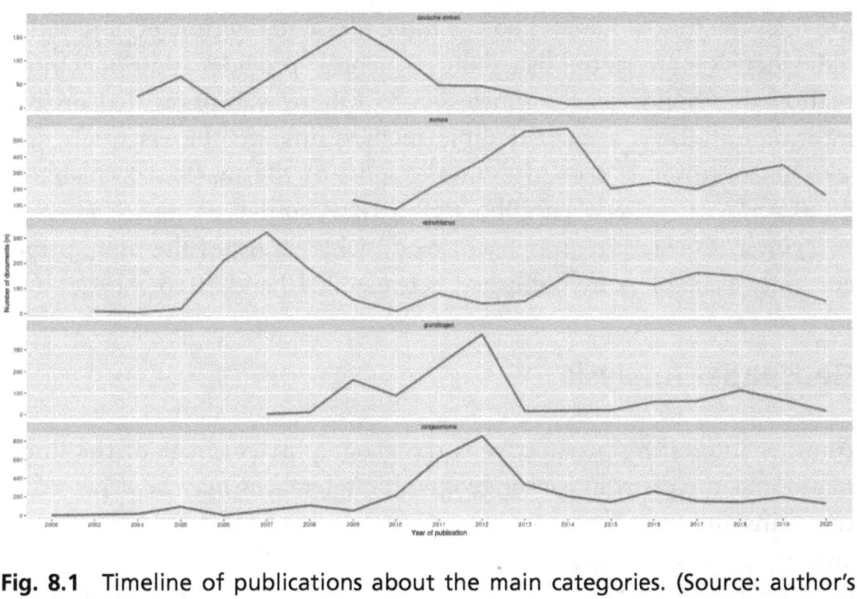

Fig. 8.1 Timeline of publications about the main categories. (Source: author's calculations)

publications concerning 'German unification' reflects the 20th anniversary of the 'European year', 1989. Another good example is the peak in 'extremism' between 2006 and 2008, reflecting the rise of right-wing extremist parties in Germany in the early 2000s (also Stöss 2007). A similar peak is also visible for 'Europe', around the European elections in 2014 and 2019.

Generally speaking, the publication timelines of various principal topics reveal three important aspects with regard to civic education. First—especially if we bear in mind that our data represents a snapshot of a brief period in May 2020—the bpb seems to successfully cover a wide range of topics, and provide a significant amount of information online. The older material still available online seems to consist of basic knowledge and essential facts, both being fundamental for the capacity to evaluate political questions. Second, the bpb responds rather quickly to current developments in politics and society by providing relevant material for those searching for information about current affairs. In accordance with the theoretical framework for civic competence, the bpb seems to provide material for knowledge-development and for becoming informed. Also, the timelines seem to follow a similar logic among topics. Material that provides the fundamentals about a topic is essentially timeless and rather old, whereas material published during a 'peak' provides additional information that builds on the timeless core. Often, web pages that provide information about a current topic include links to the essentials. The 'extremism' topic is a good example: most of the material available in 2020 was written between 2006 and 2018. A similar pattern is apparent in *Zeitgeschichte* (contemporary history), where most of the publications currently available were published between 2010 and 2016.

Geospatial Analysis

Another interesting perspective is the geographic coverage of the information, as the distribution of geographic references may be expected to reveal insights into the most important countries or regions. Hence, an analysis of geographic references in publications linked to 'Europe' may help us to understand which countries/regions are considered most important to Germany. To explore this question, we created a geospatial data set, first, by extracting all country or regional names from the data and, second, by enriching this geographic data with geocoding (coordinates). This data set includes all the countries/regions mentioned in the data analysed. The geospatial data set also includes information about how many online documents mention each country/region.

Figure 8.2 presents a geospatial visualisation of the world's countries/regions mentioned in at least twenty documents. The ten most-mentioned countries/regions are also labelled in the graph. Both the size of point associated with the country/region and the label's font size are proportional to the total number of mentions. Figure 8.3 is based on the same data and uses the same graphic effects, but the view is restricted to the European space, and the graph shows countries/regions mentioned in at least ten documents. In this 'zoomed' map, the twenty most-mentioned countries/regions are labelled.

On the global scale, *Deutschland* (Germany), *Russland* (Russia), the United States of America, *Ukraine* (Ukraine), *Frankreich* (France) and

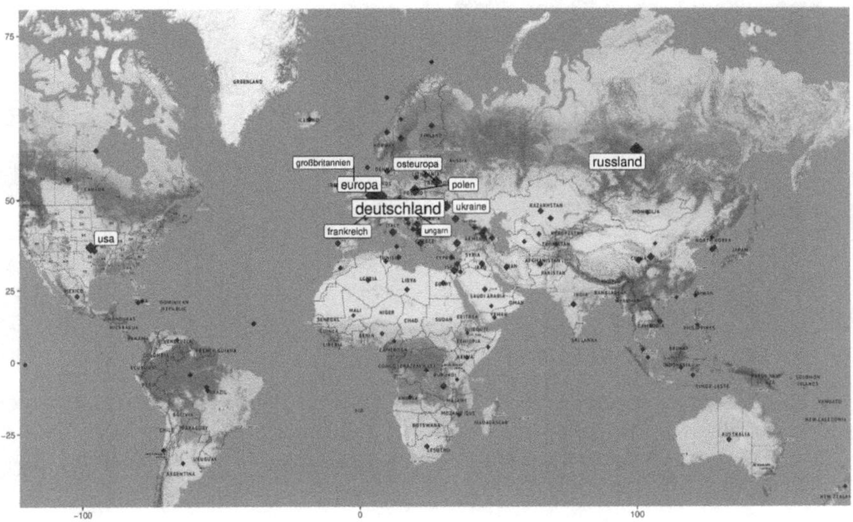

Fig. 8.2 Global geographic references. Countries/regions mentioned in twenty or more documents, the ten most-mentioned countries/regions with labels. (Source: author's calculations. Background map source: Open Street Map)

Fig. 8.3 Geographic references in Europe. Countries/regions mentioned in ten or more documents, the twenty most-mentioned countries/regions with labels. (Source: author's calculations. Background map source: Open Street Map)

Ungarn (Hungary) are the most-referenced countries/regions worldwide. Measured against the developments in global affairs during the past decade, this is no big surprise. With regard to Russia and Ukraine, the period spanning 2015 to 2017 marks a clear peak in publication activity, evidencing a clear link to the war in Ukraine and the annexation of the Crimean peninsula. The Crimean peninsula also belongs to the often-mentioned regions, and the 2014 annexation is clearly evident as a peak in the bpb's activities. With regard to the United States, the 2016 presidential elections seem to explain the peak. In the case of Hungary, the bpb's activity jumped in 2011, and has remained at a relatively high level since then, with approximately 50 publications per year. Here, too, a clear link to current political developments may be constructed: In 2010 the national-conservative party, *Fidesz*, won the national election, and Viktor Orbán was elected as the new prime minister. Since then, Hungary has conflicted with the European Union, owing to Hungary's negative developments with regard to democracy and rule of law, which violate core European values. Taken together, all these cases indicate that the bpb has reacted to current developments and sought to provide its users with background material and up-to-date information about current topics and political questions.

Since the Second World War, European integration and commitment to multilateralism have been the most important elements of the framework of Germany's international engagement. Accordingly, Germany has been willing to subject its political preferences and goal-setting to the norms of international law, and to integrate into the European political, economic and security-political structures (Maull 2018, 461–63). From this perspective, 'Europe' is also understood as a construct that manifests Germany's membership in a community with similar cultural and political values (Baumann 2010, 74). Based on the number of country references, *Deutschland* (Germany), *Frankreich* (France), *Polen* (Poland), *Großbritannien* (Great Britain) and *Ukraine* (Ukraine) are the most-mentioned countries in this European community. Also, *Europa* (Europe) and *Osteuropa* (eastern Europe) are among the most-mentioned regions. Although we may find references to most European countries, the geospatial distribution of the references accurately reflects Germany's most important geopolitical and economic European partners, especially with regard to European integration, and European developments and political hotspots. For example, not only Ukraine, but also eastern Ukraine (*Ostukraine*) and Crimea (*Krim*) are among the 20 most-mentioned countries and regions in the European space. Once again, the geospatial analysis indicates that the bpb reacts to current developments by providing informational material to develop civic knowledge.

Analysis of Selected Categories of Content

To better understand the informative content provided by the bpb, we applied standard methods of text mining to our material corpus.[9] We selected three themes—Brexit, Russia and the European Union—for a more focused analysis. Since the UK's 2016 referendum, 'Brexit', that is, the UK's withdrawal from the European Union, has remained a persistent topic in public debates. Four years after the referendum, many questions remained unanswered, and many new questions had emerged. Given this background, it may be concluded that the bpb has also regarded it as necessary to provide the essentials concerning Brexit, but also to continuously update the information available on the bpb website. The situation surrounding the topic of Russia is somewhat similar to that of Brexit. In this case, too, essential facts and knowledge about Russia and Russian–European relations are needed. Also, the conflict in Ukraine, the deteriorating relations between the European Union and Russia, and, in particular, the disinformation spread by Russia have created a strong need for a balancing counteraction to ensure the availability of fact-based and up-to-date information. The third theme, the European Union, is an 'umbrella theme' that brings together material somehow related to European questions. In our opinion, the fact that there is no separate 'Europe' topic in the educational material provided by the bpb reflects the fundamental role of the European Union in Germany's involvement in Europe. The broader 'Europe' topic is found under the main category of 'International affairs', whereas 'European Union' is included in the educational material.

The results of a comparative analysis of the three themes are presented as a comparison cloud (Fig. 8.4). A comparison cloud is based on term frequencies, and visualises the most important terms of each theme. Each term's 'parent theme' is determined by the maximum deviation between the term frequency in each theme and the average among themes. A term

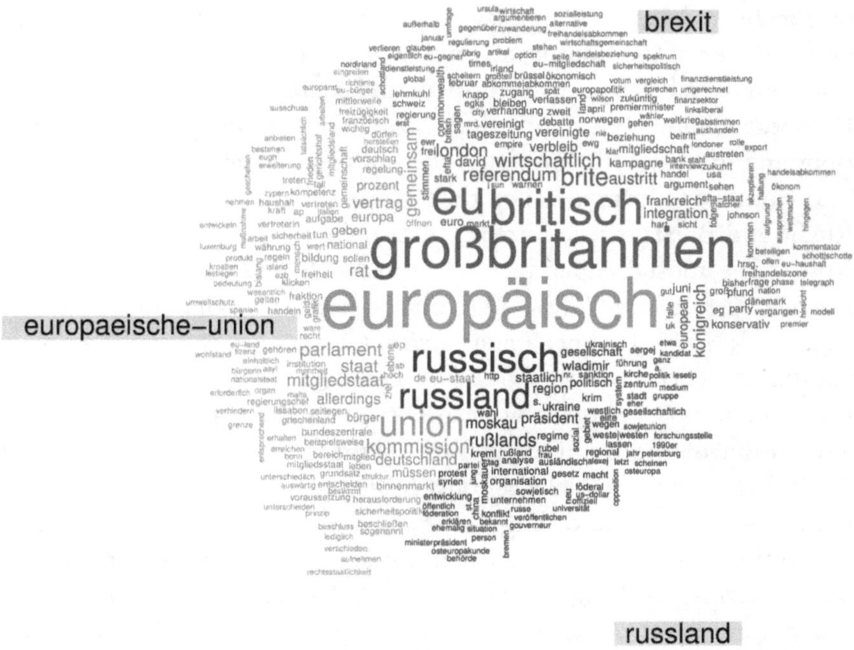

Fig. 8.4 Comparison cloud for 'Brexit', 'Russia' and 'European Union' (400 most-mentioned terms. Source: author's calculations)

belongs to the theme in which that maximum deviation occurs. A comparison cloud visualisation is an easy way to study the differences or similarities between two or more domains—here, among three different themes—by simply plotting the word cloud of each against the other. However, one should bear in mind that because the size of each term in the visualisation is mapped to its frequency within its theme, the sizes of the words are not comparable among themes.[10]

A closer look at the comparison cloud (Fig. 8.4) gives evidence of clear differences in the terminology used for various topics. With regard to the European Union, the most frequently used terms include *europäisch* (European), *Union* (union), *Komission* (Commission), *Parlament* (parliament), *Binnenmarkt* (internal market) and *Mitgliedstaat* (member state), thus indicating a clear link to European-Union-specific vocabulary and terminology. Also, terms such as *gemeinsam* (together), *Freiheit* (freedom) or *Rechtstaatlichkeit* (rule of law) connect to European values and the essential idea of the European Union as a value-based community. From a more general perspective, most of the material that focuses on the European Union seems to include structural knowledge about institutions and processes that underpin the European Union.

In contrast to its material on the European Union, the bpb's studies of Russia and Brexit reflect current political developments. With regard to Russia, the most frequently used terms include *Präsident* (president), *Moskau* (Moscow), *Kreml* (Kremlin), *Sanktion* (sanction), *Ukraine* (Ukraine), *Krim* (Crimea) and *Syrien* (Syria). As expected, the core vocabulary reflects the central role of President Vladimir Putin, but also the most important political events, such as the war in Ukraine, the annexation of the Crimean peninsula, the civil war in Syria and the 2018 Russian presidential elections. A similar structure may be found in material on Brexit. According to the comparison cloud, two topics seem to dominate the bpb's dedicated material on this subject. On the one hand, terms such as *Referendum* (referendum), *Commonwealth* (Commonwealth), *Premierminister* (prime minister) and *Johnson* (referring to Boris Johnson) focus on British domestic politics surrounding the Brexit process; on the other hand, vocabulary that includes *EU* (EU), *Austritt* (leaving), *Integration* (integration), *Freihandelszone* (free-trade zone) and *Handelsabkommen* (commercial agreement) is typical of studies of negotiations between the UK and the European Union concerning their future political and economic relations. Actually, it is interesting to note that the abbreviation 'EU' is used mostly in the 'Brexit' topic, and not, as one might assume, the 'European union' topic.

The comparison cloud analysis reveals significant differences in the vocabulary used for various topics. The results contextualised and discussed above were meaningful, and showed the usefulness of this method when it comes to exploring differences in vocabulary among documents in a corpus. However, the comparison cloud method is not so well suited to content analysis that seeks an understanding of repeated structural patterns hidden in a document corpus. To explore structural patterns, this chapter introduces an innovative approach that builds on the idea of using network analysis to identify the pathways of meaning circulation, and in text documents. The original idea was presented by Paranyushkin

(2011) in a method paper that described this approach as an attempt to discover 'repetitive patterns derived from the text's structure, using their connectivity and the intensity of interactions between them as the only criteria for their belonging together' (Paranyushkin 2011, 5). Text network analysis introduces an entirely new viewpoint for exploring the content of a document corpus, and seeks 'to identify salient words and concepts in order to extract underlying meanings and frames from the structure of concept networks' (Shim et al. 2015, 58). What is fascinating about this approach is its methodological simplicity. The researcher need only possess knowledge of how to convert textual documents in word co-occurrence networks and how to analyse network structures with the help of network analysis. As is evident in Shim et al.'s study (2015) of the identification of policy frameworks for the nuclear energy policies of six countries, Paranyushkin's relatively simple approach may be used as a powerful tool 'to analyse the hidden meanings of the community of words in an interpretive way as in qualitative frame analysis' (Paranyushkin 2011, 75). Paranyushkin notes another methodologically important point that favours the simple conversion of the target document into a network and first beginning the analysis once the network has been created. Many, if not most, of the abovementioned studies pre-process their source data with a specific text analysis tool, and visualise and analyse these results as networks. However, 'this is definitely helpful in gaining a better understanding of text, such an approach is also adding an extra layer of ontologies and complexity on top of the textual data [... and introducing] a strong subjective (and even cultural) bias into the structure of the resulting text graphs' (Paranyushkin 2011, 4).

Network Analysis

We selected one topic—'European Union'—for the text network analysis, partly because it fits well with this chapter's overarching subject. The network data were created from textual documents provided on the bpb's web page in the 'European Union' category, by applying a specific data-preparation workflow. First, we removed all stopwords[11] that is, words with no exact semantic meaning. Second, we filtered out all words except for nouns, adjectives and verbs. In the third step we created the network structure for each document by applying a sliding window method that focused on blocks of five words. The window started from the first term in the document, and moved forward term by term, until the end of the document was reached. In each window, the first word was connected to all other words in the window, resulting in four (4) collocations between the words in the window. The final, fourth, step reduced the network size by removing term pairs that co-occurred fewer than five times. Term co-occurrences (i.e. collocations, in the sense used by Stuart and Botella 2009) are regarded as undirected: that is, a link between word A and word B is identical to a link between word B and word A.

This chapter starts from the belief that a nonlinear analysis of textual data based on Text Network Analysis (TNA) can help us to better understand structural and thematic properties hidden in a large text corpus, and also to explore how statements are organised within and across contexts. One of the key strengths of network analysis is its capacity for presenting complex relationships as graphs (a.k.a. network visualisation) consisting of—to use the terminology of network theory—nodes and edges that connect two nodes (Ruohonen 2013; Feicheng and Yating 2014). In the following text network analysis, each unique word represents a node in the network, and each co-occurrence is represented as an edge that connects two words. As the human brain is an extremely powerful pattern-detection tool, graphic visualisation is also an important method for exploratory research.

Table 8.1 presents the most important structural properties of the 'EU' text network. The network size is determined by the number of nodes (words) and ties (co-occurrences). The network is modest in size, indicating the existence of a core vocabulary used across documents. According to average degree, each co-occurs with nine (9) other words, on average. A typical characteristic of natural language is reflected in the variance of degree, which ranges from 1 to 541: the distribution has a long tail to the right, indicating a structure with many words that occur rarely, and fewer words that occur frequently. A similar pattern applies to word co-occurrences measured with link width, which ranges from 3[12] to 457. The relatively strong links indicate that there are certain argumentation patterns based on selected words that are systematically used together

Table 8.1 Network properties for core text network, 'European Union'

Network Properties	European Union
Word	1273
Co-occurrences	5933
Average degree (min/max)	9.3 (1/541)
Average edge weight (min/max)	44.3 (3/457)
Number of communities/clusters (Louvain modularity)	16 (0.394)
Words in largest community (% of words)	305 (24.96)
Words in second largest community (% of words)	229 (17.99)
Words in third largest community (% of words)	107 (8.41)

Unit: number of words

across documents. In other words, material seems to rely on a certain core word structure that is used systematically, thus helping the reader to assimilate information about similar or related topics.

From the perspective of text network analysis, words (as nodes) in a text network may be categorised into four different groups, depending on their degree and betweenness centrality. A node's degree is the simplest centrality measure, and equals the number of connections between its node and other nodes. Betweenness, as the term indicates, defines centrality by analysing where a node is positioned within a network. Consequently, a node's betweenness centrality score is computed by considering the rest of the network, and by looking at how many times a node sits on the shortest path that links two other nodes, thus helping to identify nodes with 'a high probability of occurring on a randomly chosen shortest path between two randomly chosen vertices' (Hsu and Kao 2013; also Prell 2012, 103–04). Compared to Eigenvector betweenness, which is quite reliant on a node's connections, betweenness centrality depends on the node's capacity to connect two or more otherwise disconnected nodes. Considering meaning circulation throughout the entire network, the latter capacity is believed to be more significant, and therefore we use betweenness centrality to measure a word's status in a text network. As both Paranyushkin (2011) and Shim et al. (2015) note, analysing both degree and betweenness centrality is a suitable approach to identifying words that play a central role in circulating meaning throughout the entire network. Words with high betweenness and degree centrality play a meaning-circulation role, whereas words with low centrality measures are peripheral. Between these two extremes are words with high betweenness but low degree centrality, and words with low betweenness but high degree centrality. The former play an important role in connecting words between local communities; the latter, in turn, are local hubs within a cluster (Shim et al. 2015, 59–60).

The visualisation in Figure 8.5 shows the text network constructed on the basis of word co-occurrences in documents tagged for the topic, 'European union'. The original network comprised 4969 words (nodes) and 72,275 co-occurrences (edges). To improve the readability of graphic visualisations, all word pairs co-occurring fewer than three times were removed. The reduced network comprises 1273 words connected by

Fig. 8.5 Text Network of the bpb's material on 'European Union' (Layout: Quadrilateral Simmelian backbone layout. Node label size: betweenness centrality. Node size: word frequency)

5933 co-occurrences. On the one hand, this means that most words have been used together only occasionally; on the other hand, the relatively small size of the core network indicates that a relatively small number of words plays an important role in meaning circulation, also across documents.

To provide a more meaningful, accurate visualisation, we mapped the size of a node to the word's frequency. The size of the node label, in turn, was mapped to the node's betweenness centrality. As a result, words with a high betweenness centrality value—that is, words connecting various regions of the network—are easier to identify. Using betweenness instead of degree reveals 'the variety of contexts where the word appears' (Paranyushkin 2011, 13; for a more general discussion, see Puretskiy et al. 2010).

Table 8.2 summarises the ten (10) most influential words (in the table listed in lemmatised form) in terms of meaning circulation among documents. Considering the relatively strong variation in degree centrality values, these words seem to take different structural positions in the text network. Words with both high degree and high betweenness form the core vocabulary of the whole document corpus, and thus reflect the principal content of the bpb's material on the 'European Union'. It should be no great surprise that *europäisch*, *eu* and *union* occupy such a central position. Words with high degree but lower betweenness—here, *gemeinsam*, *deutschland* and *mitgliedstaat*, for example—have the role of a local hub that binds together words from similar contexts. In this case, these

Table 8.2 Ten (10) structurally most influential words

Word	Betweenness	Degree
europäisch (European)	113,218.158	541
eu (EU)	64,061.062	369
staat (state)	14,734.744	159
europa (Europe)	14,406.074	137
union (union)	13,777.237	236
gemeinsam (common)	6827.321	127
deutschland (Germany)	6726.061	97
mitgliedstaat (member state)	5648.245	91
vertrag (contract, agreement)	4774.47	71
komission (commission)	3561.038	65

contexts include various aspects of common European politics, Germany's European policy and the role of the European Union member states. From a methodological perspective, exploring words with high betweenness *and* high degree may help us to gain an understanding of general themes in a document corpus, whereas exploring words with high degree but lower betweenness may be helpful in terms of identifying thematic clusters in a document corpus.

A closer look at the co-occurrence structure of the text network supports the interpretation that the bpb's material is based on an institutional view of the European Union. All 'institutional combinations'—such as *europäisch–union* (for the EU), *europäisch–parlament* (for the European Parliament), *europäisch–kommission* (for the EU Commission), *europäisch–rat* (for the European Council) or *vertrag–lissabon* (for the Treaty of Lisbon)—are among the most frequent co-occurrences. Also, co-occurrences such as *gemeinsam–aussenpolitik* (for common foreign policy), *europäisch–integration* (for European integration), *deutschland–frankreich* (for the French–German dyad) or *deutsch–frage* (for the German question) strengthen the view that many documents provide fundamental knowledge of the European Union, European integration and Germany's European policy, and less about current affairs.

Cluster Analysis

One of the suggested key advantages of analysing texts as networks is bound up with the possibility of exploiting community detection techniques for identifying hidden structures in a network, by analysing the intensity of relationships between nodes.[13] We apply the 'Louvain method', a community-detection method that relies on the assumption that nodes that are more densely interconnected than they are connected to the rest of the network comprise a cluster or community (Blondel et al. 2008). The promising results presented by Paranyushkin (2011) and Shim et al. (2015), who applied the Louvain method to text networks for frame-identification purposes, encouraged us to test this method with our data. As the Louvain method is well supported by *Visone*, applying it to our text networks was straightforward. The results indicate a relatively high modularity throughout the documents (Table 8.1), and the network seems to be partitioned by relatively tightly knit communities. In other words, the text network structure consists of groups of nodes with dense connections *within* the groups, but with sparse(r) connections to other groups.

Words in bold indicate top-ranking words, in terms of both degree and betweenness centrality, that is, words that are central to meaning circulation throughout the text network

Table 8.3 presents the four main clusters of the text network, 'European Union'. The labels used to describe each cluster were determined based on words constructive for each cluster. It should be noted that the table presents only the ten most influential words in each cluster; the total number of words in a cluster is presented in parenthesis. The words were selected according to their betweenness centrality values, that is, the words listed for each cluster include the words with the highest betweenness centrality values. Also, salient words—that is, words that play a central role in the meaning circulation in the network—are marked in bold. These words are characterised by both high degree centrality and high betweenness centrality. Also, this analysis supports the interpretation that most of the bpb's material on the European Union focuses more on institutions and policies than actual questions. An exception is the third largest cluster, which consists of vocabulary strongly related to 'Brexit' and the Eurocrisis.

Discussion and Conclusion

This chapter has two main objectives. First, it seeks to exemplify how computational methods may be used to explore large amounts of textual data, to extract, analyse and visualise content and context-related knowledge. In addition to traditional text mining and analytical methods based on word frequency, this chapter exemplifies the utility of geospatial analysis for exploring the geographic coverage of educational material. Also, this chapter confirms the usefulness of text network analysis for content mining and topic modelling with an unstructured, textual document corpus. Although several studies have examined word co-occurrence

Table 8.3 Four largest communities of the text network, 'European Union' (largest cluster first)

Label	*Core words (lemmatised)*	*Total # of words*
'European institutions'	***europäisch, union, sollen***, *geben*, ***vertrag, allerdings, komission, gemeinschaft, parlament, rat***	*305*
'Global Europe'	***eu, mitgliedstaat, müssen, land, weit, groß, wirtschaftlich, wichtig***, *führen, besonder*	*229*
'Current European issues'	***geben, deutschland, grenze***, *klar*, ***großbritannien, euro***, *rumänien*, ***wahl***, *osten, bestimmt*	*107*
'European space'	***europa, gut, mitglied, gelten, möglich, frage***, *gleichzeitig, island, reisen*, ***truppe***	*96*

networks or discourse networks based on manually coded documents, our article illustrates how text network analysis may be exploited with minimal manual intervention, by applying digital tools during data preparation, and dedicated network analysis tools to explore the structural properties of text networks. Although the results are encouraging, both empirically and methodologically, the limitations of text network analysis need to be addressed. As Diesner et al. (2012) note, validating results may be difficult for densely connected, large-scale networks. Also, techniques for text pre-processing, node identification (words selection) and edge constructions (co-occurrence calculation) must be selected before mining network structure from text data, but 'could strongly influence the structure of resulting networks' (Shim et al. 2015, 75). In other words, different methods may produce different results, so that data pre-processing and network analysis techniques should be selected with care, and be closely aligned with research questions and objectives.

The second objective of this chapter was to analyse the German bpb as a civic education agency that provides citizenship education and information on political questions. Also, although the bpb's main target group is all people in Germany, its thematic focus is not limited to Germany or the German-speaking region. The geospatial analysis presented in this chapter indicated that the bpb's educational material has global coverage. Differences in the importance of various regions—measured against information density—seem to be relative to their global importance, although a small, yet understandable, bias in favour of Germany's most important partners is evident.

The results of the content analysis support the conclusion that the online material provided by the bpb is designed to strengthen knowledge of politics and civic affairs and to support the ability to assess and evaluate political questions. The exploratory text analysis of three selected topics—'European union', 'Brexit' and 'Russia'—highlighted the presence of both essential knowledge of, and information about, current political developments. The material on 'Brexit' that was analysed seems to more strongly reflect current developments, with the purpose of informing people about current subjects. Material on the European Union has a quite different design, follows a strong institutional approach to European integration and focuses on conceptual knowledge of the

European Union and European integration. Material on Russia lies somewhere between these two poles. The results indicate a moderate focus on current developments (Ukraine, Crimea, Syria, etc.), but there is also a dedicated domain that addresses conceptual knowledge of the Russian political system. To summarise—taking into account the fact that our analysis explored only a selection of all the information supplied by the bpb—the results justify the conclusion that the bpb is an institution that provides information and other resources that support all dimensions of civic competence.

Overall, the findings of our exploratory analysis presented in this chapter are promising, and offer interesting perspectives on computational educational research. We have provided results that present the analytical power of methods designed for the distant reading of large data sets and document corpora, especially when it comes to mining, exploring and analysing unstructured material that is available in digital form. We hope that our article encourages our colleagues to apply computational tools and digital methods, to improve and enrich our understanding and knowledge of topics, patterns and argumentative structures used in educational material.

Notes

1. Quoted from: https://www.bpb.de/die-bpb/138852/federal-agency-for-civic-education (accessed September 22, 2020).
2. It should be noted that the concept of 'civic competence'—or, as many scholars call it, 'political competence'—still lacks a commonly accepted theoretical definition. As dedicated reflection on these debates exceeds the scope of this chapter, the reader is encouraged to become familiar with the following literature: Remy and Turner (1979); Gaventa (1995); Popkin and Dimock (1999).
3. A wahl-o-mat is an online question-and-answer tool for comparing one's political positions with those of political parties or candidates, and are mostly used to help voters to find appropriate candidates (e.g. https://www.bpb.de/politik/wahlen/wahl-o-mat/294576/wie-funktioniert-der-wahl-o-mat, accessed August 12, 2021).
4. https://www.gnu.org/software/sed/.

5. https://www.gnu.org/software/gawk/.
6. https://github.com/ericchiang/pup.
7. https://cis.uni-muenchen.de/~schmid/tools/TreeTagger/.
8. For a comprehensive overview, see http://dhdebates.gc.cuny.edu/debates/text/30 (accessed 22 September, 2020).
9. For a general introduction to text mining with the 'R' statistical package, as applied in this chapter, see https://www.tidytextmining.com/.
10. Also see https://www.r-bloggers.com/2012/01/words-in-politics-some-extensions-of-the-word-cloud/.
11. Stopwords are 'terms that are widespread and frequent in any kind of text, and hence are not informative about the specific text content (e.g. articles, prepositions, pronouns)' (Ferilli et al. 2014, 118).
12. As noted above, when data pre-processing was described, the network data included only links with a weight of 3 or greater.
13. Both Fortunato (2010) and Wu et al. (2013) offer excellent comparative summaries of various community detection methods.

References

Barber, Benjamin R. 1984. *Strong Democracy: Participatory Politics for a New Age*. Berkeley, CA: University of California Press.

Baumann, Dominik. 2010. "Aufbau Ost" vs. "Röstigraben". Vergleich der Regierungssprache in Deutschland und der Schweiz. In *Wahl der Wörter—Wahl der Waffen? Sprache und Politik in der Schweiz*, ed. Kersten Sven Roth and Christa Dürscheid, 63–78. Bremen: Hempen.

Becker, Helle. 2012. Politische Bildung in Europa. *Aus Politik Und Zeitgeschichte* 62 (46–47): 16–22.

Benei, Veronique, ed. 2005. *Manufacturing Citizenship: Education and Nationalism in Europe, South Asia and China, Vol. 10 of Routledge Research in Education*. Florence: Routledge.

Blondel, Vincent D., Jean-Loup Guillaume, Renaud Lambiotte, and Etienne Lefebvre. 2008. Fast Unfolding of Communities in Large Networks. *Journal of Statistical Mechanics: Theory and Experiment* 10: 10008–10019.

Campbell, David E. 2008. Voice in the Classroom: How an Open Classroom Climate Fosters Political Engagement Among Adolescents. *Political Behavior* 30 (4): 437–454.

Converse, Philip E. 1975. Public Opinion and Voting Behavior. In *Handbook of Political Science: Nongovernmental Politics*, ed. Fred I. Greenstein and Nelson W. Polsby, 75–171. Reading, MA: Addison-Wesley.

Davis, Leniece T. 2005. Motives and Motivation: Social Context, Civic Orientation, and Political Behavior. PhD diss., University of Chicago, Department of Political Science.

Delli Carpini, Michael X., and Scott Keeter. 1991. Stability and Change in the U.S. Public's Knowledge of Politics. *The Public Opinion Quarterly* 55 (4): 583–612.

Detjen, Joachim, Peter Massing, Dagmar Richter, and Georg Weißeno. 2012. *Politikkompetenz—ein Modell*. Wiesbaden: VS Verlag für Sozialwissenschaften.

Diesner, Jana, Kathleen M. Carley, and Laurent Tambayong. 2012. Extracting Socio-Cultural Networks of the Sudan from Open-Source, Large-Scale Text Data. *Computational and Mathematical Organization Theory* 12 (3): 328–339.

Downs, Anthony. 1957. *An Economic Theory of Democracy*. New York: Harper & Row.

Elo, Kimmo, and Lauri Rapeli. 2008. *Suomalaisten politiikkatietämys*. Helsinki: Edita Prima.

———. 2010. Determinants of Political Knowledge: The Effects of the Media on Knowledge and Information. *Journal of Elections, Public Opinion and Parties* 20 (1): 133–146.

Faas, Thorsten, and Arndt Leininger. 2020. Wählen mit 16? Ein empirischer Beitrag zur Debatte um die Absenkung des Wahlalters. In *OBS-Arbeitspapier 41*. Otto Brenner: Stiftung.

Feicheng, Ma, and Li Yating. 2014. Utilising Social Network Analysis to Study the Characteristics and Functions of the Co-occurrence Network of Online Tags. *Online Information Review* 38 (2): 232–247.

Ferilli, Stefano, Floriana Esposito, and Domenico Grieco. 2014. Automatic Learning of Linguistic Resources for Stopword Removal and Stemming from Text. *Procedia Computer Science* 38: 116–123.

Fortunato, Santo. 2010. Community Detection in Graphs. *Physics Reports* 486: 75–74.

Galston, William A. 2001. Political Knowledge, Political Engagement, and Civic Education. *Annual Review of Political Science* 4: 217–234.

Garimella, Kiran, Gianmarco De Francisci Morales, Aristides Gionis, and Michael Mathioudakis. 2018. Political Discourse on Social Media: Echo Chambers, Gatekeepers, and the Price of Bipartisanship. *ArXiv e-prints*. Accessed May 5, 2022. https://arxiv.org/abs/1801.01665v2.

Gaventa, John. 1995. Citizen Knowledge, Citizen Competence and Democracy Building. *The Good Society* 5 (3): 28–35.

Genova, B.K.L., and Bradley S. Greenberg. 1979. Interest in News and the Knowledge Gap. *Public Opinion Quarterly* 43 (1): 79–91.

Graber, Doris A. 1994. Why Voters Fail Information Tests: Can the Hurdles Be Overcome? *Political Communication* 11 (4): 331–346.

Grönlund, Kimmo. 2007. Knowing and Not Knowing: The Internet and Political Information. *Scandinavian Political Studies* 30 (3): 397–418.

Hentges, Gudrun. 2012. Neuanfang staatlicher politischer Bildung: Die Bundeszentrale für Heimatdienst 1952–63. *Aus Politik Und Zeitgeschichte* 62 (46–47): 35–43.

Hodgson, Naomi. 2016. *Citizenship for the Learning Society: Europe, Subjectivity, and Educational Research*. Chichester, West Sussex, UK: Journal of Philosophy of Education/Wiley Blackwell.

Holmberg, Sören, and Henrik Oscarsson. 2004. *Väljare: svenskt väljarbeteende under 50 år*. Stockholm: Norstedts Juridik.

Hsu, Yi-Yu, and Hung-Yu Kao. 2013. CoIN: A Network Analysis for Document Triage. *Database*: 1–11.

Iyengar, Shanto. 1990. Shortcuts to Political Knowledge. In *Information and Democratic Processes*, ed. John A. Ferejohn and James H. Kuklinski, 160–185. Champaign, IL: University of Illinois Press.

Jensen, Michael, and Rodolfo Espino. 2006. Unpacking Education: Exploring the Links between Civic Knowledge and Participation. *Conference Paper, presented at the annual meeting of the Midwestern Political Science Association, Chicago, IL*, 1–28.

Keating, Avril. 2014. *Education for Citizenship in Europe: European Policies, National Adaptations and Young People's Attitudes*. Basingstoke: Palgrave Macmillan.

Kennedy, Kerry J., and Andreas Brunold. 2016. *Regional Contexts and Citizenship Education in Asia and Europe*. New York: Routledge.

Lupia, Arthur. 1994. Shortcuts Versus Encyclopedias: Information and Voting Behavior in California Insurance Reform Elections. *American Political Science Review* 88 (1): 63–76.

Massing, Peter. 2012. Die vier Dimensionen der Politikkompetenz. *Aus Politik Und Zeitgeschichte* 62 (46–47): 23–29.

Massing, Peter, and Gotthard Breit, eds. 2003. *Demokratie-Theorien. Von der Antike bis zur Gegenwart*. Bonn: Bundeszentrale für politische Bildung.

Maull, Hanns W. 2018. Reflective, Hegemonic, Geo-economic, Civilian…? The Puzzle of German Power. *German Politics* 27 (4): 460–478.

Paranyushkin, Dmitry. 2011. *Identifying the Pathways for Meaning Circulation using Text Network Analysis*. Research report, Nodus Labs. Accessed May 5, 2022. https://noduslabs.com/research/pathways-meaning-circulation-text-network-analysis/

Popkin, Samuel L., and Michael A. Dimock. 1999. Political Knowledge and Citizen Competence. In *Citizen Competence and Democratic Institutions*, ed. Karol Edward Soltan and Stephen L. Elkin, 117–146. University Park, PA: Pennsylvania State University Press.

Prell, Christina. 2012. *Social Network Analysis: History, Theory and Methodology*. London: SAGE.

Puretskiy, Andrey A., Gregory L. Shutt, and Michael W. Berry. 2010. Survey of Text Visualization Techniques. In *Text Mining. Applications and Theory*, ed. Michael W. Berry and Jacob Kogan, 107–127. Chichester: Wiley.

Remy, Richard C., and Mary J. Turner. 1979. Basic Citizenship Competencies: Guidelines for Educators, Policymakers, and Citizens. *Mershon Center Quarterly Report* 5: 1–8.

Ruohonen, Keijo. 2013. Graph Theory. Tampere University of Technology. Accessed May 5, 2022. https://archive.org/details/flooved3467

Shim, Junseop, Chisung Park, and Mark Wilding. 2015. Identifying Policy Frames Through Semantic Network Analysis: An Examination of Nuclear Energy Policy Across Six Countries. *Policy Sciences* 48 (1): 1343–1357.

Stöss, Richard. 2007. *Rechtsextremismus im Wandel*. Berlin: Friedrich-Ebert-Stiftung.

Stuart, Keith, and Ana Botella. 2009. Corpus Linguistics, Network Analysis and Co-occurrence Matrices. *International Journal of English Studies* 9: 1–20.

Tranter, Bruce. 2007. Political Knowledge and its Partisan Consequences. *Australian Journal Of Political Science* 42 (1): 73–88.

Wu, Zhiang, Jie Cao, Wu Junjie, Youquan Wang, and Chunyang Liu. 2013. Detecting Genuine Communities from Large-Scale Social Networks: A Pattern-Based Method. *The Computer Journal* 57 (9): 1–15.

Part III

Learners' Concepts and Reception Processes

9

'Europe' in Our Minds: Identifying Knowledge Models Using Concept Maps

Corinna Dettbarn, Jörg Kilian, and Erla Hallsteinsdóttir

Introduction

In Germany, the educational standards of the *Kultusminister Konferenz* (KMK)—a standing conference that comprises the ministers of education and cultural affairs—are crucial for establishing subject content and competence descriptions in the curriculum for each school subject. These guidelines are incorporated into the curricula of the sixteen federal states and are realised by defining curricular arrangements and content focuses. The curriculum content recommended by the Standing Conference includes *Europabildung in der Schule* (Education about Europe in Schools, KMK 2008), which is designed to foster students' awareness and understanding of Europe and prepare them for their role as European citizens

C. Dettbarn • J. Kilian
Christian-Albrechts-Universität zu Kiel, Kiel, Germany
e-mail: dettbarn@germsem.uni-kiel.de; kilian@germsem.uni-kiel.de

E. Hallsteinsdóttir (✉)
School of Communication and Culture, Aarhus University, Aarhus, Denmark
e-mail: ehall@cc.au.dk

K. Gorbahn et al. (eds.), *Exploring Interconnectedness*, Palgrave Studies in Educational Media, https://doi.org/10.1007/978-3-031-13960-4_9

(KMK 2008, 7).[1] However, 'Europe' is not a subject in its own right. Instead, 'Europe-oriented skills' (KMK 2008, 5) are to be developed through various subjects. Educational media are supposed to play an important role in this process.

When learners work with educational media, they activate their existing knowledge, that is, their individual knowledge is always the basis for acquiring new knowledge, which is acquired and deepened by reading, analysing, and interpreting, for example. The activation of existing knowledge and linking new knowledge to this existing knowledge is one of the most important and best-investigated aspects of learning and concept formation (e.g. Edelmann 1986, 210–11 on Bruner's concept of knowledge transfer; Montada 1995, 548–54 on Piaget's genetic model). Activating learners' existing knowledge of Europe (also in the sense of preconcepts, that is, ideas acquired before learning occurs) usually takes place in the classroom. This activation is mostly controlled by the teacher's instruction, which may also fulfil the function of an *advance organiser*, in the sense that Ausubel used this term (1974, 159–60). According to the actual state of the research, both curriculum guidelines and teaching practices primarily focus on declarative knowledge of the European Union as a political organisation, about its representative bodies, and about the relationship between the European Union and/or Europe and the country in which the teaching is taking place (Banneck 2014; Geyr et al. 2007). Thus, Bacia and Abs concluded that the curricula in at least one federal state in Germany—North Rhine–Westphalia (NRW)—have critical deficiencies in terms of developing a national and a European identity (Bacia and Abs 2017, 44). The curricula have no clear instructions for how to integrate or address the subject of the students' identities at the national or European level.

Studies of learner knowledge that go beyond examining their declarative knowledge of Europe often apply a rather restrictive approach to ascertaining possible values and attitudes to Europe. Those studies primarily use survey instruments such as knowledge tests and questionnaires (Ziegler and Reinhardt 2012, 11–24; Goll 2014, 125–37; Ziemes et al. 2017, 47–76). As learners are asked to indicate only the degree of their agreement or disagreement with statement items (e.g. 'I see myself as a European'; Jasper et al. 2017, 120), existing positions are reproduced, and possibly even become manifest. Learners are unable to communicate their individual knowledge, ideas, conceptions, and expectations, which may exceed the available response options. Thus, the findings are restricted by the survey tools, and some aspects of participants' mental models may not appear in the data.

This study aims to examine concepts and mental models of Europe as linguistic constructions of knowledge. To this end, we use the concept map as a survey instrument to determine students' linguistically bound knowledge of Europe, focus on lexical–semantic aspects, and interpret them as semiotic constructs of their mental models of Europe. Hence, the scope of this chapter is twofold. First, we test whether and to what extent concept maps are suitable instruments for collecting linguistically bound knowledge. Next, we demonstrate how the concept map survey provides analysable data about concepts of Europe.[2] Those concepts may be seen as components of knowledge (constructions of mental models) that correspond to the ACTUAL state of the learners' knowledge. Finally, we relate our findings to the recommendations in 'Education about Europe in Schools' (KMK 2008) and the teaching objectives (EXPECTED states) defined in the curricula of the federal state of North Rhine–Westphalia (NRW), from which the participants in two of our surveys came.

From Language to Knowledge with Concept Maps

If knowledge is considered in the context of teaching–learning psychology, a broad spectrum of possible classifications and definitions of various types of knowledge may be identified. In this chapter, we work with the constructs presented by Anderson et al. (2001), who regard conceptual knowledge as comprising complex and organised units of knowledge that do not occur in isolation, but are instead integrated into networks—for example, in the form of mental models (Anderson et al. 2001, 48). Thus, conceptual knowledge includes a knowledge of categories, classifications, and the relationships among them and helps to connect information, recognise connections, and relate to other subject areas (Anderson et al. 2001, 48). Anderson et al. emphasise the network-like character of this kind of knowledge by describing how conceptual knowledge of the seasons is mentally modelled:

> For example, a mental model for why seasons occur may include ideas about the earth, the sun, the rotation of the earth around the sun, and the tilt of the earth toward the sun at different times during the year. These are not just simple, isolated facts about the earth and the sun but rather ideas about the relationships between them and how they are linked to the seasonal changes. (Anderson et al. 2001, 48)

Conceptual knowledge cannot be understood directly, but is linguistically bound, and may be captured in its linguistic form. However, a distinction must be made between factual and language-related knowledge. There is a difference between the question, 'What does the word "Europe" mean?' and the question, 'What is Europe?' (Konerding 1993, 141ff.) when they appear in a survey. The first question aims to determine semantic knowledge related to the word 'Europe' as a part of one's linguistic competence. The second question presupposes the linguistically constructed existence of an entity called 'Europe', and demands encyclopaedic attributes, in the sense of non-linguistic information—so-called world knowledge—as an answer. The use of concept maps focuses on the latter. This facilitates a holistic, semantic description of the findings as linguistically coded knowledge, for instance, as developed in the context of frame semantics.

Our approach draws on frame semantics. Frame semantics determine and describe semantically encoded, encyclopaedic attributes. These attributes fulfil the representational function of language, and may be interpreted as lexically bound knowledge of meaning (Konerding 1993, 161ff.). The representational function of the meanings of lexemes comprises the entirety of our stereotypical, everyday knowledge. It also includes expert knowledge related to an object, or facts that we learn at school. These aspects of knowledge correspond to what Anderson et al. (2001) call 'conceptual knowledge'.

When concept maps are used to determine learners' representational–functional knowledge (or 'conceptual knowledge'), a keyword prompt is provided as a cognitive stimulus. Then the elicited 'ideas' and 'associations' identified in the linguistic data are interpreted as parts of the cognitive structures associated with the lexical stimulus. Thus, one may interpret the initial keyword as the central node of a knowledge framework that activates a number of other nodes connected to it as components of a mental model. The linguistic data may be interpreted as declarative knowledge, as existing knowledge, in the sense of a preconcept, or even as more elaborated, declarative knowledge acquired at school. Also, associations, affects, and emotions may be linguistically encoded and then indicate associative–semantic stereotypes, which are individually or collectively connected to a language sign (Kilian 2005). Often, the boundaries between intersubjectively verifiable declarative knowledge and associative–semantic stereotypes are not clearly distinguishable (e.g. the concept, 'Europeans are rich').

With respect to conceptual knowledge, concept maps are not used to determine linguistically formed preconcepts (i.e. learners' pre-instruction ideas). For example, with regard to institutionally defined skills, these may identify incorrect or incomplete concepts. Also, attitudes arising from extracurricular teaching–learning settings may be revealed, as may subjective beliefs that are closely linked to questions of identification with a (European, local, global) community, such as pride, respect, or shame (Bacia and Abs 2017, 33). Thus, the open survey instrument (see section 'Degree of Directedness: Open and Closed Tasks') has the potential to elicit not only (socially and/or educationally expected) declarative and conceptual knowledge of Europe but also subjective theories, emotional and affective elements, and evaluative stereotypes. Precisely for this reason, concept maps may make it possible to draw important conclusions about elements of concepts and mental models of Europe. Moreover, the data may offer insights into aspects of a European identity. Thus, a reconstruction of aspects of study participants' 'European identity' (KMK 2008, 7) may even be interpreted in relation to existing constructs of Europe (Quenzel 2005, 98–136).

Using Concept Maps to Capture Concepts of Europe

General Background on Concept Maps

The use of concept maps is an approach in which the participants form a kind of network by writing words in ellipses (the so-called nodes) and then connect the words with directional lines (the so-called edges). The participants label the connecting lines, which are interpreted as semantic relationships in a later step, with prepositions, conjunctions, or verbs that indicate the relationships between the nodes (Brüning and Saum 2019).

Concept mapping differs from other mapping techniques (such as clusters or mind maps) primarily in requiring the connecting lines to be clearly labelled, so that 'the focus of the method is on the representation of interdependencies and connections' (Dunker 2017, 130). Dunker (2017, 130) points out that requiring the connecting lines to be labelled is accompanied by a high cognitive demand:

> The structuring function of concept maps is one of its great strengths. The process of construction plays a major role here, as important decisions have to be made with regard to the selection and connection of the individual concepts. This is possible only if there has been deeper reflection on the content.
>
> (*Die Strukturierungsfunktion von Concept Maps ist eine ihrer großen Stärken. Der Prozess der Konstruktion spielt dabei eine große Rolle, da hier wichtige Entscheidungen im Hinblick auf die Auswahl und die Verbindung der einzelnen Konzepte getroffen werden müssen. Dies ist nur möglich, wenn zuvor eine vertiefte Reflexion der Inhalte stattgefunden hat.*)

For example, a concept map of the topic of 'Europe' might look like that shown in Fig. 9.1.

Using concept maps to represent knowledge structures is based on the cognitive–psychological assumption that semantic memory functions as a similar array of nodes and connecting lines, whose lexical units in the mental lexicon are arranged in a network and interconnected in a variety of ways (Aitchison 1997, 105–25). Thus, the design of a concept map

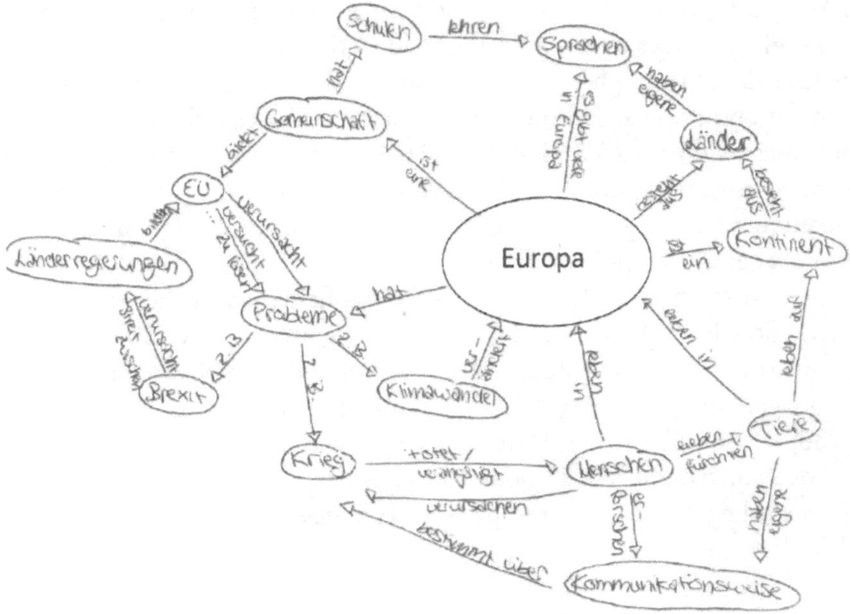

Fig. 9.1 Example of a concept map on the concept of Europe

resembles an active (reconstruction) process in which a person attempts to visualise his or her linguistically bound, semantic–encyclopaedic knowledge of a specific subject area. This will never be a 1:1 image of cognitive structures, or even 'objectively' ascertainable knowledge (Barte et al. 2020, 83); instead, it should be regarded as 'the result of an attempt of a directed reconstruction process' (Ziem 2008, 39):

> Concept mapping techniques are interpreted as representative of students' knowledge structures and so might provide one possible means of tapping into a student's conceptual knowledge structure. (Yin et al. 2005, 166)

Nowadays, the concept map is used not only in teaching–learning situations but also in research as an important tool for gathering, structuring, and presenting knowledge. As far back as the early 1970s, Joseph Novak used concept maps to improve the structure of interview transcripts and to obtain a better understanding of the changes in the participants' knowledge (Novak and Cañas 2008, 2). Cognitive psychology and linguistics research findings led to the idea of modelling semantic knowledge through graphical networks. This idea became increasingly popular and popularised the use of concept maps, especially for didactic purposes (e.g. Frey 2010; Dunker 2010), for example, in the sense of an advance organiser tool (Ausubel 1960).[3] In contrast to other mapping techniques, concept maps are still rather uncommon in didactic approaches to the topic of 'Europe'.

As a research tool, the concept map was first used in the natural sciences (Stracke 2004; Graf 2014), before being used to determine learners' pre-instruction ideas in studies that focus on didactics related to politics, language, and history (Hahn-Laudenberg 2017; Barte et al. 2020; Landgraf (unpublished)). Here, we explore concept maps as instruments for detecting linguistically bound models of knowledge by interpreting the lexical data from the concept maps as representations of mental models of Europe.

Concept Maps as Survey Instruments

The use of the concept map as a survey instrument for research involves a number of methodological decisions, which will be presented and discussed in this section. We wish to situate the concept map formats we chose for our pilot studies of the research landscape and to highlight the rich diversity of this instrument.

Usually, concept maps are classified according to the dimensions task, response format, and analysis process (Ruiz-Primo et al. 2001, 99). Next, we discuss aspects of the first two dimensions, and the analyses are presented below.

Degree of Directedness: Open and Closed Tasks

The types of tasks in concept mapping range from open (low directed) to closed (high directed). The type depends on whether or not the nodes and connecting lines and the structure of the concept map are predefined. Figure 9.2 illustrates the spectrum from closed (marked 'high' on the scale) to open ('low') tasks.

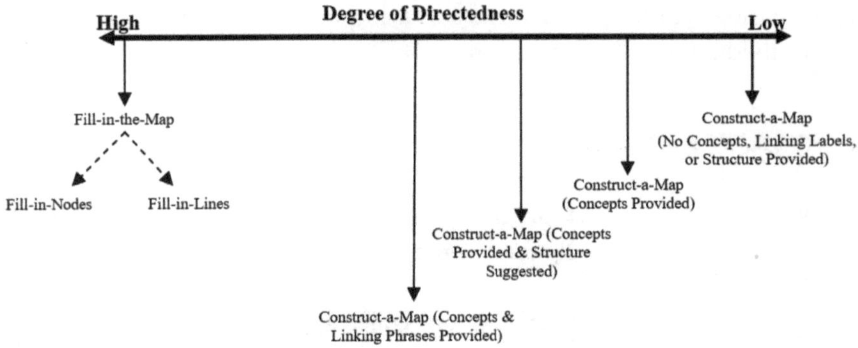

Fig. 9.2 The spectrum of open to closed tasks (Ruiz-Primo 2004, 3)

The scale is regarded as a continuum that includes various possibilities in terms of restriction and gradations of the degree of directedness. In research, it is believed that knowledge structures may be more validly mapped if an open task format is available, which does not restrict the person working on the concept map by imposing predefined structures on the creation of the map (Hahn-Laudenberg 2017, 94). The necessity of verbalising one's ideas and thoughts leads to a deeper and more reflective examination of a subject (Hahn-Laudenberg 2017, 95). An open task format also allows 'a more precise (re)construction of subjective conceptual structures; the resulting map corresponds more to the individual representation of knowledge' (Hahn-Laudenberg 2017, 95). However, owing to the absence of restrictions, the complexity of the task may also overwhelm the participants, who may lose focus when working on the concept map (Ruiz-Primo et al. 2001, 102). This leads to descriptive, rather than explanatory, maps (Hahn-Laudenberg 2017, 95).

With a restrictive task format, where nodes and connecting lines are predefined, aspects of knowledge relevant to the question under discussion may be determined more specifically, with respect to the content. This ensures greater reliability: 'The more directed the task the easier the assessment is to grade and thus reliability and task directness increase proportionally' (Himangshu and Cassata-Widera 2010, 59). This format may be suitable for determining whether terms relevant to a topic may be arranged and correctly contextualised; however, it seems unsuited to the epistemological focus of this study, as it imposes too many restrictions on the individual use of lexical forms.

Focus Questions

A *focus question*, that is, an introductory question, may help to avoid overwhelming the participants, as mentioned above:

> A good way to define the context for a concept map is to construct a *Focus Question*, that is, a question that clearly specifies the problem or issue the concept map should have to resolve. Every concept map responds to a focus question, and a good focus question can lead to a much richer concept map. (Cañas and Novak 2006, 10–11)

The exact formulation of the focus question must be carefully selected because it may significantly affect the focus and quality of a concept map. Derbentseva et al. (2006) show that participants that answer the key question, 'How does a car work?', generate more comprehensive concept maps with more dynamic propositions than those who answer the key question, 'What is a car?'.[4] Miller and Cañas (2008) confirm this finding and recommend a question that requires both a factual explanation and draws on personal experience: 'the more open to personal experience and the more demanding of explanation a focus question, the more explicative the resulting propositions in the corresponding map' (Miller and Cañas 2008, 7). However, Cañas and Novak (2012, 250) note the difficulty of analysing data that are yielded by an open focus question. In this case, a comparative quantitative analysis of aspects of content is possible only to a limited extent, and is very complex (Hahn-Laudenberg 2017, 95).

Response Format

Response format refers to the way the words the students add to the concept maps are processed during data collection, and the tools used to create the concept map. Concept maps may be produced digitally or with paper and pencil. For example, the digital program, *CoMapEd*, allows concept maps created on any internet-compatible device to subsequently trace the individual processing sequence and to individually adapt the task (Mühling 2014, 149–56). The maps are readily modified, as participants may easily move nodes and connecting lines and also use colour marking. Using paper and pencil is less flexible because it is more difficult to make changes to the concept map. As Stracke (2004, 61) points out, establishing the connecting lines at an early stage may impose unintended restrictions on the participants' mental activity. The minimal necessary preparation and material costs of paper and pencil, and the students' familiarity with them, are the main reasons these were chosen for testing concept maps in the pilot studies discussed here.

Training in Concept Mapping

As concept mapping is a method by which participants become self-directed and are not guided through a survey—as is the case with an interview or questionnaire, for example—it is advisable to practise concept mapping in advance to minimise possible method effects and ensure a reliable outcome. As the current research shows, this step is essential, because

> if the participants cannot use the method with certainty, generally, the results obtained are not valid. If, for example, an attempt is made to ascertain learning progress with concept mapping, and the test group does not yet have sufficient command of the procedure before the start of the intervention, both the learning progress and the progress of mastering the procedure are measured. Thus, one has two confounding variables. (Graf 2014, 330)
>
> (… *wenn die Probanden die Methode nicht sicher anwenden können, sind die erzielten Ergebnisse grundsätzlich nicht valide. Versucht man beispielsweise den Lernfortschritt mit Concept Mapping zu erheben und die Versuchsgruppe beherrscht das Verfahren vor Beginn der Intervention noch nicht hinreichend, wird nicht nur der Lernfortschritt, sondern auch der Fortschritt in der Beherrschung des Verfahrens gemessen. Man hat also zwei Variablen, die konfundiert sind.*)

To ensure methodological competence, it is not sufficient to simply present concept mapping; instead, it is advisable to have the participants thoroughly practise this method by actively designing a concept map for another domain of knowledge (Graf 2014, 329; Hahn-Laudenberg 2017, 112). Sumfleth et al. (2010) tested a training programme for concept mapping and found that learners who were instructed and trained in the method produced higher-quality concept maps than those who were not instructed (Sumfleth et al. 2010, 70). They concluded that a three-step training programme, consisting of an introduction, a demonstration, and a hands-on exercise, had a positive effect on methodological competence, and thus on the structure and content of the concept maps. Hahn-Laudenberg (2017, 113) implements a standardised exercise to minimise method effects. The participants in her survey completed intensive training in using concept maps before completing the survey.

Pilot Studies

In 2019, we carried out five pilot studies with Danish and German participants. The goal of the studies was to test concept mapping as an innovative method for collecting data on the participants' concepts of Europe, and to examine the influence of various settings and participants. In 'Description of the pilot studies', the five pilot studies and the survey characteristics are first presented and explained with the selected maps. In the section 'Discussion of the Methodology of the Pilot Studies' section, we discuss the influence of various variables on setting tasks, on the answer format and the resulting methodological consequences. The section 'Analysis of the Concept Map Data' presents examples of qualitative and quantitative analyses of the concept map data. Finally, the results, regarded as the participants' ACTUAL state of knowledge, are compared to the EXPECTED state of their knowledge, as presented in the curricula of the federal state of North Rhine–Westphalia. An interpretation of the data as a basis for reconstructing 'Europe-oriented skills' and 'Europeanness' related to learner's knowledge concludes the empirical portion of the paper.

Description of the Pilot Studies

Because the research we present here is a pilot study, various concept map formats and frameworks were tested in the surveys, including open and semi-open tasks, to determine whether and to what extent the task type affects concept-map creation. For example, some participants had the option of integrating words provided in the map, such as *Kultur* (culture), *Unterschiede* (differences), *Gefühle* (feelings), *Aufgaben* (tasks), *Gemeinsamkeiten* (commonalities), *Sport*, *Werte* (values), *Vor- und Nachteile* (advantages and disadvantages), and *Reise* (travel), into their concept map, for inspiration, whereas in other surveys, only the initial prompt, *Europa*, was displayed on the sheet. Before one of the surveys, study participants received training in concept mapping to familiarise them with the characteristics of a concept map and to strengthen their methodological skills (see the section 'Training in Concept Mapping'). Table 9.1 provides an overview of all the pilot studies and their characteristics. Next, we discuss each pilot study in detail.

Pilot Study 1

Twenty-six eighth-year students at a high school in Remscheid took part in the study. The survey was conducted in German. Before the participants created their concept maps, they received a written introduction with a little information on the EurEd project and this study, and brief oral instructions on how to develop the concept map. Metadata were collected on a separate sheet. They received no prior instruction or training in concept mapping.

The concept maps were created on sheets of A4 paper, oriented horizontally. The task may be characterised as fairly open. The focus question, *Was kommt Dir in den Sinn, wenn Du an Europa denkst?* (What comes to mind when you think of Europe?), was centred at the top of the sheet. As the only prompt, and to suggest the structure, a node with the word 'Europa' appeared in the middle of the sheet as the starting point for the concept map (Fig. 9.3).

Table 9.1 Overview of the pilot studies

	Study 1	Study 2	Study 3	Study 4	Study 5
Place	High school, Remscheid, Germany	Aarhus University, Denmark	High school, Næstved, Denmark	Kiel University, Germany	High school, Düsseldorf, Germany
Language	German	German	Danish	German	German
Sample	n = 26 (8th year)	n = 14 (university students)	n = 11 (11th year)	n = 89 (university students)	n = 34 (8th year)
Average age	13.65	24.7	17.09	22.35	13.5
Prompts	not provided	provided	provided	provided: 4[a] not provided: 16	not provided
Focus Question	*Was kommt Dir in den Sinn, wenn Du an Europa denkst?* (What comes to mind when you think of Europe?)	*Welche Assoziationen verbinden Sie mit Europa?* (What do you associate with Europe?)	*Hvad forbinder du med Europa?* (What do you associate with Europe?)	*Welche Assoziationen verbinden Sie mit Europa?* (What do you associate with Europe?)	*Was kommt Dir in den Sinn, wenn Du an Europa denkst?* (What comes to mind when you think of Europe?)
Training in concept mapping	not provided	not provided	not provided	not provided	provided

[a]Of sixty-three concept maps, only four were analysed in this paper

Fig. 9.3 Example of a concept map from pilot study 1

The concept maps that emerged from this pilot study were not very complex, and rarely went beyond the first level. A network-like structure was rarely evident. Even the connecting lines were unlabelled, or had a reading direction defined by an arrow. Often, the nodes were nominal phrases.

Pilot Study 2

This study involved fourteen students reading German Studies at Aarhus University in Denmark. The survey language was German, a foreign language for most of the participants (at CEF level B1). Before they developed their concept maps, the participants received a little information on how to develop them. Metadata were collected on a separate sheet before the assignment. There was no prior instruction or training in this method.

The concept maps were created on a sheet of A4 paper, oriented horizontally. The task may be characterised as rather open. The focus question, *Welche Assoziationen verbinden Sie mit Europa?* (What do you associate with Europe?), appeared at the top left of the sheet. As a prompt,

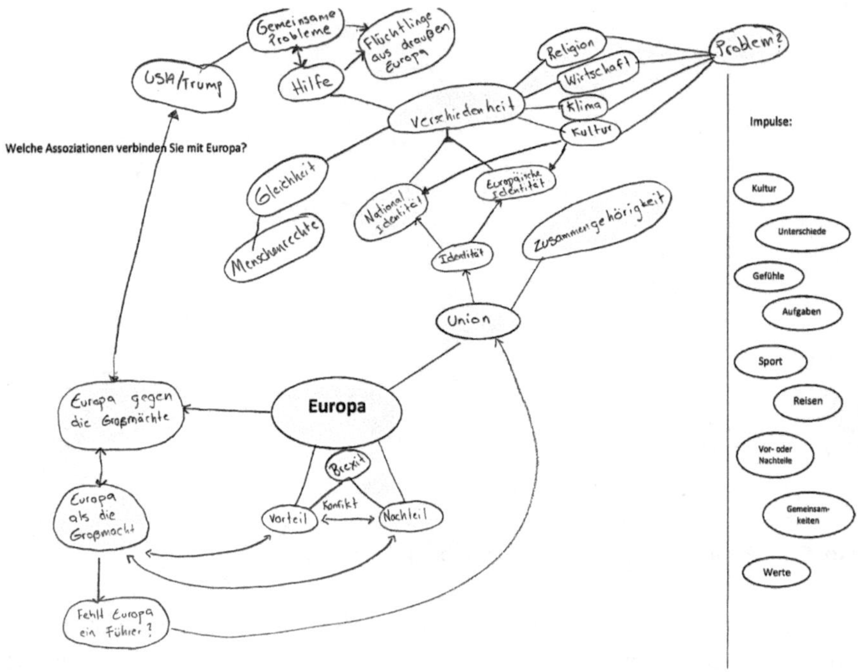

Fig. 9.4 Example of a concept map from pilot study 2

and to suggest the structure, a node with a connecting line (without an arrow) enclosing the word 'Europa' appeared in the middle of the sheet, as the starting point for the map (Fig. 9.4).

The words *Kultur* (culture), *Unterschiede* (differences), *Gefühle* (feelings), *Aufgaben* (tasks), 'Sport', *Reisen* (travel), *Vor- und Nachteile* (advantages and disadvantages), *Gemeinsamkeiten* (commonalities), and *Werte* (values) appeared as prompts on the right side of the sheet, separated by a vertical line from the space for the concept map. Although a heading identified these words as prompts, the shapes in which they appeared (ellipses) suggested potential nodes. In the concept maps that emerged from this pilot study, complex networks were created, the depiction of which reached its limits on A4 paper. Here, the lexical prompts were partly, but not exclusively, used as nodes. The connecting lines were rarely labelled, and the reading direction was only partially defined by arrows.

Pilot Study 3

This study involved eleven students from a high school in Denmark. The survey language was Danish. Prior to the survey, the participants received a brief oral presentation about the EurEd project and the study. The metadata were collected on a separate page after the maps were created. There was no prior instruction or training in concept-map creation.

The concept maps were created on a sheet of A4 paper, oriented horizontally. The instructions appeared at the top of the sheet, in Danish: *Udarbejd din egen Concept Map til temaet Europa. Du kan anvende de begreber, der står herunder, men du skal ikke nødvendigvis. Glem ikke at forbinde begreberne med pile.* (Create your own concept map on the topic of Europe. You may use the terms listed below, but you don't have to. Do not forget to connect the terms with arrows.) The task may be characterised as rather open. The focus question, 'Hvad forbinder du med Europa?' (What do you associate with Europe?), was centred below the instructions. As a prompt, and to suggest the structure, a node enclosing the word 'Europa' appeared in the middle of the sheet, as a starting point for the map. At the bottom of the sheet, the words *Rejse* (travel), 'Sport', *Følelser* (feelings), *Fordele og ulemper* (advantages and disadvantages), *Værdier* (values), *Kultur* (culture), *Opgaver* (tasks), and *Politik* (politics) appeared in ellipses. The words were not separated from the concept map area, and there was no explanation of their function, that is, they were not identified as prompts (Fig. 9.5).

The concept maps that emerged from this pilot study show hardly any network-like structures. The lexical prompts were, without exception, understood as predefined nodes. The participants transferred the lexical prompts to the concept map and used lines to connect them to the initial keyword, 'Europa'. Thus, hierarchical-looking structures were created. Although the lines were always labelled, they were only sometimes provided with a reading direction. The space required for detailed labelling of the lines showed that the A4 format does not offer enough space for some maps.

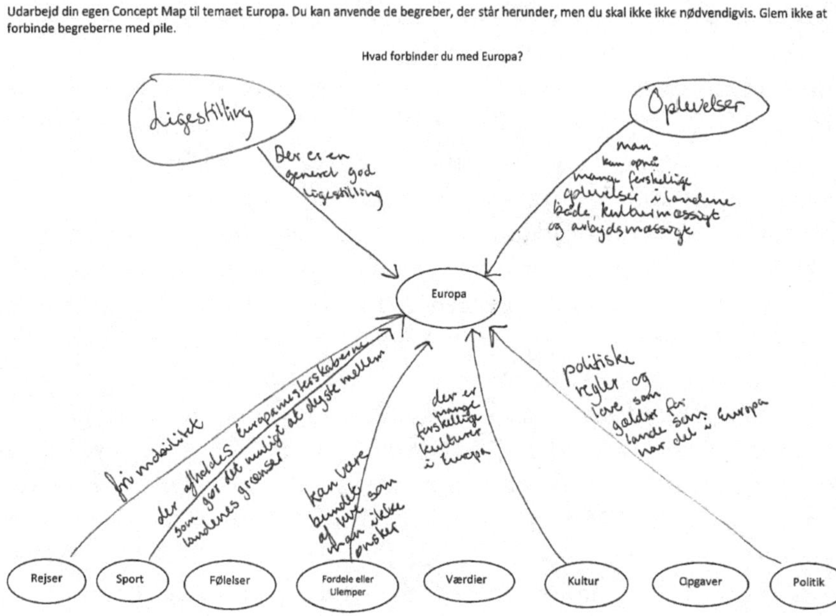

Fig. 9.5 Example of a concept map from pilot study 3

Pilot Study 4

Eighty-nine students reading German Studies at the Christian-Albrechts University of Kiel participated in this study. The survey was conducted in German. The participants were given brief introductory information on the EurEd project and the study, and instructions on how to develop the concept map.

The concept maps were created on a sheet of A4 paper, oriented horizontally. The task may be characterised as rather open. The focus question, *Welche Assoziationen verbinden Sie mit Europa?* (What do you associate with Europe?), appeared at the top left of the sheet. As a prompt, and to suggest the structure, a node with a connecting line (without an arrow) enclosing the word 'Europa' appeared in the middle of the page, as the starting point for the map.

Pilot study 4 had a partly similar setup to study 2 but took place in Germany, and the participants' native language was German. Also, the study was divided into two sub-studies, one with and one without prompts. Sixteen participants completed a concept map with similar characteristics to those used in study 2. Here, the prompts *Kultur* (culture), *Unterschiede* (differences), *Gefühle* (feelings), *Aufgaben* (tasks), 'Sport', *Reisen* (travel), *Vor- und Nachteile* (advantages and disadvantages), *Gemeinsamkeiten* (commonalities), and *Werte* (values) were positioned at the right side of the sheet. The second sub-study provided no prompts on the sheet, and yielded only four analysable concept maps (Fig. 9.6).

Most of the concept maps had complex network structures, and the A4 paper was not always large enough to accommodate them. It is worth noting that the participants often visualised the words in the nodes without using enclosing ellipses. Only some of the words provided as prompts were adopted as nodes. Here too, the lines were seldom labelled or drawn as arrows with a reading direction.

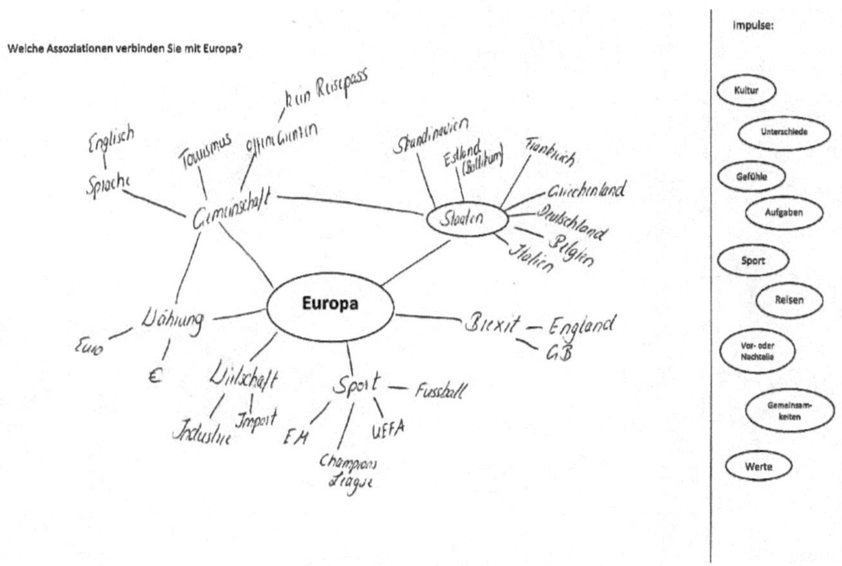

Fig. 9.6 Example of a concept map from pilot study 4

Pilot Study 5

Thirty-four eighth-year students from a high school in Düsseldorf participated in this study. The survey was conducted in German. The participants received written instructions with a brief explanation of concept mapping and a sample map of the topic of *Naturschutz* (protecting nature). No metadata were collected.

The concept maps were created on a sheet of A4 paper, oriented horizontally. The task may be characterised as fairly open. The focus question (also see pilot study 1), *Was kommt Dir in den Sinn, wenn du an Europa denkst*? (What comes to mind when you think of Europe?), was centred at the top of the sheet. As a prompt and to indicate the structure, a node with the word 'Europa', with four connecting lines radiating from it (not arrows) appeared at the centre of the sheet as the starting point for the concept map. No other prompt words were provided (Fig. 9.7).

The vast majority of the concept maps in this pilot study included very complex network structures that comprised several levels. Most of the

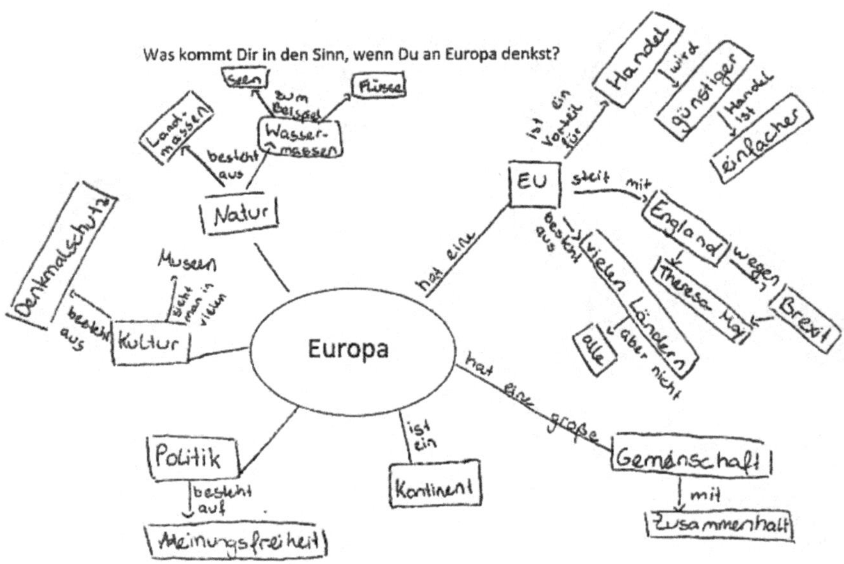

Fig. 9.7 Example of a concept map from pilot study 5

connecting lines were labelled arrows. It is notable that the sample map of the topic of *Naturschutz* (protecting nature) seemed to strongly influence the participants' concept map of Europe. Thus, lexemes such as *Natur* (nature), *Landmassen* (land masses), or *Seen* (lakes), the detailed labels on the arrows and the rectangular nodes may be traced back to the design of the sample map (in detail, Krämer et al. 2021).

Methodology of the Pilot Studies

The data from our pilot studies suggest that the extent of a task's directedness and response format (see sections 'Degree of Directedness: Open and Closed Tasks' and 'Response Format') have a particularly significant influence on the final quality of the concept maps. This relates to the survey design, that is, the predefined structural elements and lexical prompts and to the use and structure of training in concept mapping.

In the pilot studies, all the groups used pencil and paper to create the concept maps. With the exception of pilot study 5, all the studies indicated that the DIN A4 format does not always offer enough space to fully develop concept maps. In the case of surveys carried out with paper and pencil, it is important to ensure that the sheet is large enough to allow the participants unrestricted space to develop their maps.

The suggested structure of the concept map, that is, whether or not, and how, nodes and connecting lines are defined, has a significant effect on the results. This seems especially to be the case in pilot studies that included no training in concept mapping, as this effect is not as evident in study 5, which included some instruction in this method. The data indicate that study participants tended to use the lexical prompts as nodes when they were presented at the side of, or below, the space designated for the concept map (see pilot studies 2, 3, and 4). Thus, the participants connected the prompts on the map with lines, instead of integrating them into the concept map at appropriate places in the space designated for the concept map, as intended. Therefore, we conclude that prompts presented in this form impose some limitations on data collection. The participants seemed to focus exclusively on forming a network with the prompts provided, instead of using their own words in the nodes. This may have limited the activation of the participants' knowledge and self-prompted lexical units. Therefore, one should consider using a line to separate the nodes from the concept map area (as in pilot study 4), listing them on a separate sheet or even not providing any lexical prompts at all.

In all our pilot studies, a node with the lexeme *Europa* appeared in the middle of the drawing area as an initial prompt. The structure surrounding the initial prompt was designed differently in the various pilot studies. Sometimes, connecting lines to only the first level were provided, but sometimes connecting lines that suggest a map design up to the second level were given, for example, in pilot study 4. Here, we observe a tendency that suggests that the characteristics of a given structure may influence the final complexity of the concept maps: the more complex the structure of the map presented beforehand, the more the participants tended to adopt and develop these structures. Furthermore, the fact that we did not include arrows may have been the reason that the participants rarely indicated a reading direction for the connecting lines. These findings, which relate to the design of our survey instrument, suggest that study participants were strongly oriented by the structures and prompts provided. Therefore, they should be used with care.

Instruction in the use of concept maps prior to the survey was tested only for pilot study 5. The instructions consisted of a one-page written introduction that explained concept maps and presented their most important features. A sample concept map on the topic of *Naturschutz* (protecting nature) was also provided, followed by the invitation to create a map of the topic of Europe. The results indicate that the participants were significantly influenced by the content of the sample map. This is particularly evident in the parallels in the labelling of the connecting lines (*Politiker sind wichtig* [politicians are important], *Vorteil* [advantage], *Artikel 13 sollte durchgesetzt werden* [Article 13 should be enforced]). To avoid priming effects, care must be taken that the instructional material has no thematic relationship to the topic examined. Furthermore, instruction in using the instrument seemed to yield a comparatively higher degree of complexity in the subsequent concept maps, even if no lexical prompts or structural indications were provided, and only an initial prompt, *Europa*, was used. Here, we observe a significant difference in the quality of the data compared to that from the pilot studies that included no instructions. Therefore, we recommend that the participants be instructed, and even practise creating a concept map, before this method is used to collect data.

It should also be noted that in the concept maps, the connecting lines were rarely labelled. Once again, the exception to this was pilot study 5, in which the necessity of labelling the connecting lines was emphasised during the introduction to the instrument. As it is impossible to evaluate the connecting lines if they are not labelled, this finding confirms that during instruction, it is advisable to explicitly point out the necessity of labelling the connecting lines, and to practise this step with the participants prior to collecting data.

Three focus questions were used in the pilot studies: *Was kommt Dir in den Sinn, wenn Du an Europa denkst?*, *Welche Assoziationen verbinden Sie mit Europa?* and *Hvad forbinder du med Europa?* (What comes to mind when you think of Europe?, What do you associate with Europe?, What do you associate with Europe?) The position of the focus question may influence the design of the concept maps, but the data analysis showed no clear trends. However, the appearance of predominantly declarative knowledge in the data, especially in pilot study 1, suggests that the maps are more descriptive than explanatory in nature. This may be due to the rather open focus questions, which have no specific focus, but, as previously explained, allow a creative design in all directions, with regard to the maps' content. Given the focus of our research, stronger, content-based guidance may narrow the thematic scope of the data.

Based on the pilot studies, we may make the following methodological recommendations for the questions that drove the research presented in this chapter.

1. A detailed explanation of and training in the use of the instrument significantly improves the quality and interpretative value of the lexical data in the concept maps. The training should be carried out prior to the survey, should not thematically overlap the subject being researched, and should explicitly identify the need to label connecting lines, and provide a reading direction by using arrows.

2. A specified, predefined structure in the space designated for the concept map encourages the participants to create more complex concept maps.
3. Lexical prompts should either be clearly separated from the space designated for the concept map, or not be provided at all.

Despite the above-mentioned limitations, using the concept map as a survey instrument to determine mental models and lexically bound knowledge has proven useful. On the one hand, we have gained critical insights into the methodological conception of the instrument, which contributes to the focused use of concept maps in a broader research framework; on the other hand, the data collected include an extensive lexical inventory, which is directly or indirectly related to the morpheme {europ} at various levels.

In the next sections, we will discuss whether and to what extent the lexical inventory may be interpreted as representative of a collective mental model, and whether we may draw conclusions about constructions of Europe—or even of a European identity—from the collected data.

Analysis of the Concept Map Data

In cognitive semantics, semantic categories are seen as 'basic structures of complex knowledge structures that store information about certain areas of life or experience … in such a way that a mental world model … is represented' (Schwarz-Friesel and Chur 2014, 68). This perspective allows us to interpret the lexical data from concept maps as encoding the study participants' mental models of Europe. From a linguistic perspective, and in the sense of lexically bound knowledge, concepts are semantic categories that may be used to group 'things, qualities and events' (Seel 2003, 378) with similar attributes in semantic fields. The linguistic representations of these fields may vary from language to language.

We analysed the linguistic data in the concept maps that were created by the study participants by extracting keywords and classifying them into conceptual fields according to the *Dornseiff* thesaurus.[5] Because they lacked labels, we could not analyse the connecting lines in all concept map in all the pilot studies. Therefore, the question of how the nodes relate to each other, which is usually addressed by analysing the connecting lines, must remain open in these studies (for the analytical method, e.g. Stock 2008, 2009).

As a first step, we analysed the words in the nodes of the concept maps as lexemes, and in a second step, we interpreted the lexemes as linguistic forms of concepts, that is, as lexically bound summaries of 'perceptions' and 'experiences' in the sense described by Konerding (1993, 101). In the analysis, we assigned the extracted lexemes to conceptual fields (classes, subject areas; also *Hauptgruppen*) and their (lexical) subfields (sections; also *Sachgruppen*), according to the thesaurus *Der deutsche Wortschatz nach Sachgruppen* by Franz Dornseiff (2020).

Categorising Nodes According to Conceptual Fields (*Dornseiff*)

Dornseiff refers to Franz Dornseiff's thesaurus, *Der deutsche Wortschatz nach Sachgruppen*, a German thesaurus divided into subject areas. The thesaurus was first published in 1934, and has been revised and updated several times, most recently in 2004, by Uwe Quasthoff, and the most recent edition was published in 2020. Uwe Quasthoff's revisions are based on language-use data from the corpora of the project, *Deutscher Wortschatz.*[6] The subject areas in *Dornseiff* are also integrated into the German corpus, available online (www.wortschatz.uni-leipzig.de), meaning that the *Dornseiff* conceptual fields, and the lexical subfields for the words contained therein, are displayed in the search results.

The *Dornseiff* presents a large part of the German vocabulary in its semantic contexts in twenty-two conceptual fields and nine hundred and seventy lexical subfields. The conceptual fields consist of words and groups of words that have various (quasi-)synonymous and encyclopaedic semantic relationships to the titles of the conceptual fields. The lexical fields may be interpreted as parts of a semantic network (Dornseiff 2020, 21). The words included in a lexical field have similar meanings. Although Dornseiff's original intention was to create a thesaurus that provided rhetorical and stylistic support for translation (Storjohann 2012, 479), which functioned as a text-production tool (Reichmann 1990, 1067), the updated edition allows for the combination of an analysis of the concept map data and a corpus-based description of concepts in current language usage. This is extremely valuable in terms of our research questions, because the conceptual fields in the Dornseiff thesaurus

> provide an empirical basis for linguistic findings, in which statistical randomness is suppressed, and the typical, significant, and frequency-based aspects are focused on. The dictionary's content is no longer incorporated randomly or arbitrarily according to the editor's subjective perceptions, but confirmed and and justified on the basis of a statistical analysis that goes beyond the editor's language competence. (Storjohann 2012, 481–482)
>
> (*…eine empirische Grundlage sprachlicher Erkenntnisse vor, bei der statistische Zufälligkeiten ausgeblendet und Typisches, Signifikantes und Frequenzbasiertes fokussiert werden. Inhalte des Wörterbuchs sind nicht mehr zufällig oder willkürlich nach subjektivem Empfinden eines Bearbeiters aufgenommen, sondern aufgrund der statistischen Auswertung über die eigene Sprachkompetenz hinausgehend abgesichert und begründbar*)

More than any other thesaurus, the *Dornseiff* allows us to determine semantically related lexical expressions, and to combine them in semantic fields that are as close as possible to linguistic reality (Storjohann 2012, 482). Accordingly, assigning the words that appeared in the nodes of the concept maps from our pilot studies to the conceptual fields in *Dornseiff* allowed us to categorise our data so it very strongly reflects the way we structure the real world through language.

In the analysis in this study, we consider only the German maps from pilot studies 1, 2, 4, and 5. As a first step, we extracted the words entered in each node, which we identified as the linguistic form of a concept and carrier of the node's core meaning. In the second step, we carried out a semantic classification by assigning each word to a conceptual field and a lexical subfield in the *Dornseiff*. In all, we extracted and classified 989 words from the concept maps.

In the data, lexemes from all twenty-two conceptual fields in *Dornseiff* occur with varying frequency (Fig. 9.8), but only five fields contain more

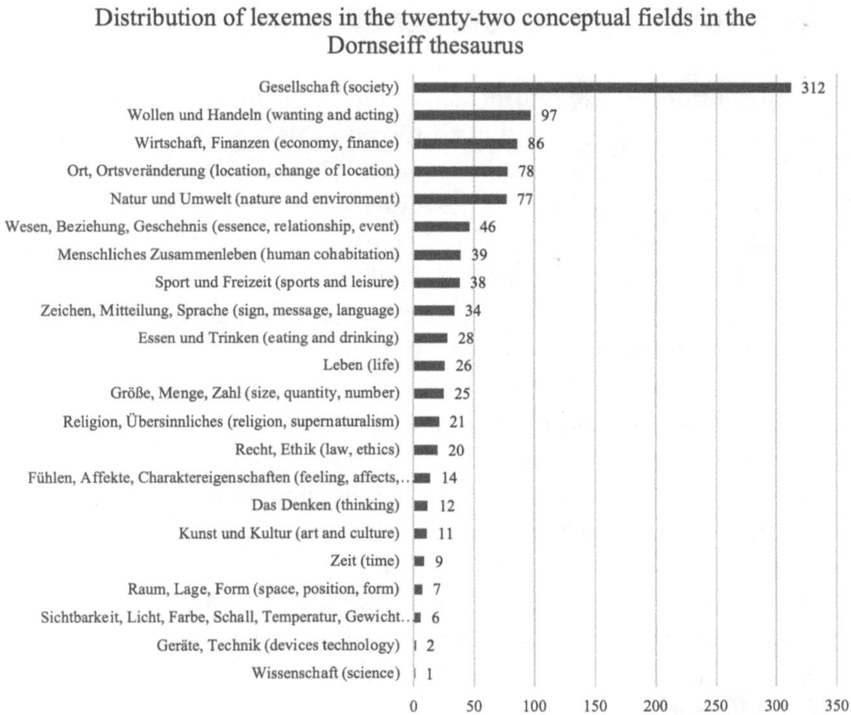

Fig. 9.8 Distribution of lexemes according to the conceptual fields in the *Dornseiff* thesaurus

than fifty lexemes. However, the most lexemes by far may be assigned to the conceptual field, *Gesellschaft* (society) (312). Similarly, a considerable number of lexemes may be assigned to the conceptual fields, *Wollen und Handeln* (wanting and acting) (97) and *Wirtschaft und Finanzen* (economy and finance) (86), followed by the fields, *Ort, Ortsveränderung* (place, change of place) and *Natur und Umwelt* (nature and the environment) (78 and 77 lexemes, respectively). To provide more detailed information about semantic classification, the incidence of the lexemes in the conceptual fields and the subordinate lexical fields in *Dornseiff* is summarised in the following sections.

Conceptual Field: *Gesellschaft* (Society)

The distribution of lexemes in the conceptual field, *Gesellschaft*, whose focus is on socio-political and institutional subject areas, is divided into the following[7] lexical subfields: *Staat* (state) (173), *Kulturelle Entwicklung* (cultural development) (42), *Krieg* (war) (19), *Weltorganisation* (world organisation) (14), *Parlament* (parliament) (12), *Freiheit* (freedom) (12), *Politiker* (politicians) (9), and *Politik* (politics) (9).

The *Staat* subfield is mostly composed of country names (e.g. *Deutschland, Italien, Griechenland*). It is noteworthy that Danish study participants listed *Dänemark* in almost all cases, and German study participants always mention *Deutschland.* Here, we observe a manifestation of nationality in the concepts. The much lower frequency of the keyword *Union* may also be seen as an indicator of national influence.

The *Kulturelle Entwicklung* subfield refers to culture as the result of the development of civilisation. The result of our analysis suggests an ambivalent view of Europe. On the one hand, we find nationally defined ideas that emphasise the cultural differences within Europe (*viele verschiedene Kulturen* [many different cultures], *verschiedene Kulturen treffen aufeinander* [different cultures meet]), but on the other hand, the data also illustrate a community of shared values, a common understanding of values, and cultural exchange.

In the data, the lexemes belonging to the *Krieg* (war) subfield reference the past, indicated by the temporal adverb, *früher* (in the past, before) or explicitly mention the First or Second World War, and also possible future wars, often in connection with the lexemes *Schutz* or *Hilfe* (e.g. *im Kriegsfall gibt es Schutz* [in the case of war there is a defence]). This is closely related to the *Angriff* (attack) subfield, which also refers to a war scenario, but is represented by only one noun in the data. In contrast, words in the *Freiheit* subfield, occur less frequently in the data, which is particularly interesting if one considers *Freiheit* as an essential part of *Frieden* (peace), and therefore presents a strong contrast to the semantic content of *Krieg* and *Angriff.* Here, the data indicate that learners more frequently associate *Europa* with *Krieg* than with *Freiheit.*

Conceptual Field: *Wollen und Handeln* (Wanting and Acting)

The lexemes in the conceptual field, *Wollen und Handeln*, are divided into the following lexical fields: *Methode* (method) (19), *Zusammenwirken* (interaction) (17), *Hilfe* (help) (13), *Sicherheit* (security) (9), *Vorteil* (advantage) (6), and *Misslingen* (failure) (5).

Although the *Methode* subfield, contains only *Politik*, the *Zusammenwirken* subfield, which has the same number of lexemes, reveals the view that Europe is seen as a community or a union characterised by cooperation and a collective sense of being a team and community. This finding, which is particularly interesting in times of nationalistic tendencies and social disintegration in Europe, is underpinned by frequent instances of lexemes in the lexical field, *Hilfe*, such as *alle helfen sich*, *einander helfen*, *gegenseitige Unterstützung* and *Schutz* ('everyone assists', 'to help each other', 'mutual support', and 'protection'). The *Sicherheit* subfield indicates that study participants also often associate Europe with a feeling of security—from the structure of the corresponding maps, it is apparent that references such as these are often the result of the *Vorteil* subfield, and therefore may be interpreted positively. Other positive aspects are *offene Grenzen* (open borders), *Frieden und Freiheitsbewahrung* (peace and protecting freedom), *Lösung von Konflikten über die Landesgrenzen hinaus* (resolving conflicts across national borders). The keyword, *Krise*—often specified as, or connected to, *Flüchtlingskrise* (refugee crisis), *Grenzschutzkrise* (border security crisis), and *Griechenland* (Greece)—is a central lexeme in the *Misslingen* (failure) subfield. Our analysis did not reveal further details that might indicate what kinds of triggers, reasons, or feelings prompted those lexemes.

Conceptual Field: *Wirtschaft und Finanzen* (Economic and Financial Affairs)

The conceptual field, *Wirtschaft und Finanzen*, also offers interesting insights into study participants' concepts of Europe. The field consists of the following subfields: *Währung* (currency) (44), *Weltwirtschaft* (world economy) (17), *Tausch*, *Handel* (exchange, trade) (11), and *Reichtum* (wealth) (5)

The currency, *Euro*, is often directly associated with the initial prompt, *Europa*, at the first level, and labelled a common feature of EU member states. The *Weltwirtschaft* subfield includes keywords such as *Wirtschaft* (economy), *transnationale Wirtschaftsverbindungen* (transnational economic relations), and *gemeinsame Wirtschaftsunion* (common economic union). Those lexemes may be interpreted as indicators of the study participants' view that Europe is characterised by many common features. However, a question that is relevant at this point is whether the lexemes provided as prompts, including *Gemeinsamkeiten* (commonalities), influenced the data. However, in the data from all our pilot studies, we observed the mention of the many similarities of the European member states, regardless of whether linguistic prompts were provided.

Conceptual Field: *Ort, Ortsveränderung* (Place, Change of Place)

Lexemes assigned to the conceptual field, *Ort, Ortsveränderung*, are particularly frequent in the subfield, *Reisen* (travel), (77), but also in the fields *Hinaus* (out) (22), *Ansiedlung*, *Stadt* (settlement, city) (18), and *sich entfernen* (to move away) (5). Many of the study participants associated *Reisefreiheit* (freedom to travel) with Europe, in the sense of ease of travel without a passport, and the possibility of crossing national borders at any time. Many of the nodes containing those lexemes are connected directly to the initial prompt at the first level, and often link to lexemes that belong to the concept field, *Sport und Freizeit* (sport and leisure), and refer to vacation activities. Here, the data give us insights into the personal lives and experiences of the study participants, which are primarily in the field of travel.

At the time of the survey, Great Britain withdrew from the European Union, which was extensively discussed in the media. This topic dominates the *Hinaus* subfield. It remains unclear whether the learners are aware of a difference between 'Europe' and 'the European Union', or whether they used the terms synonymously. The subfield, *Ansiedlung, Stadt,* primarily comprises city names. Particularly frequent here is the reference to *Brüssel* as the headquarters of the European Union, closely followed by *Frankfurt* and *Aarhus* as *Kulturhauptstadt* (capital of culture). The *sich entfernen* subfield primarily consists of the lexeme *Flüchtling* (refugee). We concluded that this reveals the participants' view that Europe has a refugee problem and is facing a refugee crisis. Europe is also seen as a popular destination for refugees.

Conceptual Field: *Natur und Umwelt* (Nature and the Environment)

The conceptual field, *Natur und Umwelt,* is largely constituted by the subject groups, *Festland* (mainland) (46) and *Klima, Klimaänderung* (climate, climate change) (7). Thus, Europe is primarily considered a continent in the geographic sense. Lexemes from the lexical field, *Klima, Klimaänderung,* are *Klimwawandel* (climate change), *Klimaabkommen* (climate agreement), and *Klimaschutz* (climate protection), the latter often linked at the next level to concrete measures for climate protection, such as *Strom/Energie sparen* (save electricity/power). Furthermore, climate is often characterised as a *Problem* and declared *schutzbedürftig* (in need of protection), which suggests personal involvement in the topic, which also received considerable media coverage at the time the surveys were done.

Summary and Conclusions

The incidence of lexemes in all twenty-two conceptual fields of the *Dornseiff* thesaurus suggests that the participants activated many different concepts of Europe while creating their concept maps, where Europe was associated with various topics and subject areas. In pilot studies 1 and 5, we observed that the participants tended to merely list their lexically coded knowledge of Europe, without integrating it into a network. This tendency to reproduce declarative knowledge by using keywords for the nodes of the concept maps is striking; for example, learners often listed historical dates (e.g. dates of the World Wars, the year of the founding of the EEC), alliances and associations associated with Europe (UN, NATO), or names of other continents (Africa, Asia, etc.) without connecting them to other nodes, or further elaborating on them. This finding, and the participants' overarching tendency to avoid individual evaluations, opinions, or personal experiences of Europe, led to the conclusion that Europe does not yet have an established a narrative representation in the participants' personal lives and experiences. We concluded that the participants' mental models and their concepts of Europe are derived primarily from school subjects.

Only the frequent connection of 'Europe' to 'ease of travel without a passport' indicates the influence of study participants' individual experience or of narratives adopted from others. This coincides with the results of studies on the understanding of *democracy*, which found that a European identity is not explicitly negotiated, and personal attitudes are not addressed at school (Ziemes et al. 2017, 48). In contrast, the concept maps in pilot studies 2 and 4 provided more information on affective, evaluative, and conative aspects of the concepts of Europe, as they are often composed of lexemes that may be assigned to the conceptual field of *Wollen und Handeln*. This conceptual field includes processes, intentions, and plans and is characterised by a high semantic binding strength with the initial prompt, 'Europe'.

The study participants' concepts of Europe are more national than European. According to Zappettini (2019, 171) the phenomenon of 'Europeanness' would have to be described as 'nation-centric'. Europe appears less as a unified whole than as an association of individual sovereign states. We base this conclusion on the frequent naming of individual member states, with *Deutschland* (in pilot studies 1, 4 and 5) and *Dänemark* (in pilot study 2), the participants' native countries, being the most frequently named. Furthermore, we support this finding with the somewhat rare perception of Europe as a union or community of values. Nevertheless, it is striking that the younger participants saw the individual countries as a community that works together in accordance with the motto, *alle für einen* (all for one). When Europe is referred to as a *Union* or *Allianz*, this is often followed by a reference to a nation's possible withdrawal or *Brexit*. If one considers this finding alongside Quenzel's conclusion that 'the process of collective identity formation ... includes not only identification with the ideas about this community but also strategies of demarcation' (Quenzel 2005, 96), then it becomes apparent that this tendency—namely, constructing boundaries in a community, to distinguish between 'inside' and 'outside'—is a clear indication of collective identity formation. The 'European others' (Quenzel 2005, 96) are also part of the collective (national) identity, which is an important construct for negotiating various models of identity.

Lexemes related to socio-political phenomena and institutions are very often directly and indirectly associated with Europe. Here, the older participants' (university students') concept maps included more comprehensive data, in the sense that they facilitated the analysis of more elaborate concepts and relationships. These may be regarded as declarative aspects of knowledge, and interpreted as important affective, evaluative, and conative components of the construction of study participants' European identity.

When analysing the data, it is apparent that concepts of Europe are characterised by ambivalent views that do not always allow a clear interpretation of the data as whole. For example, words such as *Konkurrenz* (competition) and *Verbundenheit* (solidarity) indicate a dichotomy in the mental models of Europe. A more precise analysis of such differences requires more extensive studies with significantly more participants to obtain representative results.

Education About Europe as a Framework of Concepts of Europe

Europe in Curricula as the EXPECTED State of Learners' Knowledge

The resolution, *Europa im Unterricht* (Europe in the Classroom), first developed in 1978 and revised in 2008, the Standing Conference of the Ministers of Education and Cultural Affairs of the Länder (KMK) of the Federal Republic of Germany, defines how the European dimension may be incorporated when teaching at schools. The resolution, *Europabildung in der Schule* (Education about Europe in Schools), includes recommendations for how schools may meet their pedagogical obligation (KMK 2008, 5) to promote an awareness of Europe among learners, through all subjects. For example, teaching 'basic values of state, social and individual life', which 'enable a successful life in Europe' (KMK 2008, 5), is mentioned, as is the awareness that 'European references are effective and European decisions are required in many areas of our lives' (KMK 2008, 5). Accordingly, 'Europe-oriented skills' (KMK 2008, 5) include:

- 'the willingness to reduce prejudices and to recognise what we have in common' (KMK 2008, 5)
- 'cross-cultural open-mindedness' (KMK 2008, 5) and
- the 'advocacy of freedom, democracy, human rights, justice … and peace' (KMK 2008, 5)

These recommendations propose the 'examination of central aspects and content of European history and the process of European unification' (KMK 2008, 6) in all subjects and years to ensure the development of Europe-oriented skills.

Each German federal state implements the KMK recommendations independently. Therefore, it is up to the state ministries of education to define the role of Europe in the curricula for each subject, and for various types of schools and years. The curricula are generic documents and provide approximate sequences of learning opportunities, content, and goals to be presented through educational media and teaching to 'determine the programme of school education and contribute to a standardisation of what happens in the lessons and/or with regard to the results of school education' (Bacia and Abs 2017, 27). Thus, the recommendations form the general framework for imparting knowledge of Europe and attitudes to Europe. In this sense, the content of the recommendations and their concrete deployment in the curricula equate the EXPECTED state of the learner's concepts of Europe that are formed through formal education. Next, we use corpus linguistic tools to analyse the recommendations and the curricula that correspond to the concept-map data in pilot studies 1 and 5. The objective of this analysis is to identify the Europe-related material presented at the study participants schools, which should be—at least partly—reflected in the concept map data.

Corpus Analysis: Europe in the Curricula

The data from pilot studies 1 and 5 presented here relate to thirteen- to fourteen-year-old learners at high schools in Remscheid and Düsseldorf. Accordingly, the curricula for secondary level I of the German state of North Rhine–Westphalia will be analysed to identify Europe-relevant content in the school subjects. As discussed above, we believe that this content represents the general framework of the EXPECTED state of these learners' knowledge of Europe.

We carried out a sample, corpus-based analysis of the curricula for G8 (eight-year 'fast track' secondary school), which are accessible on the Qua-Lis NRW home page.[8] Although these curricula will expire with the fast track in 2020/2021, they form the basis of this analysis, because they include the subject specifications for the participants in pilot studies 1 and 5. There are curricula for thirty-one subjects: German, social studies (history, geography and politics/economics), mathematics, natural sciences (biology, chemistry, and physics), English and a second foreign language (eleven languages to choose from), practical philosophy, art and music, religious studies (relating to seven different religions), and sports.

We downloaded the curricula as .pdf files on September 4, 2020 and analysed them with the *Voyant* corpus tool. The corpus of the thirty-one curricula comprises 321,423 running words with 20,950 different word forms.[9] *Voyant* allows users to accumulate several search forms and to search for parts of words. The search function also shows whether and how often a given character string occurs in the corpus. The corpus was first searched for Europe words. The search form, *euro**, covers all words beginning with *e/Euro*. For the search for word formations containing the form, **euro** but not beginning with *euro**, the forms with the usual endings were verified according to their occurrence in the corpus, yielding the following three search forms: **europäischen*, **europäische*, and **europa*. The search yielded 237 instances[10] of words with **euro** as a component. All these words refer to Europe. By far the most common lemma is the adjective, *europäisch* (European), with 159 instances, followed by *Europa* (Europe) with thirty instances and *Europarat* (Council of Europe) with twenty-nine instances.

The rather low frequency of the remaining **euro** words is distributed among the lemmas as follows (number of instances in parentheses): *außereuropäisch* (5, non-European), *Außereuropa* (1, not Europe), *Europäer* (2, European), *Mitteleuropa* (4, central Europe), *mitteleuropäisch* (1, central-European), *Westeuropa* (2, western Europe), *westeuropäisch* (1, west European), *Nordeuropa* (1, northern Europe), *innereuropäisch* (1, 'Inner' Europe), and *osteuropäisch* (1, east European).

The search for *EU** yielded only four instances, in the curricula for Portuguese (2), geography (1), and politics/economy (1). With the search procedure described above, we found 241 instances of 'Europe' lexemes in the curriculum corpus.[11]

Table 9.2 illustrates the distribution of the instances 'Europe' lexemes, by subject.

Table 9.2 demonstrates that Europe is predominantly addressed in the curricula for foreign languages, for example, in English (21) and all eleven other foreign languages offered from years seven and ten: Chinese (11), French (18), Greek (11), Italian (24), Japanese (12), Latin (16), Dutch (14), Portuguese (22), Russian (20), Spanish (20), and Turkish (15). Furthermore, thirty-two 'Europe' word forms were found in the curricula for history (11), geography (9), and politics/economics (3), and for the subjects of Orthodox and Syrian Orthodox religious studies, with seven and two instances.

Table 9.2 Results of the corpus-based analysis of the curricula

Subject	Number **euro** words	Findings ('Europe' words)
(Foreign) languages from the 5th year on	**22**	
German	1	europäischen
English	21	europäischen (7), europäischer (1), Europarat (12), Europas (1)
(Foreign) languages from the 7th or 10th year on	**183**	
Chinese	11	*außereuropäische* (2), *europäischen* (7), *europäischer* (1), *Europarat* (1)
French	18	*europäischen* (8), *europäischer* (2), *europäisches* (5), *Europarat* (2), *Europas* (1)
Greek	11	*europäischen* (6), *europäischer* (2), *Europas* (3)
Italian	24	*Europa* (1), *europäische* (1), *europäischen* (11), *europäischer* (2), *europäisches* (5), *Europarat* (2), *Europas* (2)
Japanese	12	*außereuropäische* (2), *Europa* (1), *europäischen* (6), *europäischer* (1), *Europarat* (1), *mitteleuropäische* (1)
Latin	16	*außereuropäischen* (1) *Europa* (1), *europäische* (3), *europäischen* (6), *europäischer* (2), *Europas* (3)
Dutch	14	*europäischen* (8), *europäischer* (2), *europäisches* (2), *Europarat* (2)
Portuguese	22	*EU* (2), *europäischen* (8), *europäischer* (2), *europäisches* (5), *Europarat* (2), *Europas* (2), *innereuropäischen* (1)
Russian	20	*europäischen* (8), *europäischer* (2), *europäisches* (5), *Europarat* (2), *Europarates* (1), *Europas* (1), *osteuropäischen* (1)
Spanish	20	*europäischen* (8), *europäischer* (2), *europäisches* (5), *Europarat* (2), *Europas* (3)
Turkish	15	*europäischen* (9), *europäischer* (2), *Europarat* (2), *Europas* (1), *Mitteleuropa* (1)

(*continued*)

Table 9.2 (continued)

Subject	Number *euro* words	Findings ('Europe' words)
Natural sciences	**3**	
Biology	1	*europäischen*
Chemistry	1	*europäischen*
Physics	1	*europäischen*
Mathematics	1	*europäischen*
Social sciences	**23**	
Geography	9	*außereuropa* (1), *europäischen* (3), *europäischer* (1), *europas* (1), *europa* (2), *EU* (1)
History	11	*Europa* (4), *Europäer* (2), *europäische* (2), *europäischen* (2), *europäischer* (1)
Politics/Economics	3	*europäischen* (1), *Europa* (1), *EU* (1)
Practical philosophy	0	
Sports	0	
Religious studies	**9**	
Protestant, Catholic, Jewish, Alevi, and Islamic religious studies	0	
Orthodox religious studies	7	*Mitteleuropa* (3; 2 as part of *West- und Mitteleuropa*), *Nordeuropa* (1, as part of *Zentral- und Nordeuropa*), *Westeuropa* (2), *westeuropäische* (1)
Syrian Orthodox religious studies	2	*Europa* (2)
Artistic subjects	**0**	
Art	0	
Music	0	

A substantial number of the instances of 'Europe' relate to information on, or references to the guidelines and directives of the European educational systems. For example, the only mention of Europe in the curricula for German, mathematics, chemistry, physics, and biology is the following standard statement, which appears in the foreword of seventeen curricula:[12]

> Responsible handling of the learning and lives of young people requires an adjustment of the school training periods to the corresponding regulations

in most European countries. (Ministerium für Schule und Weiterbildung des Landes Nordrhein-Westfalen [MSBNRW] 2007a, 3)

(*Ein verantwortlicher Umgang mit der Lern- und Lebenszeit junger Menschen erfordert eine Anpassung der schulischen Ausbildungszeiten an die entsprechenden Regelungen in den meisten europäischen Staaten.*)

The analysis of the curricula corpus shows that Europe is not addressed in the learning material of fourteen of thirty-one curricula. In five subjects, 'Europe' occurs only once in the standard statement in the foreword, and not at all in nine curricula (Practical philosophy, Sport, Art and Music, and Protestant, Catholic, Jewish, Alevi, and Islamic religious studies).

In the recommendations in 'Education about Europe in Schools' (KMK 2008), the subjects of history and political education are defined as central to knowledge and understanding of Europe. To gain a more precise understanding of the findings, we examined the instances of 'Europe' in these two subjects and compared them to the content mentioned in the recommendations.

Content Analysis: Europe in the Curricula

According to the recommendations in 'Education about Europe in Schools' (KMK 2008), learning about Europe and the development of Europe is obligatory in the subjects of history and political education. Also, Education about Europe is a required element of subjects with geographic, economic, and legal content. In the federal state of North Rhine–Westphalia, this means that Europe-related material must be taught in the social science subjects of geography, history, and politics/economics. In the curriculum corpus we identified nine (geography), eleven (history), and three (politics/economics) instances of Europe in those subjects; in history and in politics/economics, one of these instances is the above-mentioned statement about the 'regulations in most European countries'.

The recommendations specifically state that when studying history, the students should learn 'about the origins of European peoples and states and the origins of the political-social, ideological and religious movements, power struggles, ideas and cultural creations that determined their path, and about the history of European integration' (KMK 2008, 8). The comparison of these recommendations with the curriculum content of the subject of history reveals that the relevance of the history of the European continent is already emphasised in the selection of subjects. The curriculum also highlights the importance of 'taking the European perspective into account at a very early stage in order to make one's position and its rationale more comprehensible' (MSBNRW 2007b, 23). Accordingly, the subjects of 'Europe in the middle ages' and 'Europe is changing' (MSBNRW 2007b, 23) are part of the obligatory content. 'Europe' is also a focus of the following topics:

- 'What people in ancient times knew about each other', with a focus on 'world views and geographic knowledge of Africa, Europe, Asia' (MSBNRW 2007b, 27);
- 'What people in the Middle Ages knew about each other', with a focus on 'world views and geographic knowledge of Asia (including Arabia) and Europe' (MSBNRW 2007b, 30);
- 'New worlds and new horizons', with a focus on 'Europeans and non-Europeans—discoveries and conquests' (MSBNRW 2007b, 30);
- 'National Socialism and the Second World War', with a focus on the 'disfranchisement, persecution and murder of European Jews, Sinti and Roma, and dissenters, between 1933 and 1945', and 'Flight and expulsion from Europe' (MSBNRW 2007b, 31);
- 'Reorganisation of the world and the situation in Germany, with a focus on "transnational cooperation: European unification and the United Nations"' (MSBNRW 2007b, 31).

According to the recommendations, the subject of politics/economics should include knowledge of

> the existing and changing political, social and economic processes and systems of order, their values, norms and realities; ... the economic and legal foundations, especially of the European Union [and] the ability to participate in social and economic events in Europe. (KMK 2008, 8)

> *([...] die bestehenden und sich verändernden politischen, gesellschaftlichen und wirtschaftlichen Abläufe und Ordnungssysteme, ihre Werte, Normen und Realitäten; die ökonomischen und rechtlichen Grundlagen insbesondere der Europäischen Union [sowie] die Befähigung zur Teilhabe am sozialen und wirtschaftlichen Geschehen in Europa)*

In the curriculum for the subject of politics/economics, there are three instances of 'Europe'. Two of them refer to skills and topics. Along with the ability to understand democracy (MSBNRW 2007a, 27), students should be able to discuss 'the development, opportunities and central problems of the European Union using selected examples' (MSBNRW 2007a, 28). Eight topics are linked to this specific ability, and of these, the topic of 'International Politics in the Age of Globalisation' addresses 'developments, expectations and current problems' (MSBNRW 2007a, 33) in Europe, as one of three focal points.

The recommendations for the subject of geography apply a global perspective that includes 'dealing with Europe's worldwide economic networks and its role with regard to the global challenges of our time' (KMK 2008, 8). They also envisage thematising Europe at a more local level, 'with the diversity of its landscape types and its cultural, environmental and economic space that has been shaped by man for centuries' (KMK 2008, 8). In the geography curriculum, Europe is combined with 'knowledge about Germany as a reference area with perspectives on Europe' (MSBNRW 2007c, 24). In years five and six, Europe is part of the overall framework of knowledge of 'Germany with European perspectives' (MSBNRW 2007c, 23). For years seven to nine, Europe appears in the topics, 'Non-European and Europe' (MSBNRW 2007c, 23) and 'change in economic and political structures under the influence of globalisation'. Here, the focus is on 'competition between European regions in the context of structural change, transformation and integration' (MSBNRW 2007c, 31). For years seven to nine, examples of 'theme-related topographical interdependencies' (MSBNRW 2007c, 27), include 'economically active and passive areas in the member states of the EU' (MSBNRW 2007c, 31), and for years five and six, 'important industrial and densely populated areas in the member states of the European Union and main destinations of German tourists in various European countries' (MSBNRW 2007c, 27).

In the recommendations, languages have a central role 'in giving access to Europe's cultural world' (KMK 2008, 8). This applies not only to modern foreign languages but also to ancient languages, which 'are of great importance for a deeper understanding of the common European heritage' (KMK 2008, 8). At first glance, the number of instances of 'Europe' in the foreign-language curricula suggests the comprehensive inclusion of material relevant to Europe, with the exception of the curriculum for German, which shows no instances of 'Europe', although according to the recommendations, in this subject in particular, there is a 'special obligation and opportunity to present the relationships between the German language and literature, and the environment of European languages and literatures' (KMK 2008, 8).

In the English curriculum, eighteen of twenty-one instances of 'Europe' refer to (educational) policy instruments and bodies such as the *Council of Europe* (12 instances), the *Common European Framework of Reference for languages* (4 instances) or the *European Language Portfolio* (2 references). These are not actually part of the learning material for the subject of English, but form a framework for the European standardisation of the skills to be acquired when learning a foreign language. The other three instances are:

(a) the standard statement in the foreword (e.g. MSBNRW 2007a, 3);
(b) a statement that 'the political, cultural and economic development of Europe in the context of international cooperation and global competition places increased demands on foreign language teaching' (MSBNRW 2007d, 11); and
(c) the statement that the knowledge 'about living environments influenced by the English language in the European context' (MSBNRW 2007d, 31) should be extended to include knowledge of other, non-European, English-speaking countries, as part of the students' intercultural competence.

A search in the curricula for the other subjects listed in the recommendations—'Religion and Ethics, Philosophy, Mathematics, Science and

Technology, Art and Music, and Physical Education'—(KMK 2008, 8) did not yield any instances of 'Europe', apart from the standard statement in the foreword. Although the recommendations treat those subjects as 'indispensable components of an overall European concept at school' that are intended to provide valuable 'contributions to the promotion of European awareness' (KMK 2008, 9), the results of our analysis suggest that the implementation of Europe in the curricula does not reflect the content of the recommendations at all.

The Educational-Media Perspective

The curricula are educational policy texts that provide an overarching framework for developing educational media and using them in the classroom. Even though the curricula we analysed do not fully implement the recommendations for 'Education about Europe in Schools' (KMK 2008), and in some cases even completely dispense with the specification of 'Europe' in the descriptions of skills and topics, it is possible to identify some aspects of an EXPECTED state of the learners' knowledge, especially in the core subjects of social studies (history, geography and politics/economics). In our study, only a limited comparison between EXPECTED and ACTUAL states is possible (e.g. for thematic learning vocabulary related to 'Europe', Krämer et al. 2021), as it requires more data. Thus, only preliminary hypotheses may be developed for the relationship between the EXPECTED state suggested by the curricula, and the ACTUAL state of study participants' knowledge, revealed by the concept map data. For further research, it is essential to also consider educational media and their use in teaching, when determining the EXPECTED state, because these are essential building blocks of the learners' ACTUAL state. We illustrate this with two examples.

The example in Fig. 9.9 demonstrates a German textbook's use of a mind map to gather together ideas associated with Europe (Biermann and Schurf 2000, 144). The mind map, which is part of the teaching unit, *Wege ins europäische Haus* (lit. 'Ways into the European House'), serves as an example for the subsequent task in Fig. 9.9 (e.g. the question in 5a): 'What does Europe mean to you personally? Collect your ideas

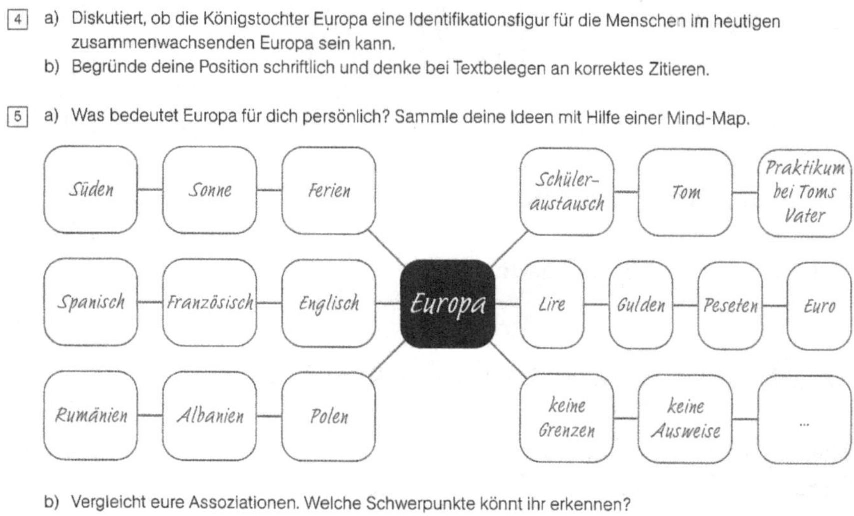

4 a) Diskutiert, ob die Königstochter Europa eine Identifikationsfigur für die Menschen im heutigen zusammenwachsenden Europa sein kann.
b) Begründe deine Position schriftlich und denke bei Textbelegen an korrektes Zitieren.

5 a) Was bedeutet Europa für dich persönlich? Sammle deine Ideen mit Hilfe einer Mind-Map.

b) Vergleicht eure Assoziationen. Welche Schwerpunkte könnt ihr erkennen?

Fig. 9.9 Example of the use of a mind map of the subject of Europe in a German textbook (Biermann and Schurf 2000, 144; separate authorship is not shown in the textbook's image source index)

with the help of a mind map'. This cognitive activation is supplemented by a task that calls for reflection, presented under the sample map in Fig. 9.9 (e.g. the instructions in 5b): 'Compare your associations. Which key aspects do you recognise?' The instructively used lexemes, *idea* and *association*, indicate that this task is intended to activate lexically bound knowledge, as existing knowledge in the sense of preconcepts.

According to Hilary Putnam, such lexically bound preconcepts may also be understood as 'stereotypes':

> In ordinary parlance a 'stereotype' is a conventional (frequently malicious) idea (which may be wildly inaccurate) of what an X looks like or acts like or is. Obviously, I am trading on some features of the ordinary parlance. I am not concerned with the malicious stereotypes (save where the language itself is malicious); but I am concerned with conventional ideas, which may be inaccurate. (Putnam 1975, 249)

In the example provided, there are certainly some associations that may be understood as stereotypes of Europe in the sense intended by Putnam (e.g. *Süden—Sonne—Ferien* (South—Sun—Holiday). Also, individual experiences are indicated, which are linked to *Europa*: *Schüleraustausch* (Europe: school exchange)—*Tom—Praktikum bei Toms Vater* (Tom—internship with Tom's father). However, statements that present declarative knowledge of Europe in the areas of languages, currencies, states, and freedom of movement predominate.

The second example references Europe more indirectly. In a sixth-year textbook for German, a unit called, 'Table manners and eating habits' leads to a text with the title, 'Europe: no lip-smacking and slurping'. The text addresses cultural norms as a focus of awareness, and, indirectly, identity formation (Henninger et al. 2012, 214). Not a single state name appears in the text, but a collective 'we' presents a reference to people in Europe. In some other textbooks for teaching German, too, the topic of 'Europe' is addressed less in terms of political structure than in terms of cultural knowledge and stereotypical (here, in Kilian's sense, 2005) classifications (e.g. Diekhans and Fuchs 2015, 238). Our project's ongoing research will focus on (thematic) correlations at the junctions of the recommendations, curricula, educational media, classroom practices and learners' knowledge, based on data from concept maps.

Conclusions: Europe and Europeanness

The recommendations for 'Education about Europe in Schools' (KMK 2008), define Europe-oriented 'skills and attitudes' intended to develop an 'awareness of Europe' among students, and 'enable them to lead a successful life in Europe' (KMK 2008, 5). In these recommendations, the term 'identity' is interpreted in a culture-specific way, as 'one's own cultural identity' among various European cultural identities, but in a subsequent step this is also extended to Europe, and understood in terms of 'European identity':

> The aim of educational work at schools must be to awaken and promote in young people an awareness of a European identity. This includes preparing young people to actively assume their responsibilities as citizens of the European Union. (KMK 2008, 7)

> (*Ziel der pädagogischen Arbeit an Schulen muss es sein, in den jungen Menschen das Bewusstsein einer europäischen Identität zu wecken und zu fördern. Hierzu gehört auch die Vorbereitung der jungen Menschen darauf, ihre Aufgaben als Bürgerinnen und Bürger in der Europäischen Union aktiv wahrzunehmen.*)

One of the most delicate tasks of cultural linguistics and language didactics is to answer the question of whether and to what extent actual knowledge may be inferred from linguistic data elicited through a study. It is even more difficult to use language or elicited data to infer what a person thinks, feels, and wants with regard to his or her self-image and self-positioning in a social group, a region, or a nation, for example.

Our research aims to reconstruct concepts and mental models of Europe, and to interpret them as indicators and factors of the formation of national and European identities, among other things. In the various studies presented in this volume, and in some of our previous studies (e.g. the SMiK project on national stereotypes: www.stereotypenprojekt.eu; Hallsteinsdóttir and Kilian 2016), the data may be interpreted in terms of indicators and factors of regional and national identity, but cannot yet be understood in terms of indicators and factors concerning the existence of European identities in the narrower sense. Jasper et al.'s findings, based on data on German students, suggest similar conclusions (2017, 122ff.).

Although some of the data from the concept maps in our pilot studies may be interpreted as references to mental models of {europ}, as more or less solid concepts of Europe, the data primarily indicate declarative knowledge, and primarily declarative knowledge acquired at school. Only a very small number of entries, compared to our data on national stereotypes, for example (Hallsteinsdóttir and Kilian 2016), may be interpreted as to at least some extent reflecting associative–semantic stereotypes of the prompt {europ}. We regard this as suggesting that our study participants only weakly associate {europ} with themselves as individuals, and do not develop stereotypes, as those require personal points of reference.

For the delicate step of interpreting linguistic data as indicators and factors of identity, it seems desirable to use the concept of 'European identity' as a variable framework (certainly also in the sense of frame semantics) and, in further investigations, to favour the concept of 'being

European', described by Zappettini as 'Europeanness' (Zappettini 2019, chapter 6.5). Here, 'Europeanness' appears to be the construction of a 'European identity' that, on the one hand, reformulates aspects of national identities, and, on the other hand, includes cosmopolitan experiences in a transnational-European context (Zappettini 2019, 171–72). We suggest that the nodes and connecting lines of the concept maps should be used to establish the concrete value of a concept of 'being European' that goes beyond declarative school-derived knowledge, and that may be interpreted as experience-based. Furthermore, we consider the connecting lines relevant indicators of concepts of Europe that include 'stereotypes', both in the sense Putnam describes (see above) and national stereotypes and indicators of preconcepts and subjective theories.

We must also discuss the extent to which the results of our studies may be interpreted as statements about narrative identity, in the sense described by Paul Ricoeur (1988), and thus perhaps as indicators of a 'European identity'. Based on our data, it may be possible to reconstruct aspects of European identity in the sense of 'narrative identity', that is, an identity that is composed of the stories of one's—European—life experience and others' narratives of their—European—life experiences (communicated through conversation, in the news, in literature, in films etc.). Zappettini's approach is compatible with this as he attempts to reconstruct 'European identity' and 'Europeanness' as bottom-up constructions from various discursive sources.

Summary and Outlook

The aim of this chapter is to contribute to an interdisciplinary research framework that explores linguistic constructions of concepts and mental models of Europe. We focused on testing and analysing the concept map as an instrument for collecting data that have been analysed as mental models and lexically bound knowledge. The results of five pilot studies were presented, the analysis of which revealed critical insights into the methodological conception of the survey instrument, and how it could be implemented in larger research frameworks of a similar kind.

Our analysis of the lexical data collected through the concept maps also revealed an extensive lexical inventory that is directly or indirectly related to the morpheme {europ}. We suggest that those data may be interpreted as representing the ACTUAL state of the study participants' knowledge of Europe. In a further step, we demonstrated how interpreting the data could be used to draw conclusions about the lexical construction of a European identity.

The (exemplary) analysis of documents from an educational policy framework—curricula and recommendations for 'Education about Europe in Schools'—has revealed discrepancies that need to be further explored, for instance, with a comprehensive investigation of teaching practices and educational media related to learners' mental models of Europe.

Notes

1. At this point we would like to mention the revised recommendations for *Europabildung in der Schule* (Education about Europe in Schools), which came into force on October 15, 2020; however, at the time of our data collection, the 2008 version was valid, which is why this article refers exclusively to the 2008 version.
2. Konerding (1993, 92–101) uses 'concept' to indicate a combination of several elements of one's knowledge, that is, a constellation of knowledge that may be activated and called into consciousness. It is also based on the assumption that the construction and production of these concepts is essentially accomplished through lexical–semantic (linguistic) means.
3. The concept map may also be used as an evaluative instrument that accompanies a teaching unit, which, to our knowledge, has not yet been done. To understand whether and to what extent knowledge structures related to a subject change over the course of a lesson, students could create a concept map for a given subject before a lesson and continue working on it during and/or after a lesson. They may change, delete, or keep structure and content elements of their concept map. By using different colours (analogue) or a transparent editing process (digital), it is possible to trace the impact of a lesson on the structure, content, and extent of individual, language-bound knowledge structures.

4. Regardless of the focus question, the centre and starting point of the concept map may still be 'cars'.
5. Further possibilities for analysing and interpreting concept-map data are found in Krämer et al. (2021).
6. Online, as a part of The Leipzig Corpora Collection: https://wortschatz.uni-leipzig.de/de.
7. Number of lexemes in brackets; only lexical fields with five or more lexemes are included.
8. See www.schulentwicklung.nrw.de/lehrplaene/lehrplannavigator-s-i/gymnasium-g8/index.html.
9. Sinclair and Rockwell (2020). *Voyant Tools*. Accessed September 29, 2020. https://voyant-tools.org/?panels=cirrus%2Creader%2Ctrends%2Cdocuments%2Ccontexts&corpus=8158cf50904cf59dbe9367077e3083b7.
10. Result after the additional manual check, and assignment of word divisions with hyphens.
11. As *Voyant* sometimes does not recognise hyphenated words as whole words, we cannot exclude the possibility that some instances of *Europa* words were not identified by our search method.
12. This statement was also included in the curricula for Chinese, English, Geography, French, History, Greek, Italian, Japanese, Latin, Politics/Economics, Portuguese, Russian, and Spanish.

References

Aitchison, Jean. 1997. *Wörter im Kopf. Eine Einführung in das mentale Lexikon*. Tübingen: De Gruyter.

Anderson, Lorin W., David R. Krathwol, Peter W. Airsasian, Kathleen A. Cruikshank, Richard W. Mayer, Paul R. Pintrich, James Raths, and Merlin C. Wittrock. 2001. *A Taxonomy for Learning, Teaching, and Assessing. A Revision of Bloom's Taxonomy of Educational Objectives*. New York: Langman.

Ausubel, David P. 1960. The Use of Advance Organizers in the Learning and Retention of Meaningful Verbal Material. *Journal of Educational Psychology* 51: 267–272.

———. 1974. *Psychologie des Unterrichts*. Weinheim: Beltz.

Bacia, Ewa, and Hermann Josef Abs. 2017. Politische und zivilgesellschaftliche Bildung in Kernlehrplänen. In *Das politische Mindset von 14-jährigen.*

Ergebnisse der International Civic and Citizenship Education Study 2016, ed. Hermann Josef Abs and Katrin Hahn-Laudenberg, 27–46. Münster and New York: Waxmann.

Banneck, Catharina. 2014. Im Praxistest: Thema im Unterricht extra "Wahlen für Einsteiger" und "Europa für Einsteiger". Accessed October 1, 2020. https://www.bpb.de/lernen/formate/rezensionen/183308/im-praxistest-thema-im-unterricht-extra-wahlen-fuer-einsteiger-und-europa-fuer-einsteiger

Barte, Burghard, Julia Landgraf, and Andreas Mühling. 2020. Concept Mapping als ein Weg zur Erfassung professionsbezogener Wissensanteile im Praxissemester. In *Formen der (Re-)Präsentation fachlichen Wissens. Ansätze und Methoden für die Lehrerinnen- und Lehrerbildung in den Fachdidaktiken und den Bildungswissenschaften*, ed. Tobias Heinz, Margot Janzen, and Jörg Kilian, 79–93. Münster and New York: Waxmann.

Biermann, Heinrich, and Bernd Schurf. 2000. *Deutschbuch. Sprach- und Lesebuch 10*. Berlin: Cornelsen.

Brüning, Ludger, and Tobias Saum. 2019. *Erfolgreich unterrichten durch Visualisieren. Die Kraft von Concept Maps*. Essen: Neue Deutsche Schule Verlagsgesellschaft.

Cañas, Alberto J., and Joseph D. Novak. 2006. The Theory Underlying Concept Maps and How to Construct Them. Accessed October 1, 2020. http://cmap.ihmc.us/publications/researchpapers/TheoryUnderlyingConceptMaps.pdf

Cañas, Alberto J., Novak, Joseph D. 2012. Freedom vs. Restriction of content and structure during concept mapping – possibilities and limitations for construction and assessment. In Concept Maps: Theory, Methodology, Technology. Proceedings of the Fifth International Conference on Concept Mapping. Valletta. http://cmc.ihmc.us/cmc2012papers/cmc2012-p192.pdf

Derbentseva, Natalia, Frank Safayeni, and Alberto J. Cañas. 2006. Two Strategies for Encouraging Functional Relationships in Concept Maps. In *Concept Maps: Theory, Methodology, Technology. Proceedings of the Second International Conference of Concept Mapping*, ed. Alberto J. Cañas and Joseph D. Novak, 582–589. San José: Editorial Universidad de Costa Rica. Accessed May 5, 2022. http://cmc.ihmc.us/cmc2006Papers/cmc2006-p164.pdf

Diekhans, Johannes, and Michael Fuchs. 2015. *P.A.U.L.D. Persönliches Arbeits- und Lesebuch Deutsch 9*. Brauchschweig: Schöningh.

Dornseiff, Franz. 2020. *Der deutsche Wortschatz nach Sachgruppen. Mit einer lexikographisch-historischen Einführung und einer ausführlichen Bibliographie zur Lexikographie und Onomasiologie*. Berlin and New York: De Gruyter.

Dunker, Nina. 2010. *Concept Maps im naturwissenschaftlichen Sachunterricht. Didaktische Rekonstruktion am Beispiel des Lerngegenstandes Feuer.* Oldenburg: BIS.

———. 2017. Erweiterung der Grounded Theory durch Concept Maps als Auswertungsmethode. Öffnungen innerhalb eines Forschungsparadigmas. In *Forschungspraxen in der Bildungsforschung. Zugänge und Methoden von Wissenschaftlerinnen und Wissenschaftlern*, ed. Martin Heinrich, Carolin Kölzer, and Lilian Streblow, 119–136. Münster: Waxmann.

Edelmann, Walter. 1986. *Lernpsychologie. Eine Einführung.* Munich and Weinheim: Beltz.

Frey, Hanno. 2010. *Lesekompetenz verbessern? Lesestrategien und Bewusstmachungsverfahren nutzen!* Münster: Waxmann.

Geyr, Mv, Hornung, L., Noack, F., et al. 2007. Die Europäische Dimension in den Lehrplänen der deutschen Bundesländer. Vergleichende Studie im Auftrag der Europäischen Kommission. https://www.jugendpolitikineuropa.de/downloads/4-20-2352/eab_studie%5B1%5D.pdf

Goll, Thomas. 2014. Die Entwicklung des politischen Wissens bei Schüler/innen in den Schulformen der Sekundarstufe I (POWIS II). Ergebnisse einer Längsschnittstudie. In *Politische Bildung als lebenslanges Lernen*, ed. Dirk Lange and Tonio Oftering, 125–137. Schwalbach am Taunus: Wochenschau Verlag.

Graf, Dittmar. 2014. Concept Mappings als Diagnosewerkzeug. In *Methoden in der naturwissenschafts-didaktischen Forschung*, ed. Dirk Krüger, Ilka Parchmann, and Horst Schecker, 325–337. Berlin and Heidelberg: Springer.

Hahn-Laudenberg, Katrin. 2017. *Konzepte von Demokratie bei Schülerinnen und Schülern. Erfassung von Veränderungen politischen Wissens mit Concept-Maps.* Wiesbaden: Springer.

Hallsteinsdóttir, Erla, and Jörg Kilian, eds. 2016. '{deutsch} und {dänisch} im Stereotyp. Stereotypenwelten und ihre sprachlich-kulturellen Konstituierungsformen/{german} and {danish} in stereotypes. The worlds of stereotypes and their linguistic-cultural constitution forms'. Linguistik online 79 (5). Accessed October 1, 2020. https://bop.unibe.ch/linguistik-online/issue/view/678

Henninger, Heike, Michael Jahnsdorf, and Maximilian Nutz. 2012. *Deutsch. kompetent 6.* Stuttgart and Leipzig: Ernst Klett.

Himangshu, Sumitra, and Amy Cassata-Widera. 2010. Beyond Individual Classrooms: How Valid are Concept Maps for Large Scale Assessment? In *Concept Maps: Making Learning Meaningful. Proceedings of the 4th*

International Conference on Concept Mapping (Viña del Mar), ed. Alberto Cañas and Joseph Novak, 58–65. Providencia: Lom Ediciones.

Jasper, Janina, Johanna F. Ziemes, and Hermann Josef Abs. 2017. Identität und politische Selbstwirksamkeit. In *Das politische Mindset von 14-jährigen. Ergebnisse der International Civic and Citizenship Education Study 2016*, ed. Hermann Josef Abs and Katrin Hahn-Laudenberg, 112–134. Münster: Waxmann.

Kilian, Jörg. 2005. Assoziative Stereotype. Sprachtheoretische, sprachkritische und sprachdidaktische Anmerkungen zum lexikalisch verknüpften Mythos, Aberglauben, Vorurteil. In *Brisante Semantik. Neuere Konzepte und Forschungsergebnisse einer kulturwissenschaftlichen Linguistik*, ed. Dietrich Busse, Thomas Niehr, and Martin Wengeler, 117–132. Tübingen: Niemeyer.

Konerding, Klaus-Peter. 1993. *Frames und lexikalisches Bedeutungswissen. Untersuchungen zur linguistischen Grundlegung einer Frametheorie und zu ihrer Anwendung in der Lexikographie*. Tübingen: De Gruyter.

Krämer, Corinna, Jörg Kilian, and Erla Hallsteinsdóttir. 2021. Europa als mentales Modell in den Köpfen von Lernenden. Zur Ermittlung lexikalisch gebundenen Wissens mit Concept Maps. *Zeitschrift für Angewandte Linguistik* 74 (1): 61–92.

Kultusministerkonferenz (KMK). 2008. Europabildung in der Schule. Empfehlung der Ständigen Konferenz der Kultusminister der Länder in der Bundesrepublik Deutschland. Accessed October 30, 2016. https://www.kmk.org/themen/allgemeinbildende-schulen/weitere-unterrichtsinhalte-und-themen/europabildung.html

Landgraf, Julia. (Unpublished). Verzahnung als Methode, Vernetzung als Ziel. Eine Concept Map-Studie zum fachbezogenen Professionswissen von Lehramtsstudierenden des Faches Deutsch im Bereich Lesen und Textverstehen. Master's thesis, Kiel University.

Lehrplannavigator. 2020. Qualitäts- und Unterstützungsagentur—Landesinstitut für Schule. Accessed October 1, 2020. https://www.schulentwicklung.nrw.de/lehrplaene/lehrplannavigator-s-i/gymnasium-g8/index.html

Miller, Norma L., Cañas, Alberto J. 2008. Effect of the nature of the focus question on presence of dynamic propositions in a concept map. Proceedings of the Third International Conference on Concept Mapping. Tallinn. http://cmc.ihmc.us/cmc2008papers/cmc2008-p251.pdf (11.09.2020).

Ministerium für Schule und Weiterbildung des Landes Nordrhein-Westfalen (MSBNRW). 2007a. *Kernlehrplan für das Gymnasium—Sekundarstufe I (G8)*

in Nordrhein-Westfalen. Politik/Wirtschaft (LP-W/P). Frechen: Ritterbach Verlag.

———. 2007b. *Kernlehrplan für das Gymnasium—Sekundarstufe I (G8) in Nordrhein-Westfalen*. Geschichte (LP-G). Frechen: Ritterbach Verlag.

———. 2007c. *Kernlehrplan für das Gymnasium—Sekundarstufe I (G8) in Nordrhein-Westfalen*. Erdkunde (LP-Erd). Frechen: Ritterbach Verlag.

———. 2007d. *Kernlehrplan für das Gymnasium—Sekundarstufe I (G8) in Nordrhein-Westfalen*. Englisch (LP-Eng). Frechen: Ritterbach Verlag.

Montada, Leo. 1995. Die geistige Entwicklung aus der Sicht Jean Piagets. In *Entwicklungspsychologie. Ein Lehrbuch*, ed. Rolf Oerter and Leo Montada, 518–560. Weinheim: Beltz.

Mühling, Andreas. 2014. Investigating Knowledge Structures in Computer Science Education. Master's thesis, Technische Universität München.

Novak, Joseph D., and Alberto J. Cañas. 2008. The Theory Underlying Concept Maps and How to Construct and Use Them. Accessed October 1, 2020. http://cmap.ihmc.us/Publications/ResearchPapers/TheoryUnderlyingConceptMaps.pdf

Putnam, Hilary. 1975. *Mind, Language and Reality*. Cambridge: Cambridge University Press.

Quenzel, Gudrun. 2005. *Konstruktionen von Europa. Die europäische Identität und die Kulturpolitik der Europäischen Union*. Bielefeld: transcript Verlag.

Reichmann, Oskar. 1990. Das onomasiologische Wörterbuch. Ein Überblick. In *Wörterbücher. Ein Internationales Handbuch zur Lexikographie*, ed. Franz Josef Hausmann, Oskar Reichmann, Herbert Ernst Wiegand, and Ladislav Zgusta, 1057–1067. Berlin and New York: De Gruyter.

Ricoeur, Paul. 1988. *Time and Narrative*. Chicago: University of Chicago Press.

Ruiz-Primo, Maria Araceli. 2004. Examining Concept Maps as an Assessment Tool. In *Concept Maps: Theory, Methodology, Technology. Proceedings of the 1st International Conference on Concept Mapping, Pamplona*, ed. Alberto Cañas, Joseph Novak, and Fermin Gonzàles, 1–8. Pamplona: Servicio de Publicaciones de la Universidad Pública de Navarra.

Ruiz-Primo, Maria Araceli, Richard J. Shavelson, Min Li, and Susan Schultz. 2001. On the Validity of Cognitive Interpretations of Scores From Alternative Concept-Mapping Techniques. *Educational Assessment* 7 (2): 99–141.

Schwarz-Friesel, Monika, and Jeanette Chur. 2014. *Semantik: Ein Arbeitsbuch*. Tübingen: Narr.

Seel, Norbert M. 2003. *Psychologie des Lernens. Lehrbuch für Pädagogen und Psychologen*. Munich: UTB.

Sinclair and Rockwell. 2020. *Voyant Tools*. Accessed September 29, 2020. https://voyant-tools.org/?panels=cirrus%2Creader%2Ctrends%2Cdocuments%2Ccontexts&corpus=8158cf50904cf59dbe9367077e3083b7

Stock, Wolfgang. 2008. *Wissensrepräsentation. Wissen auswerten und bereitstellen.* Munich: De Gruyter.

———. 2009. Begriffe und semantische Relationen in der Wissensrepräsentation. *Information, Wissenschaft und Praxis* 60: 403–420.

Storjohann, Petra. 2012. Dornseiff—Der deutsche Wortschatz nach Sachgruppen. In *Große Lexika und Wörterbücher Europas. Europäische Enzyklopädien und Wörterbücher in historischen Porträts*, ed. Ulrike Haß, 477–490. Berlin and Boston: De Gruyter.

Stracke, Iris. 2004. *Einsatz computerbasierter Concept Maps zur Wissensdiagnose in der Chemie. Empirische Untersuchungen am Beispiel des chemischen Gleichgewichts*. Münster and New York: Waxmann.

Sumfleth, Elke, Jasmin Neuroth, and Detlev Leutner. 2010. Concept Mapping—eine Lernstrategie muss man lernen. *CHEMKON* 17 (2): 66–70.

Yin, Yue, Jim Vanides, Maria Araceli Ruiz-Primo, Carlos C. Ayala, and Richard J. Shavelson. 2005. Comparison of Two Concept-Mapping Techniques: Implications for Scoring, Interpretation, and Use. *Journal of Research in Science Teaching* 42 (2): 166–184.

Zappettini, Franco. 2019. *European Identities in Discourse. A Transnational Citizens' Perspective*. London: Bloomsbury Academic.

Ziegler, Béatrice, and Volker Reinhardt. 2012. *Was Schweizer Jugendliche von der EU wissen. Die schweizerische TEESAEC-Studie*. Zürich and Chur: Rüegger.

Ziem, Alexander. 2008. *Frames und sprachliches Wissen. Kognitive Aspekte der semantischen Kompetenz.* Berlin: De Gruyter.

Ziemes, Johanna F., Janina Jasper, Daniel Deimel, Katrin Hahn-Laudenberg, and Hermann Josef Abs. 2017. ICCS 2016—Design und methodisches Vorgehen. In *Das politische Mindset von 14-jährigen. Ergebnisse der International Civic and Citizenship Education Study 2016*, ed. Hermann Josef Abs and Katrin Hahn-Laudenberg, 47–76. Münster and New York: Waxmann.

10

Eye-Tracking as a Scientific Method for Analysing Educational Media: State of the Art and Potential

Stefan Hackl

Introduction

Eye-tracking is a research method that offers numerous possibilities for applications in various scientific disciplines. For example, in pedagogy and subject didactics, this method is used to record learning processes or to reveal learners' problems with cognitively processing presentations of learning content. Current research in the field of educational-media analysis focuses particularly on reading research to identify reading strategies and strategies for supporting learners' text comprehension; increasingly, it also focuses on the influence of images on the (online) reading process. Pioneering theories of reading research, such as the top-down reading strategy presented by Goodman (1967), may be substantiated with the help of eye-tracking by demonstrating corresponding reading paths (cf. Radach et al. 2012).

S. Hackl (✉)
Institute of German Philology, University of Munich, Munich, Germany
e-mail: stefan.hackl@germanistik.uni-muenchen.de

K. Gorbahn et al. (eds.), *Exploring Interconnectedness*, Palgrave Studies in Educational Media, https://doi.org/10.1007/978-3-031-13960-4_10

Based on the direct feedback of fixations (stopping points) and saccades (eye movements) of the eyes on cerebral activity, eye-tracking and its analysis may be used to investigate and purposefully improve the quality of real-world and virtual learning environments (e.g. of textbooks and online platforms). Therein lies the hitherto barely tapped potential of this scientific method. Ballis et al.'s contribution in this book demonstrates how this potential may be better exploited by German-language educational-media research.

The Scientific Method of Eye-Tracking

Eye-tracking is the process of determining where someone is looking. It refers to the scientific method of recording gaze points and eye movements, but it may also measure the characteristics of eye movements and the eye itself. Eye-tracking is usually done with the help of a device called an eye-tracker. These devices may be monitor-based or special glasses worn by the subjects. Most commercially available eye-trackers work by emitting light in the near-infrared range to determine the position of the gaze based on the relative position of the pupil centre and the corneal reflection.

The human gaze jumps from place to place a few times per second. The purpose of these jumps, called saccades, is to bring visual stimuli into the fovea (a small area of peak visual acuity on the retina) and thus into focus. The information thus collected is extracted during fixations, which are short pauses between saccades, where a particular gaze point is fixated for a little longer. Even though eye-tracking captures only foveal vision (what we directly fixate/focus on) and the paths of the eye movements, it provides useful information about visual attention, because, usually, fixation coincides with attention, and thus also reveals information about our reception/perception processes.

As we receive/perceive, saccade targets (i.e. where the next fixation will occur) are selected based on a combination of bottom-up and top-down cognitive processes. In other words, where one looks depends on the characteristics of what one is looking at, and one's goals, experiences and expectations (cf. Bojko 2013, 19).

In general, we distinguish among three structural elements of visual perception, which may be recorded with the help of eye-tracking:

fixations (points of gaze with a certain dwell time of the eye, centred focusing of the fovea on a perceived object), saccades (partial distances between two fixations) and micromovements (especially microsaccades, which are mostly undirected and support physiological fixation control). Each reflects a different cognitive process. However, when interpreting individual gaze (movement) patterns, the results are not always unambiguous (cf. Geise 2011, 167–68). A particular problem of interpreting eye-tracking data is that in most situations, the researcher is a passive observer, and thus can only partially understand what the test person is doing, why he is doing it and what he is thinking. Also, interpretations of psychophysiological data are often contradictory. Therefore, without further contextualisation, few specific insights may be gained into the processes of reception, processing and impact of visual perception. Nevertheless, to the best of our knowledge, eye-tracking data makes it possible to draw general conclusions about the distribution, depth and ranking of cognitive processing, as eye movement and the totality of visual information processing are highly interdependent (cf. Geise 2011, 192).

Just and Carpenter (1980) posited three fundamental assumptions for interpreting fixation in the results of eye-tracking studies on reading. The immediacy assumption states that fixation is interpreted directly in relation to the words registered while reading. However, this assumption is considered to be at least partially refuted by the occurrence of regressions, the context-dependence of fixation duration and the so-called spillover effect, which occurs after words that are difficult to read and understand, when the following word is fixated longer than would be the case in a simpler context (cf. Just and Carpenter 1980, 330; Rayner and Duffy 1986). The eye-mind assumption states that fixation duration an indicator of the depth of cognitive information processing, that is, longer fixation correlates with correspondingly deeper cognitive information processing. This assumption associates regressions with difficulty in reading and comprehension (cf. Just and Carpenter 1980, 330). According to the capacity assumption, fixation duration in reading may also indicate the degree of working memory capacity use. Thus, individuals with higher working memory capacity utilisation have longer fixation durations than those with lower working memory capacity use (cf. Just and Carpenter 1980, 332).

Another important basis for eye-tracking is the knowledge that its results are strongly dependent on the tasks that the test persons are given and, therefore, that these must be chosen carefully and appropriately. Furthermore, the data analysis must always relate to the personal variables that influence gaze behaviour. For eye-tracking, the quality of the data (independent variables) also depends to a large extent on the homogeneity of the study group. For example, in reading studies, central factors such as foreknowledge, word length, text difficulty or objective must be comparable (cf. Just and Carpenter 1980, 340ff.).

Eye-Tracking in Educational (Media) Research and Learning

Eye-tracking has a wide range of applications in educational (media) research, and thus also in connection with research into, and its application in, the fields of teaching and learning. Among other things, eye-tracking is a method for recording cognitive processes in multimedia learning environments, for determining reading levels, for checking the effectiveness of the layouts of learning materials and for checking subject-specific concepts (e.g. reading strategies). Also, eye-tracking is a suitable method for analysing problem-solving strategies in the natural sciences, for investigating reading strategies for solving tasks and for recording learning activity and literacy.

Findings from eye-tracking research may also provide valuable suggestions for the design of explanatory videos that are effective for learning. For example, eye-tracking studies have shown that image elements that are unnecessary for understanding content should be hidden, which is also referred to as the 'coherence principle' (cf. Fäth et al. 2013, 746). Also, eye-tracking helped to determine that the multimedia principle applies only if an image and text are consistent (cf. Schüler 2017, 218–31). Furthermore, eye-tracking studies provide evidence that uncoordinated multimedia elements may lead to memory overload (cf. Wang et al. 2016, 9–18), and visual cueing elements to direct learners' attention to relevant learning content correlate with learning performance (cf.

Tabbers et al. 2004, 71–81). All these findings from eye-tracking research should be included when designing and producing explanatory videos, for example.

Text-Image Units

With regard to important text-image units in educational media, eye-tracking may yield helpful insights that are now considered part of the essential knowledge used in developing multicodal teaching-learning materials. The following theories were confirmed with the help of eye-tracking studies.

Dual encoding in the form of images and text may improve the retention of certain material (Dual Encoding Theory; cf. Paivio 1990, 53ff.). The importance of images during reading was confirmed by two eye-tracking studies: schematic images, in the sense described by the Dual Encoding Theory, may support strong readers. On the other hand, weak readers find it difficult to encode text-picture combinations. They concentrate only on 'simple' text elements (cf. Jian and Ko 2017; Mason et al. 2013). Positive learning effects are achieved through congruent text and image information (cf. Schnotz 2005, 21). Positive effects on the learning process may be achieved through the spatial proximity of text and image (parallelism/integration, instead of continuous presentation) (cf. Holšánová et al. 2009, 10ff.). In multicodal educational media, images that are irrelevant to the learning content are to be regarded as obstacles to learning (cf. Mayer 2010, 170ff.).

Reading Research

Influence of the Reading-Strategy Concept Maps on Reading Competence Compared to the Reading Strategy Questions in the Text

The effectiveness of the use of various scaffolding measures that support reading may be examined with the help of eye-tracking. Concept maps help learners to read a text efficiently, and to take in its meaning; pure

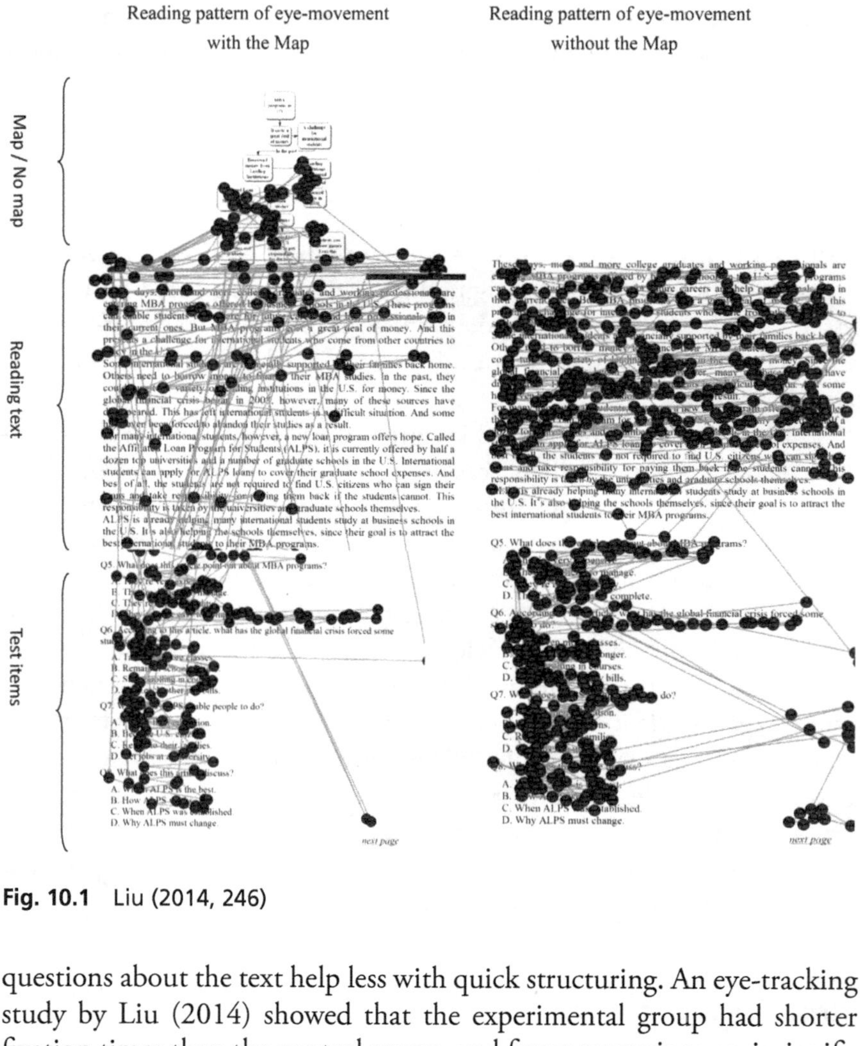

Fig. 10.1 Liu (2014, 246)

questions about the text help less with quick structuring. An eye-tracking study by Liu (2014) showed that the experimental group had shorter fixation times than the control group, and fewer regressions on insignificant parts of the text. They were the more efficient readers. The control group, with the longer fixation times, demonstrated a greater use of cognitive resources, and more regressions. They had difficulty extracting and linking important information (cf. Liu 2014, 245ff.) (Fig. 10.1).

Differences in the Gaze Patterns of High-Performing and Low-Performing PISA Participants When Addressing Reading Tasks

Eye-tracking helped to identify differences in the gaze patterns of high-achieving and low-achieving PISA participants as they addressed reading tasks. Weak readers' strategies are characterised by global searching for important information and memorising as much information as possible. On the other hand, strong readers focus exclusively on the important parts of the text. Further findings show that, on the whole, weak readers have more heterogeneous strategies than strong readers and tend to have small perception margins (cf. Mason et al. 2013, 529ff.) (Fig. 10.2).

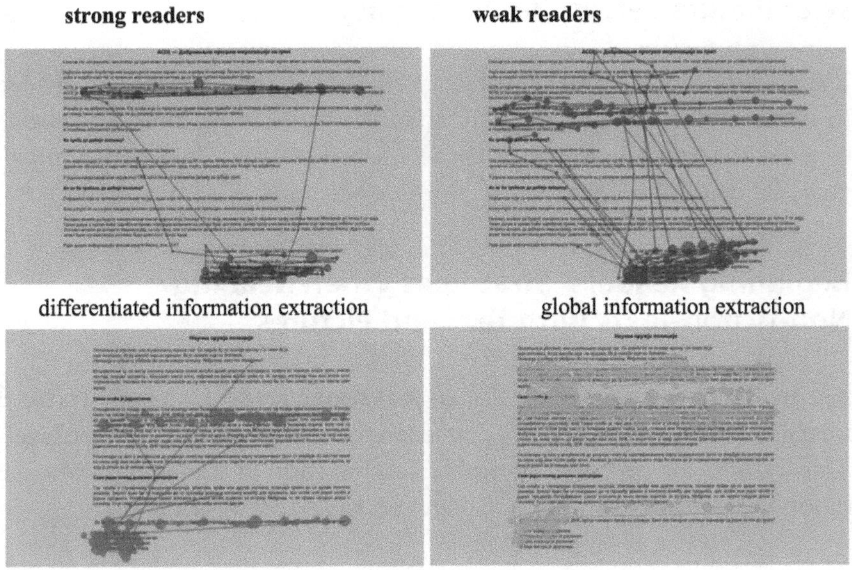

Fig. 10.2 Krstić et al. (2018, 532)

Influence of Text Design and Connectors on Learning and Reading Speed

With regard to the design criteria of teaching/learning material, eye-tracking may offer important insights in terms of the influence of the layout on the reading process. The layout of a text has an influence on the readers' reading speed and the extent of their use of their cognitive resources, both in terms of the text's form and content. According to these research findings, a continuous layout and connectors increase reading speed, and make fewer demands on working memory (cf. van Silfhout et al. 2014, 1043ff.).

Learning Letters with the Help of Readers with Picture-Letter Combinations

Eye-tracking studies provide evidence that there are correlations between fixations on distinct letter locations and letter registration. Thus, knowledge of letter shapes facilitates learning new letters. Literacy is of great importance for reading and writing (cf. Both-de Vries and Bos 2014, 159ff.).

Beginning Readers' Strategies When Reading Non-fiction Texts with Text and Pictures

Eye-tracking studies have confirmed that strong readers integrate text and images, whereas weak readers concentrate only on simple text passages. This leads to the pedagogical-didactic assumption of teaching text-image linking as a reading strategy (cf. Jian and Ko 2017, 276ff.).

Influence of Image Type on Sensory Processes During Reading

Eye-tracking studies indicate that abstract images lead to improved integration of text and images, and more effective reading than representational images do (cf. Mason et al. 2013, 367ff.) (Figs. 10.3 and 10.4).

Un piano inclinato è un qualsiasi piano che formi un angolo compreso fra zero e novanta gradi con un qualsiasi piano orizzontale.

Poniamo che un corpo scenda lungo un piano inclinato, verso un piano orizzontale. Poniamo pure che l'attrito fra il corpo che scende e il piano inclinato sia trascurabile. Per determinare la causa della discesa del corpo lungo il piano inclinato, occorre considerare anzitutto il suo peso. Il peso del corpo che scende è una forza che, in mancanza di ostacoli, lo farebbe cadere, in direzione perpendicolare al piano orizzontale. In quella direzione, però, il corpo trova l'opposizione del piano inclinato. In questo modo, la forza peso è scomposta in due forze componenti. La prima componente è una forza la cui direzione è parallela al piano inclinato. Questa è la componente della forza peso che fa scendere il corpo lungo il piano inclinato, verso il piano orizzontale. La seconda componente è anch'essa una forza la cui direzione è, però, perpendicolare al piano inclinato. Questa componente della forza peso "spinge" il corpo contro il piano inclinato. Quest'ultimo, a sua volta, esercita una forza sul corpo, uguale e contraria rispetto alla componente della forza peso perpendicolare al piano inclinato: la cosiddetta "reazione vincolare del piano". Queste due forze, essendo della stessa intensità ma di verso opposto, si annullano a vicenda.

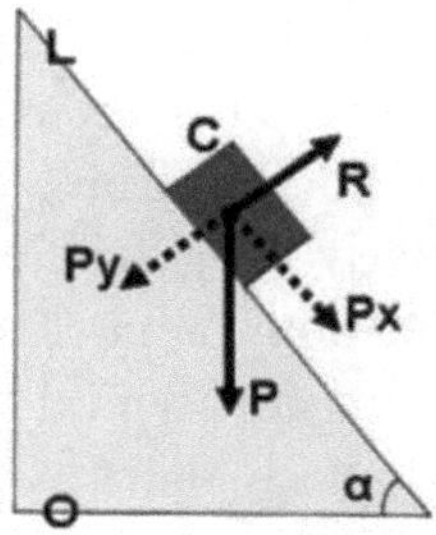

Di conseguenza, la discesa del corpo lungo il piano inclinato è dovuta alla sola forza esercitata dalla componente della forza peso parallela a esso.

Fig. 10.3 Mason et al. (2013, 364)

Un piano inclinato è un qualsiasi piano che formi un angolo compreso fra zero e novanta gradi con un qualsiasi piano orizzontale.

Poniamo che un corpo scenda lungo un piano inclinato, verso un piano orizzontale. Poniamo pure che l'attrito fra il corpo che scende e il piano inclinato sia trascurabile. Per determinare la causa della discesa del corpo lungo il piano inclinato, occorre considerare anzitutto il suo peso. Il peso del corpo che scende è una forza che, in mancanza di ostacoli, lo farebbe cadere, in direzione perpendicolare al piano orizzontale. In quella direzione, però, il corpo trova l'opposizione del piano inclinato. In questo modo, la forza peso è scomposta in due forze componenti. La prima componente è una forza la cui direzione è parallela al piano inclinato. Questa è la componente della forza peso che fa scendere il corpo lungo il piano inclinato, verso il piano orizzontale. La seconda componente è anch'essa una forza la cui direzione è, però, perpendicolare al piano inclinato. Questa componente della forza peso "spinge" il corpo contro il piano inclinato. Quest'ultimo, a sua volta, esercita una forza sul corpo, uguale e contraria rispetto alla componente della forza peso perpendicolare al piano inclinato: la cosiddetta "reazione vincolare del piano". Queste due forze, essendo della stessa intensità ma di verso opposto, si annullano a vicenda.

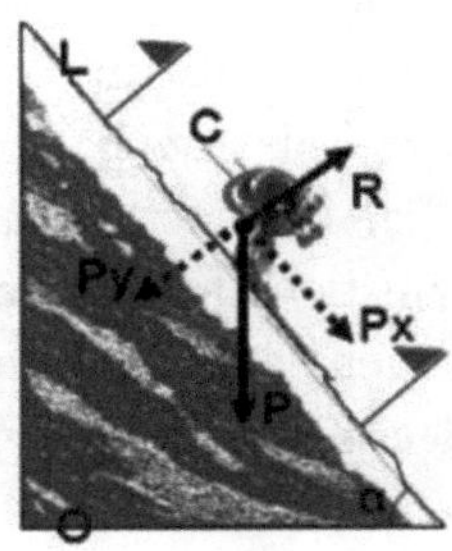

Di conseguenza, la discesa del corpo lungo il piano inclinato è dovuta alla sola forza esercitata dalla componente della forza peso parallela a esso.

Fig. 10.4 Mason et al. (2013, 363)

Computerised and Online Reading

With the help of eye-tracking, it is also possible to identify reading processes in computerised reading settings (reading excerpts from a book on a computer screen) that indicate inattentive reading: so-called mind-wandering. This is expressed by a discontinuous reading process and relatively long fixations on frequently occurring words, relatively short fixations on rarely appearing words and fewer regressions. Such gaze patterns are atypical when reading. As a rule, the opposite is true, that is, relatively short fixation on frequently occurring words and relatively long fixation on rarely appearing words is observed (cf. Faber et al. 2017, 145ff.). Furthermore, eye-tracking studies confirm that the sense-making online reading process may be supported by a number of other online reading strategies: graphic organisers, and the combination of highlighting and note-taking help to integrate relevant sections of a text and have proven to be superior to note-taking alone.

Second-Language Acquisition Research

Another field of research that may be served by eye-tracking is that of second-language acquisition. The fact that speech and hearing are closely linked is known not only because of the importance of phonological awareness for the acquisition of written language; the so-called visual-word paradigm also demonstrates that acoustic contextual information prompts gaze patterns directed at parallel textual and visual information, that is, that acoustic information processing correlates with visual-linguistic information processing (cf. Ellert 2012, 123ff.). For example, when lexical ambiguities occur, the gaze patterns of second-language learners may provide clues to how they resolve them.

With the help of eye-tracking and the bilingual visual-word paradigm, it may be demonstrated that the mental lexicon of the first language is also active when learning a second language, that is, the linguistic input in the second language cognitively activates both languages. Thus, learning a second language leads to the cognitive activation of the mental lexicons of both the first and the second languages. Here, the significant added value of eye-tracking is its recording of learning processing in real time and providing new insights, in the sense of a process orientation in second-language acquisition. Challenges associated with the use of eye-tracking with second-language learners may arise from the prerequisite that the vocabulary used in the studies must already be known. The appropriateness of the speech rate and the examination of the extra-linguistic contextual influences on gaze patterns also contributes to the success of eye-tracking studies of second-language learners (cf. Ellert 2012, 125ff.).

In the case of second-language acquisition, eye-tracking has also provided valuable information on the distribution of attention to verbal and pictorial elements in second-language dictionaries. It may be shown that pictures are not used more frequently for learning the meaning of a word than a corresponding verbal or graphic representation of the word, but that there is a balance in viewing preferences. There is no significant preference for the pictorial or the verbal or graphic elements of words in second-language dictionaries. As a rule, there is an equally frequent fixation on images and text (cf. Lew et al. 2017, 60ff.). This finding is also consistent with Paivio's Dual Encoding Theory (1990, 53ff.; see Chap. 3, this volume).

Challenges associated with using eye-tracking in second-language acquisition research are primarily due to a lack of standards, and to the validity of the interpretation, as it is difficult to control the independent variables and to reach correct conclusions from the results. Owing to a lack of standardisation (e.g. with regard to fixation duration, i.e. when this is to be considered short or long), misinterpretations of gaze patterns may also easily occur.

Multimedia Learning

There are two main research foci in multimedia learning—attentional guidance (which attention guidance tools favour learning, comprehension and retention of content presented in multimedia learning environments?) and factors that influence eye-tracking—that provide clues to the design of multimedia learning environments.

Attention Guidance in Multimedia Learning Environments

The most important results of eye-tracking studies on attention guidance in multimedia learning environments indicate that certain attention guidance devices, such as changing colours or presenting content step-by-step, have positive effects on learner comprehension, retention and the perceived learnability of the content. Furthermore, eye-tracking reveals that learners fixate on highlighted content much longer and more often, and that their attention is immediately directed to highlighted elements. Contrary to what one might expect, visual cues such as highlighting content do not detract from the rest of the information presented. Visual cues merely determine the order in which learners direct their attention to individual elements (so-called attention allocation), and therefore may be used specifically to direct attention (cf. Jamet et al. 2008; Koning et al. 2010; Lowe and Boucheix 2011; Madsen et al. 2012).

Factors Affecting Eye-Tracking Measurements in Multimedia Learning

In 2018, Alemdag and Cagiltay published a paper in which they reviewed numerous studies of factors that may influence eye-tracking measurements in multimedia learning. Five main influencing factors emerged: Meyer's multimedia learning principles (which provide essential design principles for multimedia learning environments: signalling, modality, spatial contiguity, coherence, multiple representation, segmenting, pre-training, learner control of pace, redundancy, personalisation, multimedia and temporal contiguity), the multimedia content, individual differences, metacognition and emotions (cf. Alemdag and Cagiltay 2018, 420).

Regarding the type of multimedia content, learners tend to favour a text-dominant learning process in multimedia learning environments. No effects of a specific text type on information processing were found in the analysis of text types. With regard to types of visual content, learners demonstrated increased visual attention when processing dynamic images, rather than static images, which strongly suggests that animations yield better learning outcomes. Where there are individual differences, foreknowledge plays a decisive role, which significantly influences the processing of multimedia content. Also, visual imagination influences the distribution of visual attention (the greater the visual imagination, the greater the visual attention, especially with animations). Although the factors of metacognition and emotion have been identified as two major influences on eye-tracking in multimedia learning, there is still a lack of additional research that would support more precise statements about the exact nature and manner of their influence (cf. Alemdag and Cagiltay 2018, 416–24).

Conclusion

The use of eye-tracking in educational (media) research undoubtedly has many possibilities. One of these is its pronounced process orientation, that is, its observation of the learning process, which offers new findings and insights into learning activities, problem-solving strategies and cognitive processes. This also suggests new approaches to subject-specific concepts, and analytical approaches and support for learners with learning difficulties, because from them, one may gain further insights into cognitive processes, and identify possible starting points for support.

Finally, eye-tracking research may help to develop the essential design principles of analogue and digital educational media, which promote and positively influence learning, and may significantly increase the effectiveness of teaching and learning material. However, very little such research is available, especially in the field of written German or German-language educational media; most studies refer to English-language educational media or written English. In this volume, Ballis et al. (Chap. 11) present a practical example of the application of eye-tracking in German-language educational media research.

References

Alemdag, Ecenaz, and Kursat Cagiltay. 2018. A Systematic Review of Eye Tracking Research on Multimedia Learning. *Computers and Education* 125: 413–428.

Bojko, Aga. 2013. *Eye Tracking the User Experience. A Practical Guide to Research.* Brooklyn, NY: Rosenfeld Media, LLC.

Both-de Vries, Anna C., and Adriana G. Bos. 2014. Visual Processing of Pictures and Letters in Alphabet Books and the Implications for Letter Learning. *Contemporary Educational Psychology* 39 (2): 156–163.

Ellert, Miriam. 2012. Eye Tracking in der Zweitspracherwerbsforschung. Am Beispiel anaphorischer Bezüge. In *Einblicke in die Zweitspracherwerbsforschung und ihre methodischen Verfahren*, ed. Bernt Ahrenholz, 123–144. Berlin and Boston: De Gruyter.

Faber, Myrthe, Robert Bixler, and Sidney K. D'Mello. 2017. An Automated Behavioral Measure of Mind Wandering During Computerized Reading. *Psychonomic Society* 50 (1): 134–150.

Fäth, Johannes, Bianca Watzka, and Raimund Girwidz. 2013. Eyetracker-Untersuchung zu Gestaltungsprinzipien einer Animation. In *Inquiry-based Learning—Forschendes Lernen*, ed. Sascha Bernholt, 746–748. Kiel: IPN-Verlag.

Geise, Stephanie. 2011. Eye-Tracking in der Kommunikations- und Medienwissenschaft: Theorie, Methode und kritische Reflexion. *Studies in Communication and Media* 2: 149–263.

Goodman, Ken. 1967. Lesen: Ein psycholinguistisches Ratespiel. *Zeitschrift des Lesespezialisten* 6: 126–135.

Holšánová, Jana, Nils Holmberg, and Kenneth Holmqvist. 2009. Reading Information Graphics: The Role of Spatial Contiguity and Dual Attentional Guidance. *Applied Cognitive Psychology* 23 (9): 1215–1226.

Jamet, Éric, Monica Gavota, and Christophe Quaireau. 2008. Attention Guiding in Multimedia Learning. *Learning and Instruction* 18 (2): 135–145.

Jian, Yu-Cin, and Hwa-Wei Ko. 2017. Influences of Text Difficulty and Reading Ability on Learning Illustrated Science Texts for Children: An Eye Movement Study. *Computers and Education* 113: 263–279.

Just, Marcel Adam, and Patricia A. Carpenter. 1980. A Theory of Reading. From Eye Fixations to Comprehension. *Psychological Review* 87 (4): 329–354.

de Koning, Björn, Huib K. Tabbers, Remy Rikers, and Fred Paas. 2010. Attention Guidance in Learning from Complex Animation. Seeing Is Understanding? *Learning and Instruction* 20 (2): 111–122.

Krstić, Ksenija, Anđela Šoškić, Vanja Ković, and Kenneth Holmqvist. 2018. All Good Readers Are the Same, But Every Low-Skilled Reader Is Different: An Eye Tracking Study Using PISA Data. *European Journal of Psychology of Education* 33 (4): 521–541.

Lew, Robert, Rafał Kaźmierczak, Ewa Tomczak, and Mateusz Leszkowicz. 2017. Competition of Definition and Pictorial Illustration for Dictionary Users' Attention: An Eye Tracking Study. *International Journal of Lexicography* 31 (1): 53–77.

Liu, Pei-Lin. 2014. Using Eye Tracking to Understand Learner's Reading Process Through the Concept-Mapping Learning Strategy. *Computers and Education* 78: 237–249.

Lowe, Richard, and Jean-Michel Boucheix. 2011. Cueing Complex Animations. Does Direction of Attention Foster Learning Processes? *Learning and Instruction* 21 (5): 650–663.

Madsen, Adrian, Adam Larson, Amy Rouinfar, Allison Coy, Lester Loschky, and N. Sanjay Rebello. 2012. Influence of Visual Cues on Eye Movements and Reasoning in Physics Problems. Accessed May 5, 2022. https://web.phys.ksu.edu/papers/2012/madsen-AERA.pdf

Mason, Lucia, Patrik Pluchino, Maria Caterina Tornatora, and Nicola Ariasi. 2013. An Eye Tracking Study of Learning from Science Text with Concrete and Abstract Illustrations. *The Journal of Experimental Education* 81 (3): 356–384.

Mayer, Richard E. 2010. Unique Contributions of Eye Tracking Research to the Study of Learning with Graphics. *Learning and Instruction* 20 (2): 167–171.

Paivio, Allan. 1990. *Mental Representations: A Dual-Coding Approach*. New York, NY: Oxford University Press.

Radach, Ralph, Thomas Günther, and Lynn Huestegge. 2012. Kommentierte Übersichtsarbeit. Blickbewegungen beim Lesen, Leseentwicklung und Legasthenie. *Lernen und Lernstörungen* 1 (3): 185–204.

Rayner, Keith, and Susan A. Duffy. 1986. Lexical Complexity and Fixation Times in Reading: Effects of Word Frequency, Verb Complexity, and Lexical Ambiguity. *Memory and Cognition* 14: 191–201.

Schnotz, Wolfgang. 2005. An Integrated Model of Text and Picture Comprehension. In *The Cambridge Handbook of Multimedia Learning*, ed. Richard E. Mayer, 48–69. New York, NY: Cambridge University Press.

Schüler, Anne. 2017. Investigating Gaze Behavior During Processing of Inconsistent Text-Picture Information: Evidence of Text-Picture Integration. *Learning and Instruction* 49: 218–231.

van Silfhout, Gerdineke, Jacqueline Evers-Vermeul, Willem M. Mak, and Ted J.M. Sanders. 2014. Connectives and Layout as Processing Signals: How Textual Features Affect Students' Processing and Text Representation. *Journal of Educational Psychology* 106 (4): 1036–1048.
Tabbers, Huib K., Rob L. Martens, and Jeroen J.G. van Merriënboer. 2004. Multimedia Instructions and Cognitive Load Theory: Effects of Modality and Cueing. *British Journal of Educational Psychology* 74 (1): 71–81.
Wang, Ching-Yeh, Meng-Jung Tsai, and Chin-Chung Tsai. 2016. Multimedia Recipe Reading: Predicting Learning Outcomes and Diagnosing Cooking Interest Using Eye Tracking Measures. *Computers in Human Behavior* 62 (9): 9–18.

11

Images and Perceptions of Europe: Exploring a Multi-perspective Design That Comprises Visual, Textual and Subjective Elements

Anja Ballis, Tobias Heinz, and Mira Schienagel

Migration, Europe and Education: Research Questions

During the 2015 refugee crisis, it became evident that many people identified Europe as a place they longed to be. People living in precarious and miserable conditions desired a better life for themselves and their families. Consequently, people set out from the borders of Africa for Italy and Greece, via the Mediterranean Sea. The tragedy of these people, and their difficulty in finding a place in European society, is a challenge for the European Union, and has been frequently discussed in the media.

A. Ballis • M. Schienagel (✉)
Ludwig-Maximilians-Universität München (LMU), München, Germany
e-mail: anja.ballis@germanistik.uni-muenchen.de;
mira.schienagel@campus.lmu.de

T. Heinz (✉)
Christian-Albrechts-Universität zu Kiel (CAU), Kiel, Germany
e-mail: heinz@germsem.uni-kiel.de

K. Gorbahn et al. (eds.), *Exploring Interconnectedness*, Palgrave Studies in Educational Media, https://doi.org/10.1007/978-3-031-13960-4_11

Migration is not new; indeed, scholars have identified migration as a key aspect of societies, which has a significant impact on everyday life. Given this understanding, our use of the term 'migration' covers an analytical category that refers to the movement of people intertwined with processes of societal change. These changes influence lifestyles, biographies and languages of both those already living in a given country, and the people moving to it. Consequently, migration may be understood as a phenomenon that influences and *rebuilds* society as a whole (Foroutan and İkiz 2016, 138). From this perspective, migration is no longer regarded as a crisis: the movement of people is an integral part of twenty-first-century societies (Mecheril et al. 2010).

Especially in educational settings, an understanding of migration plays an important role for students' success at school. Of central concern is the extent to which students may be taught to understand migration as a normal condition that enriches people's lives, rather than as a threat. The cultural backgrounds and languages of migrants should be appreciated, and not regarded as inferior. At German universities, teacher education puts special emphasis on the topic of migration. Various disciplines, such as pedagogy, the German language and political science, address student diversity at schools, and its implications for teaching and learning. Despite these efforts, we know little about the beliefs of students becoming teachers and their understanding of migration in Europe.

The focus of our study was how students studying to become teachers perceive Europe with respect to migration. Thus, we asked them to look at educational material and reflect on Europe. We aimed to understand their image[1] of Europe in light of migration, which we regard as a metaphor and as a visual practice. Consequently, we bundled these considerations into three research questions to shed light on students becoming teachers' evaluation of the role of migration for Europe in educational contexts: (i) Which typical viewing patterns do the recipients use while observing a text–image task cue in educational material? (ii) What are the recipients perceptions and images of Europe? (iii) What connections and conclusions related to teacher education may be drawn from the study results?

Study Design, Participants and Objects of Investigation

Study Design

To answer our research questions, we developed a multi-perspective design with quantitative and qualitative aspects. Thus, the methods used complemented each other, and compensated for each other's blind spots (Flick 2020). Our study was based on a double-page spread of a geography textbook that focused on 'Europe—Migration and Population'. To explore the perception of this page and university students' understanding of migration, we combined various methods: eye-tracking, the retrospective think-aloud method and interviews (Fig. 11.1).

Our first step was to use eye-tracking to gain insights into how university students read educational material concerning migration in Europe, and how they focus on textual and visual elements. The quantitative data provide us with information on the task-based perception of textbooks (Asphalter et al. 2021, 120). For example, attentional focus and visual selections may be identified. An advantage of eye-tracking is that the participants cannot control their eye movements. Thus, their actions are not manipulated and shaped by social desirability (Ackermann et al. 2018, 148).

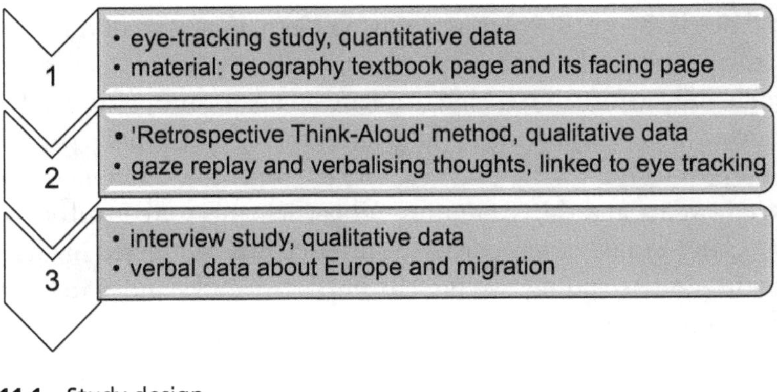

Fig. 11.1 Study design

To avoid any misinterpretation of the quantitative data, we combined visual analysis with the retrospective think-aloud (RTA) method and gaze replay. In this second step, the recipients watched replays of their gaze and described what they thought as they looked at the pages. This operation was important for quality assurance (Menold 2019, 107).

In the third step of our study, we interviewed the students using the techniques of qualitative social research to find out what Europe meant to them. In this step, we continued to give participants a voice and to allow them to elaborate on their thoughts. Their descriptions shed light on patterns of perception and thinking processes (Sprenger 2021, 92). The study participants provided more detailed descriptions of their personal images of Europe and their experience of teaching migrants. These individual descriptions helped to reconstruct these students' perceptions of Europe at a more general level and to link them to the topic of migration.

Study Participants

Participants in this study were students training to become teachers (SBT) at a German university ($n = 16$; $n = 3$ male; $n = 13$ female) between the ages of nineteen and twenty-four (72%) and twenty-five and thirty-five (28%). The interviewees are reading primary (55%) and secondary (27%) education. Eighteen percent will eventually teach students with special needs. Most (80%) were studying German as a second language.

Participation in the study was voluntary, and students were contacted through university courses and student email forums. The study was conducted in December 2019 and January 2020 at a university. Each part—eye-tracking, including the RTA, and the interview—lasted between twenty and thirty minutes. All participants were involved in the eye-tracking and interview parts. The research was conducted in German; for better understanding, we present important tasks and statements in English and German.

Object of Investigation—A Text–Image Composition in a Textbook

For most school subjects, teaching and learning in an educational setting are based mainly on texts accompanied by images. For this reason, we focused our study on a text–image composition (Ballstaedt 2005). The stimulus used in this study appears in the textbook, *Terra—Europa. Themenband Oberstufe* (Kreus and von der Ruhren 2010, 18–19), a geography textbook used at German schools. A double-page spread introduces the unit, 'Europa—Migration und Bevölkerung' ('Europe—Migration and Population'). Usually, such introductory pages present an outline of the content of the unit to evoke an emotional response and/or to activate the recipients' knowledge (Fig. 11.2).

Our selection of material is based on the fact that it reveals the challenges and problems of design, and the reception of multicodal visual surfaces (Schmitz 2006, 194). The written text, as a modality of the 'language' code, and the static image as a modality of the codes that constitute an image are unequal here, but are complementary in their communicative functions (Ballstaedt 2005, 61; Heinz 2019). These two

Fig. 11.2 Textbook page with double-page spread (Kreus and von der Ruhren 2010, 18–19)

different sign systems succeed as a complementary unit only if the textbook design supports effective processing of information for learners. Behnke, who studies the reception of illustrations in geography textbooks, uses the term 'visual attention' to emphasise its importance as a prerequisite for understanding (Behnke 2015, 56).

In our study, we deliberately chose a decorative picture, and distinguish between images that may be categorised as 'instructional' (primarily informative) and 'decorative' (primarily aesthetically appealing): 'The two functions do not exclude each other' (Lenzner et al. 2013, 812).

On the textbook page we selected, the understanding of this decorative image is strongly guided by the bold, red headline, 'Europe—Migration and Population', and the caption, 'Europe as a Modern Noah's Ark (graffiti in Rostock)'.[2] The image is a photograph of a mural of realistic-looking people and animals sitting or standing in a boat.[3] The photograph shows the mural's surroundings and includes the high-rise building in the background. It is surprising that the cropped photograph is not limited to the artwork but also depicts the urban environment. This does not seem to be accidental, because a high-rise building may be associated with an urban social hotspot, and is linked to the topics of migration and population. The group of figures on the boat is colourful. One's gaze falls on a man wearing a jester's cap, a soldier, a man in a suit with his mouth open and various stereotypically depicted people (a Western woman in a bikini vs. a veiled person). There is an apparent hierarchy in the distribution of tasks: black people do the rowing. The caption makes the scene seem strange and mysterious. The red background could also be interpreted as a reddish sea or sand.

The very first sentence in the text to the left of the image states that the pictures are frightening (*Die Bilder sind erschreckend*), which may be seen in the media almost daily: overcrowded boats full of people trying to reach Europe. At the same time, the text reveals the ambivalence with which refugees are met in Europe. The key words in the text are *Mitleid* (compassion) and *Bedrohung und Gefahr* (threat and danger). To this end, the text uses the metaphor, *Flüchtlingsstrom* (stream of refugees), which suggests the threat of Europe being flooded with refugees—*Migranten* (migrants)—through illegal immigration. Regulated, that is, legal, immigration, is also discussed briefly.

The double-page spread was adjusted to the technical affordances of the technology of the eye-tracker to avoid scan faults and to correspond closely to the focus of the research topic (Fig. 11.3). According to Mayer, it is advisable to show text and image on the same page at the same time to support the principle of temporal and spatial contiguity, which allows for better understanding (Mayer 2009). Therefore, the participants were presented with text and image together as stimuli.

Only part of the mural was reproduced in the textbook (Fig. 11.4). The use of the section dealing with this artwork is also an example of how artistic–aesthetic pictures are used for decorative and illustrative purposes in textbooks. The theme of the mural in Rostock is the plea for sustainable development—illustrated by the clearing of forests and pollution by the sewage pipes—and the world community's global responsibility. This community is shown in its diversity and sits in the same boat (a person at the left side of the picture is trying to save himself by jumping into it). The topic of these textbook pages is different from the mural's message. In the textbook, the painting is no longer aligned with global responsibility; it is framed by explosive questions about migration in Europe from the perspective of the first world.

Europa – Migration und Bevölkerung

Die Bilder sind erschreckend: Auf hoffnungslos überfüllten und kaum noch seetüchtigen Schiffen versuchen Männer und Frauen aus Afrika die Küsten Europas zu erreichen und hier Fuß zu fassen. Diese Bootsflüchtlinge erwecken zwar Mitleid, sie werden aber von den Staaten und Gesellschaften auf dem Alten Kontinent auch als Bedrohung und Gefahr empfunden. Dabei ist der Flüchtlingsstrom aus Afrika nur ein Teil der in den letzten Jahrzehnten auf Europa ausgerichteten Migration. Trotz immer aufwändiger ausgebauten Sicherungsanlagen an der Außengrenzen sowie verschärfte Grenz- und Visakontrollen wandern nach einschlägigen Einschätzungen jährlich etwa 500.000 Migranten illegal ein. Hinzu kommen die im Rahmen einer geregelten Zuwanderung angeworbenen Arbeitskräfte. Europa noch im 19. Jahrhundert und beginnenden 20. Jahrhundert ein ausgesprochener Auswanderungskontinent, ist also heute ein bevorzugtes Ziel internationaler Migration.

- Wie viel Zuwanderung verträgt ein Kontinent, ein einzelnes Land?

Europa als moderne Arche Noah (Graffiti in Rostock)

Fig 11.3 The study's adjusted textbook page

Fig 11.4 Mural Global painting in the city of Rostock, by Britta Naumann and Charles Bheb (photograph: private collection)

The Eye-Tracking Study

Eye-Tracking and the Retrospective Think-Aloud Method (RTA)

Eye-trackers are used in various disciplines and provide insights into brain activity, a black box, by recording gaze behaviour (Strohmaier 2014). In educational media research, eye-trackers are applied proofing teaching materials for effectiveness in educational and media research, and for measuring students' reading skills (see Hackl, this volume, for an overview of the eye-tracking method). To interpret the data collected by the eye-tracker, it is necessary to understand the cognitive processes behind gaze behaviour.

Often, eye-tracking data are visualised in two ways—heat maps and gaze plots (Bojko 2013). According to the eye–mind hypothesis, heat maps show the distribution of the participant's attention as real-time, cognitive language processing that corresponds to the time of fixation. It has been observed that a reader takes longer pauses at certain points, where the cognitive load of processing visual input increases (Just and

Carpenter 1980). The conclusion from that is that extended attention indicates either deeper or more difficult cognitive processing (Klein et al. 2018, 3). Such pauses in attention are called fixations, and the eye movements between the pauses are called saccades.

In terms of eye-tracking and research on learning processes, fixations are the most important eye-tracking measures besides saccades (Klein et al. 2018, 3). In our study, we used gaze plots as a part of the visual analysis to explore the participants' response to the educational material. Gaze plots visualise the types of gaze (saccades or fixations), orders of gaze (by numbers in the gaze points) and the duration of the gaze (by the sizes of the gaze points). The system we used, *Tobii Pro X2*, stores the recorded data in the form of maps or as raw data in tab-separated values files (.tsv) (Tobii Pro AB 2014, 137ff.). By combining all these data, a reader's reading path may be traced (Bojko 2013).

We used the method of visual analysis of the eye-tracking data, combined with an analysis of the retrospective think-aloud (RTA) method based on gaze replay (Jo and Stautmeister 2011, 172). For the RTA, participants verbalise their thoughts about a task they performed earlier (Elbabour et al. 2017, 96). A gaze replay is recommended during the RTA: a video of the eye-tracking record is replayed as a reminder to improve the precision of the RTA, as participants tend to miss or add parts of their performance in their memories, when they lack visual cues. Experts highly recommend such a combination to avoid false conclusions when analysing and interpreting heat maps and gaze plots (Hyrskykari et al. 2008). Therefore, we recorded the participants' eye movements while watching their perception of the stimulus, and afterwards asked them to verbalise their thoughts. These verbal statements were recorded, transcribed, analysed and interpreted.

Eye-tracking stimuli may be static (images, text) or dynamic (videos, hypertexts such as web pages) (Strohmaier 2014). We worked with a static stimulus drawn from a geography textbook (for grades 11 and 12). The stimulus consisted of a picture and a text with an introduction to the topic, tasks and a caption to the picture (Fig. 11.2 on the original textbook page). The size, content and layout of the stimulus had to be adjusted to the eye-tracking system. Therefore, the scan of the page was enlarged in comparison to the original book size due to the set-up function fit to the screen during stimuli presentation (Tobii Pro AB 2014, 36). Also, the ratio of text and images was changed, so half of the page was available for each element. Of the five questions about the text, we selected only one. To ensure the perceptibility of the question/exercise, it was also necessary to move the caption and position it beneath the photograph (Fig. 11.3).

We prepared the environment for the eye-tracking record, which included the technical set-up (eye-tracker, screen, recording laptop), and constant and adjustable lighting conditions, as well as a quiet setting with no distractions. These surrounding conditions were crucial to avoiding involuntary eye movement and other undesirable behaviour that could influence data quality (Holmqvist et al. 2011, 125). It is also recommended that the participants and the eye-tracker be placed in predetermined positions, so the participants' eyes may be recorded with the best possible outcome. Holmqvist et al. (2011) report that data quality is improved when participants do not move during the recordings. Therefore, we first placed chair and eye-tracker in the ideal positions. The average distance between the participant and the monitor with the eye-tracker was sixty-five centimetres. At the beginning of each eye-tracking session, we briefly instructed our participants on the importance of remaining in their position during the recording, and of not talking, except in case of emergency. Subsequently, we calibrated the participants' view accuracy and precision with *Tobii Pro Lab* and rejected all values less than 0.9° as the determined precision value was 0.8 centimetre. Finally, we presented the written instructions for the task on the screen: 'Consider the text and image in the double-page spread. Afterwards, you will be required to answer the printed question in your mind. Duration: max. 5 minutes'.[4]

The design of this part of the study was exploratory, and the aim of our data analysis was to find commonalities in the existing visual data types and in the RTA protocols. Three independent coders overviewed all the data and discussed the results in order to sort the gaze patterns into various types of reception.

Results

To structure the eye-tracking data, we first scrutinised the visualisations in the individual data sets, namely, the eye movement statistics with fixations and saccades (gaze plots) and the histograms with gaze fixations (heat maps). Then, in a second step, we compared the results of all the participants' data sets. We also examined the participants' statements about their eye movements in the RTA protocols to determine their relationship to the data in the visualisations. In our analyses, four types of recipients emerged (Table 11.1).

First, we identified the 'text-guided recipient', who focused on individual words and had a scanning reading style. This type rarely looked at the image, and only a few focus points may be identified. The combined analysis of the visual data and the RTA protocols emphasise a goal-oriented way of reading the educational material. Secondly, some study participants focused on both text and images to execute the task. We call this type the 'task-guided recipient', characterised by a selective approach to the material. According to the RTA protocols, these recipients excluded elements—here, the image—that they did not understand; instead, they concentrated on executing the task. The third type is the 'text- and image-focused recipient'. This type had both a special focus on keywords and an interest in the image (Fig. 11.5a). Finally, the 'intensely examining recipient' concentrates on all elements of text, image and task (Fig. 11.6a).

Regarding our interest in the interplay between text and image, we concentrated on 'text- and image-focused recipients' and 'intensely examining recipients'. To make the results easier to read, we present the responses of one participant of each type. When describing the characteristics of the text- and image-focused type, the heat map—called a histogram—shows focus points scattered over text, image and caption, with equal attention paid to each element (Figs. 11.5b and 11.5c). We also noticed an interest in the words *Mitleid* (compassion), *verschärfte Sicherungsanlagen* (strengthened security systems), *Afrika* (Africa) and *Europa* (Europe). The attention to these words is visualised with the help of peaks that show the time spent lingering over them (Fig. 11.5d). Only a few saccades occur between text and image. As may be seen in the

Table 11.1 Overview of types and participants

Types	Participants
text-guided recipient	SBT02, SBT04, SBT07, SBT08, SBT12, SBT16
task-guided recipient	SBT01, SBT05, SBT06, SBT09
text- and image-focused recipient	SBT03, SBT10, SBT13
intensely examining recipient	SBT11, SBT14, SBT15

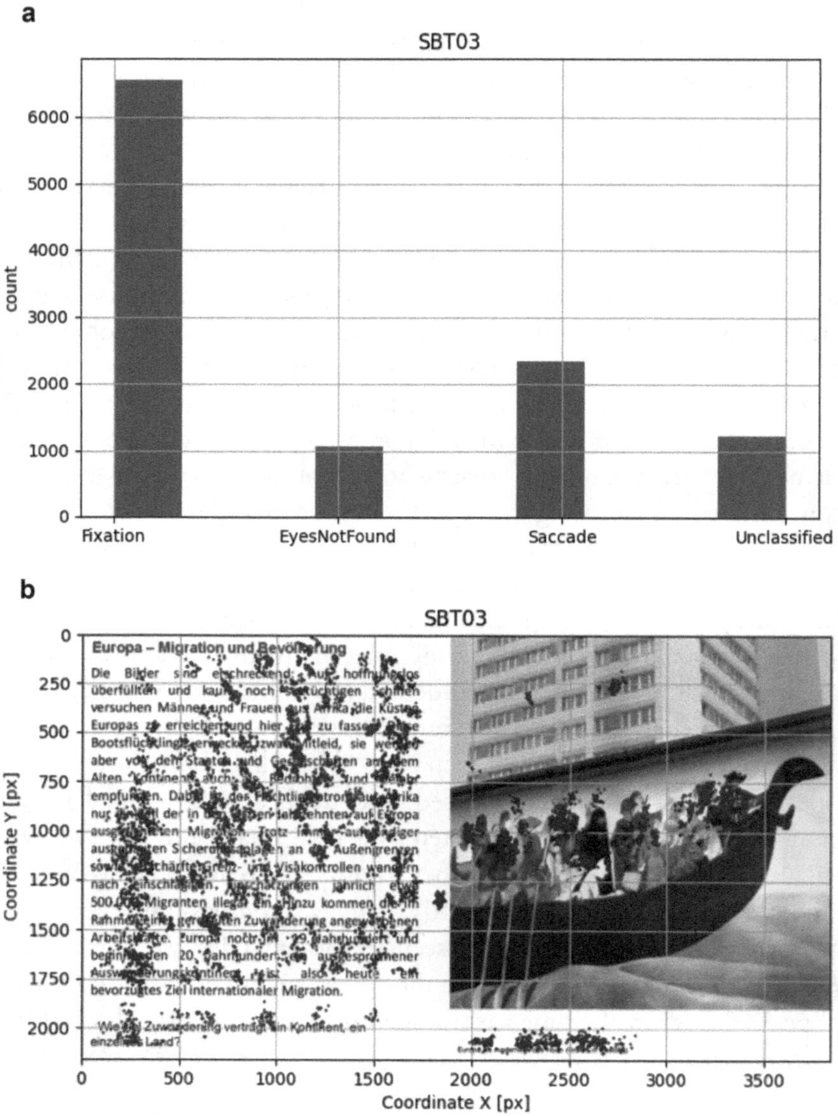

Fig 11.5 Text- and Image-Focused Type (SBT03). (a) Total number of participant SBT03's eye movements, measured by Tobii Pro X2; (b) All gaze fixations of participant SBT03 are indicated by blue marks; (c) Histogram showing number of gaze fixations, counted with squares measuring 70 by 70 pixels (px). The values are relative to the total number of fixations; (d) Surface plot showing the histogram of 5c, enlarged to 245 pixels (px)

c

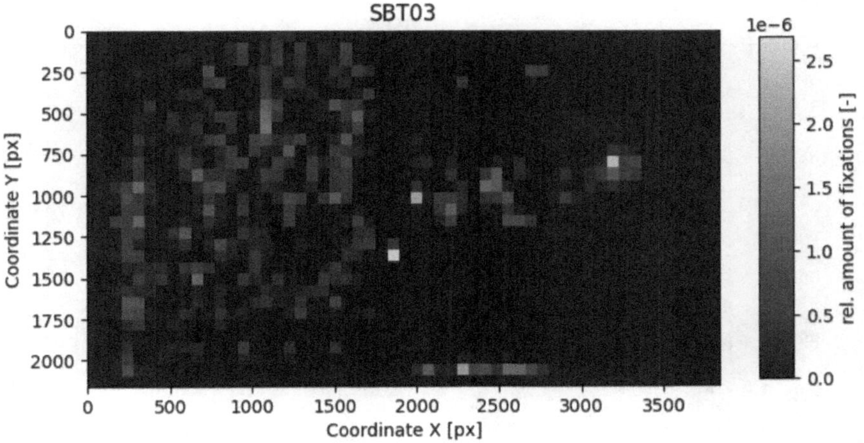

d

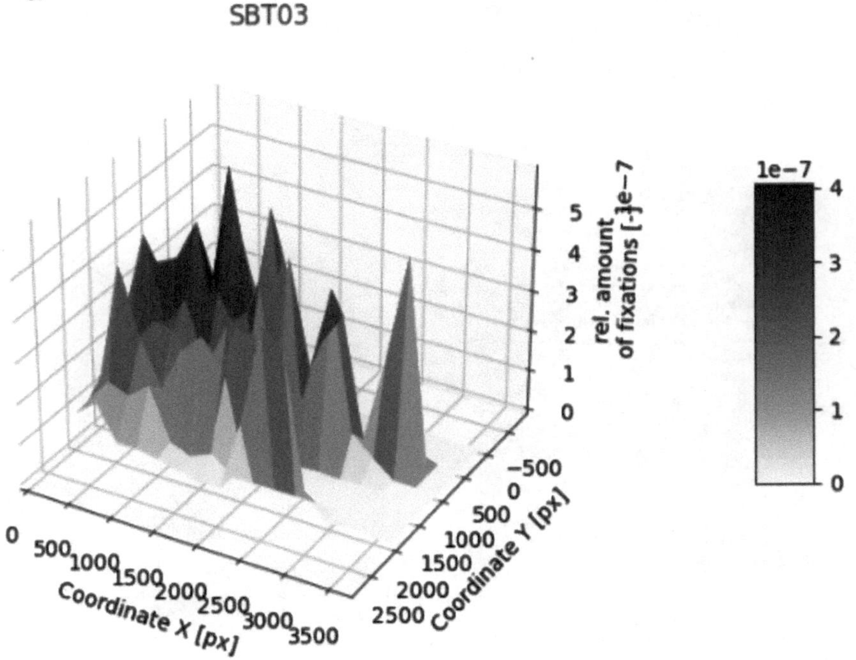

Fig. 11.5 (continued)

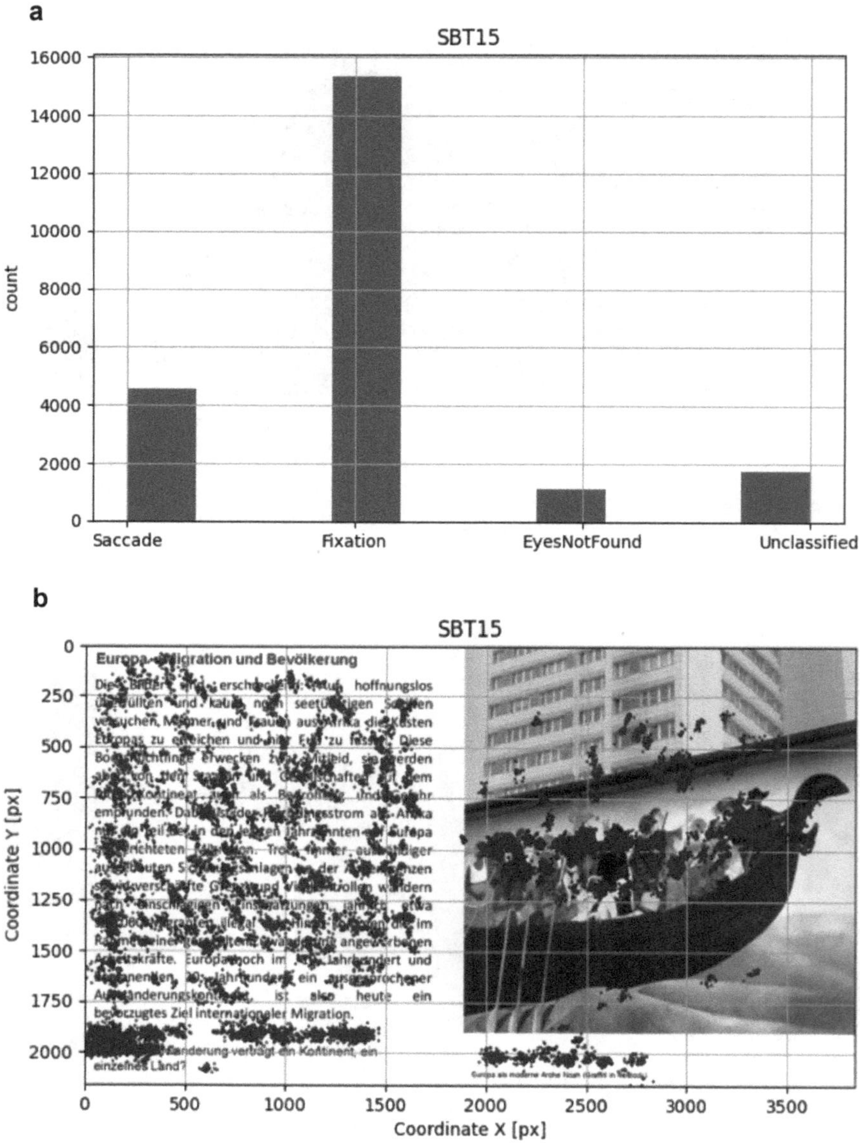

Fig. 11.6 Intensely Examining Type (SBT15). (a) Total number of participant SBT15's eye movements, measured by Tobii Pro X2; (b) All gaze fixations of participant SBT15 indicated by blue marks; (c) Histogram showing the number of gaze fixations counted with squares measuring 70 by 70 pixels (px). The values are relative to the total number of fixations; (d) Surface plot showing the histogram of 6c, enlarged to 245 pixels (px)

c

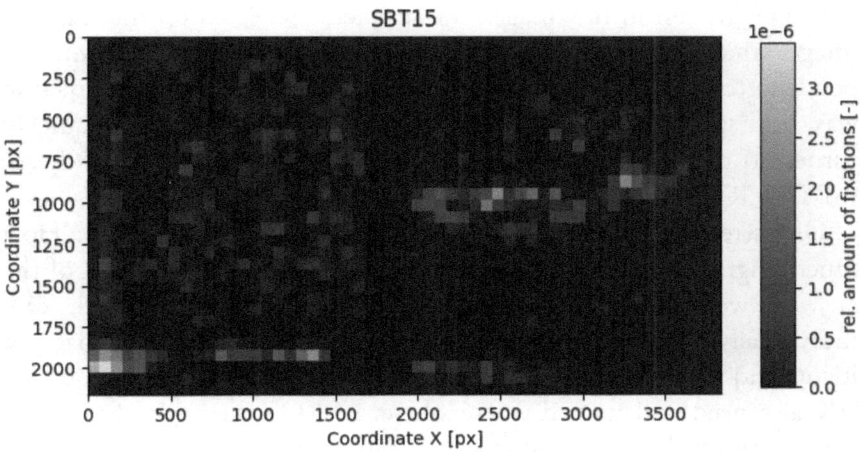

d

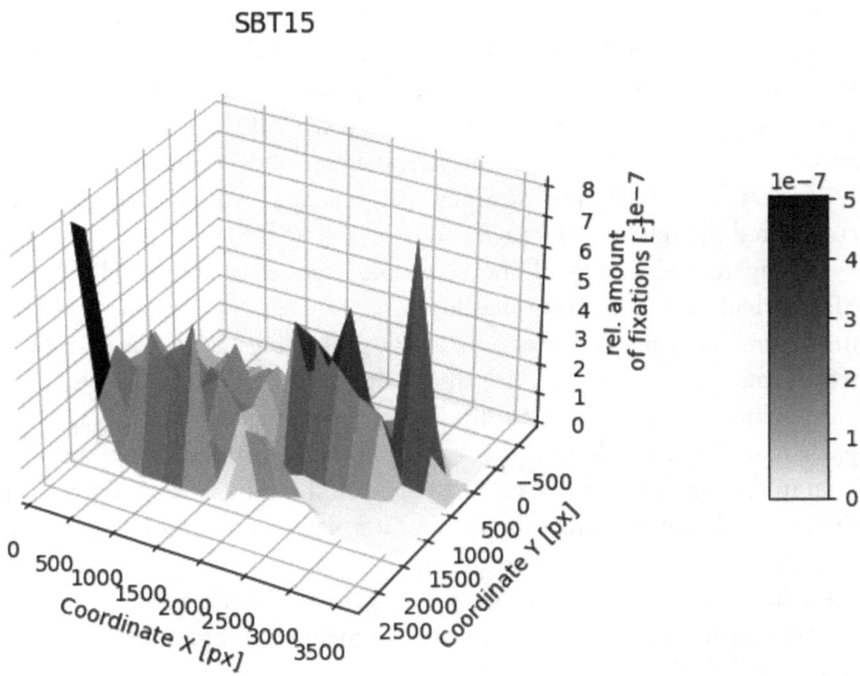

Fig. 11.6 (continued)

following statement, the density of the gaze fixations was due to the participants' interest in the image. The recipients reflected on the text and image, which led to a non-linear gaze path. We also noted this interdependence of perception in the participant's RTA protocol: 'The picture was the first thing that appealed to me directly … then, I think, I quickly turned to the text before I looked at the picture again in more detail' (SBT03_RTA).[5]

Of interest are the students' answers to the question on the page: 'How much migration can a continent, a single country, handle?' Most of the answers were vague; the students preferred to consider each case individually, to describe their thoughts about the current standard of living, and how to protect the safety of the respective European country: 'We also need well-trained workers here. […] On the topic of refugees, we think that their percentage in the total population should be super low, and that's something our country can tolerate' (SBT03_RTA).[6]

The intensely examining participants showed many fixations on text, image, task and caption (Fig. 11.6b). Many saccades occurred between text and image, and a non-linear reading style is apparent. The RTA protocols confirm the roles of image and text while reading: 'I thought about my answer, as I shifted back and forth between image and text […], then I actually just scanned the text and also the image and considered the relation of image and text […]' (SBT15_RTA).[7]

Owing to the design of the textbook page, participants SBT01 to SBT16 had some difficulty developing a coherent understanding. The histogram (heat map) shows only a few peaks (Figs. 11.6c and 11.6d), which may be explained with the help of the RTA protocols. The participants mentioned a contradiction between text and image. In particular, they thought that the woman in the bikini, the soldier and the man in the bow of the boat in the image could hardly be associated with migration. Focusing intensely on the interplay of text and image, these participants had difficulty assigning meaning based on the elements presented: 'The picture is just strange. I don't really know why. Also, the contrast with the skyscraper behind it is somehow strange, and the text as well' (SBT15_RTA).[8]

Due to the above-mentioned difficulties, the participants answered the question with which they were presented—'How much migration can a continent, a single country, handle?'—with the help of their knowledge and their beliefs. Participants mentioned problems in their society: 'It's fine for the people who have lived on this continent or in this country—as long as they have no problems [...]. If there are problems, then somehow a line has been crossed' (SBT15_RTA).[9]

Discussion

Participants who focused on both text and image showed more saccades between text, image and task than participants who focused on either text or task. Other research has shown that as the number of saccades increases, the more a text and an image do not correspond to each other in terms of meaning (Oestermeier and Eitel 2014, 18). This incongruence prompts the gaze to switch between both elements, and demands significant cognitive resources, in the sense described by cognitive load theory (Sweller 1994); cognitive resources are unsuccessfully used to attempt to link text and image. As the image in the textbook was cropped and presented as a message about migration, rather than as its intended message about environmental pollution, the students may have lacked information and could not use the image to execute the task.

According to Schnotz's integrated model of text and image comprehension, recipients need information from both text and images, working in different ways. Text and images have fundamentally different roles in comprehension and learning: image comprehension process information provides differently to mental model construction than text comprehension; texts are first processed and leave some ambiguity, which may be resolved by consulting images. Texts guide the readers' conceptual analysis, and images serve as an external tool for enriching and adding missing information (Schnotz 2014, 93–94). As the message of the image in our stimulus was not congruent with the message of the text, some of the participants tended to ignore the information in the image, so their mental model would not conflict with their understanding of the text and their understanding of the topic.

Some students who intensely examined the textbook page became aware of the inconsistencies inherent in the material, although they could not find an explanation for this. Therefore, when designing effective educational material, texts and images should be congruent, and images should clearly relate to the message in the text (Schnotz 2014, 96). As mentioned above, the educational material we used as a stimulus in our study did not follow these principles. We realise that the designers may have deliberately chosen an incongruent text, image and task. As the page introduces a chapter, it may serve as a provocation to encourage recipients to raise questions and position themselves.

Regarding the task the study participants had to execute, the histograms (heat maps) and the RTA protocols yielded interesting findings. Some participants focused predominantly on the keywords *Mitleid* (compassion), *verschärfte Sicherungsanlagen* (strengthened security systems), *Afrika* (Africa) and *Europa* (Europe). Guided by the task, most of the participants interpreted the boat as a refugee boat, despite the caption, 'Noah's Ark'. Moreover, the participants identified a few persons on the boat as unsuitable for illustrating migration. Most of the participants argued for ensuring that migrants have useful qualifications for working in their host countries. Repeatedly, respondents identified refugees as a current threat to European societies. In their answers to the task question—'How much migration can a continent, a single country, handle?'—the students expressed their beliefs that migration should be regulated to avoid conflicts in their societies.

The Interview Study

Structure and Analysis of the Interviews

As we were interested in the perceptions of students becoming teachers, we conducted interviews on the topics of Europe and migration. The social science approach of the interview study enriched the analysis of the eye-tracking data and the RTA protocols and helped us to reconstruct the participants' perceptions. We recognised the verbal data from the interviews as providing a tool for identifying the individual reasons behind the perceptions of migration (Ackermann et al. 2018, 149). We structured the interviews with key questions to connect to the topics of migration and Europe and to enrich the data of the eye-tracking part.

Therefore, the questions form an orientation framework (Helfferich 2019, 670). Initially, we asked the participants about their personal views of Europe: 'What does Europe mean to you? What image would you use to describe Europe? What image do you have in mind?'[10]

In the second part of the interview, we took into account perceptions related to political and economic factors in Europe: 'What values do you associate with Europe? How do you assess Europe's economic development? Do you feel safe in your neighbourhood? Would you want to leave Europe?'[11]

When we focused on the textbook page, we asked the participants specifically about the topic of immigration: 'To what extent does the topic of immigration play a role in your studies? Have you ever had contact with immigrants? How much immigration can Germany absorb? Do you perceive immigration as a threat?'[12]

The interviews were recorded and transcribed using GAT (Deppermann 2008). The data were coded according to grounded theory and supplemented with situational analysis. Grounded theory guides researchers in generating a sketch of a new, innovative theory in a methodologically bottom-up way. This methodological discovery approach may be structured in various ways. In one of their studies, Strauss and Corbin use the idea of a story as a descriptive narrative about the central phenomenon they study. A storyline is a conceptualisation of the results along the core category, grounded in the data (Strauss and Corbin 1990, 116). Therefore, a storyline is a tool that is used to aid theoretical development, and partly its dissemination. When analysis, reflection and writing are complete, a theory emerges, which is still connected and linked to social reality. The openness of this method establishes a new view of a topic that has been thoroughly researched and discussed (Birks et al. 2009, 416).

While analysing the data, we were confronted with multi-perspective and heterogeneous perceptions of Europe. Therefore, it seemed helpful to enrich the coding with Adele Clarke's ideas. As a supplemental approach to grounded theory, Clarke is convinced that situation is key to social processes. The situation is not only a surrounding or framing condition, it is always constitutive (Clarke 2016, 208):

> People and things, humans and nonhumans, fields of practice, discourses, disciplinary and other regimes/formats, symbols, technologies, controversies, organizations and institutions—each and all can be present and mutually consequential. (Clarke 2016, 210)

For situational analysis, Clarke recommends cartographic tools to shift researchers' attention. When mapping the data, researchers construct the situation of inquiry empirically. The maps are analytic tools, well-suited to contemporary, multi-perspective research projects. They are seen as supplementing traditional grounded theory analyses that centre around action. Maps help to broaden the perspective with a focus on discourses, structures and conditions that characterise a situation (Clarke 2016, 211). According to Clarke, the situation becomes the ultimate unit of analysis, and the main goals are understanding its elements and their relationships to one another: 'Situational analysis allows researchers to draw together studies of discourse and agency, action and structure, image, text and context, history and the present moment to analyse complex situations' (Clarke 2009, 55). Positional maps visualise most of the important discursive positions taken or not taken. Clarke advocates separating positions from persons, and from individual and collective institutions (Clarke and Keller 2014, 71). In so doing, the focus is not on persons or groups but on the full range of discursive positions, grounded in the data.

Results

Focusing on a discourse enabled us to identify and organise multiple perspectives on the key questions of 'Europe' and 'migration' that the participants presented. The first positional map (Fig. 11.7) has two axes that combine values related to, and images of, Europe. When organising the data, various positions on 'To which Europe do which values belong?' emerged. A community of human rights is one subject mentioned, with global and positive connotations: the role of human rights is to offer unifying values for a community, with the goal of bringing people together. These values are rooted in democratic forms of government: 'All values

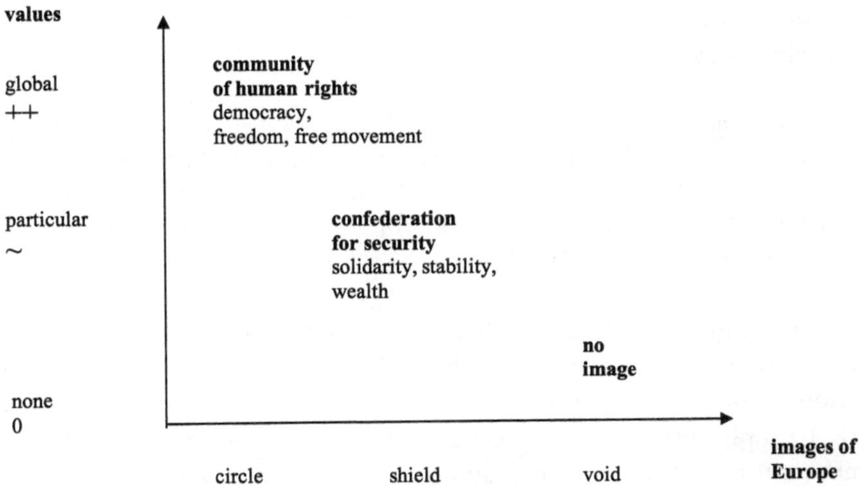

Fig. 11.7 Positional map of values and images of Europe

that are part of a democracy in a way, so really this togetherness' (SBT14_INT).[13] Examples of those values were quite often presented as a list, for example, human rights, civil liberties, freedom of opinion, freedom of speech, freedom of the press and freedom of religion (SBT13_INT). In particular, the free movement of persons played an important role in shaping the idea of the community: 'That I can go to every country and I do not need to carry my passport' (SBT15_INT).[14] These values were matched by both a sense of community—'That a European sense of community just brings people from different countries closer to each other' (SBT02_INT)[15]—and by common actions (SBT01_INT).

To represent the idea of the community, the symbol of a circle linked various elements of Europe. Elements were perceived as either the stars of the European flag (SBT01_INT, SBT06_INT, SBT09_INT, SBT13_INT) or people holding hands: 'A circle, I don't know, a group of people who are holding hands' (SBT02_INT, SBT05_INT).[16]

The idea of community was less developed in the confederation for security. Study participants considered a confederation to be a loose alliance of states based on certain values. This confederation might or might not be the European Union, and revolve around the interplay of stability and solidarity:

> Well, to me Europe stands for safety. I have already spent longer periods of time in some other countries that were not as safe, and when I, uhm, yes, when I came back again to, let's say, to Germany, then security was always a topic to me, and you can say that for almost any European country. (SBT03_INT)[17]

Stability and solidarity are needed to guarantee security. Thus, they were regarded as important elements that led directly to economic considerations: 'I don't think that there is a uniform standard of living in Europe, [...] simply distribute the prosperity, that sounds kind of communist now, but maybe the thought is not that bad after all' (SBT09_INT).[18]

Wealth was understood as both material prosperity and as an idealistic value. Also, 'wealth' was used with respect to European cultural traditions (SBT04_INT, SBT08_INT). The image associated with these values was that of a shield that protected the countries in the confederation in various ways (SBT07_INT). First, the shield served as an instrument that established and defended a system of security in which members of the confederation suffer no economic hardship. Further on, the shield expressed a symbolic idea. States with a shared heritage gathered beneath this shield and shared traditions of Greek antiquity, especially the mythical world of Zeus and Europe. This historical tradition of Europe established the cultural and geographic categories for states under the umbrella of Europe (SBT04_INT, SBT05_INT, SBT06_INT).

Positional maps also document aspects of discourses that have not been developed. Such a result was evident in our study, when neither values nor images were mentioned: 'As I said, actually no real [values] at first' (SBT11_INT; SBT15_INT).[19] The participants did not comment on values and images, so there was a noticeable void concerning this with regard to Europe.

The second positional map (Fig. 11.8) refers to the topics of Europe and migration and addresses the question, 'What kind of Europe can tolerate how much migration?' This question is intertwined with the eye-tracking part of the study, in which the participants' task was to find an answer to the question, 'How much migration can a continent, a single

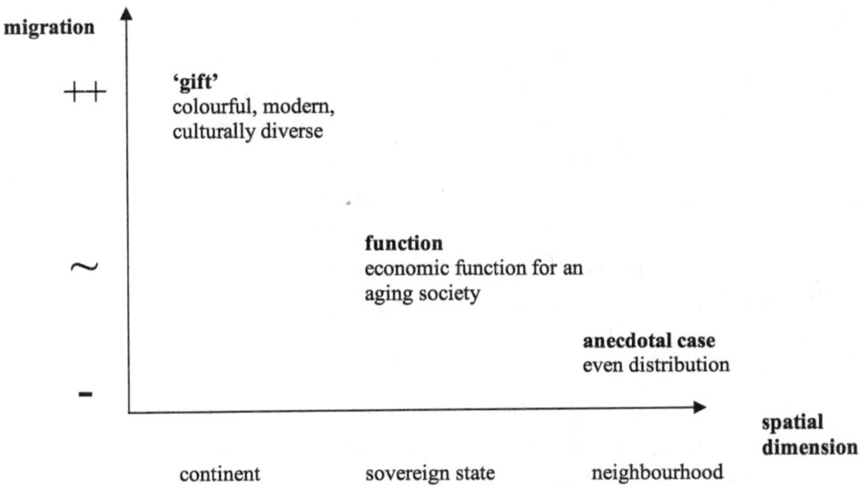

Fig. 11.8 Positional map of migration and spatial dimensions

country, handle?' In the interviews, the participants outlined a nuanced view of Europe along the axis of migration and the spatial dimension (of Europe).

The connection between the spatial dimension and migration offers important insights. Positive statements about migration were accompanied by the idea of a European continent with enough space for everyone. The opportunity to travel was regarded as a gift, it evoked positive feelings, it elicited appreciation of the presentee, and it did not require compensation: 'Europe, to me, is home, well, I am from Bavaria and have studied in England, and after I graduated from school I was in Ireland, and I think that is a great gift' (SBT12_INT).[20] Other positive elements that characterise this discourse are ideas of modernity: Europe was regarded colourful and young in terms of lifestyles and political systems (SBT07_INT, SBT08_INT, SBT16_INT), and culturally diverse, with many languages and traditions (SBT10_INT). The diversity of lifestyles and systems found its place in the idea of the European continent, whose borders were not clearly defined.

Another perspective on migration that was found in the data was a more functional one. Migration enriches the economic system, and thus supports the existence of European societies. The necessity of migration was calculated by considering the needs of the European employment market. The aging of European societies has made migration without any alternatives. With regard to societal affordances and economic requirements, migrants faced a broad range of expectations. They had to accept the conditions of schooling and training (SBT16_INT), they had to be flexible, they had to fit into missing professions (SBT09_INT) and they had to learn the local language to pursue a successful career (SBT10_INT). Their integration into the existing (economic) system was the top priority, whereas migrants' desires and needs were less relevant and important:

> Ah, the challenge, so to speak, is that you have to accommodate them all, at our place and also integrate them, and so on and also sort of make them work in our labour market, well that they have some sort of graduation, which I think is really good, because when you look at the Germans, the demographic shift here is very negative, because we keep having fewer children, and migration brings in a lot of younger people, who could, in theory, then earn some sort of educational qualification somewhere, or have already done that, only this is not always accepted and this is where we have to see the chance that they get included in our work so there will be an upturn here again, yes. (SBT05_INT)[21]

This detailed statement also illustrates a shift found in the data: when it came to migration in a functional context, the sovereign state, for example, Germany, provided the geographic orientation to play through the advantages and disadvantages of migration. No figures were given as upper limits in response to the question of 'how many'; instead, the system provided arguments for regulating migration and familiarising migrants with the conditions in Germany.

The more people felt confronted by migration in their own neighbourhoods, the louder were their critical voices. Nevertheless, the rejection of migration was a soft discourse in the interview data. Criticism of migration was mostly framed by anecdotes about the participants' surroundings, which they contextualised with other societal problems. They differentiated between refugees and migrants: migrants left their home countries to lead a better life; refugees had to leave their homes because they were persecuted and feared for their lives. An 'as well as' structure characterises the pattern of the argument: people felt safe in their neighbourhoods, except with regard to the migrants and unemployed people nearby (SBT03_INT, SBT08_INT); people read newspapers reports of crimes committed by refugees and Germans (SBT11_INT); people living in rural areas were confronted with refugees, at the latest after the crises of 2015, so that migration was no longer just a problem in large cities (SBT11_INT). The decisive factor for the positive development of migration was seen in a favourable distribution of people. Nevertheless, they rarely explained what this distribution should look like.

> In France there is always this model, 'all them, those evil foreigners, we'll send them to the suburbs, so to speak, so that you do not have to see them as French', I think this is different in [the city of] M., at least, in that you have places where you meet each other not far from where you live, I live less than a kilometre from a refugee camp, and you run into those people, and when I do, I sometimes talk to them. (SBT09_INT)[22]

The conditions in the city of M. seem better than those in France. However, what was not criticised was the accommodation of refugees in special centres, apart from the rest of the local population. Also, there is a position in the statement above that is mentioned in the data as a narrow line of discourse: 'I would not say that I am in very close contact with migrants, I'd call it fleeting encounters' (SBT14_INT).[23]

Our interviewees had little personal contact with migrants (SBT01_INT, SBT02_INT). Their encounters with migrants have been mainly mediated by institutions: during their traineeships at schools, a required part of their university studies, they were confronted with the cultural diversity of the student body. During the interviews, the participants described the migrant students with respect to their German language skills (SBT06_INT), to their traumatic experiences surrounding their flight from their home countries (SBT16_INT) and to their families' socio-economic circumstances (SBT08_INT). Also, some of the participants' mothers worked with migrants on a volunteer basis and spoke of their experiences to their children (SBT05_INT, SBT13_INT). This volunteer activity began because of the 2015 refugee crisis, and was declining at the time of the interviews, in 2020.

Interpretation

With the help of mapping, the interview data were arranged in discursive units, and the study yielded some important results. At this point, we would like to pick up the idea of the story line, and present the results as 'an elegant, abstract theoretical explanation' (Birks and Mills 2019, 145). When reflecting on the results of the two positional maps, it becomes apparent that security—in German, *Sicherheit*—may serve as a unifying element of this discourse. In English, *Sicherheit* has at least two translations that are related but do not have the same meaning. One of these focuses on the idea of averting security risks, for example, protecting computers against spying, worms and viruses; the term 'security' also includes checks at airports and buildings to exclude dangerous and criminal elements. It may also be associated with security services that protect companies and their employees from danger and damage by maintaining safety and order (Enthof 2013, 3).

Currently, one risk to the security of Western nations and European countries is the ageing of its societies. Ageing changes social conditions and threatens economic prosperity. Migration may remedy to these threats to security (Buchen et al. 2014, 8). Throughout European history, migrants have often been recruited and had to undergo security checks: not everyone was wanted, not everyone was needed. At the security checkpoint, it is decided to what extent a migrant is of value to the wealth of a country. Migrants with expertise in geriatric care and IT experts are welcomed and favoured in Europe. To ensure that the security measures are effective, the states in the European Union act as a security system. National governments are responsible for regulating migration and calculating its risks to society and its potential benefits. In the interview data, this line of discourse refers to the current national conditions in Germany and may be described as pragmatic security.

Sicherheit may also be translated as 'a sense of safety'. This may be regarded as a desired and ideal condition of life, where humans are protected from all sorts of harm and suffering (Enthof 2013, 3). The desire for safety is universal, fundamental and common to all people, and it shapes our ideas of what life in future communities should be like:

there will be enough resources for all human beings; people will be connected by their humanity and their acceptance of cultural diversity; all human beings will have the same rights and live in paradise-like conditions. Under such circumstances, state security and order are hardly necessary, and people unite in a peaceful community. To summarise this line of discourse in the data, it may be called the concept of an ideal secure community.

The two branches of the discourse that we have identified in the data—pragmatic security and an ideal, secure community—characterise the interview sample in our study. *Sicherheit* and freedom are often contrasted: How much security can freedom take? How much security does freedom need? Answers to these questions were only touched on by our data. The participants did not question *Sicherheit* closely related to the identity of young Europeans living in Germany. These results fit into the general pattern of further surveys of young people's attitudes and values. The current 'Shell Studie' reports that people aged between fifteen and twenty-five regard the European Union as a guarantor of peace, particularly because of its democratic form of government. In this study, young people mentioned the positive effects of economic prosperity and cultural diversity, as well as the opportunity for free movement within the European Union (Schneekloth and Albert 2019, 75). They also commented on migration: 20% of the respondents would like to have a refugee family as neighbours, and they complained about the impossibility of criticising foreigners without being regarded as racist (Schneekloth and Albert 2019, 81).

Concerning values, *Sicherheit* is the fixed star of the value cosmos. The data also illustrate a varied understanding of *Sicherheit*. The term is intertwined with various social and political conditions, which range from the pragmatic to the idealistic. The fact that some participants expressed no values at all should be emphasised once again. In this mixed-value perspective extracted from the data, young people show themselves to be twenty-first-century actors who deal in this way with the complexity of society (Lechleiter 2016, 20). Even it has shining scope, they did not doubt security as a consistent part of their lives. Europe, including the European Union and the sovereign states, seemed able to meet the challenges of our times, and provide good living conditions.

Conclusions of This Multi-perspectival Study

In this final section, we bring together the results of our multi-perspective study. A page from a geography textbook with its facing page served as a stimulus and was explored with various tools, and combined eye-tracking with RTA protocols and interviews. The variety of tools helped us to describe viewing patterns of students becoming teachers and to understand their positions in the discourse on migration. The interviewees indicated that migration is not a matter of course for them but that they are challenged by it.

With regard to the first research question—Which typical viewing patterns do the recipients use while observing a text–image–task stimulus in educational material?—our analysis revealed various types of reception. The students showed various visual patterns when they focused on a text and an image: either they tried to focus on both text and image, to establish a coherent understanding of the text, or a conscious examination of all the elements on the page confused them when they read the text.

When answering the second research question—What are the recipients' perceptions and images of Europe?—we must bear in mind the exploratory design of our study. As we found the combination of text, image and task thought-provoking, we chose and prepared educational material for the eye-tracking part. We wanted to give the interviewees a voice and an opportunity to express their perspectives on the topic. Therefore, we combined social science research approaches and eye-tracking data related to textbook reception. This combination is rarely used in educational media research, and strengthens the interdisciplinary force of our study.

When migration is addressed in geography textbooks, the problematic consequences for both the countries of origin and the destinations are considered. Migration is often presented as a multidimensional crisis (Beauftragte der Bundesregierung für Migration, Flüchtlinge und Integration 2015, 57). This characterisation also applies to the textbook page and its facing page that we used in our study. The page is complex and contradictory in its design and in its answers to questions about Europe and migration. In the eye-tracking part, the participants lingered over the words *Mitleid* (compassion), *verschärfte Sicherungsanlagen* (strengthened security systems), *Afrika* (Africa) and *Europa* (Europe). These words may be associated with the storyline of *Sicherheit* (safety) that is frequently found in the interview data. Reflecting on *Sicherheit* (safety), the participants expressed their views of a Europe to which they feel they belong. Also, the students valued migration more positively as a global phenomenon, whereas they regarded migration less positively when it took place in their own neighbourhoods. These results should be followed up in further studies of Europe and migration in textbooks. This would increase educators' awareness of the question surrounding controversies in their society, and their effects on teaching with various materials in class.

Our final question deals with the connections and conclusions that may be related to teacher education based on the study results. First, the results of our study emphasise that we should implement critical textbook and media analyses in teacher training at universities (Bucher et al. 2017; Fuchs et al. 2014, 136–37; Heitzmann and Niggli 2010, 17). Students becoming teachers should be encouraged to reflect on the sources of their teaching/educational material, the integration of text and image, and the institutional teaching settings. Although we find many text and image combinations in teaching material, visual literacy is rarely integrated into school and university curricula (Dehn 2014, 133). As illustrated by our research, the image of the original painting was cropped and inserted into a specific context. This cropped image is presented at the beginning of a unit on 'Europe—Migration and Population'. Therefore, the participants' response to this page again illustrates the complexity of text–image comprehension in educational media. Far too often, images merely serve as illustrations; texts and images contradict each other, and the material's function in the learning process is ambiguous, unspecified (Beauftragte der Bundesregierung für Migration, Flüchtlinge und Integration 2021, 80–81). Therefore, we argue that the contexts in which images appear—in terms of their position and their connection to other textbook content, and in terms of their relation to the subject matter and the curriculum—must be clearly and critically addressed. Second, the interviews bring the various aspects of eye-tracking and educational media back to societal discourses on Europe and migration (Geuenich 2015). When the study participants reflected on Europe, these discussions were all about *Sicherheit* in its dimensions of security and safety. Also, the students' statements indicated their distance from migrants and refugees in everyday life. Most of the students learned about the fate of refugees and migrants second-hand. Media and family members provided them with information and impressions. As many interviewees had studied German as a second language and will be teaching students with immigrant backgrounds, one of our tasks is to initiate a theoretical and self-reflecting process on migration among students becoming teachers. Moreover, universities must provide sufficient work experience for intercultural and transcultural teaching.

The results of our study may serve as a starting point for interesting discussions of migration in Europe, as presented in educational media. The challenges of our time lead to feelings of insecurity in European communities (Kershaw 2018, 760–66; Krastev 2017). During 2019 und 2020, there were many crises in the European Union, which may be summarised with the terms, 'Brexit', 'rise of right-wing parties', 'refugee problems', 'global climate crisis' and 'COVID-19 pandemic'. When discussing these events, some historians and sociologists describe a new era of insecurity in Europe's history. Our interview data emphasise this aspect of security, and illustrate how closely security and insecurity are linked in the discourse on migration. Many of our study participants felt threatened by migration, though they had not met migrants. The questions of whether, how and when migrants will become accepted by European societies are relevant. Answers to these questions are socially significant and should be discussed in further studies.

Acknowledgements We would like to thank Lea Zuromski for supporting the survey, Niklas Oranienburg for his assistance in transcribing the interviews and Johannes Schreiber for organising the eye-tracking data. Tilman von Brand took the photograph of the mural.

Notes

1. We use the term 'image' in our paper, which may be understood as a picture that we see with our eyes. Further on, we also use 'image' when we discuss the internal processes of using our imagination.
2. 'Europa als moderne Arche Noah (Graffiti in Rostock)'.
3. The artwork is a mural by Britta Naumann and Charles Bhebe. The painting at the Brunnenhof in the August-Bebel-Straße in Rostock 'is part of a worldwide mural project for the Agenda 21, a catalogue of tasks, which was decided on at the conference of the United Nations for environment and development 1992 in Rio de Janeiro. [...] Artists from a wide range of cultural backgrounds create murals all over the world on the theme of the environment and sustainable development' (http://britta-naumann-art.de/arbeiten/baugebundene-arbeiten/).
4. 'Erfassen Sie Text und Bild vorliegender Schulbuchdoppelseite. Im Anschluss haben Sie die abgedruckte Frage 'Wie viel Zuwanderung verträgt ein Kontinent, ein einzelnes Land?' im Kopf zu beantworten. Dauer: max. 5 Minuten'.
5. 'Das Bild [war] das Erste, was so mich direkt angesprochen hat, [...] [dann] bin ich relativ schnell auf den Text gegangen, bevor ich mir das Bild im Detail angeguckt habe'.
6. 'Gut ausgebildete Arbeitskräfte [werden] hier auch gebraucht. [...] Wenn man wieder auf das Thema Flüchtlinge geht, dann sagt man, der prozentuale Anteil an der Gesamtbevölkerung sollte super gering sein und das kann unser Land tolerieren'.
7. 'Ich hab quasi während ich über meine Antwort nachgedacht habe, immer wieder zwischen Bild und Text hin- und hergeschwenkt [...], dann hab ich eigentlich nur noch den Text abgescannt und auch das Bild abgescannt und überlegt in welchem Verhältnis das zum Bild und Text steht [...]'.
8. 'Das Bild ist einfach eigenartig. Ich weiß auch nicht warum und auch der Kontrast mit dem Hochhaus dahinter ist irgendwie komisch und auch dieser Text dazu'.
9. 'Die Menschen, die auf diesem Kontinent oder in diesem Land gelebt haben—solange es für die zu keinen Problematiken kommt—[...] ist es ok. Wenn es dann Probleme gibt, ist eine Grenze irgendwo erreicht'.
10. Was bedeutet Europa für Sie? Mit welchem Bild würden Sie Europa beschreiben? Welches Bild kommt Ihnen in den Sinn?

11. Welche Werte verbinden sie mit Europa? Wie schätzen Sie die ökonomische Entwicklung in Europa ein? Fühlen Sie sich sicher in Ihrer Nachbarschaft? Würden Sie Europa verlassen wollen?
12. Inwiefern spielt das Thema 'Migration' in Ihrem Studium eine Rolle? Haben Sie schon einmal Kontakt mit Migrant(inn)en gehabt? Wieviel Zuwanderung verträgt Deutschland? Empfinden Sie Migration als Bedrohung?
13. 'Alle Werte, die zu einer Demokratie dazu gehören irgendwie, also einfach dieses Miteinander'.
14. 'Dass ich halt in jedes Land gehen kann und brauche nicht meinen Pass mitnehmen'.
15. 'Das ein europäisches Gemeinschaftsgefühl ja Menschen aus verschiedenen Ländern einfach näher zusammenbringt'.
16. '[E]in Kreis, ich weiß nicht, eine Gruppe von Menschen, die sich an den Händen hält'.
17. 'Also Europa steht für mich auch für Sicherheit, ich hab auch schon in einigen anderen Ländern längere Zeit mal verbracht, die dann auch nicht so sicher waren und wenn ich da ähm ja, wenn ich dann wieder zurück kam, sag ich mal, nach Deutschland, dann war für mich auch immer so ein Thema Sicherheit und das kann man ja fast für jedes europäische Land so sagen'.
18. '[I]ch glaub nicht, das wir in Europa einen einheitlichen Lebensstandard haben […] einfach den Wohlstand zu verteilen, das klingt jetzt ein bisschen kommunistisch, aber vielleicht ist der Gedanke ja auch gar nicht so schlecht'.
19. 'Wie gesagt, eigentlich erstmal gar keine [Werte]'.
20. 'Europa bedeutet für mich Heimat, also ich komme halt nicht aus Bayern und hab in England studiert und war auch nach dem Abi in Irland und ich finde es ist ein ganz großes Geschenk'.
21. 'Ähm also die Herausforderung ist ja quasi, dass man die halt alle unterbringt quasi bei uns und halt auch integriert und so und auch quasi in unseren Arbeitsmarkt einarbeitet, also dass sie halt nen Bildungsabschluss haben, was ich halt sehr gut finde, weil so wenn man jetzt nur die Deutschen betrachtet quasi da ist ja der demographische Wandel sehr negativ für uns quasi, weil wir immer weniger Kinder haben und dadurch durch die Migration kommen halt sehr viele Jüngere, die halt dann einen Berufsabschluss haben könnten theoretisch und die bereits auch einen haben nur dass es nicht immer anerkannt wird und da müssen wir

halt die Chance sehen, dass wir die halt einarbeiten, dass es hier wieder Aufschwung gibt genau'.

22. 'Es gibt in Frankreich gibt es immer das Modell, 'die ganzen, die bösen Ausländer, die verteilen wir auf die Banlieues sozusagen, damit man sie nicht sehen muss als Franzose', ich finde, dass ist in München zumindest schon anders, dass man wirklich nicht weit von sich selber Begegnungsstätten hat, ich wohn keinen Kilometer von einem Flüchtlingsheim weg und da trifft man die Leute und wenn ich mal jemanden treffe, dann rede ich auch mal mit dem'.
23. '[I]ch würd' sagen jetzt nicht, dass ich mit Migranten sehr, sehr engen Kontakt habe, also mehr so flüchtige Begegnungen würde ich es nennen'.

References

Ackermann, Lena, Renate Delucci Danhier, Sabrina Heiderich, Stephan Hußmann, and Barbara Mertins. 2018. Begabung in Sprache und Mathematik relational testen (Be_SMart). In *DoProfiL—Das Dortmunder Profil für inklusionsoriente Lehrerinnen- und Lehrerbildung*, ed. Stephan Hußmann and Barbara Welzel, 141–159. Münster: Waxmann.

Asphalter, Christian, Reinhard Bauer, Sandra Reitbrecht, and Erich Schönbächler. 2021. "Es durch die Augen von Schüler*innen sehen"—Eye-Tracking in (fach-)didaktischen Forschungsfeldern am Beispiel einer Rechercheaufgabe zur "Berliner Mauer". In *Multimediale Kommunikation in den Hypermedien und Deutschunterricht. Theoretische, empirische und unterrichtspraktische Zugänge*, ed. Katharina Staubach, 117–135. Baltmannsweiler: Schneider.

Ballstaedt, Steffen-Peter. 2005. Text-Bild-Kompositionen im Unterrichtsmaterial. *Der Deutschunterricht* 57 (4): 61–70.

Beauftragte der Bundesregierung für Migration, Flüchtlinge und Integration. 2015. *Schulbuchstudie Migration und Integration*. Paderborn: Bonifatius.

———. 2021. *Lehrplanstudie Migration und Integration*. Frankfurt am Main: Zarbock Media.

Behnke, Yvonne. 2015. Welchen Grad an visueller Aufmerksamkeit widmen Lernende den Abbildungen in Geographieschulbüchern? *Bildungsforschung* 12 (1): 54–76.

Birks, Melanie, and Jane Mills. 2019. Rendering Analysis Through Storyline. In *The SAGE Handbook of Current Developments in Grounded Theory*, ed. Antony Bryant and Kathy Charmaz, 243–258. London: SAGE Publications.

Birks, Melanie, Jane Mills, Karen Francis, and Ysanne Chapman. 2009. A Thousand Words Paint a Picture: The Use of Storyline in Grounded Theory Research. *Journal of Research in Nursing* 14 (5): 405–417.

Bojko, Aga. 2013. *Eye Tracking the User Experience. A Practical Guide to Research*. Brooklyn, NY: Rosenfeld Media, LLC.

Buchen, Tim, Dagmara Jajeśniak-Quast, Mark Keck-Szajbel, and Katharina K. Kowalski. 2014. Demographischer Wandel in Polen, Deutschland und Europa. Geschichte, Verflechtungen und neue Forschungsperspektiven—eine Einführung. In *Demographischer Wandel in Polen, Deutschland und Europa. Geschichte, Verflechtungen und neue Forschungsperspektiven*, ed. Tim Buchen, Dagmara Jajeśniak-Quast, Mark Keck-Szajbel, and Katharina K. Kowalski, 7–16. Berlin: epubli.

Bucher, Kristina, Sophia Finck von Finckenstein, and Thomas Heiland. 2017. Das Augsburger Analyse- und Evaluationsraster in der Lehramtsausbildung. In *Das Augsburger Analyse- und Evaluationsraster für analoge und digitale Bildungsmedien (AAER). Grundlegung und Anwendungsbeispiele in interdisziplinärer Perspektive*, ed. Carl-Christian Frey and Eva Matthes, 185–195. Bad Heilbrunn: Klinkhardt.

Clarke, Adele E. 2009. Situational Analysis. In *Innovations in social science research methods*, ed. Maria Xenitidou and Nigel Gilbert, 55–56. Surrey: University of Surrey, ESRC National Centre for Research Methods. Accessed May 5, 2022. http://epubs.surrey.ac.uk/2271/1/ISSRM_Report_Public.pdf.

Clarke, Adele E. 2016. 'From Grounded Theory to Situational Analysis. What's New? Why? How? In *Developing Grounded Theory. The Second Generation*, ed. Janice M. Morse, Phyllis Noerager Stern, Juliet Corbin, Barbara Bowers, Kathy Charmaz, and Adele E. Clarke, 194–235. New York: Routledge.

Clarke, Adele E., and Reiner Keller. 2014. Engaging Complexities: Working Against Simplification as an Agenda for Qualitative Research Today. Adele Clarke in Conversation with Reiner Keller. Interview, *Forum Qualitative Sozialforschung / Forum: Qualitative Social Research* 15 (2). Accessed May 5, 2022. https://doi.org/10.17169/fqs-15.2.2186.

Dehn, Mechthild. 2014. Visual Literacy, Imagination und Sprachbildung. In *BilderBücher. Band 1: Theorie*, ed. Julia Knopf and Ulf Abraham, 125–134. Baltmannsweiler: Schneider Verlag.

Deppermann, Arnulf. 2008. *Gespräche analysieren. Qualitative Sozialforschung*. Wiesbaden: Verlag für Sozialwissenschaften.

Elbabour, Fatma, Obead Alhadreti, and Pam Mayhew. 2017. Eye Tracking in Retrospective Think-Aloud Usability Testing: Is There Added Value? *Journal of Usability Studies* 12: 95–110.

Enthof, Horst. 2013. Der Wert der Sicherheit: Anmerkungen zur Ökonomie der Sicherheit. *Munich Personal RePEc Archive*: 1–19. Accessed May 5, 2022. https://mpra.ub.uni-muenchen.de/49690/.

Flick, Uwe. 2020. *Introducing Research Methodology. Thinking Your Way Through Your Research Project*. London: SAGE Publications.

Foroutan, Naika, and Dilek İkiz. 2016. Migrationsgesellschaft. In *Handbuch Migrationspädagogik*, ed. Paul Mecherlin, 138–151. Weinheim: Beltz.

Fuchs, Eckhardt, Inga Niehaus, and Almut Stoletzki. 2014. *Das Schulbuch in der Forschung. Analysen und Empfehlungen für die Bildungspraxis*. Göttingen: V&R unipress.

Geuenich, Helmut. 2015. *Migration und Migrant(inn)en im Schulbuch: Diskursanalysen nordrhein-westfälischer Politik- und Sozialkundebücher für die Sekundarstufe I*. Wiesbaden: Springer.

Heinz, Tobias. 2019. "So bunt ist Europa": Europa multimedial. Bildlinguistische Perspektiven auf NATION- und EUROPA-Konzepte. In *Europa und Bildungsmedien*, ed. Annemarie Augschöll Blasbichler, Eva Matthes, and Sylvia Birgit Schütze, 285–297. Bad Heilbrunn: Klinkhardt.

Heitzmann, Anni, and Alois Niggli. 2010. Lehrmittel—ihre Bedeutung für Bildungsprozesse und die Lehrerbildung. *Beiträge zur Lehrerbildung* 28 (1): 6–19.

Helfferich, Cornelia. 2019. Leitfaden-und Experteninterviews. In *Handbuch Methoden der empirischen Sozialforschung*, ed. Nina Baur and Nina Jörg Blasius, 669–686. Wiesbaden: Springer.

Holmqvist, Kenneth Marcus, Richard Andersson Nyström, Richard Dewhurst, Halska Jarodzka, and Joost Van de Weijer. 2011. *Eye Tracking: A Comprehensive Guide to Methods and Measures*. Oxford, UK: Oxford University Press.

Hyrskykari, Aulikki, Saila Ovaska, Pävi Majaranta, Kari-Jouko Räihä, and Merja Lehtinen. 2008. Gaze Path Stimulation in Retrospective Think-Aloud. *Journal of Eye Movement Research* 2 (4): 1–18.

Jo, Yong-Min, and Anke Stautmeister. 2011. Don't Make Me Think Aloud!—Lautes Denken mit Eye Tracking auf dem Prüfstand. In *Tagungsband UP11*, ed. Henning Brau, Andreas Lehmann, Kostanija Petrovic, and Matthias C. Schroeder, 172–177. Stuttgart: German UPA e.V.

Just, Marcel A., and Patricia A. Carpenter. 1980. A Theory of Reading: From Eye Fixations to Comprehension. *Psychological Review* 87 (4): 329–354.

Kershaw, Ian. 2018. *Achterbahn. Europa 1950 bis heute*. Munich: Deutsche Verlags-Anstalt.

Klein, Pascal, Jouni Viiri, Saleh Mozaffari, Andreas Dengel and Jochen Kuhn. 2018. Instruction-Based Clinical Eye-Tracking Study on the Visual Interpretation of Divergence: How Do Students Look at Vector Field Plots? *Physical Review Physics Education Research*, 14. Accessed May 5, 2022. https://doi.org/10.1103/PhysRevPhysEducRes.14.010116.

Krastev, Ivan. 2017. *Europadämmerung. Ein Essay*. Frankfurt am Main: Suhrkamp.

Kreus, Arno, and Norbert von der Ruhren. 2010. *Terra—Europa. Themenband Oberstufe*. Stuttgart: Klett.

Lechleiter, Philipp. 2016. *Wertekonstellationen im Wandel*. Wiesbaden: Springer.

Lenzner, Alwine, Wolfgang Schnotz, and Andreas Müller. 2013. The Role of Decorative Pictures in Learning. *Instructional Science* 41: 811–831.

Mayer, Richard E. 2009. *Multimedia Learning*. Cambridge: Cambridge University Press.

Mecheril, Paul, María do Mar Castro Varela, Inci Dirim, Annita Kalpaka, and Claus Melter. 2010. *Migrationspädagogik*. Weinheim: Beltz.

Menold, Natalja. 2019. Effekte der Verbalisierung von Ratingskalen auf die Messqualität. Eine Forschungssynthese. In *Qualitätssicherung sozialwissenschaftlicher Erhebungsinstrumente*, ed. Natalja Menold and Tobias Wolbring, 103–131. Wiesbaden: Springer.

Oestermeier, Uwe, and Alexander Eitel. 2014. Lernen mit Text und Bild. *e-teaching.org*. Accessed May 5, 2022. https://www.e-teaching.org/etresources/media/pdf/langtext_2014_oestermeier-uwe_eitel-alexander_lernen-mit-text-und-bild.pdf.

Schmitz, Ulrich. 2006. Schriftbildschirme. Tertiäre Schriftlichkeit im World Wide Web. In *Neuere Entwicklungen in der linguistischen Internetforschung. Germanistische Linguistik*, ed. Jannis K. Androutsopoulos, Jens Runkehl, Peter Schlobinski, and Torsten Siever, 184–208. Hildesheim: Georg Olms Verlag.

Schneekloth, Ulrich, and Mathias Albert. 2019. Jugend und Politik: Demokratieverständnis und politisches Interesse im Spannungsfeld von Vielfalt, Toleranz und Populismus. In *Jugend 2019. 18. Shell Jugendstudie: Eine Generation meldet sich zu Wort*, ed. Mathias Albert, Klaus Hurrelmann, Gudrun Quenzel, and Kantar, 47–101. Weinheim: Beltz.

Schnotz, Wolfgang. 2014. Integrated Model of Text and Picture Comprehension. In *The Cambridge Handbook of Multimedia Learning*, ed. Richard E. Mayer, 72–103. Cambridge: Cambridge University Press.

Sprenger, Priska. 2021. *Prozesse bei der strukturierenden Mengenwahrnehmung und strukturnutzenden Anzahlbestimmung von Kindern im Elementarbereich. Eine Eye-Tracking Studie*. Wiesbaden: Springer.

Strauss, Anselm, and Juliet Corbin. 1990. *Basics of Qualitative Research: Grounded Theory Procedures and Techniques*. Newbury Park, CA: SAGE Publications.

Strohmaier, Stefan. 2014. Visuelle Analyse von Eyetracking-Experimenten mit einer Vielzahl von Areas of Interest. Master's thesis, Universität Stuttgart, Institut für Visualisierung und Interaktive Systeme. Accessed April 5, 2020, https://doi.org/10.18419/opus-3312.

Sweller, John. 1994. Cognitive Load Theory, Learning Difficulty, and Instructional Design. *Learning and Instruction* 4: 295–312.

Tobii Pro AB. 2014. *Tobii Pro Lab User Manual v. 1.145*. Accessed April 5, 2020, https://www.tobiipro.com/siteassets/tobii-pro/user-manuals/Tobii-Pro-Lab-User-Manual/?v=1.145.

Index[1]

[1] Note: Page numbers followed by 'n' refer to notes.

K. Gorbahn et al. (eds.), *Exploring Interconnectedness*, Palgrave Studies in Educational Media, https://doi.org/10.1007/978-3-031-13960-4